Social Scientific Research

Sara Miller McCune founded SAGE Publishing in 1965 to support the dissemination of usable knowledge and educate a global community. SAGE publishes more than 1000 journals and over 800 new books each year, spanning a wide range of subject areas. Our growing selection of library products includes archives, data, case studies and video. SAGE remains majority owned by our founder and after her lifetime will become owned by a charitable trust that secures the company's continued independence.

Los Angeles | London | New Delhi | Singapore | Washington DC | Melbourne

Social Scientific Research

Dawn Brancati

Los Angeles | London | New Delhi
Singapore | Washington DC | Melbourne

Los Angeles | London | New Delhi
Singapore | Washington DC | Melbourne

SAGE Publications Ltd
1 Oliver's Yard
55 City Road
London EC1Y 1SP

SAGE Publications Inc.
2455 Teller Road
Thousand Oaks, California 91320

SAGE Publications India Pvt Ltd
B 1/I 1 Mohan Cooperative Industrial Area
Mathura Road
New Delhi 110 044

SAGE Publications Asia-Pacific Pte Ltd
3 Church Street
#10-04 Samsung Hub
Singapore 049483

Editor: Natalie Aguilera
Editorial assistant: Eve Williams
Production editor: Katie Forsythe
Copyeditor: Christine Bitten
Marketing manager: Susheel Gorkarakonda
Cover design: Stephanie Guyaz
Typeset by: C&M Digitals (P) Ltd, Chennai, India

Library of Congress Control Number: 2018938678

British Library Cataloguing in Publication data

A catalogue record for this book is available from the British Library

ISBN 978-1-5264-2684-0
ISBN 978-1-5264-2685-7 (pbk)

Contents

Preface

While research design and methods may seem like a rather prosaic subject, it is an important tool for *understanding* fascinating and important questions in the world, such as why third place winners in athletic competitions are happier than second place winners; why poor people with the least amount of money to waste tend to play the lottery more than rich people; and why authoritarian states with poor human rights records in their own countries extend humanitarian aid to other countries. Knowledge of this subject can also help you to *evaluate* existing research in order to make informed personal and professional decisions, such as what political candidates to vote for based on the likely effects of their proposed policies; how to challenge claims put forward by the opposing side in a legal case; and whether donating to a charity is really helping the recipient and in what ways. Fluency, moreover, in research design and methods is essential for *conducting* your own research in order to make decisions based on sound scientific evidence rather than personal experiences, anecdotal evidence, and hunches. The latter may be uninformative at best and misleading at worst.

Background

Social Scientific Research was born largely from my experience teaching research methods courses and workshops, building and directing an undergraduate thesis program in political science, and advising numerous senior theses and doctoral dissertations. For me, it was impossible to find a single textbook that discussed at length questions related to research design, as well as the diverse range of qualitative and quantitative methods used in my field, in an engaging and entertaining manner, and at a level where students would not only be able evaluate existing research using these methods, but to also conduct their own research using them. *Social Scientific Research* seeks to rectify these issues.

Objectives

The goals of *Social Scientific Research* are threefold. The first is to provide a thorough introduction to research design. To this end, *Social Scientific Research* devotes entire chapters to identifying research puzzles, organizing literature reviews, constructing useful concepts, building compelling arguments, and writing effectively. The second is to provide a comprehensive introduction to a full range of qualitative and quantitative methods that adhere to a positivist research paradigm. Many textbooks include only qualitative approaches or quantitative methods, and a limited number of methods within each approach. *Social Scientific Research*, however, includes both and introduces an array of methods within each approach. The qualitative methods include: interviews, focus groups, participant observation, process tracing, and the comparative case study method. The quantitative methods include: content analysis, surveys, observational studies and experiments. The discussion of these methods emphasizes the strengths and weaknesses of these methods, especially in comparison to other methods, rather than technical detail. Yet, the methodological chapters still provide sufficient practical content for readers to implement the methods based on them.

The third is to present the subject of research design and methods in an entertaining and engaging style. To this end, *Social Scientific Research* includes numerous interesting and lively examples based on everyday experiences, contemporary world events, and academic research. *Social Scientific Research* also includes many exercises in which readers are asked to apply the concepts and techniques learned in each chapter in order to deepen their understanding of them. Both the examples and the exercises address a range of subjects important in the social sciences and require no background information other than that which is provided in the exercise.

Contents Overview

Part I provides an introduction to the research process. Chapter 1 explains what defines and distinguishes research in the social sciences from research in other disciplines. Chapter 2 discusses the main issues of concern regarding research ethics. Chapter 3 provides guidance on developing good research questions, while Chapter 4 explains the process of constructing a literature review around these questions.

Part II focuses on the nuts and bolts of developing causal arguments. Chapter 5 outlines the criteria and process of developing concepts used to build these arguments, while Chapter 6 discusses different types of causal relationships and common errors of causal inference.

Part III discusses issues related to method and case selection. Chapter 7 outlines the primary differences between qualitative and quantitative approaches to research, as well as a number of issues researchers may consider in choosing which approach to use. Chapter 8 discusses mixed methods research designs and the ways in which qualitative and quantitative research are combined in them. Chapter 9 moves on to discuss case selection in terms of both the number of cases selected and the process by which they are selected.

Part IV introduces different types of qualitative research methods. Chapters 10 and 11 present interviews and group interviews, known as focus groups, respectively. Chapter 12 describes participant observation, which involves the immersion of researchers into the environment of their subjects for an extended period of time. Chapter 13 discusses process tracing, which is a single-case study design, while Chapter 14 presents the comparative case study method, which is a multi-case study design.

Part V switches perspectives and introduces different types of quantitative research methods. Chapter 15 discusses the types of and criteria used to evaluate measures while Chapter 16 discusses these issues in regards to quantitative data. Chapter 17 explains the method of content analysis, which is used to transform qualitative data into quantitative measures and data. Chapters 18 and 19, meanwhile, discuss two quantitative methods in which researchers interact with their subjects and/or their environments – surveys and experiments, while Chapter 20 describes observational studies in which researchers do neither.

Part VI concludes by offering guidance on writing up the results of one's research, from the overall organization of the presentation of the results to the nitty-gritty of style and verbiage.

Features

At the beginning of every chapter, there is a list of objectives. Within each chapter, there are tables and boxes that summarize key points discussed in the text, and provide additional information that is not included in, but that is no less important than, the information included in the text. There are also many examples in each chapter to elucidate the key concepts. At the end of each chapter, there is a list of key points and suggestions for further reading. There are also numerous exercises at the end of each chapter in which readers can practice the key concepts and techniques introduced in each chapter. For ease of reference, there is also a glossary at the end of the book summarizing the most important terms and concepts used in each of the chapters.

I

INTRODUCTION

1

What is Social Science Research?

Objectives

- explain the goals, subjects, and orientations of social science research
- differentiate between positivist and non-positivist research
- introduce the steps in the scientific method
- debate the 'scientific' nature of social science research

Social science research strives to understand human behavior. While the term 'social' refers to the object of social science research – human behavior – the term 'science' refers to the methodological approach by which human behavior is analyzed. The social sciences encompass a range of disciplines including anthropology, business, criminology, economics, education, political science, psychology, sociology, and so forth. Research in these disciplines is distinguished from each other not in terms of the type of human behavior that it examines – since no type of human behavior is the exclusive domain of any one of these disciplines – but in terms of the emphasis they place on particular behaviors, as well as the *methods* they tend to use to study them.

Consider the subject of education. Anthropological research on education is more likely to focus on the effects of culture on academic opportunities and learning behaviors than economics. Research on education in economics is likely to focus instead on the employment opportunities and gains to earnings derived from education, while research in political science and criminology is more apt to study the reductive effect of education on violent behavior. To understand these issues, economics, political science, and criminology rely heavily on quantitative methods while anthropology tends to rely on qualitative methods.

Regardless of discipline, social scientific research adheres to a positivist epistemology and as such, uses the scientific method to understand human behavior. *Epistemology* is the study of the nature, scope, and production of human knowledge. It is concerned with philosophical questions such as: 'What is knowledge?', 'How is knowledge acquired?', 'How much do we, or can we, know?'

Epistemology is often mentioned in conjunction with the term ontology, but is quite distinct from ontology. The term *ontology* refers to the study of the nature of being or existence. It is concerned, in contrast, with questions such as 'What is existence?' and 'What can be said to exist?' and whether or not it is possible to construct a taxonomy of all things that exist.

A positivist epistemology maintains that an objective reality or truth exists in the world independent of the observer, and that this reality can be understood using the scientific method. In accordance with the scientific method, a positivist methodology is open to the use of either qualitative or quantitative research methods. These methods are distinguished from each other in terms of the type of data that they employ. Qualitative research methods employ verbal, written, or visual data, while quantitative research methods utilize data that are numeric in form.

A non-positivist epistemology, in contrast, maintains that an objective reality does not exist independent of human perception, and that it is impossible to study a phenomenon without influencing it or being influenced by it. Non-positivist research also rejects the scientific method and the use of quantitative methods. It relies instead on qualitative research techniques. Many of these techniques are used in positivist research, such as interviews, focus groups, and participant observation, but others are the exclusive bailiwick of non-positivist research, such as hermeneutics and narrative analysis.

Positivists assert, for example, that there is an objective phenomenon known as food insecurity, which is defined generally as a lack of access to adequate, safe, nutritious, and culturally appropriate food, and that food insecurity can be measured using numeric data, such as caloric intake, anthropometry, and so forth. Non-positivists argue instead that food insecurity is a socially constructed term that cannot be quantified with the aforementioned measures. Non-positivists further argue that food insecurity ought to be understood in terms of communities' own conceptions of what it means to feel hungry and that groups ought to be allowed to define for themselves appropriate markers of food insecurity through interviews, focus groups, and so forth.

The Scientific Method

The *scientific method,* which positivists embrace and non-positivists reject, is a set of procedures used to test hypotheses about phenomena based on the collection and analysis of data through observation, interaction, or experimentation. The scientific method includes six basic steps. These steps are illustrated in Figure 1.1 and elaborated on in further detail in subsequent chapters. To elucidate the steps in the scientific method, the question of why food insecurity has declined in developing countries in the last 20 years is used as an example.

The first step in the scientific method involves *identifying a problem* in need of analysis and developing a research question around it. The question of food insecurity is an important issue because, although food insecurity has declined, millions of people, primarily in

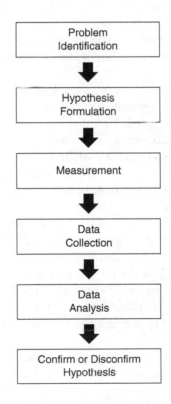

Figure 1.1 Scientific method

Africa and Asia, are still food insecure. The fact that food insecurity has declined in developing countries in the last 20 years is puzzling since droughts have become increasingly more severe in the last few decades, and the total number of ongoing civil wars in the world has increased. Civil wars, and intrastate conflict in general, contribute to food insecurity because they disrupt food production and prevent the delivery of humanitarian aid to food insecure areas.

The second step in the scientific method entails *developing hypotheses* in order to explain the problem at hand. *Hypotheses* are suppositions put forward to explain a given phenomenon. Any research project may include more than one hypothesis since there can be more than one factor that explains a given outcome. A potential hypothesis to explain the decline in food insecurity in the last two decades is the concurrent improvement in governance in this period.

Governance is a broad term referring to the process by which political decisions are made and implemented. One aspect of governance likely to be related to food insecurity is the extent to which the poor – those most likely to experience shortages in nutritious food – are able to vote for representatives in government, and the extent to which these representatives are beholden to their constituents. As Amartya Sen famously declared, 'No famine has ever taken place in the history of the world in a functioning democracy' (1999: 16). If the poor are given the opportunity to vote in democratic elections, food insecurity is expected to decline because the poor are likely to elect candidates who endorse legislation addressing issues of food security (Blaydes and Kayser 2011). This legislation might support improvements in infrastructure, innovative agricultural programs, food subsidies, welfare policies, and so forth.

The next step in the scientific method involves developing measures to test the hypotheses. These measures ought to represent the outcome of interest, the factor(s) argued to cause the outcome, as well as any other factors that increase the likelihood of the outcome to occur. The aforementioned example of food insecurity requires measures of at least food insecurity and governance. It also begs for measures of other factors such as drought conditions and intrastate conflict, which may also be related to food insecurity, in order to ensure that any observed effect of governance on food insecurity is not a function of these other factors, but of governance.

Two potential quantitative measures of food insecurity are the average daily caloric intake and the average height and weight of individuals by gender and age. The former captures the extent to which individuals have sufficient access to food, but not whether the food is healthy, while the latter measures the outcome of a lack of access to healthy and safe food. Qualitative measures of food insecurity may include interview questions regarding how frequently heads of households are unable to purchase food due to a lack of money, or how often a person worries about not having adequate food to eat.

Governance may be measured in terms of the extent to which national, regional, and local elections are democratic. Qualitative measures of governance may include interview questions regarding: whether or not the poor vote and why not if they do not vote; the extent to which people believe that national leaders are doing enough to address the issue of food insecurity in their constituencies; and the importance voters place on this issue when casting their ballots.

Drought conditions may be measured in terms of annual rainfall while intrastate conflict may be measured in terms of civil wars. For violence to disrupt aid flows and inhibit migration, the violence must be very intense as in the case of civil wars. Civil wars are distinguished from other forms of intrastate violence by, among other things, the number of battle deaths they involve. For violence within a state to constitute a civil war, typically, it must involve at least 1000 battle deaths.

The next step in the scientific method entails *collecting data* on these measures. In the case of the qualitative measures previously identified regarding food security, this process entails conducting the proposed interviews. In the case of the quantitative measures, this process involves nothing more than accessing numeric, publicly available data from governmental, intergovernmental, and academic institutions. The United Nations Food and Agricultural Organization (UNFAO) collects quantitative data on average caloric intake and the prevalence of underweight children.[1] Other UN-affiliated organizations and national environmental agencies provide data on rainfall.[2]

Academic institutions, meanwhile, are a valuable source of data on governance and civil wars. There are various sources of quantitative data on democracy at the national level, but not on democracy at the subnational level. These datasets include: the Polity Index,[3] the Democracy-Dictatorship dataset (Cheibub et al. 2010), and the Polyarchy dataset.[4] They provide data on the level of democracy in countries around the world as far back as 1800.

There are far fewer datasets available on civil wars. The best is the UCDP/PRIO Armed Conflict Dataset.[5] It provides very high quality data on armed conflict defined as the use of armed force between two parties, one of which is the government, resulting in at least 25 battle-related deaths. It provides two additional measures, which allow researchers to identify conflicts that constitute civil wars. These measures provide data on the intensity of conflict in terms of 1000 battle-related deaths either total or per year.

The penultimate step in the scientific method involves *analyzing the data*. For the quantitative indicators, this would consist of an observational study analyzing the relationship between the aforementioned measures of governance and food security, as well as rainfall and civil wars. Observational studies are discussed in Chapter 20. For the qualitative indicators, this step would involve identifying and interpreting patterns in the interview responses.

The final step of the scientific method involves *confirming or disconfirming (i.e., falsifying) the hypotheses*. In the quantitative analysis of food insecurity, results in support of the governance hypothesis would demonstrate a correlation between higher levels of democracy at the national level and greater caloric intake and fewer underweight children. In the qualitative analysis, results in support of the governance hypothesis would indicate that there are fewer indications of people being unable to purchase food for lack of money and/or worrying about not having adequate food to eat, where people vote more often, place a lot of importance on food security issues, and believe that politicians have dedicated sufficient attention to issues regarding food for the poor.

Violations in the Scientific Method

Violations in the scientific method arise any time a subsequent step occurs prior to an antecedent step. Certain violations in the scientific method are more problematic and more common than others. A very common violation occurs when researchers, instead of first defining their measures and then collecting data to represent these measures, allow the availability of data to determine the hypotheses that they construct, and the measures that they employ to test their hypotheses.

In the above example regarding food insecurity, we would have violated the scientific method in this way had we first identified what quantitative data existed on governance, and then argued that food should be more secure in countries where national-level elections are democratic, ignoring the importance of regional and local elections because data on these elections does not exist.

This kind of violation in the scientific method generally results in a narrowing of hypotheses to fit the available data as in the prior example. This example was more limited because it omitted the importance of regional and local elections. Researchers might be tempted to define their hypotheses or measures in terms of the available data in order to avoid criticisms that their analysis is not a strong test of their argument, because the distance between their theory and data is large while avoiding the costly and time-intensive process of collecting original data for which this distance would not be as large.

A much more problematic violation of the scientific method occurs when researchers collect data, observe patterns in it, and then change their hypotheses to be consistent with the results that they find in their analyses. This is highly problematic because it prevents the analyses from serving as tests of the researchers' hypotheses. In this case, there is no way for the analyses to do anything other than confirm the researchers' hypotheses. Unfortunately, knowing whether violations in the scientific method of this kind have occurred is very difficult unless a researcher leaves a paper trail – that is, unless earlier versions of the research, including the research proposal, are available so that changes in how the findings have been reported over time can be observed.

How 'Scientific' are the Social Sciences?

Although social science research, like the natural sciences, uses the scientific method, questions still abound as to what extent patterns in human behavior are scientific. The social sciences are scientific to the extent that human behavior is *observable, consistent, predictable,* and, thus, *testable* using the scientific method.

Observability of Human Behavior

The first criterion on which the scientific nature of the social sciences is judged against is the observability of human behavior. To be observable means that human behavior is capable of being observed, not that it has been observed. Many forms of human behavior and the motivations for them are observable. Wars, trade, investment patterns, elections, protests, coups d'état, and so forth, are all observable with the human eye.

Although researchers cannot personally observe certain human behaviors, including those that have occurred in the past, they can often observe them through others who have directly experienced them. To do so, researchers might interview witnesses to events or examine archival documents about accounts of them. Of course, many witnesses to events may be unwilling or unable to testify about them because of societal pressures, restrictions on civil liberties, and potential harm to themselves or their livelihoods, among other reasons. Witnesses may misconstrue events, either intentionally or unintentionally, as well.

When researchers cannot directly observe certain behaviors themselves or through others that have experienced them, researchers may still be able though to identify the observable implications of these behaviors. The latter are behaviors that one expects to observe (or not to observe) if certain behaviors have occurred. Emotional or physical distance, for example, and spending less time with a spouse are all observable implications of a marital affair. Testing for the observable implications of a behavior is not as convincing, of course, as observing a behavior directly since the observed behavior may be consistent with other behaviors. Emotional or physical distance and spending less time with a spouse, for example, are also consistent with general unhappiness in a marriage and wanting a divorce.

Electoral fraud offers another valuable example of this concept. It is very difficult to observe whether or not a political party has cheated in an election, but it is possible to observe if the turnout rate in certain districts has exceeded 100 percent. While it might seem unlikely that a party would cheat in such an obvious way, turnout exceeded 100 percent in several districts in the 2011 legislative elections in Russia, which sparked massive street protests, as well as the 2014 presidential election in Afghanistan. Although this was not the case in these elections, it is also possible for voter turnout to exceed 100 percent for reasons other than fraud, including computer error.

The behavior of the drugs cartels in Mexico further illustrates this concept. The Mexican drug cartels are known to threaten to kill local politicians if the politicians do not comply with the cartels' demands for money, government contracts, and so forth. Researchers cannot directly observe these threats, but they can observe the number of mayors that have been murdered while in office (an estimated 100 in the last decade). This number should be indicative of the minimum number of mayors that have been threatened by cartels, since those who were killed were likely those who refused to comply with the cartels' threats and were murdered as a result. While some of these mayors may have died for other reasons, most likely did not given the fact that the style of the murders was consistent with those of the cartels.

Consistency and Predictability of Human Behavior

Human behavior must also be predictable and consistent for the social sciences to be scientific. The former hinges on the latter. That is, for human behavior to be predictable, it must first of all be consistent. To be consistent means that people facing the same set of circumstances, conditions, or options tend to behave in the same way each time they face them. It does not mean that everyone always behaves in the same way as each other when confronted with the same set of circumstances. Nor does it mean that the same person acts in the same way each time they are confronted with the same set of circumstances.

An important reason why individuals tend to behave the same way when faced with the same set of circumstances, conditions or options, is because individuals are generally rational. In layman's terms, rationality means that people behave according to logic and reason. In economics, rationality is defined more formally as the ability of a person to order his or her preferences over a set of choices and to always choose the option that maximizes his or her utility. Rationality presumes that people see the same choices as better than others given the same set of circumstances, conditions, or options, and tend to perceive the same course of action as the best to produce a certain outcome.

To continue with the example of food security, rational individuals when confronted with a lack of adequate, safe, and nutritious food, are likely to migrate to other areas where food shortages are less severe unless internal conflict or other factors restrict their movement. In the Horn of Africa drought of 2011, an estimated one million Somalis migrated to neighboring countries to escape the food crisis in their country. These migrants lived primarily outside the Al-Shabaab-controlled South, where fighting prohibited Somalis from fleeing. In 2017, another severe food crisis occurred in Somalia, and in nearby states, with about the same number of Somalis fleeing their country.

However, people do not always behave rationally, which poses a challenge to social science research, because they do not have the time, knowledge, and computational abilities to consider all the options available to them, and because of the ways in which issues are framed. Psychological research on charitable giving suggests that people's willingness to support food aid is higher when it is framed as either a purely altruistic act (Newman and Cain 2014), as an action that prevents a death as opposed to an act that saves a life (Chou and Murnighan 2013), or as an activity that is uncommon and infrequent (Sussman et al. 2015).

Human behavior can still be predictable, though, even if people are not always rational, as long as researchers can identify the conditions under which people are less likely to behave rationally, as in these examples. A potentially greater challenge than rationality to the consistency and predictability of human behavior is learning. People do not always behave in a consistent fashion because they learn from past experiences and change their behavior accordingly.

Corporations, for example, change their marketing strategies when one fails to attract new customers. Educators adopt new ways to teach students when old strategies fail to produce real changes in learning outcomes rather than simply improvements in test scores, while educational testing services continually change their exams to keep abreast of students who learn to game the questions with the help of businesses hired for this purpose.

Even policy-makers change their behaviors when past ones fail to produce their desired results. Until the United States adopted the Smoot-Hawley Tariff during the Great Depression, politicians in the US and elsewhere believed that tariffs helped protect and profit domestic industries. After the Act, however, free trade became economic mantra.

The Smoot-Hawley Tariff actually sunk the US's economy into a further depression because it provoked other countries to impose retaliatory tariffs on US goods (Irwin 2011).

The problem of learning is not unique to the social sciences. Even nature changes. Viruses, for example, adapt and change forms in response to medications. As a result, over time medicines that had previously worked to combat diseases are no longer useful, and researchers are compelled to develop new ones. The structure of the human brain also changes following severe trauma in order to prevent arguably future trauma (Hull 2002).

Learning, moreover, is not as problematic for social scientific research as it may at first appear. Learning does not always lead to changes in individual's behaviors. Knowing the cause of a phenomenon does not mean that actions can be taken to prevent the phenomenon from occurring in the future. Somalis were aware of the vulnerability of their country to food crises even before the 2011 food crisis, but with limited resources and a weak government, were unable to avoid the 2017 crisis.

Learning can also be incorporated into social science arguments. Many researchers have identified diamonds as a primary source of funding for civil wars in the late 1990s and early twenty-first century (Collier and Hoeffler 2002; Lujala et al. 2005). However, at the same time, they also recognize that due to increased social awareness and the development of the Kimberley Process their use in this regard has since declined (Bieri 2016). The Kimberly Process certifies mines and their products as conflict-free. Social scientists also have a bevy of methodological techniques that allow them to incorporate and account for learning in their empirical analyses.

Testability of Human Behavior

Human behavior is testable because it is observable. Social science research is arguably more scientific than the natural sciences in terms of being observable because it is possible for researchers to observe human behavior without the expensive high technology equipment needed to observe phenomena in the natural sciences. The Higgs Boson was theorized to exist in the early 1960s. Yet, it went unobserved for more than 40 years until a supercollider, costing billions of euros, was developed in 2012 powerful enough to detect the particle. Scientists did not actually even observe the Higgs Boson with this supercollider since the Higgs' lifetime is only ~10^{-22} seconds. Instead, they detected the observable implications of the Higgs Boson, namely, the interactions of its decay products.

Social science arguments about human behavior are also testable because they are falsifiable, although ill-conceived social science arguments, such as tautologies, are not. Falsifiable means that an argument is capable of being proven false, not that it is false. Normative arguments about how people should behave, not how they actually do behave, are also not falsifiable and are not social scientific arguments for this reason. However, the premises on which certain normative arguments are built may be falsifiable.

A normative argument, for example, that governments should provide their people access to adequate, safe, and nutritious food because food security reduces intrastate violence is an example of a normative argument for which the premises are falsifiable. This argument is based on a claim that food security reduces intrastate violence and this claim can be proven false. An argument, however, that governments should ensure that their citizens have access to adequate, safe, and nutritious food because food security is a human right is an example of a normative argument that is not falsifiable because this argument is based on values and rights.

How scientific researchers think social science research is, or can be, can influence what methodological approach and/or methods they choose to use in their research. A *method* is the specific process researchers use to collect and analyze information. In the social sciences, there are two basic methodological approaches – one qualitative and the other quantitative – as previously described, and a third approach, which combines the two, known as mixed methods research. The differences between these approaches, including their advantages and disadvantages, are discussed in Chapters 7 and 8. Each of these approaches consists of various methods. Qualitative research, for example, includes interviews, focus groups, participant observation, process tracing, the comparative method, and so forth. Quantitative research, meanwhile, includes content analysis, surveys, observational studies, and experiments. These methods are discussed in separate chapters in the remainder of the book.

Key Points

- Social science research seeks to understand human behavior.
- There are two different philosophical approaches to research. *Positivism* claims that an objective reality exists in the world independent of the observer. *Non-positivism* maintains that it does not.
- Positivist research uses the scientific method to analyze problems. The scientific method is a set of procedures to test hypotheses based on the collection and analysis of data through observation, interaction, or experimentation.
- The extent to which social science can be understood using the scientific method is debatable. Issues that inform this debate concern the extent to which human behavior is observable, consistent, predictable, and testable.

Further Reading

The first reading provides a comprehensive guide to the scientific method. The second describes interesting and entertaining examples of positivist research in the social sciences, and the third provides an introduction to non-positivist research methodologies.

Carey, Stephen S. 2011. *A Beginner's Guide to Scientific Method*. Boston: Wadsworth.

Levitt, Steven D. and Stephen J. Dubner. 2010. *Freakonomics: A Rogue Economist Explores the Hidden Side of Everything*. New York: William Morrow.

Yanow, Dvora and Peregrine Schwartz-Shea, eds. 2006. *Interpretation and Method: Empirical Research Methods and the Interpretive Turn*. Armonk, NY: M.E. Sharpe.

EXERCISE 1.1

To what extent do you believe in the positivist tradition that a world exists independent of observers, and that it is possible for researchers to conduct research without influencing the behavior of their subjects? Why? Can you identify examples or incidences when the latter is not the case, and do these examples mean that a world does not exist independent of the observer?

EXERCISE 1.2

The following behaviors and/or motivations for them are all difficult to directly observe. Identify one or two observable implications of these behaviors. Consider what other behaviors might also be consistent with the observable implications that you identify.

1. Bribery in order to obtain business licenses to operate in a foreign country.
2. Genocide defined as the *intention* to exterminate a group through acts of killings, wartime rape, the cutting off of groups' food supplies, and so forth.
3. The selling of mortgages by securities traders at higher rates than the mortgages are valued in order to deceive the purchaser.
4. Whether or not the explosion of a car bomb is an act of terrorism (i.e., the purposeful use or threat of violence against civilians or property in order to instill fear among the population for political goals), where the driver is killed in the explosion without having left a statement explaining the motivation for the act.
5. An authoritarian regime's investment in nuclear weapons in order to build domestic legitimacy.

EXERCISE 1.3

On a scale of 1–10, overall how scientific do you think your discipline is in terms of the ability of researchers in this discipline to observe and test consistent and predictable patterns in human behavior? On this scale, 1 represents 'not at all scientific' and 10 represents 'fully scientific'. Break down your assessment in terms of the following four criteria: *observable, consistent, predictable,* and *testable*. How do you think (and why) your discipline compares to other disciplines in the social sciences in terms of being scientific, and how do you think (and why) your discipline compares to the following natural sciences disciplines – biology and chemistry (or physics)?

2

Research Ethics

Objectives

- present the ethical concerns surrounding the use of human subjects
- discuss non-human subjects concerns regarding the conduct of research
- describe the peer review process for evaluating research quality and integrity
- detail the ethical issues regarding publication, such as transparency, credit stealing, and so forth

---

Research ethics is a term that refers to the norms, standards, and legal rules regarding appropriate behavior in the conduct and publication of research. It refers to a range of issues that arise at each stage of the research process and extend beyond concerns for the physical and psychological welfare of human subjects. Standards for ethical research have evolved significantly since the days when scientists subjected people to high altitudes until they lost consciousness, exposed people to freezing temperatures until their organs failed, and infected them with diseases to investigate the effectiveness of potential treatments for these diseases.[1] However, these standards still vary widely across countries, institutions, academic disciplines, and even within discipline journals, not only in terms of their content, but also in terms of the degree to which these standards are formalized and the punishment that follows from violating them. For this reason, this chapter does not define what these standards are or should be, but rather presents for discussion and debate the ethical concerns most often and most widely raised regarding research in the social sciences.

What Research is Permissible?

Social science research may be restricted for many reasons, including the values, ideologies, and anxieties of governments, especially in authoritarian states, which perceive research on certain topics as a threat to regime stability. These restrictions are due to the subject of the research, not the subjects of the research – that is, the participants in the study and the way in which research involving humans is conducted. Research that involves human subjects is often restricted in countries – in democratic states more often than in authoritarian ones – in order to prevent physical and psychological harm to individuals. Although human subject standards and the interpretation of these standards vary significantly within and across countries, the core principle behind these standards is that the potential benefits of the research ought to outweigh any potential risks of physical and psychological harm to the participants. The risks are assessed both in terms of the likelihood of the harm occurring, as well as the severity of it.

Physical Harm

In the social sciences, concerns regarding the physical harm that research poses to participants relate less to the lives of individuals than in the natural sciences, and more to the livelihoods of individuals. Concerns regarding the physical harm that research poses to individuals evolved from biomedical research studies where people were exposed to inhumane conditions. In these studies, people were exposed to high altitudes and freezing temperatures until they lost consciousness. They were intentionally infected with diseases, such as malaria and cancer, and denied known treatments, such as penicillin, to test the progression of diseases, such as syphilis.

  Although social scientific research does not pose as much of a bodily threat to participants as research in the natural sciences, it is not unheard of for social scientific studies to pose a bodily threat to participants or others those participants encountered. Marianne Bertrand and colleagues (2007), for example, conducted a study of the effects of corruption on the allocation of driving licenses in New Delhi, which posed a significant threat to the participants and to those they encountered. In the study, participants were offered either a financial reward for obtaining their driver's licenses quickly, a free driving lesson, or neither. Those offered the financial reward acquired their licenses 40 percent faster, and at a 20 percent higher rate, than those who did not receive anything. They did not learn to drive safely in the process, however. In fact, 69 percent of those in the reward group failed an independent driving test. Follow-up surveys indicated that these participants obtained their licenses faster by using the reward to pay informal agents to bribe bureaucrats so that they did not have to take the driving exam.

Bodily threats, as in the Bertrand study, are less common in social scientific research than threats to the livelihoods of individuals. A salient case of these threats is the Tea Room study (Humphreys 1970). In this study, the researcher, Laud Humphreys, a sociology graduate student at Washington University in Saint Louis, conducted an ethnographic study of the tea room trade (i.e., homosexual encounters in public places) in Saint Louis in the 1970s. The findings from the study challenged conventional views of homosexual men at the time by demonstrating that many men who participated in the tea room trade were heterosexual, employed, married, and parents.

In the study, Humphreys immersed himself in the tea room trade by acting as a lookout to alert men having sex inside public bathrooms to passersby who might detect their activities. Humphreys also recorded the license numbers of the men engaged in the tea room trade, as well as other identifying information, which he used to obtain men's names and addresses. He then went to the men's homes and presented himself as an interviewer to collect information about their backgrounds and family lives. In his published accounts of the tea room trade, Humphreys did not report the real names of the men involved, but the information he provided was so detailed that in some cases, the men's identities could be identified. Due to the stigmatization of homosexuality at the time, the participants whose identities were revealed risked losing their jobs and families. They could have been arrested for sodomy, which was illegal in the state of Missouri until 1999.

The Tea Room study raised concerns about the privacy expectations of people in public places. Whether or not the Tea Room participants had a right to privacy is debated since the tea room trade was carried out in public restrooms located in a park. Similar questions have arisen today in terms of the internet and online support groups in particular. While, in general, these support groups are open to anyone, and individuals who post comments on the groups' websites usually do so anonymously, many support groups ask that only those who suffer from certain conditions, or their friends and families, join the groups. In this case, many ethicists argue that these people have a right to privacy, and that even if they did not, researchers should not be permitted to study them because the groups did not give the researchers permission to study them (Walther 2002; Eynon et al. 2008). Some ethicists even argue that researchers should not be allowed to research any personal data from the internet, including information from resumés or curriculum vitae, for the same reason.

A major controversy arose in 2018 when an investigation revealed that a researcher named Alessandr Kogan sold data he culled from millions of Facebook users to a UK-based data science firm called Cambridge Analytica. Cambridge Analytica used the Facebook data to target specific groups of voters with partisan ads in the 2016 US presidential elections. Kogan culled the data through an app that collected information on what Facebook users 'liked'. This information was combined with a personality test that Kogan administered to a subset of Facebook users, who voluntarily completed the personality test having been told that the test was for academic purposes. Kogan deduced the personalities of the millions of Facebook users who had not completed the personality test based on similarities in their 'likes' with those who completed the test. In selling the data to Cambridge Analytica, Kogan violated Facebook's terms of service. Cambridge Analytica denied having any knowledge of how the data were collected and of using it to influence electoral outcomes.

Psychological Harm

Often, as the aforementioned examples suggest, the potential for physical harm coincides with the potential for psychological harm. Psychological harm can take the form of stress or unpleasant thoughts incurred in the process of the study or through what the results reveal about the study participants. A classic example of the psychological harm that can be experienced in social science research is the Milgram experiments. The Milgram experiments were a series of experiments conducted in the 1960s by Stanley Milgram in order to understand obedience to authority in general and German participation in the Holocaust in particular.

In the Milgram experiments, participants believed that they were administering shocks to individuals, who were actually actors, in order to teach the individuals word pairs. Approximately two-thirds of the participants administered the maximum 450 volts. Participants in the study experienced undue psychological stress because they believed that they were seriously harming the individuals they shocked, and because the results of the study revealed to them that they might have behaved like the Germans in World War II and obeyed orders from the Nazis to exterminate the Jewish people.

Although the Milgram experiments would not be permitted in most academic settings today, a French documentary in 2010 conducted a similar experiment with shockingly (no pun intended) similar results.[2] The documentary depicted a fictitious television game show in which the contestants were led to believe that they had shocked other contestants, who incorrectly answered questions posed to them. Approximately four-fifths of the contestants administered the maximum 460 volts to the other contestants.

Another classic example of psychological harm is the Stanford Prison Experiment (1971) in which students at Stanford University assumed the roles of prison guards and prisoners in a week long study to examine the importance of the inherent qualities of individuals versus the characteristics of situations to people's attitudes, values and behaviors. In the course of the study, several of the guards undertook draconian measures to enforce the rules of the fictitious prison and subjected some prisoners to psychological torture. Many of the prisoners passively accepted the abuse and, at the officers' request, actively harassed other prisoners who tried to stop the abuse, leading the chief researcher, Philip Zimbardo, to end the study early. The results of the study are consistent with those of the Milgram experiments, as they suggested that the context, rather than the personality traits of the individuals, was responsible for the guards' and the prisoners' behaviors.

In 2002, psychologists Alex Haslam and Steve Reicher conducted a similar experiment, known at the BBC Prison Study.[3] In the experiment, the participants, all volunteers, lived in a prison-like setting for nine days. The procedures in place in the BBC study to protect the participants against harm differed in many ways from the original Stanford study. Among other things, the BBC researchers informed the participants that the environment would be challenging – that it might involve hunger, hardship and anger, and that it would resemble either a barracks, prison, or boot camp, but that they could drop out of the study at any time. The results built on the findings of the Stanford Prison Experiment by demonstrating that individuals only acted in terms of the role they were assigned when they internalized this role as a result of social identification with the group, and that groups with a strong group identity were better able to achieve their goals.

A more recent, but less dramatic, example of the psychological, as well as physical, harm that social science research poses to participants is a study conducted by Steven Levitt of *Freakonomics* fame. In the study, participants were asked to flip a coin to decide an important life issue, such as breaking up with a romantic partner, quitting a job, or deciding which graduate school to attend or employment offer to accept (Levitt 2016). The objective of the study was to determine if people are happier if they make a decision, regardless of the outcome of the decision, than if they do not. The study posed a potential harm to the participants because the participants could have made poor life decisions as a result of the coin toss. However, those who made a major change, like filing for divorce or leaving their jobs, reported being significantly happier two months later, and even happier six months later, than those who did not make a major change in their life, regardless of whether they made the change based on the coin toss or of their own volition.

Protections Against Harm

To reduce the potential physical and psychological harm that social science studies pose to participants, many governments and institutions require that researchers adopt a number of measures. These include obtaining written consent from subjects acknowledging their willingness to participate in studies; informing participants that they can refuse to take part in studies at any time; limiting or banning the use of deception; and debriefing participants after studies about their purpose. Debriefs are especially important when deception is used.

Deception occurs when participants are not given information about the real purpose or nature of the research, or are deliberately given false information about some aspect of the research. It is problematic because it undermines the intent behind informed consent. A major scandal arose, which resulted in a joint letter of apology from two university presidents, when hundreds of thousands of Montana state voters were deceived by a study that researchers at Stanford University and Dartmouth College conducted on non-partisan

Cartoon 2.1

ballots. Although the Montanans were deceived in the study, this was not the intention of the researchers.

In this study, the researchers distributed tens of thousands of postcards to Montana state residents to determine if people are more likely to participate in judicial races when they have more information about the ideology of the judicial candidates. The postcards showed how liberal or conservative judicial candidates for the 2014 judicial elections in Montana were using a scale in which Democratic President Barack Obama and 2012 Republican presidential nominee Mitt Romney were the two end points, denoting very liberal and very conservative candidates.

On the postcards, the researchers used the Montana state seal without permission. The researchers disclosed the fact that the postcards were part of a research study, but in a discrete and oblique way. The disclosure statement was in small print towards the bottom of the postcards and said: 'Paid for by researchers from Stanford University and Dartmouth College'. As a result, many Montanans thought that the postcards were official communications from the state and contacted their representatives to inquire and complain about them.

Intellectual Theft

Although it does not cause physical or psychological harm to participants, intellectual theft violates any reasonable standard for ethical research. Intellectual theft occurs when researchers take more credit than they are owed for research. Plagiarism is the most overt form of intellectual threat. It occurs when someone appropriates, in part or in full, the

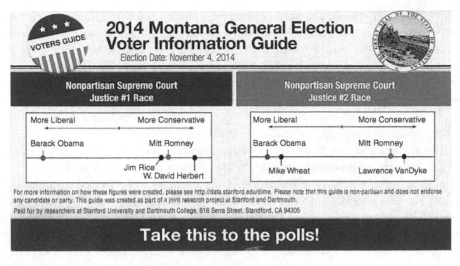

Figure 2.1   Montana non-partisan voter study flyer

Source: Montana Public Radio (http://mtpr.org/post/dartmouth-stanford-violated-montana-election-laws)

academic, artistic, or scientific work of another person. In the case of plagiarism, the person accused of appropriating the work has no claim to have influenced the appropriated work. In other forms of intellectual theft, this is not the case.

Intellectual thievery of this nature occurs when researchers take credit for being collaborators on projects to which they did not contribute. This situation may arise if senior researchers use their position to pressure or compel junior researchers (e.g., another faculty

Plagiarism

Copying the ideas, writing, or data of another researcher's work (published or unpublished) without citing it.

Credit-stealing

Taking credit for research that one did not directly contribute to by including one's name on a byline or ordering the names on a byline to indicate a contribution greater than one's actual contribution.

Credit-denying

Denying a researcher's contribution by not including his or her name on a byline or downplaying his or her contribution by manipulating the order of names on a byline.

Figure 2.2   Forms of intellectual theft

member or a post-doctorate, graduate, or undergraduate student) to include their name on the junior researchers' work. Senior researchers may do this because they feel that the junior researchers got the idea for the work directly from their lectures and public statements or their conversations with them. Senior researchers may also do this because they believe that the junior researchers benefited from their mentorship on the project in another way, including financially. The reverse may also occur where senior researchers give credit to junior researchers for a project that the junior researchers did not contribute to in order to advance the junior researchers' career.

Credit in academic research is generally based on co-authorship. In some fields, particularly in the sciences, anyone regardless of the size of their contribution to a project is listed as a co-author – at times making for articles with a hundred or more co-authors. In other fields, only people who make a significant contribution are listed as co-authors and those who did not are mentioned in the acknowledgements section. The difficulty in the latter is that there is no standard as to what level or type of contribution merits co-authorship, and if a person is paid for their contribution, whether or not that person should be listed as a co-author.

The dilemma of credit attribution is not unique to academia. Many well-known artists, including those with techniques as diverse as August Rodin, Andy Warhol, and Antony Gormley have had assistants, who have been deeply involved in the production of the artist's work, yet their names do not appear on the final work. In contrast, Salvador Dalí's wife never assisted in the production of her husband's art, but nonetheless Dalí signed her name alongside his on his paintings.[4] Meanwhile, German artists, Hans Zank and Willi Gericke co-painted many works and with few exceptions, signed none of them.

In some fields in the social sciences, the degree to which authors contribute to a project is acknowledged by the order in which the names are listed on the project's byline. In these fields, the author who made the most significant contribution to the work is listed first, while the author who made the second most significant contribution is listed second, and so on. In some fields, especially in the natural sciences, the last person(s) listed is generally the researcher under whose auspices the research was conducted. In other fields, authors are listed alphabetically regardless of their contribution. In many more fields, though, there is no uniform practice as to whether authors are listed according to their contribution or not. When name order denotes the contribution of a person to a project, intellectual theft can also arise when a person is listed ahead of another who made a more significant contribution.

In order to avoid conflicts among co-authors from arising, some academic institutions, professional organizations, and journals have guidelines regarding authorship but, unfortunately, these guidelines are often not respected. Thus, it is important for researchers to agree on how they will assign credit among collaborators before beginning a project. Of course, these initial discussions can be fraught with power dynamics and not result in equitable outcomes. Disagreements can also still arise after the research has been completed. In the end, some contributors may contribute more or less than they had originally agreed to because of the way in which the project evolved, while others may have contributed less than they originally promised to because they shirked their responsibilities.

Research Fraud

Research fraud refers to misconduct involving the intentional falsification or fabrication of research or the reporting of false or misleading results. Errors that are made unwittingly do not constitute research fraud. Researchers may perpetrate fraud for a number of reasons, including the desire to obtain a certain job or not lose one; publish an article in a prestigious outlet; satisfy a grant provider; advance a company in which they have a financial stake; and obtain tenure or enhance their academic reputation more generally. A recent prominent case of flagrant research fraud is the LaCour-Green scandal.

The LaCour-Green scandal revolves around a 2014 study published in *Science*, which challenged conventional views that political beliefs are very stable and that any changes in these beliefs are small and short-term. The study consisted of a field experiment in which a canvasser had a brief conversation with participants in order to persuade them to support gay marriage. The study found that just a brief conversation with a canvasser increased significantly the likelihood of someone supporting gay marriage, and that the effect lasted for months if the canvassers identified themselves as homosexual. However, the original data upon which this conclusion was reached was fabricated.

The firm that Michael LaCour claims conducted the survey of the participants' attitudes toward gay marriage said that LaCour never hired them, and the foundations that LaCour identified as having funded the project denied doing so. The fraud was exposed by two Berkeley grad students, along with a third colleague at Yale, who identified significant irregularities in the replication data, including very high response rates, baseline outcome data that was statistically indistinguishable from a prior national survey, unusually small overtime changes in the data that were indistinguishable from perfectly normally distributed noise, and so forth. *Science* retracted the article at the request of LaCour's co-author, Donald P. Green, when Green became aware of the irregularities and was unable to obtain the raw data from LaCour, who claimed to have destroyed it in order to protect the participants' privacy.

Research fraud also involves more subtle ways of purposefully manipulating the results of studies at different stages of the research process. They include intentionally asking leading interview or survey questions to confirm expectations at the outset of a study. They also include setting up a study in order to stack the deck in favor of finding supportive empirical results, as well as massaging the data after the fact by discarding outliers, and using inappropriate statistical techniques or other means to ensure the significance of the statistical results. It also includes intentionally presenting only results that confirm a study's theories, while intentionally hiding results that do not conform to expectations.

A well-known example of research fraud of this kind is Hausergate. The case involves former Harvard professor, Mark Hauser, who at the time was an eminent psychologist whose work demonstrating that monkeys have cognitive abilities similar to humans, had a significant impact on his field. In the last decade, investigations of ethic boards at

Cartoon 2.2

Harvard and the US government found Hauser guilty of recording false values in experiments, fabricating data after the fact, and providing incorrect information regarding the methods used in studies.

Researchers in Hauser's lab suspected that Hauser changed the values in some of his experimental data when they gave him data from experiments showing insignificant results, and received back from him data with some values changed showing significant results. Video recordings of the experiments also did not match Hauser's claims of how the experiments were conducted. In one study, he claimed to have found evidence that cotton-top tamarin monkeys reacted to shifts in syllables patterns in ways similar to those of humans, but videos of the experiment showed that monkeys were only exposed to one pattern of syllables.

In order to prevent this kind of research fraud, some fields have suggested a number of different and creative measures. One measure is to have researchers using quantitative techniques register the analyses that they intend to conduct prior to running them. This would prevent researchers from presenting only those results that support their findings. Some disciplines have tried to encourage this practice voluntarily with little luck.

Another suggestion is for journal editors to agree to publish articles based on analyses researchers propose to run prior to the researchers conducting the analyses. This would remove any incentives researchers have to manipulate the results in order to publish articles, but not to obtain fame from them. This strategy is further problematic because the contribution of a research project is an important criterion for publication, which is difficult to assess apart from the results.

Peer Review

Peer review is an important component of the research process and is used to determine the suitability of research for publication or financial support. Through peer review, experts evaluate research in a given field regarding the quality and integrity of the research so far as they can discern. The experts who review the research are not associated in any way with the research being evaluated and are expected to give their independent and unbiased assessment of the research.

The peer review process may be single-blind, where reviewers are informed of the identity of the researchers and may take this into account in their evaluation, or double-blind, where neither the reviewers nor the researchers are informed of the identity of the other. Even when the review process is double-blind, in practice, reviewers often know the identity of the researchers because they are already familiar with their work through conferences and other venues.

Unfortunately, this stage of the research process can be corrupted. Researchers may positively review low quality research because they are friends with the authors of the research or hope that the authors will favorably review future research of theirs. They may also positively review low quality research that references their own work, especially if it flatters theirs, because this research will draw attention to their own work if it is published.

Researchers may also negatively review high quality research in order to prevent others from publishing research in their area of expertise or on a similar topic before they have an opportunity to publish work on it. Researchers may also negatively review high quality research to prevent findings contrary to theirs from being published. They may also do so in order to retaliate against another researcher for personal reasons or for this researcher having negatively reviewed past work of theirs, among other reasons.

Box 2.1   Ethics Violations in Peer Reviews Occur When …

- reviewers reject high quality research for personal or political reasons
- reviewers identify the author of the research, breaking the double-blind review system, and base their reviews on information about the author of the research
- researchers rig the system so that reviewers likely to favor their research are chosen

---

Even when the review process has not been corrupted in these ways, the review process is not foolproof. In 2013, a scientist submitted an article, which had obvious errors in it, to hundreds of open-access journals, which provide no-fee access to their content and its use. According to the scientist, a competent peer reviewer should have easily identified these errors and rejected the article based on them. However, more than half of the open-access journals accepted the article. This problem is not limited to open-access journals, however. Low quality articles like this one may slip through the review process for many reasons. Reviewers may not be qualified to review articles or certain aspects of them. Reviewers may not read the research they are reviewing carefully or may not have access to information (e.g., raw data, software, and codebooks) needed to identify certain problems in studies, such as poor quality data, coding errors, and so forth. This was the case with the LaCour-Green study. The LaCour-Green study was externally reviewed and accepted for publication in *Science,* a leading scientific journal, before it was exposed for fraud.

Box 2.2   Peer Reviews Cannot Detect Ethics Violations When ...

- reviewers lack access to information needed to verify research, such as raw data (e.g. interview transcripts, raw numeric data)
- reviewers do not dedicate time to fully vet an article based on information at their disposal.

Research Transparency

Replicability refers to the ability of another researcher using the same procedures under the same circumstances to research the same question and obtain comparable results. It does not refer to publishing the same research multiple times, as was the case with a 2014 article on mass analysis, which the journal *Surface Interface Analysis* unintentionally published three times.

The issue of replicability has gained increasing attention because a number of articles have been published as of late indicating that a disturbingly small percentage of articles published in prominent social science journals can be replicated. In 2015, *Science,* the same journal that accepted the LaCour-Green study for publication, published an article, which concluded that less than half of all published articles in peer-reviewed psychology journals were replicable (Open Science Collaboration 2015).

Replicability is important for improving the quality of research. The sharing of data allows researchers to identify errors in other researchers' work, and incentivizes researchers to produce higher quality research in the first place. Replicability also facilitates cumulative knowledge building through the sharing of data. When quantitative data are shared, for example, researchers can build on these data by extending the time or country coverage, adding new measures to test different theories, and evaluating the same data using new estimation techniques.

Research may not be replicable for a number of reasons besides outright fraud or research misconduct. Research may not be replicable due to errors in the original analyses or the replication material, and mistakes by those trying to replicate the research. They may also not be replicable due to researchers lacking information regarding the techniques and protocols used in analyses, the inability of researchers to reproduce the exact same environment as the original study, as well as normal and expected statistical variations. More than one of these factors may help explain why researchers have been unable to replicate the results of a very controversial study by Daryl Bem that claims to have found empirical evidence of psychic abilities.

Bem, a well-respected Cornell University professor, was very transparent about his procedures and even shared the software he used to conduct the analyses, but multiple attempts to replicate the findings did not find empirical support for his findings. Many reasons have been proposed to explain the failure to replicate his results, including the fact that the replication studies were carried out after the study had received substantial media attention, so that participants' responses were contaminated by their knowledge of the controversy. Other reasons suggested include the use of inappropriate or liberal statistical tests likely to overestimate the results, such as one-sided p-values, unrealistically low Bayesian priors, and optional stopping.

In response to the apparent replicability crisis, many professional organizations and journals have adopted standards about research transparency that articles must comply with in order to be published. Some journals have also hired in-house staff to replicate analyses before publishing them, while some researchers have independently contracted firms to replicate their results for them. In order to reduce the costs of replication and to create a non-adversarial replication process, some researchers have suggested innovative ways to facilitate the replication of study results using crowdsourcing and citizen scientists. Citizen scientists are individuals without academic affiliations that help researchers conduct studies.

Key Points

- Research ethics standards are highly debated and vary across countries, institutions, and fields.
- Ethnical concerns are not limited to outright fraud, but also include issues related to the protection of human subjects from physical and psychological harm, credit sharing, and massaging the data to produce favorable results, and so forth.
- Measures exist to improve the quality and integrity of research, such as institutional ethics boards, peer review, and publication requirements regarding the sharing of data and code, but none of these measures are foolproof.

Further Reading

The first and last readings discuss the ethical issues involved in research in authoritarian and unstable countries. The second and third books survey current issues and debates in research ethics in the social sciences.

Glasius, Marlies, Meta de Lange, Jos Bartman, Emanuela Dalmasso, Aofei Lv, Adele Del Sordi, Marcus Michaelsen and Kris Ruijgrok. 2018. *Research, Ethics and Risk in the Authoritarian Field*. Cham, Switzerland: Palgrave Macmillan.

Israel, Mark. 2015. *Research Ethics and Integrity for Social Scientists: Beyond Regulatory Compliance.* London: Sage Publications.

Mertens, Donna M. and Pauline E. Ginsberg. 2009. *The Handbook of Social Research Ethics.* Thousand Oaks, CA: Sage Publications.

Wood, Elisabeth. 2006. 'The Ethical Challenges of Field Research in Conflict Zones.' *Qualitative Sociology* 29(3): 307–41.

EXERCISE 2.1

Discuss the potential physical and psychological harm that the following study poses to participants.[5] In your assessment, do the potential benefits of this study outweigh the potential risks in terms of the likelihood of the benefits and risks occurring and the magnitude of their effects? Also, discuss whether or not there are any protections that could have been included in the design of the study to have reduced the possibility of harm to subjects, and explain their advantages and disadvantages.

> In a study to understand how businesses respond to customer grievances, a Columbia University Business School professor sent a letter to 240 restaurants in New York City falsely claiming to have been food poisoned during a meal with his wife to celebrate their wedding anniversary. Before learning that the professor's claims were false, and were part of a research project that had not been approved by the university ethics board, some restaurants offered the professor a refund and a complimentary dinner to apologize. Many of the restaurant owners, some of whom filed lawsuits against the university, said that upon receiving the letter, they worried that the food poisoning incident would tarnish their restaurants' reputations and would result in a loss of costumers and jobs.

EXERCISE 2.2

Each of the studies below poses significant harm to the participants, as well as their communities. For one of these studies, identify the potential harm that the study poses to the participants and their communities. Does the likelihood and severity of these risks outweigh the benefits of the potential findings of the study and why? How would you design a study to answer the same question but with less potential physical and psychological risk to the participants and their communities? What are the potential risks, if any, of your study? Does the likelihood and severity of these risks outweigh the benefits of the potential findings of your study, and why?

1. impose fraud on an election to determine if electoral monitors are effective in detecting electoral fraud.
2. offer a bribe to individuals of different religious denominations, agnostics, and atheists to determine if any of these groups are more or less willing to accept a bribe than the others.
3. pay people cash to turn in their guns in to local police stations with no questions asked.
4. study the effect of training programs in preventing former combatants from engaging in future violent activity by hiring local business to train former combatants in various trades.

EXERCISE 2.3

Debate the following questions:

1. Does requiring students to participate in experiments (of their choosing) as part of their classes, or paying participants a very large amount of money to participate in experiments, undermine their free will to participate and, thus, violate certain norms and standards for research ethics?

2. Is it appropriate to use information from past research, which would likely violate contemporary human subject standards, as in the case of the Milgram experiments or the Stanford Prison Experiment, if that information could make a significant contribution to existing knowledge about important phenomena that would better people's lives today?

EXERCISE 2.4

In your field, what type and level of contribution do you think merits a person being listed as a co-author on a project? Do you think the names of collaborators should be ordered to denote their contribution or listed alphabetically?

EXERCISE 2.5

Discuss the potential advantages and disadvantages of registering an analysis prior to conducting it in order to reduce the risk of fraud, and the advantages and disadvantages of accepting research for publication based on analyses that have been proposed but not yet conducted.

Identifying a Research Question

One of the hardest, but most important, aspect of any research project, is identifying a valuable question to explore. Remarking on this difficulty, Alfred Nobel once stated that '[i]f I have a thousand ideas and only one turns out to be good, I am satisfied.'[1] Unfortunately, deadlines and other pressures to publish can compel researchers to charge into the next project before they have identified a worthwhile question to explore. In order to identify such a question, researchers must take the time to explore potential ideas, have the courage to discard inadequate ones, and be willing to make progress in their research without necessarily putting words on a paper. While it is possible to ruin a great question with poor research design and methods, it is impossible to turn a bad question into a great one with excellent research design and methods.

What Constitutes a Good Research Topic?

A good research topic should be something that is important and interesting to the researcher in order to sustain his or her interest throughout the research process, and important and interesting to others in order to sustain theirs. While research can be engaging, it can also be quite challenging. It can require researchers to learn different skills and master new technologies, including foreign languages, advanced statistics, and computer programming. It can also involve a sizeable amount of tedious work, such as transcribing interviews, arranging the logistics of field trips, and reading through reams of news articles or reports to construct datasets, not to mention endless hours of entering data from these materials into databases.

Research can further demand many personal sacrifices. Although travelling abroad to conduct archival research or interviews can be exciting, it can also mean living without all the luxuries of home, like hot showers, reliable internet access, your favorite foods, and the company of friends and family. Even research that does not require travel abroad can still demand many sacrifices. It may demand spending late nights or weekends in the library, getting up at 3am in the morning to conduct a phone interview with someone living in a different time zone, and foregoing career opportunities, relaxing weekends, and holidays, among other things.

Not only can research require personal sacrifices, but it can also be emotionally taxing. Research can push people outside their comfort zones and raise feelings of self-doubt, frustration, and of being overwhelmed. It can also provoke feelings of loneliness, stress, and depression, especially when aspects of your research do not go as planned or when the project does not yield interesting results. These challenges, however daunting, though, make the sense of achievement once the research has been completed all the greater.

But, in order to supersede these challenges, individuals have to be very passionate and dedicated to the subject of their research. When asked (by himself) the 'secret of his success', Nobel Prize winner Sir Edward Appleton, answered enthusiasm .... 'I rate enthusiasm even above professional skill.'[2] Appleton's discoveries regarding the ionosphere are fundamental to our understanding of radio transmission, and contributed to the development of long-range radio communication as well as radar.

There are many different reasons why a topic might be interesting and important to someone. Personal experience is only one of them. A person might be interested, for example, in understanding national immigration or refugee policies because his or her parents immigrated in their youth to the country in which they now live, while someone else might be interested in studying offshoring because many jobs where this person lives have relocated abroad. Other people, in contrast, might be interested in examining issues that are far from their personal experiences, such as gendercide or child marriages, because these issues speak to their values, such as justice, individualism, or respect for human life.

Others may want to study a particular issue related to a career that they are considering pursuing in order to acquire further knowledge on this issue, explore this career from a different angle, or demonstrate to future employers or school admission officers their commitment to a subject. A person interested in a career in international law, for example, may want to research compliance with international treaties, or perceptions of alternative forms of justice, such as war crime tribunals, truth commissions, and so forth. A person interested in a career in international development, meanwhile, may decide to research the utility of digital games for teaching refugee children language, cognitive, and coding skills and improving mental health.

A good research topic should be something that is not only important and interesting to the researcher, but it should also be something others will likely find interesting and important as well. One indication of how important and interesting others are likely to think a particular research topic is the amount of news interest and academic research already on an issue. If this topic already garners a lot of attention, then it is likely a topic that will be of interest to others. Of course, at the same time, if there is already a lot of research on the topic, it can be more difficult to make a unique contribution to research in this area.

While public interest in a topic is important, at the same time, researchers ought to be wary of fads. What is hot one year might not be hot the next. Interest in terrorism has grown in recent years due to global political events, but research on terrorism is not a fad. Unfortunately, terrorist events are unlikely to decline in the near future, making for an abiding interest and need for research on terrorism. Research, though, on Bitcoin is likely to be more of a passing fad due to the impracticality and extraordinary volatility of the cryptocurrency and the isolated demographic (i.e., young American men) that it attracts.

Research on neuromarketing is also likely a passing trend. Neuromarketing uses functional magnetic resonance imaging (fMRI), electroencephalography (EEG), biometrics, facial coding, eye tracking, and other technologies to ascertain how consumers respond to certain products and services (Ariely and Berns 2010). Neuromarketing is touted for its

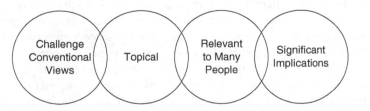

Figure 3.1 Characteristics of important research questions

ability to identify consumers' unconscious responses to products and services. However, it is not practicable given the high costs it entails, and as of yet, has failed to yield information that is more useful than that which can be obtained through much less costly surveys and focus groups.

Another way to gauge the importance of a potential research topic is to consider how many people the subject of this research may affect. Is the research about refugee policies, which affects tens of millions of refugees each year, or is it about dispensing foreign aid to countries through bond or loan guarantees, two exceedingly rare forms of foreign aid? By most accounts, a research topic that has an impact on a greater number of people is more important than one that affects fewer.

However, it is equally important to consider not only how many people the research has the potential to affect, but also how significant are the ways in which it may affect them. Some research may add to our knowledge of a subject, but not have implications for how to better the world. Research, for example, finding that Bitcoin users tend to be young is not unlikely to fundamentally change the demographic of Bitcoin users, since the innate characteristics of this digital currency are antagonistic towards older users (Yelowitz and Wilson 2015).

Other research, though, can have significant policy implications. Research on the causes of violence within refugee camps, the permissive conditions of gender-based violence, the types of foreign aid more or less likely to be corrupted by recipient states are all examples of research with the potential to significantly impact the lives of others. For many researchers, what drives them is the ability to affect positive change in the world even if this change is small and not immediately apparent. Often the biggest obstacle in this endeavor, according to development economist Jeffrey Sachs, is overcoming cynicism that change is possible.[3]

Even a seemingly trendy or narrow topic, however, may still be valuable to study if it has important applications to other issues. The research topic must be framed, though, in a way that makes its relevance to other research apparent. A study on the separatist movement in Kosovo in the 1990s might seem narrow since Kosovo's population is less than two million people. However, the findings of such a study might help explain why, in contrast to conventional views, economically poor regions with little chance of forming economically viable states have separatist movements (Herrera 2004).

A final way to gauge the importance and likely interest of others in a particular research topic is to share your idea with friends and family, and even complete strangers. It can actually be more valuable to share your idea with acquaintances and strangers (e.g., cab drivers, hair stylists, or doctors) than friends and family members since the latter might share a similar perspective as you, given your common backgrounds, or not reveal their true feelings about a topic to avoid hurting yours. If your topic is framed in a way to maximize its appeal, and if others stare at you blankly when you tell them what you are thinking about researching, or respond with a polite, 'Oh, that sounds interesting' without asking any further questions, then it might be a good idea to consider a different research topic.

From Topic to Question to Puzzle

After settling on a research topic, the next step is to transform this topic into a research question and ideally, a research puzzle. A research question is much more specific than a research topic. It relates to a particular aspect of the broader topic that a researcher seeks to understand. A research question, for example, on the topic of immigration might ask 'Under what conditions does a massive influx of refugees into a country provoke a rise in nationalist (anti-immigrant) parties at the polls?' Another important aspect of the topic of immigration is the trafficking of women. A research question about it might ask 'What is the relationship between the trafficking of women and China's one-child policy?'

Social science research questions should not be normative even though social scientists may be driven to study a particular topic for normative reasons or values, such as freedom, equality, or dignity. Normative questions ask questions about what should be rather than what is, and are not falsifiable. A normative question on the subject of refugees might ask 'Do states have a responsibility to protect refugees?' A normative question on China's one-child policy might ask, meanwhile, whether or not it is appropriate for governments to restrict the rights of individuals to protect the common good.

Social science questions do not try to predict the future either. 'Will China democratize?' and 'Will North Korea and South Korea reunite?' are both examples of questions that try to predict the future. The findings of social science research may have implications for future events, but they do not try to predict whether specific events will occur or not. Instead of asking whether China will democratize or the two Koreas reunite, a social science question might ask 'What are the conditions that make one-party states likely to democratize?' or 'What are the long-term effects of partitions?'

Social science research questions should address an important aspect of the larger phenomena that are being studied. A research question itself is not important simply by virtue of being on an important topic. International trade is an important topic. However, a research question about the effectiveness of environment standards in free trade agreements is not especially important since few trade agreements include provisions about the environment. Environmental protection is also an important issue but research on the trafficking of wildlife by rebel groups to finance civil wars is not. At least, it is not as important as research on other resources to finance these wars, such as oil and diamonds, which provide a much more profitable source of funding for rebels than wildlife trafficking.

Ideally, a research question should also constitute a puzzle. A puzzle is a question for which the answer is not immediately obvious. Puzzles are derived from unexpected or surprising phenomena, like a man biting a dog as opposed to a dog biting a man. Table 3.1 illustrates the differences between research questions versus research puzzles

Research questions that constitute puzzles often challenge conventional views. These views are frequently derived from historical trends, expert opinion, common assumptions about human behavior, and so forth. Alternatively, research questions that constitute a puzzle may involve a debate between two opposing viewpoints, one of which may represent the conventional view on a subject.

A question about what the health effects of civil wars are is not a puzzle since very few people would be surprised to learn that civil wars have detrimental effects on local populations. Nor is a question about why couples that are unhappy in their marriages are more likely to divorce than couples that are happy in their marriages. However, a question about why adults, who are unhappily married, are not necessarily happier after divorce than before is a puzzle (Amato 2000; Amato and Hohmann-Marriott 2007).

Contentious divorce negotiations can be one source of this unhappiness. In general, negotiations are believed to be more successful when handled by a mediator that is neutral to both parties. That is why a proposition that biased mediators who favor one side in an international conflict are more effective in ending militarized conflicts than unbiased mediators is an excellent puzzle (Kydd 2003). In this case, the puzzle is derived from a historical trend in the behavior and beliefs of political actors about mediators.

In some cases, the puzzle lies in the fact that a historical trend is not as striking because a given outcome is different in one set of cases than in another very similar set of cases. Why, for example, decentralization reduces intrastate conflict in some countries, such as Spain, and not in others, like Bosnia-Herzegovina, is a puzzle for this reason (Brancati 2006, 2009). So is a question about why rape is more prevalent during violent conflicts in some states, such as Rwanda (1994), and not in others, including Sri Lanka (1983–2009) and Peru (1982–2010) (Wood 2006).

Question	Puzzle
What are the effects of divorce on the psychological wellbeing of divorcees?	Why are adults who are unhappily married not happier after divorce (Amato 2000; Amato and Hohmann-Marriott 2007)?
What characteristics make for the best mediators?	Why are biased mediators more effective in ending militarized conflicts than unbiased mediators (Kydd 2003)?
What is the best political system to prevent intrastate conflict?	Why does decentralization reduce intrastate conflict in some countries and not in others (Brancati 2006)?
What strategies do rebel groups use against their opponents to achieve their goals?	Why is rape prevalent during violent conflicts in some states and not in others (Wood 2006)?
What effect, if any, do regime changes have on the propensity of states to go to war?	Why are democratizing states more war-prone when democracies are more pacific, at least towards each other (Mansfield and Snyder 2007)?
What are the characteristics of countries that determine trade flows?	Why do countries with similar capital-to-labor ratios commonly trade in contrast to expectations regarding comparative advantage (Krugman 1979)?
How do people make decisions on important issues?	Why do people make decisions that do not maximize their utility (Tversky and Kahneman 1981)?

Table 3.1 Research questions versus research puzzles

"You need to read the late edition."

Cartoon 3.1

Other research puzzles do not lie in historical trends, but rather in expectations derived from existing research or expert opinion. Research, for example, concluding that democratizing states are more prone to initiating international wars is puzzling because decades of research have shown that stable democracies are less likely to go to war with other democracies (Mansfield and Snyder 2007). Likewise, research showing that countries with similar capital-to-labor ratios commonly trade with each other is puzzling, and helped earn Paul Krugman a Nobel Prize in economics, because it challenges the principle of comparative advantage. This principle postulates that countries specialize in producing and exporting only those goods and services that they can produce at lower opportunity costs than other goods and services (Krugman 1979).

Finally, other research puzzles challenge expectations or assumptions about human behavior. Psychological theories on cognitive biases have challenged conventional views that people always make rational decisions by demonstrating that often people make decisions that do not maximize their utility based on how issues are framed in terms of losses or gains (Tversky and Kahneman 1981). Theories about international norms have similarly challenged assumptions about rationality by arguing that individuals, groups, and states behave according to social norms, which define what is appropriate behavior, even though following these norms conflicts with their material interests.

The search for a puzzle has the potential to result in straw men. Straw men are very weak arguments, which are easily defeated, but presented as strong arguments in order to make them appear as puzzles. Straw men should always be avoided. Claiming that everyone perceives free trade positively in order to introduce an argument about how preferences for free trade vary based on economic class or ethnic identity is an example of a straw man. While economists widely view free trade as positive for economic development, it is well established that the views of the general population are much more polarized.

To ensure that your research question is important and interesting, and even puzzling without being a straw man, it is a good idea to pitch it to others. What seems surprising to one person may not necessarily seem surprising to another. Someone who is not familiar with issues of development might not see the previous question about free trade as a straw man, but someone who is, immediately will. Therefore, it is best to solicit the opinions of individuals with a range of backgrounds and experiences. If others generally think your question is not especially important or interesting, and that the answer to your question is rather obvious, then it is likely a good idea to develop a new question on your topic of interest.

Making a Contribution

The ultimate value of any research project lies not just in the question it poses, but in the contribution the project makes to extant knowledge regarding this question. This contribution may be theoretical, empirical, or both. A theoretical contribution relates to the explanation provided for a given question or puzzle, while an empirical contribution refers to the evidence offered in support of this explanation. Figure 3.2 summarizes the different types of contributions that research can make along these dimensions. Ideally, research will make both a theoretical and empirical contribution, but plenty of valuable research has done only one or the other.

Research can make a theoretical contribution by challenging an existing explanation for a given phenomenon with or without proposing an alternative explanation for this phenomenon, by providing an additional explanation for a given phenomenon, or by simply refining an existing theory. Often research that challenges an existing theory without providing an alternative explanation for a given phenomenon does so because it argues against the existence of the phenomenon itself. Sheri Berman (1997) in her research on the Weimar Republic does just that, challenging a widely held view that social capital is necessary for civic engagement and, thereby, democracy (Putnam 2000).

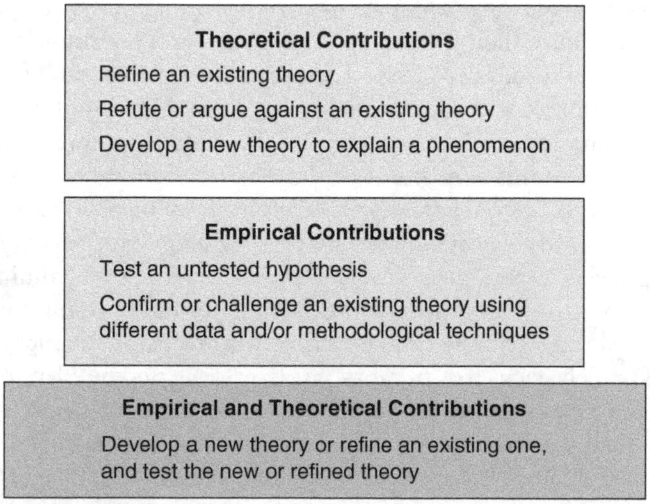

Theoretical Contributions

Refine an existing theory

Refute or argue against an existing theory

Develop a new theory to explain a phenomenon

Empirical Contributions

Test an untested hypothesis

Confirm or challenge an existing theory using different data and/or methodological techniques

Empirical and Theoretical Contributions

Develop a new theory or refine an existing one, and test the new or refined theory

Figure 3.2   Types of contributions

Social capital was very strong in the Weimar Republic, according to Berman, and did not prevent, and in fact helped, the Nazis rise to power. The dense network of civic groups in the Weimar Republic, she argues, provided the Nazis with cadres of activists that the Nazis used to gain insight into the fears and needs of particular groups in German society at the time in order to tailor their appeal to them. These cadres of activists also had the skills, organizational contacts, and social expertise needed to spread the party's message, mobilize the electorate, and discredit political opponents. In her research, Berman does not offer an alternative explanation for civil engagement or democratic stability, but simply challenges the link between social capital, civic engagement and democracy.

When researchers offer either an alternative explanation or an additional explanation for a phenomenon, it is because they accept that the phenomenon exists, but they do not accept the existing explanations for it, or think that these explanations are incomplete. Dawn Brancati's (2006, 2009) argument regarding the role of decentralization in the management of intrastate conflict is an example of the former. Brancati challenges both claims that decentralization increases intrastate conflict and those that decentralization decreases it, arguing that the effect of decentralization on intrastate conflict depends on the structure of decentralization and its effect, in turn, on the party system. Decentralized systems of government, she argues, which encourage parties to compete cross-nationally are more likely to reduce intrastate conflict in states with territorially-concentrated ethnic groups than those that do not.

Instead of developing a new explanation for a given phenomenon, research can also make a valuable theoretical contribution by refining an existing theory. One way to refine an existing theory is to demonstrate how the theory only applies under certain conditions. There are many examples of seminal research, which are refinements of existing theories. Tversky and Kahneman's (1981) research on framing is a refinement of rational choice theory in that it establishes the conditions under which people makes decisions that do not maximize their utility. One of the important conditions that they establish is that individuals are likely to choose one option over another, even if the two options are equivalent in terms of economic value, if this option is framed as avoiding losses rather than acquiring gains.

Likewise, Paul Krugman's (1979) work explaining why trade occurs between states with roughly the same ratio of capital to labor is a refinement of the Heckscher-Ohlin model. Krugman argues that this occurs because of localized external economies. Localized external economies is the territorial clustering of industries that occurs within countries due to labor pool sharing, increasing returns of scale, and the ease with which like industries in close proximity of each other are able to communicate and exchange supplies, laborers and ideas.

Instead of making a theoretical contribution, research can make a contribution to extant knowledge on empirical grounds. One way in which research can do this is by providing new evidence regarding an existing theory. This theory may (or may not) have been tested before and the empirical findings may (or may not) confirm the existing theory. The new evidence may take different forms, such as new data or new results based on different methodological approaches or techniques. The extent of the empirical contribution depends on the evidence that already exists on a subject and the strength of the researchers' clams to provide better evidence than that which already exists. It is larger the less evidence that already exists, and the stronger the researchers' claims to having higher quality evidence than that which already exists.

Thad Dunning and Lauren Harrison (2010) make just such an empirical contribution in their work on cross-cutting cleavages. Cross-cutting cleavages are social cleavages, such as religious, ethnic, and tribal cleavages, which overlap each other, as members of a particular religious group are composed of multiple different ethnic groups. Researchers have long hypothesized that cross-cutting cleavages have stabilizing and moderating influences on political behavior (Lipset 1960). The causal effects of cross-cutting cleavages, however, are difficult to demonstrate because many factors related to patterns in ethnic politics are also related to countries' cleavage structures. A government, for example, may compel a minority group to convert to another religion so that religious and ethnic identities are cross-cutting in a country. However, the forced conversion can cause strife between the ethnic groups resulting in violent conflict between them.

To overcome this problem, Dunning and Harrison conducted a lab-in-the-field experiment in Mali in which they asked Malians to evaluate the quality of political speeches. The politicians delivering the speeches either belonged to the same ethnic group and cousinage as the participants in the experiment, the same ethnic group or the same cousinage group, or neither group. Cousinage in Mali and in other West African countries refers to a set of symbolic or fictional kinships characterized by banter or joking among cousins. Consistent with expectations, Dunning and Harrison found in their experiment that Malians are more likely to vote for candidates of the same ethnicity if they are joking cousins of theirs than if they are not.

Finding Inspiration

Approaches to research differ. Many researchers take a problem-driven approach to research by identifying an issue within their field that is unexplained and which has potentially significant social effects, and immersing themselves in that problem with the hope of finding an explanation for, if not a solution to, that problem. Researchers who take this approach differ in how they identify these problems. Some researchers identify problems based on gaps in the existing literature, while others look to everyday experiences and global events for inspiration. Each strategy has its distinct advantages and disadvantages.

Researchers who derive their ideas from existing research may find it easier to convince others of the value of their research, but they may be less likely to come up with original ideas, such as the availability heuristic, because their ideas are influenced, if not constrained, by the ideas of others. Nobel Prize winner Daniel Kahneman said that the idea for the availability heuristic, which he and his life-long collaborator Amos Tversky developed, came from wondering about the divorce rate of professors at their university (Tversky and Kahneman 1973). The availability heuristic is a shortcut whereby people make judgments about the likelihood of an event based on how easily an instance or case of the event comes to mind. As per the availability heuristic, when Kahneman and Tversky tried to calculate the divorce rate of professors at their university, they did so by thinking of all the divorced professors that they could think of off the top of their heads at the university.

Similarly, Sheena Iyengar claims that she decided to study whether too many options leads to greater indecision after leaving empty-handed from a local grocery store that carried an abundance of choices in similar products, because she could not decide what she wanted.[4] Iyengar has applied her hypothesis about indecisions to many different scenarios, including decisions about whether or not to remove life support in the case of a terminally ill person.

Great ideas, like the availability heuristic and Iyengar's, do not always come when you need them, or when you have time to fully explore them. As Nobel Prize winning astrophysicist Saul Perlmutter once put it, 'you can't order [breakthroughs] up.'[5] Instead, according to Perlmutter, they are developed through the playful, undirected engagement of ideas. As a result, it can be useful to keep a 'Book of Ideas' in which to record observations, questions, hunches, or hypotheses as they occur to you so that you can further develop them later.

Instead of taking a problem-driven approach to research, some researchers take a funding-driven approach. These researchers derive their ideas of what to study from grants and fellowship announcements. These researchers may be more likely to secure funding for their work, but they may also be constrained theoretically as to what they investigate by the stipulations of their funding. Moreover, the areas in which funding opportunities exist are not necessarily important areas of research since organizations may be compelled to fund certain issues of interest to them or their donors because these issues are narrow and specific to them, such that research on them would not otherwise take place.

Other researchers do not take a problem-driven or a funding-driven approach to research but take a data- or methods-driven approach. Those that take a data-driven approach derive their ideas from the existence of data on an issue. These researchers, once they know that data exists on a topic, try to conjure up research ideas in which they can use the data. This is not a violation of the scientific method in that the researchers are not analyzing the data and developing hypotheses based on patterns that they observe in the data, but are merely directing their attention towards given subjects knowing that data already exists to study them. This approach can reduce the time and costs involved in research, but like a funding-driven approach, it can be theoretically constraining.

A methods-driven approach offers the same benefit as a data-driven approach of reducing the time and costs involved in research since it does not require researchers to learn a new set of skills to conduct their studies. A methods-driven approach involves the application of a different method to an existing problem or question. As such, it is only able to yield an empirical, not a theoretical, contribution. An empirical contribution can still challenge a theoretical argument, however, and have significant real-world implications.

Key Points

- Social science research questions are not normative or predictive, seeking instead to explain current or past human behavior.
- Research questions may take different forms. Those that constitute puzzles are questions for which the answer is not immediately obvious.
- Research questions ought to make a contribution to the academic literature in either theoretical or empirical terms and/or the real world.
- The inspiration for a research question may arise unexpectedly from many different sources, so keep your eyes open.

Further Reading

The first reading relates to the negative comments that respected researchers have received on influential work of theirs. In the second and third reading, Nobel Prize winners discuss how they develop their ideas and provide other useful advice regarding research.

Gans, Joshua S. and George B. Shepherd. 1994. 'How the Mighty are Fallen: Rejected Classic Articles by Leading Economists.' *The Journal of Economic Perspectives* 8(1): 165–179.
Krugman, Paul. 1993. 'How I Work.' *The American Economist* 37(2): 25–31.
Nobel Prize Inspiration Initiative. www.nobelprizeii.org. Accessed 31 January 2018.

EXERCISE 3.1

1. Using the following facts and figures, construct a single-sentence research puzzle and explain why it is a puzzle. You may not use all the information provided.

- Fourteen countries currently have nuclear weapons (either individually or in alliance with other countries), while four countries have destroyed their nuclear weapons stocks.
- The fourteen countries with nuclear weapons are: Belgium, China, France, Germany, the Netherlands, India, Italy, North Korea, Pakistan, Russia, Turkey, the United Kingdom, and the United States.
- The four countries that have destroyed their weapons stocks are: Belarus, Kazakhstan, South Africa, and the Ukraine.
- Israel is also believed to have nuclear weapons but has not made its possession of them public.
- North Korea has an active program dedicated toward developing nuclear weapons. Iran had an active program until the Joint Comprehensive Plan of Action (2015).
- Not all countries with nuclear weapons have long-range weapons.
- Nuclear weapons have only been used once in world history by the United States at the end of the Second World War.

2. Using the following facts and figures, construct a single-sentence research puzzle, and explain why it is a puzzle. You may not use all the information provided.

- Income inequality has increased globally over the last several decades.
- Income inequality has received enormous international media attention in the last few years and tops the political agenda of many world leaders of different ideological orientations.
- Income inequality is not good for growth (Persson and Tabellini 1994).
- Experts have proposed different solutions, including increasing taxes on the rich, raising minimum wages, and expanding public services to close the income gap.
- Publics are divided as to the best solutions to reduce the income gap.
- Experimental studies in psychology show that individuals from higher income brackets are more likely to break the law, cheat, lie during negotiations, and endorse unethical behavior, such as stealing at work, than individuals in lower income brackets (Piff et al. 2012).
- The number of democracies in the world has also grown since at least the end of the Cold War, increasing the enfranchisement of low-income individuals.[6]

EXERCISE 3.2

Provide at least one reason why each of the following research questions are puzzles and suggest one potential explanation (or solution) for this puzzle.

1. Why do people vote in elections in dictatorships?
2. Why isn't linking teachers' merit pay to the performance of students on standardized tests significantly associated with higher student test scores?
3. Why doesn't increasing the traffic fines associated with speeding tickets always reduce an individual's propensity to exceed posted speed limits?
4. Why does the United States spend more on health care than other high-income states even though Americans utilize medical services (e.g., going to doctors and hospitals) less often than individuals in high-income states?

EXERCISE 3.3

Write your own research puzzle and explain why it is a puzzle.

4

Conducting a Literature Review

Objectives

- describe the purpose and content of a literature review
- explain how to organize literature reviews either chronologically or thematically
- discuss how to summarize and synthesize research for a literature review
- provide guidance on practical issues regarding how to identify and format literature

A literature review is an essential component of any research project. The purpose of a *literature review* is to summarize and synthesize the existing academic and non-academic literature on a particular subject in order to characterize the strengths and weaknesses of this literature.[1] A literature review may be undertaken as part of a larger research project or as an independent exercise. In the case of the former, the ultimate goal of the literature review is to demonstrate the theoretical and empirical contribution of the research project at hand to the existing literature. In the case of the latter, it is to identify future avenues of research. The ultimate objective of the literature review affects both the content and structure of the review, but it does not determine the best practices and principles used to identify, discuss, and present literature in a review. These are the same regardless.

Identifying the Literature

A literature review should contain all the relevant and prominent literature on a particular subject regardless of quality. In general, quality is not a criterion for inclusion because quality is evaluated through the literature review. The criteria used to evaluate research quality are discussed at length in subsequent chapters. The criteria for evaluating the empirical contribution of any research endeavor is based on the type of method used as well as the execution of the method, while the criteria for evaluating the theoretical contribution are the same across methods.

Quality is not necessarily linked to prominence, which is a criterion for inclusion. Research may be influential for many reasons other than quality. Research may be influential because it has been published by a well-known scholar affiliated with a prestigious institution or in a prominent outlet with a wide circulation. Research may also be influential because it proposes a very controversial idea that has provoked a backlash.

The prominence of a research project is typically evaluated in terms of its influence on subsequent research and public discourse. It is generally measured in terms of the number of times that a research project, whether it is a book, article, conference paper, and so forth, is cited by other research. Several options exist to track the number of times that written work is cited by other research. They include: Google Scholar, Scopus, Web of Science, and Altmetric. Some of these tools track published as well as unpublished research, while some only detect references to the former, resulting in lower overall citation counts.

Citation counts vary significantly across fields. While 500 citations may indicate a very influential article in one field, it may signify only a modestly influential one in another. Thus, in using citation counts as a measure of influence, one must consider them in terms of the field in which the cited work is written, and even the subfield. Citation counts can vary across subfields of the same discipline because more research is undertaken in certain subfields than in others, resulting in higher citation counts in the former than in the latter. Citation counts also vary quite obviously based on publication date since it takes years once research has been published for other research citing it to be published as well.

Relevance is much harder to identify and measure than prominence. It depends significantly on the scope of the literature review. Literature reviews that are stand-alone articles tend to have a broader scope than literature reviews that are a part of a larger research project. The former generally focus on a particular research topic, such as foreign aid, corruption, stereotypes, or income inequality. The latter tend to focus on a specific research

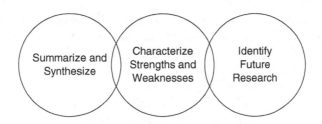

Figure 4.1 Literature review objectives

question or puzzle. A stand-alone literature review on foreign aid might examine, for example, the political dimensions of foreign aid distribution, while an in-text literature review may look specifically at whether states can use foreign aid to win the 'hearts and minds' of aid recipients.

Literature reviews that are focused on a specific question may be framed in one of a number of different ways based on the subject and/or object of the research question. A literature review that is framed in terms of the subject and object of a research question would only include literature written on the specific research question at hand. For the aforementioned question regarding winning the hearts and minds of aid recipients, a literature review that takes this approach would only include research specifically about the effectiveness of foreign aid generating favorable attitudes towards donor countries.

This approach is the preferred approach. It is more pointed and provides for a deeper analysis of the research question posed. However, there may be very little written about a particular research question. Very little may have been written on a question because the question is very narrow and attracts very little scholarly interest as a result, or because the question is original and not a question that others have thought of yet. If the literature is scant, researchers may take one of two other approaches to situate their research within the larger literature.

Box 4.1   Highlighting Absence

If the literature on a particular research question is scant, researchers ought to highlight this fact in the literature review. The dearth of immediately relevant literature is an important indicator of the contribution of the research question at hand to extant knowledge.

The first is to focus on only the subject of the research question. The subject of the aforementioned question regarding winning the hearts and minds is foreign aid. A literature review that takes this approach, instead of focusing on the effectiveness of foreign aid in currying favor with aid recipients, would review all of the outcomes associated with foreign aid in the literature. These outcomes may include, but are not limited to, generating favorable attitudes towards donor countries.

The second approach is to frame the research question in terms of the object (or outcome) of the question. In the aforementioned example of foreign aid, the object (or outcome) is winning the hearts and minds of aid recipients. A literature review that takes this approach would focus on all the strategies besides foreign aid used to win the hearts and minds of others, and what is known about their effectiveness. These strategies may include propaganda, impersonal exchanges, charity, and so forth.

The process of deciding what literature to include in the literature review is often an iterative process in which researchers first identify the literature very broadly related to their research question, decide on how to frame their research question within this literature and then seek out further literature relevant to their question and the way in which they have chosen to contextualize it.

Locating the Literature

However the literature review is framed, there are a number of useful strategies researchers may use to locate research to include in the literature review. The first approach involves a basic keyword search of a library or other database. It is best to start with a narrow set of terms to first find the research that is most closely related to the question posed, and then to broaden the search to include more general terms in order to find related literatures. This approach is less likely to overwhelm researchers and is more efficient because there may be sufficient literature very closely related to the research question at hand so that a broader search is unnecessary.

The efficiency of the search also depends on the databases searched. Certain databases allow users to view all types of literature in a single search. This includes books, journal articles, magazine articles, and unpublished research. Other databases, though, only allow users to view certain types of literature, while even narrower databases only allow users to view certain types of literature issued by specific publishers. Certain databases can also provide researchers with information about the citation counts of the literature located in the search, so that researchers can sort through the literature in terms of influence.

It is important for researchers to be aware of the types of resources available to them through a given database, so they do not overlook literature that would require them to search another database. Databases such as Google Scholar, which provide researchers with access to multiple types and sources of literature and their citation counts, allow for the most efficient search possible. The specific databases available to researchers will depend on their institutions since access to library databases is generally based on paid institutional subscriptions.

Online repositories for academic research, including commercial ventures such as Academia.edu, Research Gate, and Mendeley, as well as non-commercial platforms, such as GitHub, are also searchable using keywords. These repositories allow researchers to create profiles, upload their research as well as their data and replication code, and to connect to other scholars with common research interests. GitHub is not only an online repository, but it is also a tool for software development.

Much of the research included in these online repositories is produced by young early-career scholars and is unpublished. Researchers may include abstracts of their published research in these repositories, but they generally cannot upload copies of their published research due to copyright protections. Unpublished research is not necessarily of a lower quality, and even low quality research can have interesting ideas to impart. However, research that is unpublished has not been vetted through a peer review process and is not subject to the same standards regarding replication as published research.

An equally important way to identify research to include in a literature review is to peruse other researchers' bibliographies looking for relevant literature, and then to read the literature mentioned in these bibliographies and follow the trail of research from one study to the next until the trail runs cold or too far from the original path. Finally, it can be very useful to ask advisors, professors, or colleagues for suggestions. Like a bibliography search, this strategy is effective in identifying research which is not directly related to the research question at hand, but that has obvious parallels or implications for it.

Structuring the Literature Review

Literature reviews may be structured either chronologically, according to the publication dates of the research, or thematically. Unless the goal of the literature review is to discuss the historical development of a field, as is more typical of stand-alone literature reviews, it is best to organize the review thematically. A literature review that is organized chronologically may neglect to include important works that do not fit the trend in a field at a given time. It may also be repetitive because literature written at different periods of time may include similar themes. Moreover, a literature review that is organized thematically is better suited for synthesizing, as opposed to just summarizing, the existing literature.

Regardless of the way in which a particular research question is framed within the larger literature, a thematic literature review should be organized into layers, where the layers represent themes, subthemes, and sub-subthemes of the literature. If, for example, the literature contains a debate between opposing views on an issue, the literature review may be organized into two layers. The first layer would relate to the particular side of the debate on which the research is situated. The second layer would consist of the reasons why the research falls on either side of the debate.

Figure 4.2 depicts schematically how a literature review organized around a three-sided debate may be structured.

The themes that structure the literature review should not be presented as a laundry list of ideas, as would be the case if a researcher introduced the ideas using numbers, such as 'first', 'second', 'third', and so forth. Instead, they should be linked together according to features that they have (or do not have) in common. These features may be theoretical or empirical. Grouping the literature in this way facilitates the synthesis and the analysis of the literature.

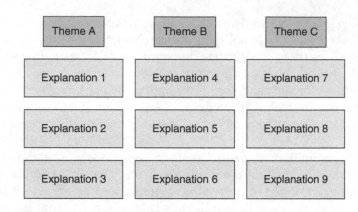

Figure 4.2   Thematic organization of the literature

Box 4.2   Rhetorical Devices

In order to draw connections between the literature reviewed, researchers may use different rhetorical devices. One of the most common ways to do this is to use particular language that emphasizes the similarities or differences between the ideas or methods presented in the literature (e.g., 'similarly', 'as in', 'unlike', or 'in contrast'). Alternatively, researchers may simply repeat a word or phrase used in different sentences to connect two ideas, or they may use words or phrases with similar structures (e.g., noun-preposition-noun rather than possessive-noun as in 'the owner of the dog' rather than 'the dog's owner') to draw parallels between them.

To better understand how to organize a thematic literature review and how to draw links among themes, consider the literature on refugees and crime as an example (Bucerius 2011). The literature on crime and refugees is divided principally between two opposing camps. The first camp claims that refugees increase crime and the second claims that refugees have no effect on crime. Those within these camps offer different explanations for why refugees either increase crime or have no effect on it.

For the sake of simplicity, the discussion below focuses on the side of the debate which argues that refugees increase crime. Figure 4.3 depicts one way in which the literature on this side of the debate may be organized.

In this example, the literature arguing that refugees or migrants increase crime is organized into two themes based on who commits the crime – the refugee or the local non-migrant population – and whether the victims of the crime are refugees or non-migrants. The themes are linked together theoretically based on two characteristics of the explanations offered to explain the increase in crime perpetrated by either the migrants or non-migrants, regarding security and deprivation.

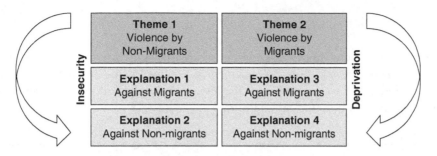

Figure 4.3   Thematic organization of migrant literature

Theme 1: The increase in violence <u>is not due</u> to violent acts perpetrated by migrants but to violence perpetrated by non-migrants.

- Explanation 1: The crime is perpetrated against refugees, especially children and women who are subject to sexual assault in camps, because of the insecurity (e.g., unlocked shelters and a lack of guards) of camps.
- Explanation 2: The crime is perpetrated by nationals outside camps, largely against other nationals, because the presence of police outside of the camps is stretched thin by the need for police at camps, making it easier to commit crimes outside camps.

Theme 2: The increase in violence <u>is due to</u> violence perpetrated by migrants, but not due to innate characteristics of the migrants but to characteristics of the environments in which they live.

- Explanation 3: Limited provisions within camps provoke violence among refugees in competition over scarce goods.
- Explanation 4: Shortages in food, medicine, clothing and other supplies in camps provoke anger towards and uprisings against governments and aid agencies over sub-human living conditions.

In this example, Theme 1 and Theme 2 are linked rhetorically because they begin with the same language except for the word 'not'. Under Theme 1, Explanations 1 and 2 are connected by the fact that the crime is perpetrated by non-migrants – against migrants according to Explanation 1 and against non-migrants in Explanation 2, and both due to insecurity – insecurity within camps in the case of Explanation 1 and insecurity outside camps in Explanation 2. Under Theme 2, Explanations 3 and 4 are connected by the fact that they are both about conditions within camps although the target of the violence is different – against other migrants in the case of Explanation 3 and against non-migrants, namely government and aid agencies, in the case of Explanation 4.

How to Discuss the Literature

Since a literature review should not merely summarize but also synthesize the existing literature, the review should only present the key arguments and findings of the research presented as they relate to the subject of the review. It should not describe every aspect of the research as in an annotated bibliography.

Box 4.3   Talking about Others

Quote sparingly. Use quotes only where the language used by another person is particularly vivid, eloquent or poignant, or when the person quoted is notable and their exact words, even if not especially articulate, are important to document. Quotes should not make your points for you, but rather heighten interest in them.

In synthesizing the literature, researchers should discuss the major strengths and weaknesses of the research reviewed. Researchers should not point out each and every strength or weakness of a research project, such as a minor error in historical fact, insufficient attention given to a particular example, or an insufficiently detailed codebook. Instead, researchers should focus on only those strengths and weaknesses that are central to the issue at hand, and that affect the extent to which the argument and evidence provided in the research are persuasive.

To illustrate how to effectively discuss research in a literature review, below are two examples of descriptions of the same article on the relationship between immigration and crime in Italy – Bianchi et al. (2012). For a literature review, the first example is preferable to the second. It summarizes only those aspects of the research relevant to the question of refugees and crime, frames the research to make the relevance of these aspects apparent, and identifies the strengths and weaknesses of the research in terms of the question posed.

Example 1

Bianchi et al. (2012) find only weak evidence that immigration, which includes but is not limited to refugees, increases crime. In their statistical analysis of the relationship between crime and immigration in Italy, the authors find that immigration significantly increases only one type of crime – robberies. This finding is consistent with arguments that suggest the refugees commit crimes in order to acquire needed provisions lacking within refugee camps. These results may underestimate, though, the impact of refugees on robberies since the level of economic deprivation of refugees is typically greater than for immigrants in countries. Although the findings are weak, they are robust – based on an analysis of a long time period (1990–2003) and an estimation technique designed to address concerns regarding causal direction.

The second example is the abstract written by the authors. The abstract summarizes all aspects of their research, not just those relevant to the question of refugees and crime. It also mentions the strengths and weaknesses of the authors' research in terms of the method employed and the applicability of the findings to other cases, but not in relation to the question posed regarding refugees and crime. While this is an appropriate strategy for an abstract, it is not an effective entry for a literature review.

Example 2

We examine the empirical relationship between immigration and crime across Italian provinces during the period 1990–2003. Drawing on police administrative records, we first document that the size of the immigrant population is positively correlated with the incidence of property crimes and with the overall crime rate. Then, we use instrumental variables based on immigration toward destination countries other than Italy to identify the causal impact of exogenous changes in Italy's immigrant population. According to these estimates, immigration increases only the incidence of robberies, while leaving unaffected all other types of crime. Since robberies represent a very minor fraction of all criminal offenses, the effect on the overall crime rate is not significantly different from zero.

This discussion of the strengths and weaknesses of the existing literature should also lay the groundwork for a presentation of avenues for future research in the case of a stand-alone literature review, or the contribution of a given research project to the extant literature in the case of an in-text literature review. In the case of the latter, the presentation of the weaknesses ought to emphasize those weaknesses in the existing literature that the research project will rectify.

Generally, researchers present the contribution of their research to the existing literature at the conclusion of the literature review section. However, as previously suggested, it is very helpful to build up to this discussion by hinting at the project's contribution throughout the literature review in discussing the strengths and weaknesses of the existing literature, and connecting them rhetorically to the researchers' contribution in the conclusion of the literature review.

Box 4.4   Talking about Yourself

In introducing your contribution to the literature, avoid trite language and phrases, like this project will 'fill in the gap' or 'make a novel contribution'. If the literature review is well written, these phrases are unnecessary as the contribution to extant knowledge will be apparent.

In defining their contribution to the extant literature, it is important that researchers do not oversimplify, distort, or downplay other researchers' work in order to make their contribution seem more significant. It is also important that researchers avoid hyperbolic and pejorative language. Researchers should avoid words such as 'poor' (as in this research does a 'poor' job answering this question), or 'fail' (as in this research 'fails to take into account'). The temptation to use this kind of language to make social scientific writing more exciting or to make one's contribution to the literature more obvious is understandable, but the language is derisive nonetheless.

Formatting References

In general, the author-date system of the *Chicago Manual of Style* is used in the social sciences for references. According to this system, sources are cited within the text with the name of the author and the year of the publication associated with a particular statement at the end of the sentence. Multiple citations are separate by semicolons and are ordered sequentially, according to the date of publication rather than alphabetically according to the name of the author. In the reference section, only articles, books, and other material that are cited in the text of the research project are included in the Chicago style.

The Chicago style is very efficient but it has certain shortcomings. For sentences making distinct points, it may not necessarily be clear to which point the citation refers. In this case, it is useful to split a sentence into parts so that each point is its own sentence. This strategy is consistent with the simple and straightforward diction of writing in the social sciences. In practice, page numbers are also used sparingly in the Chicago style. Generally, they are only used when material is directly quoted in a sentence. For references to article-length papers or shorter material, this is not particularly problematic. However, if the citation is to a book, it is much harder for the reader to locate the material referenced in the citation without page numbers.

Below are examples of the proper formatting for basic types of references using the *Chicago Manual of Style*. For other types of documents, consult the most recent addition of the manual. References using the Chicago style and alternative formats, such as the American Psychological Association (APA) style and the Harvard style, can also be generated automatically using programs, such as such as BibDesk, Endnote, and CiteULike.

Book (single author):

Brancati, Dawn. 2016. *Democracy Protests: Origins, Features, and Significance*. New York: Cambridge University Press.

Book Chapter:

Hertel, Shareen. 2017. "Re-Framing Human Rights Advocacy: The Rise of Economic Rights." In *Human Rights Futures*, edited by Jack Snyder, Leslie Vinjamuri, and Stephen Hopgood, 237–260. New York: Cambridge University Press.

Conference Paper:

Birnir, Jóhanna Kristín and Nil S. Satana. 2010. "One God for All: Fundamentalist Religious Groups and Terrorism." Presented at the Annual Meeting of the International Studies Association, New Orleans, Louisiana, November 21–24.

Edited Collection:

Falleti, Tulia G. and Emilio Parrado, eds. 2017. *Latin America Since the Left Turn.* Philadelphia, PA: University of Pennsylvania Press.

Electronic Sources:

Brancati, Dawn. 2007. *Global Elections Database.* Accessed 21 November 2017. http://www.globalelectionsdatabase.com.

Journal Article:

Rosas, Guillermo. 2006. "Bagehot or Bailout? An Analysis of Government Responses to Banking Crises." *American Journal of Political Science* 50(1): 175–191.

Working Paper:

Herrera, Yoshiko M. and Andrew H. Kydd. "'Take A Chance: Trust-Building Across Identity Groups." Unpublished manuscript, last modified July 2017. Latex file.

Key Points

- Literature reviews should summarize and synthesize the literature on a subject and also characterize its strengths and weaknesses.
- Literature reviews can also present avenues for future research or define the contribution of a research project to the extant literature.
- The best structure depends on the purpose of the literature review. Literature reviews may be structured either chronologically or thematically.
- Common sources for identifying the literature on a subject include: library databases; online repositories; bibliographies; and faculty and colleagues.

Further Reading

All three readings are informative guidebooks about how to compose literature reviews.

Galvan, Jose L. 2017. *Writing Literature Reviews: A Guide for Students of the Social and Behavioral Sciences.* New York: Routledge.

Machi, Lawrence A. and Brenda T. McEvoy. 2016. *The Literature Review: Six Steps to Success*. Thousand Oaks, CA: Corwin.

Ridley, Diana. 2012. *The Literature Review: A Step-by-Step Guide for Students*. London: Sage Publications.

EXERCISE 4.1

Design an alternative way in which to organize the literature depicted in Figure 4.3 regarding the reasons for an increase in crime due to the presence of refugees in countries.

EXERCISE 4.2

For either one of the two examples below, identify at least two themes that link each of the six explanations together and then categorize each of the six explanations by theme. Explain how the themes are related to each other and why you categorized each explanation as you did.

Example 1: The link between oil and violent conflict within states.

1. The looting of oil by rebels provides start-up costs for war.
2. The profitableness of war due to the ability of the victor to control oil sales reduces the incentives for peace.
3. Oil extraction produces grievances among locals (who often do not benefit financially from oil extraction and are dislocated from their homes and exposed to health and environmental hazards as a result of it) that rebels exploit for support.
4. Foreign countries help finance on-going wars by purchasing the rights to extract oil resources in the future ('booty futures') from the winning side.
5. Oil resources provide incentives for violent separatist movements to form because they enable regions to sustain themselves as independent states.
6. Oil makes governments less likely to agree to peace agreements, which require them to give regions political and fiscal autonomy and, thus, control over oil.

Example 2: The quality and longevity of personal relationships.

1. Relationship longevity depends not only on the specific qualities of each partner, but also on the way these qualities intersect.
2. How partners communicate about and cope with problems both internal and external to their relationships affects the quality and stability of their relationships.
3. The qualities, personalities, and temperament that individuals bring to their relationships influence their own and their partners' wellbeing in the relationship.
4. Partners bring certain goals and needs to their relationships. The dynamics between partners affect whether each partner is able to achieve their goals and, in turn, their satisfaction with their relationship.

5. The presence of attractive alternatives to a current relationship, including the option of not being in a relationship, threatens the quality and longevity of the relationship.
6. Social norms, practices and traditions can lead partners to remain in unhappy relationships.

EXERCISE 4.3

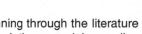

Select an academic article within your discipline, locate the literature review section, and identify the themes of the research discussed within it. Try to draw a diagram as in Figure 4.3 of the way in which the literature is organized in the literature review. If it is not possible, discuss why this is the case and what problems this presents.

EXERCISE 4.4

Using your own research, identify at least two different themes running through the literature relevant to your research question. List the arguments that belong to each theme and draw a diagram demonstrating how they are linked to each other, as in Figure 4.3.

ARGUMENTATION

5

Building Effective Concepts

Objectives

- define concepts and their importance to research
- identify the characteristics of effective concepts
- describe the steps involved in building effective concepts
- discuss the problem of concept stretching

Concepts are the cornerstone of social science research. They are the components around which arguments are built and evidence regarding them is evaluated. A *concept*, in its most basic formulation, is an abstract idea or object. Democracy, war, peace, terrorism, liberalism, clientelism, and populism are all examples of enduring political, social, and economic concepts. Although concepts like these are abstract, they are rarely unidimensional. Instead, concepts are generally comprised of a number of related properties and attributes. Clear, well-defined, and coherent concepts in which these related properties and attributes are specified are not only essential to building and defending arguments, but they also make the misuse and distortion of concepts all the more apparent.

Why Concepts Matter

In the social sciences, concepts establish the defining features or properties of political, social, psychological, and economic phenomena. They provide the basis around which arguments related to these phenomena are constructed and have significant implications, as a result, for how the world is understood.

In everyday usage, the concept of democracy is often taken to mean freedom to do as one so chooses. Democracy is understood in this way at an individual level. In other conceptualizations, though, democracy is understood at a macro-level in terms of political institutions, such as open and competitive elections, or the substantive outcomes generally associated with these institutions, such as media freedom, political and civil rights, economic wealth, and so forth.

How a phenomenon is conceptualized is important because defined one way, a concept may be unrelated to another phenomenon, but defined in a different way, it may be strongly related to it. Research, for example, which conceptualizes democracy in a minimal sense of open and competitive elections, finds a strong correlation between democracy and domestic terrorism, but not foreign-born terrorism. Countries with open and competitive elections are less likely to experience domestic terrorism than authoritarian states because the former are more responsive to the interests of society than the latter (Crenshaw 1981). They are not less likely to experience foreign-born terrorism because government responsiveness does not reduce grievances against governments arising from outside states.

However, research, which conceptualizes democracy in a maximal sense as a system of government that includes not only open and competitive elections, but a free media and robust political and civil rights, finds a strong correlation between democracy and higher levels of foreign-born terrorism (Eubank and Weinberg 1994). A free media is believed to make democracies an attractive target for foreign-born terrorism because it allows fear to spread quickly among the populace through reports of terror events. Strong political and civil rights can also impede counterterrorism efforts by preventing governments from undertaking initiatives that suspend state and local laws in order to investigate potential activists.

Characteristics of Good Concepts

There is almost always debate around how a concept should be defined and whether or not a particular concept is a good representation of the object it claims to represent. However, there is much wider agreement regarding the criteria that should be used to

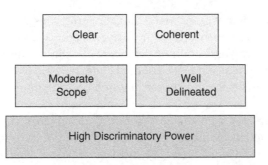

Figure 5.1 Effective concepts

evaluate whether concepts are good or not. These criteria relate to the clarity, delineation, scope, coherence, and discriminatory power of the concepts, as Figure 5.1 illustrates.

Clarity

First and foremost, concepts must be *clear* so that there is no confusion as to what they represent. Clarity requires specificity. Have you ever signed up for free internet service at the airport only to find out later that you had to watch a series of commercials in exchange for the service? Perhaps you thought 'free' meant that the service did not require anything – financial or otherwise – from you in exchange for it, while the business considered the service as 'free' because it does not require you to pay for it. The concept of 'free' is insufficiently specific in this case. The service would have been better defined in this case as 'no payment required' as opposed to 'free' to avoid confusion.

A lack of clarity over what it means to be a feminist may also help explain major discrepancies in polls among those who define themselves as feminists. When asked whether they considered themselves 'feminists' or not, no more than 20 percent of people in the UK and US considered themselves feminists.[1] However, almost two-thirds of people in these two countries described themselves as feminists in surveys that defined a feminist as 'someone who advocates and supports equal opportunities for women.'[2]

A lack of conceptual clarity may also explain why people who live in countries without open and competitive elections and robust political and civil rights consider their countries to be democracies. In the Asian Barometer (Wave IV) survey, 83 percent of Singaporeans said that their government was either 'a full democracy' or 'a democracy, but with minor problems' even though elections are not open or competitive in Singapore and political and civil rights are weak.[3] Only 67 percent of South Koreans in the same survey described their country as either a full democracy or a democracy with minor problems, even though elections are much more open and competitive in South Korea than in Singapore, and political and civil rights are much more robust.

The key to understanding why so many Singaporeans consider their country a democracy, despite it not having open and competitive elections or robust political and civil rights, rests in their conceptualization of democracy. A slight majority of Singaporeans in the same survey reported that the most essential characteristic of a democracy is a government that either 'narrows the gap between the rich and the poor' or 'does not waste any public money'. Slightly less than a third of Singaporeans surveyed said that the most essential characteristic of a democracy is a system of government where people choose their leaders in 'free and fair elections.' In South Korea, about two-fifths of people surveyed said that free and fair elections were the most essential characteristic of a democracy. Another two-fifths said that it was to narrow the gap between rich and poor and not waste public money.

Delineation

Concepts should also be *well delineated*. To be well delineated means that all the components of the concept ought to be identified and defined. Components are the building blocks of concepts and may be divided into sub-components, sub-sub components, and so forth. Some concepts are more complex than others and require more decomposition and explanation than others. Figure 5.2 illustrates the concept of delineation through the example of democracy.

A maximal definition of democracy includes two basic components – elections and rights. The elections component is divisible into two sub-components regarding the openness of the enfranchisement and the openness of competition. The first refers to who may vote in an election and the second refers to who may run for office. The rights component is divisible into at least two components – political rights and civil rights. Political rights are the rights exercised in the establishment and administration of a government. They include: freedom of assembly, freedom of association, free speech. Civil rights are rights that pertain to non-political matters, such as freedom of religion, freedom of marriage, freedom to own property, and so forth.

A well-delineated concept of democracy would not only identify these components, but would also explain what defines or constitutes each of the components, as well as each of the first- and second-tier sub-components. For example, is the vote open if all citizens are allowed to vote in a country, but if a sizeable minority of the country is

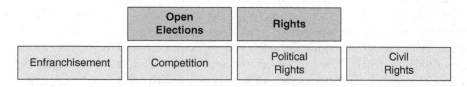

Figure 5.2   Conceptualization of democracy

denied citizenship so that they cannot vote, as in the case of the Rohingya in Burma? Are elections competitive if anti-regime parties are not allowed to participate in elections, as in Israel where parties (or candidates) that either support terrorism, incite racism, or oppose the existence of the state of Israel are not allowed to run for office? Finally, is a country a democracy if people do not have the right to own property, but if the media is unrestricted?

Scope

Concepts should not only be clear and well delineated, but they should also be moderate in scope. If a concept is too broad or too narrow, it will have limited explanatory power. If it is too broad, it will apply to everything and, therefore, explain nothing. At the same time, if it is too narrow, it will only apply to very few cases and explain a small issue or phenomenon.

Concepts are moderate to the extent that they include all the defining properties or characteristics of the objects they represent, and only these characteristics. Concepts should not include characteristics that only tend to coincide with their defining properties since these characteristics are not part and parcel of the concepts. Explaining the association of these characteristics with their given concepts should instead be the subject of empirical investigation.

To understand the problems associated with concepts that are too broad, consider the concept of 'fake news'. The concept dates back to the end of the nineteenth century and originally was used to describe deliberate misinformation and hoaxes spread via news media.[4] By the end of the twentieth century, however, the term was used to describe a genre of political satire using a news program-like format that was epitomized by *The Daily Show*, *The Colbert Report*, and *Al-Bernameg*.

Today, the concept of 'fake news' is even broader in scope. Today, it is used to describe news stories that unintentionally have factual errors in them, as well as news stories that are biased or perceived as biased because they express an opposing viewpoint. Since the term is now used to describe intentionally false news, unintentionally false news, and true news, it has lost all its explanatory value.

Some conceptualizations of democracy can also be very broad in scope and lack explanatory value as a result. These conceptualizations do not just include freedoms, such as speech, the media, assembly, that are necessary to foster open and competitive elections, but they also include outcomes that are typically associated with democracies, but are not necessarily a function of them, such as economic development. They can even include outcomes that are necessarily related to democracy, such as freedom from violence.[5] While it is well established that democracies do not go to war with other democracies (Doyle 1986; Russett 1993; Rousseau et al. 1996), democracies do go to war with non-democracies and are subject to more internal terrorist attacks than non-democracies (Li 2005).

Coherence

Coherence is related to scope. Concepts are *coherent* if all the properties that define the concept are logically connected to each other. Concepts have a tendency to be less coherent the broader their scope. The concept of 'fake news' is such an example. As it is used today, it is incoherent as well as broad in scope because the concept includes both false and true news events.

A lack of coherence is problematic because it can result in false associations. The dissimilar components of an incoherent concept can make two concepts seem to be associated with each other when they are not, or not associated with each other when they are. In the case of the former, this is because the extraneous aspects of the concept may be related to another concept. In the case of the latter, this is because the extraneous aspects of the concept are not related to another concept and obscure the association of the non-extraneous aspects of the concept with this other concept.

Corruption is an important example of this problem. Corruption is generally conceptualized in academic research as the abuse of public office for private gains (Rose-Ackerman and Palifka 2016, 7–9). In common usage, though, corruption frequently refers to unequal access to power, and more specifically, to the way in which wealthy individuals have more influence on governments than others (Warren 2014). If unequal access to power were included in the aforementioned concept of corruption, the concept would lose its cohesiveness, since unequal access to power is not about the personal benefit of public officials.

Including it in the concept would also potentially change the correlation between democracy and corruption. Democracy is strongly associated with a reduction in corruption understood as the abuse of power for public gains because democracies allow voters to punish incumbents for corrupt behavior (Schwindt-Bayer and Tavits 2016). However, if corruption includes unequal access to power, this relationship may be weaker because even in democracies, access to power is unequal. In democracies, for example, where there is no public funding for and limits on campaign spending, wealthy people are more likely to run for office than poorer people because they are better able to finance their campaigns (Avis et al. 2017).

Discriminatory Power

Concepts should not only be coherent, but they should also distinguish one object from another. Discriminatory power is related to scope. The broader the scope of a concept, the more opportunities there are for the concept to have properties in common with multiple objects, and the lower its ability to distinguish one object from another.

Figure 5.3 illustrates the difference between a concept that has low and high discriminatory power. The image at the top has low discriminatory power because the characteristics of the concept overlap two objects, whereas the image at the bottom has

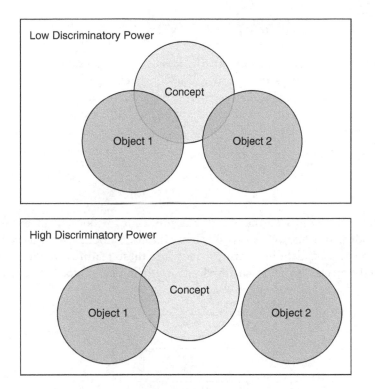

Figure 5.3 Discriminatory power of concepts

high discriminatory power because the characteristics of the concept overlap only one object.

It is important that a concept has high discriminatory power because if this concept is associated with a certain phenomenon, and is unable to distinguish among multiple objects, it will be unclear which object is associated with the phenomenon. Economic development, for example, is related to the propensity of countries to experience civil war. Countries with higher levels of economic development are less likely to experience civil wars. Economic development has low discriminatory power in this case because it is unable to distinguish between three competing explanations for civil war – repression, grievances, and rebel recruitment – and cannot, as a result, indicate which, if any of these three factors (or objects) are responsible for civil wars.

Economic development is related to the repressive capacity of states. States with high levels of development tend to have higher repressive capacities, which are argued to reduce the likelihood of civil war by making it more difficult for rebel groups to form and operate (Fearon and Laitin 2003). Economic development is also inversely related to grievances and the ability of rebels to recruit soldiers (Cederman et al. 2013). Economic grievances are argued to provide the motivation for individuals to form, join, and support rebel groups.

Building Effective Concepts

Building an effective concept is an iterative process, requiring a significant amount of time, effort and revision. Below is one strategy for constructing effective concepts using the example of terrorism to illustrate each step. It is depicted in Figure 5.4. The term terrorism is used to illustrate this process because it is applied broadly today to many events that are arguably not acts of terrorism at all. The final concept developed through this process is depicted in Figure 5.5.

Step One

Think abstractly about what the object that you want to conceptualize is without reference to the ideas of others. What is your basic intuition about what this concept entails? What are the object's defining features? How are these features similar to and different from related objects? Write down a preliminary definition of your concept.

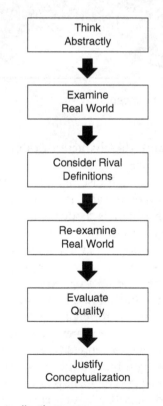

Figure 5.4   Steps in the conceptualization process

Example: Terrorism involves violent acts. The term 'terrorism' itself suggests that the purpose of these acts is not strategic, but to cause fear, as in the case of attacks against civilians. Today, most terrorist acts seem to be carried out in the name of Islam. However, historically terrorist acts have been carried out for non-religious goals, and many Muslim clerics and theologians refute the terrorists' claims that they are acting on behalf of Allah. So, although acts of terrorism do have political goals, these goals are not limited to religious ones.

Preliminary definition: *The use of violence against civilians in order to instill fear among the populace for political goals.*

Step Two

Examine real world examples of the object. Does your concept fit the examples you think it should, and not fit those that you think it should not? What characteristics do these objects possess? Which for you do (or do not) make them an example of this concept? Revise your original concept to take these examples into account.

Example: The types of actors who commit terrorist acts include individuals acting alone (e.g. Shoe Bomber 2001), individuals acting without the direct support of a terrorist group (e.g. Boston Marathon Bombing 2013), and individuals who belong to terrorist networks or work for governments (e.g. Paris Bombers 2015; London Bridge Bombings 2017). Historically, terrorist acts have occurred in Western Europe, as part of separatist movements in Northern Ireland and Spain. They have occurred against the United States by anarchists and anti-abortion activists, and in South Africa, against apartheid. The US and other Western countries have also provided financial and military support to terrorist groups, many in Latin America during the Cold War. Thus, the definition of terrorism should denote the variety of actors who commit terrorism and the fact the terrorism involves the 'intentional' killing of civilians, since all of these acts have been planned and executed by many different actors.

Revised definition: *The intentional use of violence against civilians in order to instill fear among the populace for political goals.*

Step Three

Look closely at prominent definitions in your discipline of the object you are conceptualizing. What do these definitions contain that yours does not and what does your definition contain that they do not? Are there any features of these definitions that you think should also be included in yours? Consider potential biases in these definitions and how replicating aspects of them might bias your findings. Were these concepts designed with a certain theory and/or political objective in mind?

Example: Below are two prominent definitions of terrorism:

- US State Department: 'Premeditated, politically motivated violence perpetrated against noncombatant targets by subnational groups or clandestine agents, usually intended to influence an audience.'[6]

No revisions seem necessary on the basis of this State Department definition of terrorism. The term pre-meditated is similar to intentional. Non-combatants are not civilians because they include individuals who are part of armed groups and do not fight, but who are still part of the war effort and, therefore, are not civilians. The term subnational excludes governments that have committed or supported groups that have committed terrorist acts, while the term clandestine is unclear. It also excludes many terrorist groups who openly take credit for their actions.

- UK Terrorism Act 2000: 'The use or threat of action that involves serious acts of violence against a person or damage to property; endangers a person's life; creates a serious risk to the health or safety of the public; interferes with or disrupts an electronic system, and is designed to influence the government or intimidate the public (or a section of the public) in order to advance a political, religious, or ideological cause.'[7]

The UK definition suggests some revisions. The UK government's definition of terrorism includes damage to property, which seems reasonable to include since acts of violence might not intend to harm anyone. It also seems reasonable to include the term 'physical harm' in the concept of terrorism in order to address threats to the health or safety of individuals or other types of physical harm that are not necessarily thought of as violent. It does not seem necessary to include an attack on an electronic system in the concept. Doing so would make terrorism an incoherent concept since an attack on an electronic system generally involves hacking, not violence. Finally, it does not seem useful to specify all types of political motivations for terrorism since it would be impossible to do so.

Revised definition: *The intentional use of violence against civilians by state and non-state actors in order to instill fear among the populace for political goals.*

Step Four

Once again, examine real world examples of the object that you are studying. Does the revised definition still accurately represent these examples? If not, consider whether it is because you no longer think these cases are examples of the object that you are conceptualizing, or whether the revised definition needs to be revised still further.

Example: Syrian President Bashar al-Assad used chemical weapons against his population in the Syrian Civil War. These attacks involved violence against civilians and incited fear among the populace. However, the aforementioned definition would not include, and should not include, these attacks because the motivation for these attacks was, in part, arguably strategic – that is, to defeat his opponents by demonstrating the government's strength and resolve. In its fight against apartheid, the African National Congress attacked government and non-government targets, such as churches, shopping centres, homes, and so forth. The ANC preferred to be called freedom fighters, seeing their cause as just. But their acts would be considered terrorism according to the concept of terrorism developed so far, and should be, because the purpose or morality of the attacks is not part of the concept, which in itself is subjective. For a period, Nelson Mandela, as leader of the ANC, advocated violence, although it is not clear whether Mandela committed terrorist acts personally. As a member and leader of the ANC, Mandela was included on the US terrorist list until 2008.

These examples do not suggest further revisions to the definition of terrorism.

Revised definition: Terrorism is the intentional use or threat to use violence or physical harm against civilians or property by state and non-state actors in order to instill fear among the populace for political goals.

Step Five

Evaluate the quality of your concept against the criteria of good concepts in terms of clarity, delineation, scope, and discriminatory power.

Example: This conceptualization of terrorism, which is depicted in Figure 5.5, is not too narrow or too broad because it includes all forms of violence against civilians regardless of the actor involved, political goals sought, or the success of the act, and only those that do not have a strategic purpose. It is also able to distinguish between other forms of violence against civilians even if the definition uncomfortably classifies some individuals and groups as terrorists.

Final definition: Terrorism is the intentional use or threat to use violence or physical harm against civilians or their property by state or non-state actors in order to instill fear among the populace for political goals.

Step Six

Justify why your concept is different from and preferable to other prominent definitions of this concept.

Example: The concept of terrorism used here is better than existing conceptualizations of terrorism because it is clear, well delineated, coherent and moderate in scope, while existing conceptualizations are deficient in at least one of these dimensions. It also has high discriminatory power because it is able to distinguish terrorism from other forms of violence.

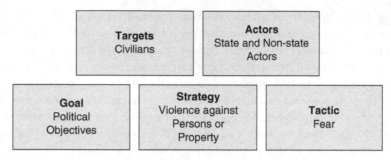

Figure 5.5   Conceptualization of terrorism

Concept Stretching

Concept stretching refers to the distortion of a concept through its application to other cases. A concept is distorted to the extent that it has lost its original meaning. Concepts can be distorted if they are broadened to include a case to which they do not apply, or narrowed to exclude cases to which they should apply, but do not.

Concept stretching is subjective. There are no criteria against which to judge whether or not a concept has been distorted. As a result, one person may consider something to be an example of concept stretching and another may not. Concept stretching is also a matter of degrees. In order words, the extent of the distortion may be greater in some cases that in others, and only certain components of the original concept may be distorted.

Applying a concept incorrectly to another case, or denying that a concept applies to a particular case, without altering the original concept in a manner inconsistent with the original concept, does not constitute concept stretching since the original concept has not been distorted in either case.

The US executive order under the Trump administration refusing entry to citizens of seven Muslim-majority countries is a case in point. The White House staff denied repeatedly at the time that the executive order was a ban, saying that the executive order is not a ban, but rather 'a vetting system to keep America safe.'[8] Of course, the two are not at odds with each other as the executive order can be both a ban – a prohibition on a certain behavior – and a vetting system to keep America safe. Regardless of whether you accept the staff's justification of why the executive order is not a ban, the White House staff's description of the executive order as a vetting system is not an example of concept stretching because it does not explicitly alter the definition of a ban in any way.

Researchers may stretch concepts for various reasons. Researchers may unintentionally distort certain concepts so that their arguments about them explain cases that they otherwise could not. These cases may be very important or salient examples of a phenomenon that researchers feel compelled to account for in their work. Even though theories do not necessarily have to explain every case to be valid, researchers might feel that their work would be marginalized if they cannot explain salient cases of events. Researchers may also distort certain concepts so that the concepts are associated with phenomena, like terrorism or populism, which are likely to receive a lot of public attention and financial support.

To avoid concept stretching, researchers can define their original concept in vague or broad terms. If a concept is very broad and ambiguous, it can apply to many things without having to be altered to account for them. However, for the reasons elaborated above, broad and vague concepts are not useful. If a concept has to be distorted in order to explain a particular phenomenon, this may be a sign that there is a problem with the theory, not the concept.

Box 5.1   Concept Stretching of Icelandic Proportions

In 2008, UK Prime Minister Gordon Brown put Iceland on the UK terrorist watch list due to Iceland's failure to guarantee British savings during the country's banking crisis. Prime Minister Gordon Brown used the Anti-terrorism Act (2001), which extended the number of acts permissible to combat terrorism from the 2000 Act delineated above, but did not alter the definition of terrorism from the previous Act, to freeze Iceland's UK assets. In response, Iceland threatened to take the UK to the European Court of Human Rights over its use of the anti-terrorism laws.

Prime Minister Brown's labelling of Iceland as a terrorist state is an example of concept stretching (and not merely a misapplication of the concept of terrorism), because Prime Minister Brown changed how the UK Terrorism Act 2000 was interpreted to include lost savings as a threat to public safety. The failure of Iceland banks obviously did not involve violence, or the threat to use violence, and was not designed for political purposes.

Some observers suggested that the Prime Minister took this action to deflect blame for the UK's own economic problems and targeted Iceland because it is a small, non-EU state, from which retaliation would pose little risk. Eventually, Iceland repaid the UK (and the Netherlands) through the liquidation of its failed banks' assets. But not without a lot of humorous, spleen-venting reactions from Icelanders declaring that 'We aren't terrorists' on online petitions, placards and postcards.

Key Points

- Good concepts are essential to high quality research. They are the components around which arguments are built and evidence regarding them is evaluated.
- Concepts should be clear, well defined, modest in scope, coherent and able to distinguish one object from another.
- Concept stretching should be avoided. It involves the distortion of a concept through its application to other cases.

Further Reading

The first and second readings provide guidance on how to construct concepts. The third reading is responsible for innovating the term, concept stretching, and elaborates on the phenomenon as well as techniques to avoid it.

Gerring, John. 1999. 'What Makes a Concept Good? A Criterial Framework for Understanding Concept Formation in the Social Sciences.' *Polity* 31(3): 357–393.
Goertz, Gary. 2012. *Social Science Concepts: A User's Guide.* Princeton: Princeton University Press.
Sartori, Giovanni. 1970. 'Concept Misformation in Comparative Politics.' *American Political Science Review* 64(4): 1033–1053.

EXERCISE 5.1

Construct a concept using the five-step procedure described for one of the following terms or a term of your own choosing. The terms are: globalization, nationalism, liberalism, populism, corporate image, human rights, identity, culture, gender nonconformity, and sexual harassment.

EXERCISE 5.2

For any three recipients of your choosing, evaluate whether you believe that the Norwegian Nobel Committee, in awarding the Nobel Peace Prize to these recipients, is guilty of stretching the concept of peace as defined by Alfred Nobel. According to Alfred Nobel, the Nobel Peace prize should be awarded to the '[p]erson who shall have done the most or the best work for fraternity between the nations and the abolition or reduction of standing armies and the formation and spreading of peace congresses.'[9]

The recipients and the announcements, explaining the Nobel Committee reasoning for the award, are as follows:[10]

1. **Rigoberta Menchú Tum (1992)**: '[i]n recognition of her work for social justice and ethno-cultural reconciliation based on respect for the rights of indigenous peoples.'

2. **Shirin Ebadi (2003)**: '[F]or her efforts for democracy and human rights. She has focused especially on the struggle for the rights of women and children.'

3. **Intergovernmental Panel on Climate Change (IPCC) and Albert Gore Jr. (2007)**: '[F]or their efforts to build up and disseminate greater knowledge about man-made climate change, and to lay the foundations for the measures that are needed to counteract such change.'

4. **Liu Xiaobo (2010)**: '[F]or his long and non-violent struggle for fundamental human rights in China.'

5. **Kailash Satyarthi and Malala Yousafzai (2014)**: '[F]or their struggle against the suppression of children and young people and for the right of all children to education.'

6

Making Strong Arguments

Objectives

- differentiate between deductive and inductive reasoning
- define necessary, sufficient, as well as (neither) necessary and (nor) sufficient conditions
- examine different directions through which explanatory factors influence outcomes
- identify common mistakes in causal arguments

An interesting puzzle can attract interest in your research, but without an equally interesting, well-reasoned, and compelling argument, all is lost. In positivist research, an argument specifies a causal relationship between two concepts. For a relationship to be causal, a change in one concept must result in a change in another. An argument that high temperatures reduce birth rates due to decreased sexual activity arising from heat-related

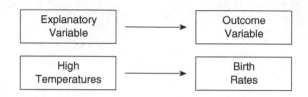

Figure 6.1   Causal argument

sluggishness and discomfort is an example of a causal argument. This argument has significant implications. It implies that the effects of climate change go well beyond the environment, resulting, in this case, in a decline in the world's population (Barreca et al. 2015).

In causal arguments, the concept that precipitates the change is known as the explanatory or independent variable, as illustrated in Figure 6.1. The concept that changes is known as the outcome or dependent variable. In the previous example, the explanatory variable is high temperatures. High temperatures precipitate a change in the outcome variable – birth rates. Reduced sexual activity due to heat-related sluggishness and discomfort is the mechanism through which high temperatures reduce birth rates.

While the concept of causality seems simple, causal arguments can be rather complex, depending on the importance ascribed to the explanatory factor in producing the outcome and the direction of the effect. This complexity can often mask common mistakes of causal inference, such as spuriousness, tautologies, and reverse causation.

Deductive and Inductive Reasoning

The two approaches to building effective arguments in the social sciences are based on opposing forms of logics. The first is based on deductive reasoning and the second on inductive reasoning. The differences between the two are illustrated in Figure 6.2.

Deductive reasoning is a top-down approach in which researchers derive specific, testable hypotheses to explain human behavior from theoretical axioms. An important advantage of a deductive approach is that it facilitates cumulative knowledge building

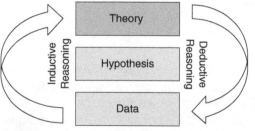

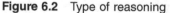

Figure 6.2   Type of reasoning

since researchers using it base their work on existing theories. Through deductive reasoning, researchers can fill in gaps or holes in existing theories, identify new conditions under which existing theories apply, or use the basic logic of existing theories to explain other phenomena yet to be explored.

Arguments that claim that legalizing marijuana will reduce its consumption based on the observed effects of increasing taxes on alcohol and cigarettes are an example of deductive reasoning. Increasing taxes on alcohol and cigarettes has been shown to reduce the consumption of these drugs by raising their costs, which prevents some people from purchasing the drugs and compels others to reduce the amount of them that they consume (Elder et al. 2010). Imposing taxes on marijuana, which would be possible through legalization, is hypothesized to have the same effect as increasing taxes on alcohol and cigarettes because marijuana is a recreational drug like alcohol and cigarettes.

Inductive reasoning, in contrast, is a bottom-up approach in which researchers construct generalizable theories from first observing patterns in human behavior and then developing hypotheses to explain these patterns. Researchers who use this approach may derive inspiration for their hypotheses from many different sources, such as news events, every day experiences, interviews or informal conversations. A researcher using an inductive approach to theorize about the effects of legalizing marijuana on consumption might do so by looking at a particular case where marijuana has been fully or partially legalized, such as the Netherlands, the United States, or Uruguay.

Box 6.1   Is Inductive Reasoning a Violation of the Scientific Method?

Inductive reasoning may seem like a violation of the scientific method because researchers using it are developing a theory from data, while the scientific method requires researchers to develop a theory prior to collecting data. Inductive reasoning is not a violation of the scientific method, however, as long as researchers do not use the same data that they use to generate their theories to test their validity. If researchers use the same data, the data would not serve as a genuine test of their arguments.

An important advantage of an inductive approach over a deductive one is that researchers' arguments are grounded in actual experiences so that the assumptions and theories that they derive from them are realistic. A potential disadvantage of this approach is that arguments developed through inductive reasoning can be more descriptive of the cases from which they are derived than theoretical. Theories identify how individual phenomena are aspects of larger concepts or phenomena. Arguments that are more descriptive than theoretical do not draw connections among observations or perceive them as parts of larger concepts, but relate them independently to particular outcomes, and are not portable as a result.

Inductive arguments also run the risk that arguments developed from particular cases are so unique that they will not apply to other cases. A case study, for example, of the legalization of marijuana in the US might result in a different hypothesis about taxes than the one above. In the US, the legalization of marijuana has not reduced marijuana consumption because it has not eliminated the black market for this drug. On the black market, marijuana can be purchased at a lower cost than the legal market. The effect may be specific to the US since government taxes on marijuana are very high, which reduces the incentives for marijuana sellers to legalize their businesses.

Types of Conditions

Arguments, regardless of whether they are derived from deductive or inductive reasoning, place different emphases on the importance of explanatory variables in producing given outcomes. The different forms that causal arguments take based on the weights they assign to explanatory variables are summarized in Table 6.1.

Neither Necessary nor Sufficient Conditions

Causal arguments in which the explanatory factor is *neither necessary nor sufficient* to produce an outcome assign the least amount of weight to the explanatory factor. An explanatory factor that is neither necessary nor sufficient does not have to be present for an outcome to be produced, and alone does not produce the outcome. These arguments are probabilistic arguments, as opposed to deterministic arguments, since they hypothesize that an outcome is more or less likely to result due to an explanatory factor, not that it will always occur. There are countless examples of this kind of argument regarding human behavior. In fact, most social science arguments take this form.

Condition	Definition
Necessary	presence required for an outcome to be produced
Sufficient	presence alone is enough to produce a given outcome
Necessary and sufficient	presence required for an outcome to be produced and alone is enough to produce the outcome
Neither necessary nor sufficient	presence not required for outcome to be produced and alone is not enough to produce the outcome

Table 6.1 Types of conditions

Below are just a few examples to illustrate the various forms that arguments, which specify conditions that are neither necessary nor sufficient for an outcome to occur, take and the language used to introduce them:

- Strong property rights give incentives to multinational corporations (MNCs) to invest in countries because they reduce the odds of these firms' investments being expropriated, and generally lead to greater investment as a result.
- Diamond-rich countries are more prone than other countries to experience civil wars because diamonds are very profitable and can help finance costly wars.
- When universities promote a culture of safety and respect across genders on their campuses, the incidence of campus rape tends to drop significantly.
- Workplace violence is likely to occur when a person has been recently denied a promotion or has been fired.

Necessary Conditions

While most causal arguments do not specify necessary and/or sufficient conditions, some do. A *necessary condition* is an explanatory factor that must be present in order for an outcome to be produced. This does not mean that the outcome will be produced when this factor is present because other factors may also be needed for the outcome to result. These other factors may interact with the explanatory factor and alter the direction of its effect on the outcome, as subsequently explained.

In the following example, sincere apologies are a necessary condition for corporations to rebuild tarnished reputations, but they are not also a sufficient condition because corporations must also change their behavior to rebuild their reputations.

> Corporations must sincerely apologize for their behavior in order to restore their reputation after a controversy, like the one United Airlines found itself mired in when one of its employees forcibly removed a passenger who refused to give up his seat on an overbooked flight. Sincere apologies engender respect and empathy for companies. However, sincere apologies must also be accompanied by actions that prevent events from reoccurring. United Airlines apologized multiple times for the incident, but its sales only recovered after it adopted a new customer-first policy allowing passengers to receive up to USD 10,000 in travel certificates for voluntarily giving up their seats.

Often, necessary conditions are not very informative because they describe very general conditions. Life is a necessary condition for death since a person cannot die unless s/he is already alive. Life, though, does not tell you very much about the causes of death since the process of dying is not precipitated by life.

A more sanguine example of a necessary condition is the phrase 'You've got to be in it to win it'. In this example, participation is the necessary condition. You cannot win any contest, performance, or competition unless you participate in it. As in the previous example, participation is not a very informative condition. Participation is only a minimal requirement to win. Many other things are also needed to win such exhibitions, including luck and skill.

Social science arguments regarding necessary conditions face the same difficulties. Elections, for example, are a necessary condition for democracy, at least according to most definitions of democracy. However, elections are not also a sufficient condition for democracy since many authoritarian states hold elections that are anything but democratic, including China, Cuba, Saudi Arabia, and Singapore. For democracy to exist, the elections must also be open and competitive, and the outcome of these elections must be upheld.

Sufficient Conditions

A *sufficient condition* is an explanatory factor that alone is enough to produce a given outcome. Sufficient conditions are not also necessary conditions because outcomes can be produced in the absence of certain sufficient conditions through other means. The philosophical statement of René Descartes, 'Cogito, ergo sum' or 'I think, therefore I am' is a sufficient condition. Thinking, according to Descartes, is enough to constitute existence. Thinking is not necessary for existence, though, as would be the case had Descartes said, 'To exist, I must think.' Descartes also allows for existence to occur through other means.

Sufficient conditions are present in academic research as well. In the following example, the depletion of non-renewable energies is a sufficient condition for companies to invest in green technologies, but not a necessary one.

> The imminent depletion of non-renewable energy sources alone is enough to make oil, gas, and coal companies invest in alternative renewable energy technologies.

This statement does not specify that non-renewable energies must be depleted for corporations to invest in green technologies, so that it is not also a necessary condition.

Necessary and Sufficient Conditions

A *necessary and sufficient condition* is an explanatory factor that must be present for a given outcome to be produced, and alone is enough for the outcome to be produced.

> With the development of DNA testing in the mid-1980s, a DNA profile for a crime, which does not match the DNA profile of the person convicted for that crime, is both a necessary and sufficient condition for this person to be exonerated if this person has already exhausted all legal opportunities to appeal the verdict.

In this example, a DNA profile that does not match the crime is necessary to exonerate the person convicted for the crime because the person exhausted all other means to challenge their conviction. It is also sufficient because a DNA profile for a crime that does not match the person convicted for the crime is alone enough to indicate that this person did not commit the crime.

Necessary and sufficient arguments, like this one, are not very common in academic research either. The following is one example of a necessary and sufficient argument developed to explain the rise in support for nationalist (i.e., anti-immigration) parties and nationalist policies throughout Europe following the influx of Syrian refugees to the continent as a result of the Syrian civil war.

Political support for nationalist parties or nationalist policies only and always increases when there is a large influx of immigrants into a country, regardless of the receiving country's level of unemployment, the national origin of the immigrants, or any other factors, such as the skill level of the immigrants and the reason for their exodus, which are commonly thought to affect public opinion on immigration.

In the previous statement, the word 'only' indicates that 'a large influx of immigrants' is a necessary condition for a rise in support for nationalist parties or policies. The word 'always' indicates that it is also a sufficient condition. The phrase 'regardless of' followed by a list of other factors that are not necessary for national support to increase also indicates that it is a sufficient condition.

Box 6.2   Alternative Explanations

Alternative explanations, as their name suggests, are arguments that claim that a given outcome was produced by a factor other than the one theorized. They are distinct from arguments that claim that other factors in addition to or besides the one theorized also contributed to a given outcome. Researchers do not have to consider every possible alternative, especially since not every one of them is likely to be plausible. However, researchers ought to consider the most likely alternatives and those that pose the greatest challenge to their arguments. To consider alternative explanations does not mean that the researcher must discredit the alternatives completely. Some alternatives may offer compelling alternative explanations to the researchers' arguments. In this case, researchers ought to honestly recognize the legitimacy of these alternative explanations. To do anything else would not be ethical. All research is limited and it is important to recognize this.

Relationship Directions

In order to build a strong argument, it is also important to consider the direction of the explanatory variable's effect on the outcome variable, as well as other factors that may alter the direction of this effect. The 'direction of the effect' refers not only to whether an explanatory factor is likely to increase or decrease the outcome, but also to whether this effect is linear, non-linear, monotonic or non-monotonic. It also refers to whether the effect of the explanatory variable changes based on the intervening variable and whether or not the explanatory variable is also affected by the outcome variable.

Figure 6.3 illustrates several different types of (non)linear and (non)monotonic relationships that exist between explanatory variables and outcomes.

Linear Monotonic Relationships

The top two graphs represent monotonic linear relationships where either an increase in the explanatory variable results in an increase in the outcome variable, as in the graph on the left, or results in a decrease in the outcome variable as in the graph on the right.

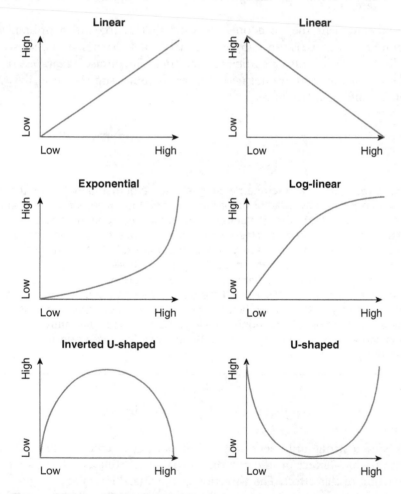

Figure 6.3 Types of linear and non-linear arguments

Most social science arguments are expressed in these terms. Newspaper headlines are filled with them. Below are only a few examples:

- Minorities are more likely to be killed by police officers than non-minorities.
- Due to young people having fewer children to focus on their careers, birth rates have fallen in wealthy countries in recent decades.
- The number of books sold each year is growing due to advancements in ebook technologies even though the number of books that people read each year is not. More ebooks are bought each year than read due to the low cost and accessibility of these books.

Non-linear Monotonic Relationships

The middle two graphs represent non-linear monotonic relationships, where the effect of the explanatory variable either intensifies (i.e., exponential functional form) or trails off (i.e., log-linear functional form) for higher values of the explanatory value. Relationships expressed in these terms are also fairly common.

The likelihood of receiving a speeding ticket based on the amount that a driver exceeds the speed limit is an example of a non-linear monotonic relationship. The more a driver exceeds the speed limit, the more likely a driver is to get a speeding ticket for a given increase in speed. In other words, the likelihood of getting a speeding ticket for a driver going 80 km/h versus 70 km/h on a road where the posted speed limit is 55 km/h is much higher than for a driver going 70 km/h versus 60 km/h. This is because an increase in speed of any given amount is more dangerous at higher speeds than at lower speeds. Among other things, the reaction time required of drivers to avoid obstacles is much shorter in the case of the former than in the case of the latter.

Economic indicators, such as GDP per capita, inflation, and unemployment, are examples of the opposite. Their effects are expected to trail off for higher values. To understand why consider the example of Zimbabwe. Zimbabwe experienced a 9-digit inflation rate in the mid-2000s that caused hundreds of thousands of Zimbabweans to flee to neighboring countries in search of food and economic opportunity. The rate by which people fled Zimbabwe trailed off at very high rates of inflation. This is likely because at very high rates of inflation most people capable of leaving Zimbabwe had already left the country, such that a given increase in inflation did not have the same impact on the number of people fleeing the country as it did at lower rates of inflation.

Non-linear Non-monotonic Relationships

The bottom two graphs in Figure 6.3 represent non-linear non-monotonic functional forms where the direction of the effect of an explanatory variable is different for middling values of the variable than it is for low and high values of it. In the case of the inverted U-shaped functional form the outcome variable is lower for middling values of the explanatory variable than it is for lower and higher values of the explanatory variable. The opposite is the case for the U-shaped functional form.

The relationship between democracy and civil wars is an example of an inverted U-shaped relationship (Hegre et al. 2001). This relationship is depicted in the left-side graph in Figure 6.4. At high and low levels of democracy, the likelihood of a civil war is low. At high levels of democracy, the government is responsive to the populace's demands through elections, reducing grievances and precluding the need for people to use violence to achieve their political goals.

At very low levels of democracy, the likelihood of civil war is also low. At low levels of democracy, governments are less responsive to the public than at high levels of democracy and grievances are greater as a result. However, at low levels of democracy, governments are also inclined to use force to prevent the population from rebelling against it.

At middling levels of democracy, the likelihood of civil war is greater than it is for high levels of democracy because the government is less responsive to the people and grievances are greater. It is also greater at middling levels of democracy than it is for low levels of democracy because governments are less inclined and less capable of repressing the population at middling levels than at low levels of democracy.

Childhood development, in contrast, has been formulated as an example of a U-shaped curve. This relationship is depicted in the right-side graph in Figure 6.4. According to Robert Siegler and colleagues (1981), college-age students perform cognitive tasks well, like balancing a scale, because they know to consider information along multiple dimensions to make decisions and know how to correctly combine this information. In the case of a balance scale, this means that college-age students consider both the weight of items on the scale and their distance from the fulcrum to determine how to balance the scale, as depicted in Figure 6.5.

Middle school-age students perform cognitive tasks less well than college-age students, according to Siegler, because they do not know how to correctly combine information across multiple dimensions even though they do know to take this information into account when making decisions. In the case of the balance scale exercise, this means that

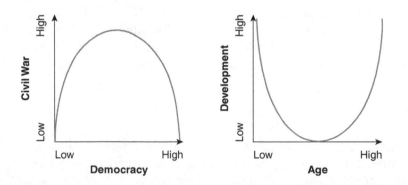

Figure 6.4 Examples of U-shaped and inverted U-shaped relationships

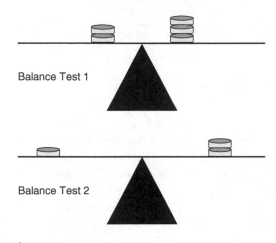

Figure 6.5 Balance scale test

middle school-age students know to consider both the weight of items on the scale and their distance from the fulcrum to determine how to balance the scale, but they are less capable than college-age students of doing so correctly.

Young children, Siegler claims, perform cognitive tasks better than middle school-age children, but not as well as college-age students. Young children only ever consider one dimension when performing cognitive tasks in contrast to both middle school- and college-age students. In the case of the balance scale example, the one dimension they consider is the weight of the items on the scale. Not surprisingly, as a result, younger children are less capable of balancing the scale than college-age students. Perhaps, more surprisingly, though, they are more capable of balancing the scale than middle school-age students, according to Siegler. Even though young children only consider the weight of the items on the scale, they do so, Siegler claims, consistently so that they make fewer mistakes trying to balance the scale than middle school-age students.

Interaction Effects

In the case of these U-shaped and inverse-U shaped relationships, the effect of the explanatory variable on the outcome variable is different for both low and high values of the explanatory variable than for middling values. This is distinct from the case of an interaction effect, where the effect of the explanatory on the outcome variable is different depending on the values of another variable, known as an intervening variable.

An *intervening variable* mediates the effect of the explanatory variable on the outcome variable, either strengthening or weakening its effect. It derives its name from the fact that it comes between the explanatory and outcome variables and alters the effect of the former

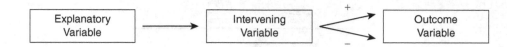

Figure 6.6 Causal argument with intervening variable

on the latter. Figure 6.6 depicts a causal relationship involving an intervening variable. In this figure, for certain values of the intervening variable, the effect of the explanatory variable on the outcome variable is higher. For certain other values of the intervening variable, the effect of the explanatory variable on the outcome variable is lower.

Relationships for which the outcome is mediated by other factors are common in everyday life. They are often identifiable by the phrase 'It depends on ...'. The factor on which things depend is the intervening variable. Whether a person uses cash to purchase an item over credit or mobile forms of payment, for example, generally depends on the size of the transaction, with people being more likely to use cash over other forms of payment when the transaction is small (Bagnall et al. 2014). Likewise, which route a person takes to get somewhere else depends on the time of day. A person who wants to go somewhere quickly is apt to choose the route that is most likely to have the least amount of traffic at a given time of day.

Macro-level relationships are also commonly mediated by other factors. Time also mediates the effectiveness of US foreign aid in democratizing countries, as Figure 6.7 illustrates.

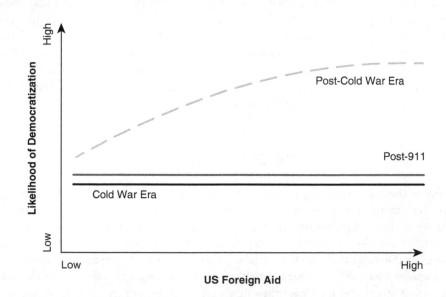

Figure 6.7 Interaction effects example

In the Cold War period, US foreign aid did not promote democracy in other countries. In this period, the US did not generally extend aid to countries on the condition of their democratizing. And, where it did, the US did not rescind, or credibly threaten to rescind this aid, from non-compliant states in order to compel them to democratize for fear of losing its influence over them to the Soviet Union (Dunning 2004). In the post-Cold War period, however, with the collapse of the Soviet Union, the US did. Foreign aid helped promote democracy in this period as a result. In the post-9/11 period, US foreign aid has again failed to foster democracy in countries. In this period, the United States has consistently given foreign aid to countries regardless of their political regime to secure allies in the fight against terrorism.

Two-way Causality

The relationships described thus far have all been unidirectional. In each, the explanatory factor influenced the outcome variable but the outcome variable did not influence the explanatory factor. However, in many cases, relationships are reciprocal or simultaneous, whereby the explanatory factor affects and is affected by the outcome variable. Such a relationship is illustrated in Figure 6.8.

There are many everyday examples of reciprocal or two-way causation. A person, not knowing how to respond to an email, is likely to delay answering that email. At the same time, a delay in answering an email is likely to make it difficult for a person to know how to respond to an email. Likewise, obesity can lead to unhappiness. At the same time, unhappiness can cause obesity by fostering bad eating habits and reducing the motivation to exercise.

The relationship between religion and economic development provides another example of reciprocal or two-way causation (Barro and McCleary 2003; McCleary 2008). Where religious practices prohibit the participation of women in the workforce, religiosity – defined as the degree to which religious principles guide and inform a person's political, social, and economic decisions – can reduce economic development. Religiosity can reduce economic development if religious principles prohibit engagement in certain economic activities. Religion, for example, is the basis on which Saudi Arabia banned women from driving, which reduced the full participation of women in the Saudi workforce. Saudi Arabia lifted the ban in 2017 without explanation. Among the reasons speculated for this decision was the need for Saudi Arabia to reduce its economic dependence on oil by diversifying its economy, which required more women in the workforce. At the same time, economic development can also reduce religiosity by exposing individuals to different

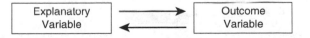

Figure 6.8 Simultaneous causation

perspectives, which supplant or reduce the influence of religion on their thinking about political, social and economic issues.

At a theoretical level, reciprocal or two-way causation is not in-and-of itself a problem; only the failure to specify a reciprocal relationship where one exists is. At the empirical level, however, it can be very difficult to disentangle the causal effects of the explanatory and outcomes variables from each other depending on the method employed.

Problems in Causal Arguments

Arguments, even if the causal direction is well specified, can be invalid for many reasons. They can be based on incorrect assumptions about human behavior. They can be internally inconsistent, or in other words, contradictory. And they can be incomplete. That is, they can fail to identify key factors that are necessary for an explanatory factor to result in a given outcome. It is impossible to specify all the reasons why arguments can be inaccurate. However, there are a few common types of errors in argumentation that researchers make that require further elaboration.

Spuriousness

A *spurious argument* is one in which the hypothesized relationship between the explanatory factor and the outcome variable is false because of the presence of another latent (or confounding) factor that causes both the explanatory factor and the outcome variable. Figure 6.9 illustrates the structure of a spurious argument.

Have you ever heard someone say that they do not want to get a flu shot because whenever they do, they get the flu? This is an example of a spurious argument. A flu vaccine contains the flu virus, but it does not cause someone to contract the flu since the cells in the vaccine are inactivated. If a person tends to get the flu whenever s/he gets a flu shot, it may be because this person only gets the flu shot when there is a flu epidemic and there is a greater risk of getting the flu in the first place. In this scenario, the flu epidemic is the latent or confounding factor that leads a person to get the flu vaccine and to also get the flu.

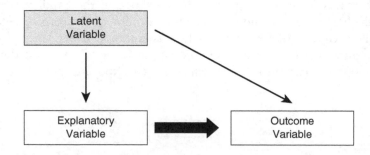

Figure 6.9   Spuriousness

Arguments that the United Nations is ineffective because it often fails to produce a sustainable peace in post-conflict countries are potentially spurious (Gilligan and Stedman 2003; Fortna 2004; Doyle and Sambanis 2011). The United Nations only mediates conflicts and establishes missions in post-conflict countries to implement peace treaties at the invitation of host states. For the UN to intervene, governments must be willing to participate in peace processes. However, the conflicts in which the UN intervenes are likely to be more intractable than other conflicts. If they were not, UN support would not be needed. If this is the case, UN intervention could fail to produce a sustainable peace in post-conflict countries not because the UN is incapable, but because the UN tends to intervene in the most intractable conflicts. The latent factor in this case is the intractability of the conflict, which is responsible for both the intervention of the UN in a post-conflict country and the failure to maintain peace.

Spuriousness should not be confused with *omitted variable bias*. Omitted variable bias occurs when a researcher fails to include a factor that has an effect on the outcome in a statistical analysis. The omitted variable is not a latent factor since it is not hypothesized to cause both the explanatory factor and outcome variable. It is, nonetheless, problematic for the statistical analysis because it can cause the other variables in the analysis to be misspecified. In the absence of the omitted variable, other variables in the model may be significant when they should be insignificant, or vice versa. Their substantive effects may also be stronger or weaker as a result.

Tautologies

Another less common problem in causal arguments are tautologies. A *tautology* is a statement that is true by definition, as Figure 6.10 depicts. Tautologies convey no information because the antecedent is the same as the postcedent. They also violate an important principle of social science research, that of *falsifiability* – the idea that all arguments have to be able to be proven false.

The English language is full of tautologies. 'Enough is enough!', 'Business is business', 'A promise is a promise' and 'It is what it is' are all examples of tautologies. Even world leaders with well-paid speechwriters at their disposal make tautological statements from time to time.

Australian Labor Party politician Kep Enderby is better known outside Australia for this tautology than for anything else. As Minister for Manufacturing Industry, Enderby once infamously stated that 'Traditionally, Australia obtains its imports from overseas.'[1] Since Australia is a continent entirely surrounded by water, all imports have to be from overseas.

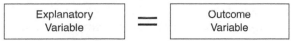

Figure 6.10 Tautology

Tautological arguments are often much less obvious than these examples. Commonly, when a person commits a horrific crime, such as the Utøya massacre, the Sandy Hook school shooting, or the intentional downing of Germanwings Flight 9525, that person is deemed mentally ill by virtue of the crime they committed. While some people who commit massacres have been diagnosed with psychiatric illnesses, to define these individuals as mentally ill by virtue of the crime they committed is tautological.

Although psychologists do not define mental illness in terms of the crimes people commit, tautologies are problematic for psychological research as well, especially personality psychology research. Research on this subject analyzes the relationship between personality traits and behaviors. Tautologies arise in personality psych studies when the behaviors argued to result from certain personality traits are an expression of the personality traits themselves.

In early studies of femininity, femininity is argued to affect self-assertiveness, nurturance, and interpersonal orientation and is defined in terms of the widely used Bem Sex Role Inventory (BSRI) (Nicholls et al. 1982). The BSRI, however, measures femininity in terms of the same characteristics that these studies claim that femininity affects. The BSRI femininity traits include assertiveness, aggressiveness, helpfulness, and compassionateness, among others. As a result, in these studies, femininity essentially explains femininity. Had these studies argued that biological sex, rather than femininity, affected individuals' self-assertiveness, nurturance, and interpersonal orientation, they would not be tautological.

Tautologies should not be confused with *functionalism*. Functional arguments claim that certain things exist because of the purposes they serve. The following is a functional argument regarding why authoritarian states hold elections.

> Strongly authoritarian states hold elections, even though these elections lack international and domestic credibility, because autocrats want to send a signal to those considering challenging them that they are strong. Winning clearly fraudulent elections by large margins of victories sends a signal to potential opponents that autocrats are strong, because it demonstrates to potential opponents that the autocrats are able to instill sufficient fear in the public to make the public vote for them, or have enough money to either buy the public's support and/or steal the elections. (Magaloni 2006; Simpser 2013)

Functional arguments may not be particularly interesting but they are not tautological because they are not true by definition. They are not necessarily wrong either. Certain institutions, policies, relationships, and so forth, might exist because they serve a given purpose. The Australian splayd (similar to the US spork) that combines three utensils into one – a knife, fork, and spoon – was reportedly created by its inventor William McArthur to make eating more efficient.[2]

However, functional arguments are problematic when the motivation or reason for these things' existence is inferred from the purpose they serve. The purpose that something serves may be different from the reason it was created. Something may serve a different purpose from the one for which it was created because new uses were found for it over time, or because a program, policy, institution, and so forth backfired.

Anti-child labor activists have effectively agitated for the adoption of child labor laws throughout the world. In developing countries, though, where poor families rely on the money earned from children for survival, children who are prevented from working in factories due to child labor laws are often forced into prostitution to earn money (Bellamy 1996). To conclude based on the effect of these laws, that governments adopt child labor laws in order to increase child prostitution would be grossly misleading.

Reverse Causation

Reverse causation refers to the situation where the explanatory variable does not cause the outcome variable, but the outcome variable causes the explanatory variable. Figure 6.11 depicts the concept of reverse causation. Reverse causation should not be confused with reciprocal causation in which the explanatory variable influences the outcome variable and the outcome variable influences the explanatory variable.

The association between engineers and terrorism may be a result of reverse causation. Engineers are significantly overrepresented among the ranks of captured and confessed terrorists, according to a study by Diego Gambetta and Steffan Hertog (2016). Nearly 20 percent of the approximately 400 men that Gambetta and Hertog studied had engineering degrees. According to the researchers, engineers made up about only 3.5 percent of the working-age population of the terrorists' respective countries.

Gambetta and Hertog hypothesize that engineering students are more likely to be radicalized and commit terrorist acts because of their unique cognitive traits and dispositions. Engineers, they argue, are especially susceptible to radicalization because they prefer clear answers to ambiguous questions and are loyal to authority. This not only makes engineers more vulnerable to recruitment by terrorist organizations, they argue, but it also makes them more likely than other students to adopt violent right-wing beliefs in response to economic frustration.

The direction of the causation may be the reverse, however. That is, those intending to join terrorist groups may study engineering in order to acquire the technical skills necessary to make bombs and carry out other terrorist-related activities. Gambetta and Hertog anticipate this criticism and argue that this is unlikely because engineers often assume managerial positions within terrorist organizations and lack contact with technical, day-to-day operations. However, those who intend to join terrorist organizations do not necessarily know this, and may major in engineering for this reason nonetheless.

Figure 6.11   Reverse causation

Key Points

- Causal arguments specify that a change in one concept results in a change in another.
- Arguments derived through deductive reasoning are disposed to facilitate cumulative knowledge building, but can be unrealistic, while arguments built through inductive reasoning are generally realistic, but can lack generalizability.
- The relationship between two factors can take complex forms, depending on the importance ascribed to the explanatory factor in producing the outcome and the direction of the effect.
- Common mistakes of causal inferences include: spuriousness, tautologies, and reverse causation.

Further Reading

The first reading highlights the importance of context in developing causal arguments. The second discusses frameworks and techniques for developing causal arguments, and the third discusses research designs for testing arguments specifying necessary and sufficient conditions.

Falleti, Tulia G. and Julia F. Lynch. 2009. 'Context and Causal Mechanisms in Political Analysis.' *Comparative Political Studies* 42(9): 1143–1166.

Jaccard, James and Jacob Jacoby. 2009. *The Construction and Model Building Skills: A Practical Guide for Social Scientists*. New York: The Guilford Press.

Seawright, Jason. 2002. 'Testing for Necessary and/or Sufficient Causation: Which Cases Are Relevant?' *Political Analysis* 10: 178–193.

EXERCISE 6.1

Make separate graphs, like those in Figure 6.2 for the three monotonic linear relationships described in the text regarding minorities, the birth rate in advanced economies, and ebook sales. Also, make separate graphs for the two non-linear monotonic relationships described in the text, regarding speeding tickets and hyperinflation. Label the x-axis and y-axis for each graph to clearly demonstrate the hypothesized relationships.

EXERCISE 6.2

Below is an example of a non-linear non-monotonic relationship. Draw a graph of the relationship described, properly label the x- and y-axes, and identify the relationship as either U-shaped or inverted-U shaped.

When paintings are very small or very large, auction prices are lower because there are fewer private collectors to drive up sales prices than when paintings are modest in size. Private collectors do not derive as much enjoyment from small paintings on their walls than larger paintings. When the paintings are too large, though, there are fewer private collectors who have the space to properly house and display the works.

EXERCISE 6.3

The following relationship between decision-making and happiness is potential spurious. Identify the latent factor that might influence both decision-making and happiness. Are there other problems with the study?

Steven D. Levitt (2016) conducted a study about whether or not people changing their lives in a major way, regardless of the outcome of the decision, made people happier than remaining with the status quo. In the study Levitt recruited volunteers on his website to participate in the study and to agree that they would allow a coin flip to determine whether they would change their lives in a major way or not.

Levitt provided the participants with a list of 30 life-altering questions. This list included questions about whether to get engaged, leave a relationship, quit a job, and return to school, among others. The participants chose among this list the questions they were willing to allow a coin toss to determine. If participants flipped the coin, and the coin landed heads, they were to change their behavior on this question. If the coin landed tails, they were not.

Two months and six months after flipping the coin, participants were asked to complete a survey about whether or not they had changed their behavior, and their level of happiness. For the less important issues, like changing one's hair style or joining a gym, about 67 percent did what the coin told them. For the important issues, such as those mentioned above, still more than half (about 55 percent) did what the coin told them. For both types of issues, those who had made a change were substantially happier than those who did not make a change.

EXERCISE 6.4

Debate whether the following are tautologies.

1. Daniel Stevens and colleagues claim that 'antidemocratic attitudes [negatively] affect elites' support for democracy' (2006: 616). The authors measure 'antidemocratic attitudes' (but never define them) based on people's support for laws outlawing 'radical political groupings' in their countries, according to an original survey. Radical political groups are not defined in the survey. To measure support for democracy, they ask survey participants if they 'would ever support an authoritarian government in their country' (2006: 619). Authoritarianism is also not defined in the survey.

2. While billionaires Bill and Melinda Gates, Warren Buffett, Michael Bloomberg, and Saudi Prince Alwaleed bin Talal have pledged to give all, or nearly all, of their wealth to philanthropic causes when they die, studies of the UK and USA have found that on average poor people give a greater proportion of their income to charity than wealthy people.[3] One of the explanations for this phenomenon is that poor people are more prosocial than rich people because they are more altruistic. Prosocial behavior encompasses a broad range of actions intended to benefit one or more people other than oneself, such as helping, comforting, sharing, and cooperating. Altruism, meanwhile, is the motivation to increase another person's welfare.

III

METHOD AND
CASE SELECTION

7

Method Selection

Objectives

- describe the attributes of qualitative and quantitative research
- define the following terms: hypothesis building, hypothesis testing, causal inference, generalizability, and replicability
- compare and contrast the strengths and weaknesses of qualitative and quantitative research in regard to each of these terms

To test their arguments, researchers have a choice between two different methodological approaches – one qualitative, the other quantitative – and a third, known as mixed methods research, which combines the two. *Qualitative research* involves the collection and analysis of data based on written, verbal, and visual content. It encompasses a number of different methods, including interviews, focus groups, participation observation, and process tracing. *Quantitative research*, in contrast, involves the collection and analysis of numeric data, some of which may be derived from assigning numerical values to qualitative information. Quantitative methods include experiments, surveys, and observational

"I'm not sure what methodology they used."

Cartoon 7.1

studies. In some disciplines, the quantitative–qualitative divide among researchers is long-standing, bitter, and contentious. Neither approach, however, is universally better than the other. Each has their advantages and disadvantages and offers different perspectives and insights into important political, social, and economic issues.

Which Methodological Approach is Best?

Given the contrasts in qualitative and quantitative approaches to research, each approach not surprisingly has advantages and disadvantages over the other. There are five key aspects of research around which these advantages and disadvantages arise. They are: hypothesis building, hypothesis testing, causal inference, generalizability, and replicability. The attributes of qualitative and quantitative research that positively influence each of these aspects of research are summarized in Table 7.1 and discussed herein. The following discussion highlights general tendencies and differences between qualitative and quantitative research. However, there is significant variation within each approach among different methods, not only as a result of intrinsic features of these methods, but also as a result of the quality of their application.

Hypothesis Building

Qualitative approaches have a much higher potential than quantitative research methods for developing rich, well-grounded, and compelling hypotheses about human behavior

Data attributes	Hypothesis building	Hypothesis testing	Generalizability	Causal inference	Replicability
Large-N		✓✓	✓✓		
Objectivity		✓✓			✓✓
Randomization		✓✓	✓✓	✓✓	
Transparency					✓✓

Table 7.1   The utility of data attributes for research

through inductive reasoning. To develop hypotheses inductively using qualitative methods, researchers can interview individuals, observe people in their natural environments, and analyze accounts of historical events, among other things. Through these experiences, researchers may gain insights into the reasons why particular events occurred, and then use these insights to develop explanations about why and under what conditions these events are likely to occur in general.

Quantitative research can also be used to generate hypotheses through inductive reasoning through a process known as data mining. Data mining involves the identification of regularities or patterns in large datasets using computer-intensive techniques. Quantitative research is not as well suited as qualitative research for theory building because the data collected through data mining lacks context and is difficult to interpret as a result. To understand the data, researchers need to draw on alternative sources of information that may include qualitative materials.

Using data mining techniques, for example, researchers may identify patterns in where intrastate violence occurs among civil populations based on satellite images of thinning forests. However, researchers still must use independent knowledge to theorize about the reasons why rebels or government forces use violence against civilian populations in ways consistent with these patterns. Likewise, educational researchers can discern patterns in response times to questions posed in tutorial programs, but again, they have to use their own knowledge and experience to develop models to explain when response times are indicative of students working through problems or gaming the system.

Box 7.1   Data Mining: Good or Bad?

'Data mining' is different than 'mining the data'. The latter term refers to researchers identifying patterns in data, devising ad hoc hypotheses to explain these patterns, while pretending to have developed the hypotheses prior to inspecting the data, and then using the data to test these hypotheses, in clear violation of the scientific method.

Hypothesis Testing

Quantitative research, conversely, has a much higher potential than qualitative research for testing hypotheses. Hypothesis testing refers to the process through which empirical evidence is used to determine if an argument is valid or not. Qualitative research is less well suited than quantitative research for hypothesis testing because qualitative research tends to include fewer cases or observations than quantitative research. It is also subjective and lacks clear-cut standards for confirming or disconfirming hypotheses, which is equally problematic for hypothesis testing.

The tendency of qualitative research to be based on a few cases presents a number of challenges for testing probabilistic theories. A study that is consistent with a probabilistic theory, but based on only a few cases, can lend support to this theory, but it cannot confirm it because these cases may not be true of other cases. A study of Macau, for example, can offer support for an argument that economic wealth is insufficient to explain public backing for authoritarian governance, since Macau has a high GDP and lacks a democracy movement, but it cannot confirm this argument since Macau might not be like very many other territories in this regard.

Likewise, a study based on a few cases that is inconsistent with the claims of a probabilistic theory, cannot disconfirm a probabilistic theory since probabilistic theories do not claim to explain all cases of a phenomenon. The fact, for example, that anti-regime protests did not occur in other countries in Latin America at the time of the anti-Maduro protests in Venezuela cannot disconfirm arguments that anti-regime protests do not diffuse, since the anti-Maduro protests may not be indicative of the ability of protests to diffuse more generally given their violent nature. The anti-Maduro protests were a series of protests, which occurred over a few years and attracted hundreds of thousands of participants at their peak, against the presidency of President Nicolas Maduro over the country's economic crisis, high level of crime, and lack of democracy, among other things.

Studies based on only a few cases can be used to disprove deterministic theories about necessary conditions and sufficient conditions, but only if an outcome results in the absence of a necessary (or necessary and sufficient) condition, or does not result in the presence of a sufficient (or necessary and sufficient) condition. A study of Bangladesh, for example, would be able to disconfirm arguments that legislation outlawing the practice of dowries is sufficient or necessary and sufficient to end dowry-related violence. A dowry is any property, money, or goods promised to a man and his family in exchange for their marrying a woman. Bangladesh outlawed dowries in 1980. Yet, women are still beaten, disfigured in acid attacks, and killed at very high rates in Bangladesh over disagreements regarding the dowries paid to their husbands as part of their marriage contracts. The disagreements often involve the financial value of the dowries or the failure of families to fulfill their promises.

The tendency of qualitative research to be based on only a few cases also makes it difficult to isolate the effect of one factor from another. If there are only a few cases, the explanatory factor may coincide with other factors that also contribute to the outcome. The coincidence of these factors makes it impossible to determine if the explanatory factor or these other factors are responsible for the outcome. If there are more cases, researchers have a greater chance to observe cases where the explanatory variable does not coincide with these other factors, and can see if the effect is produced when these other factors are not present.

In the example of dowry-related violence in Bangladesh, it is difficult to separate out the effect of female education and the lack of women in the labor force on dowry-related violence as both are highly correlated. In Bangladesh, the education rate of women compared to men is significantly lower, as is the ratio of women in the labor force, but both are growing. Higher rates of education and greater participation of women in the workforce are both expected to reduce the rate of dowry-related deaths, albeit through different channels.

The former is believed to reduce the rate of dowry-related violence by changing cultural norms regarding the appropriateness of the practice, while the latter is believed to lower it by giving women more financial independence. Women that are financially independent have more options regarding whether or not to marry and whom to marry than women who are not. These women also do not pose a financial burden to the families into which they marry, so that these families feel less of a need and right to demand dowries to offset the costs of the marriage.

Qualitative research is also less well suited for theory testing than quantitative research because qualitative data is generally subjective and open for interpretation. In the case of interviews, for example, a researcher based on his or her knowledge, experiences, and biases might understand an interviewee's response as consistent with their expectations, while another researcher based on his or her knowledge, experiences, and biases might not.

Furthermore, there are no clear-cut and established rules about when to reject or accept hypotheses based on qualitative data. For example, in interview-based research there is not a standard about how many people need to make a statement in an interview confirming a researcher's hypothesis for the hypothesis to be accepted. Nor are there standards about whether the failure of interviewees to make statements (and how many) in support of a researcher's hypothesis disconfirms it.

Causal Inference

An important component of hypothesis testing is establishing the causal effect of one factor on another. In social science research, causal inference is difficult to establish due to the *fundamental problem of causal inference*. This axiom states that for any given subject, it is impossible to observe an outcome under both the treatment and control conditions at a particular point in time. For example, it is not possible to observe a person participate and not participate in a protest at the same time. Nor is it possible to observe a business simultaneously apologize and not apologize for a given wrongdoing, or a country experience a war and not experience a war at the same time.

Of all quantitative and qualitative methods, experimental research has the highest potential for causal inference. In experiments, participants are exposed to certain conditions or treatments, and are evaluated prior to and/or after the treatment in terms of one or more outcomes of interest to ascertain the participants' response to the treatment. As a result, researchers can establish with certainty that the explanatory variable occurred prior to the outcome. Participants are assigned at random to either the treatment or control condition, which ensures the participant has received the treatment condition for reasons unrelated to the outcome of interest.

In quantitative research that is non-experimental or observational in nature, subjects are not assigned at random to treatment and control conditions, making causal inference difficult to establish. This means that an explanatory factor may be associated with an outcome because the explanatory factor is more likely to be true of certain cases than others, as in the case of being religious and being overweight (Feinstein et al. 2012). The reason why religious people tend to be more overweight than atheists may not be because religion makes people overweight, but because people who live in suburban areas tend to be more religious than those who live in urban areas, and because those in the former walk less than people in the latter.

The one exception is natural experiments. Natural experiments are observational studies in which researchers do not randomly assign subjects to treatment and control conditions, but where the assignment is random or 'as if' random anyway. Natural experiments may be derived from certain environment events, such as rainfall or earthquakes, but are not limited to environmental events. Natural experiments are just not very common in practice, and the extent to which the treatment assignment is fully random is often questioned.

In observational studies, researchers use various techniques to address selection effects and establish the causal influence on one factor or another. They measure the explanatory variable in the period prior to the outcome variable to address issues of simultaneity, and use different estimation techniques to address selection effects (e.g., Heckman selection models, propensity score matching) as well as *simultaneity bias* (e.g., instrumental variable regression). All of these methods are rarely fully convincing in practice because the data used does not meet the assumptions of the models.

Qualitative research faces the same challenges as observational studies regarding the non-random assignment of subjects to treatment and control conditions. The primary method qualitative researchers use for causal inference is process tracing. Process tracing is a form of historical analysis in which researchers hypothesize about phenomena likely to be observable if the relationship between two factors is causal, and then look for historical evidence of their presence. Evidence consistent with a hypothesis lends credence to the researchers' argument. Mixed evidence does not. When that evidence is mixed, as is so often the case, this method does not provide any guidance regarding how to reconcile the conflicting findings in order to draw an overall conclusion about the effect of the explanatory factor on the outcome produced.

Generalizability

Quantitative research has a higher potential to yield generalizable results than qualitative research. Both quantitative and qualitative research face challenges in terms of *generalizability* because of the guinea pig effect. The *guinea pig effect* is the idea that those who think they are being studied, do not behave as they would in real life. In studies, people may present themselves as they would like to be seen rather than how they are in real life, or in a way that they think will be viewed more favorably by others – a phenomenon known as *social desirability bias*.

The guinea pig effect is not an issue for all types of quantitative or qualitative methodologies. In quantitative research, it is not a problem for observational studies and in qualitative research, it is not an issue for covert participant observation. In the former, researchers do not directly observe their subjects, and in the latter where they do, participants are unaware that they are being observed as part of the study. Covert participant observation includes studies where researchers observe people in their everyday lives, unnoticed, going to cafés, travelling, using the internet.

Putting the guinea pig effect aside, quantitative research has a greater generalizability potential than qualitative research because the former tends to be based on more cases than the latter. Having few cases does not preclude a study's findings from being generalizable. A study based on as little as a single case may be generalizable if the case is representative of other cases in terms of the factors likely to affect the outcome studied. In practice, however, these cases are not often chosen through procedures that make this likely to be the case.

Random sampling techniques are used more often in quantitative research than qualitative research. In random sampling, as explained in Chapter 9, all observations have a known non-zero probability of being included in a study. While random sampling makes it more likely that the cases studied will be representative of the larger population that they claim to represent, it does not guarantee it. The representativeness of a sample can also be compromised when an insufficient number of people agree to participate in a study in the first place, or when a large number of people withdraw from a longitudinal study and are systematically different from those that remain in the study.

Replicability

The findings from quantitative research not only have a higher potential for generalizability, but they also have a higher replication potential than qualitative research due to the objectivity of quantitative data and the relative ease with which quantitative research can meet transparency standards. The subjectivity of qualitative research makes it difficult to replicate the findings of qualitative research since one researcher, trying to repeat the study of another, may reach the opposite conclusion based on the same data because they have interpreted the data differently. Quantitative data are not only objective in contrast, but whether or not they confirm or disconfirm a theory is based on mathematical principals and widely accepted standards. These standards assess whether or not patterns observed in quantitative data are likely to have occurred by chance or not.

Privacy concerns also pose a more significant challenge to the replicability of qualitative research than quantitative research. In order for researchers to replicate the findings of others, research must be transparent. Research is transparent to the extent that information regarding the data, methods, and procedures used in research is open and accessible. For quantitative researchers, privacy concerns are not generally an obstacle to making the raw data on which their analyses are based public because these data do not involve individuals and where they do, the data are generally reported anonymously. It is also difficult for others to deduce the identity of individuals based on characteristics (e.g., age, occupation, and income level) reported about them in quantitative data since quantitative data usually includes a large number of subjects and is derived from a large respondent pool.

This is not the case in qualitative research, however. The pool of potential respondents and/or the number of subjects in qualitative research is generally much smaller than it is in quantitative research. This makes it easier for another person to determine the identity of subjects from the raw data even if the data is anonymous. This is also made easier by the fact the raw data is often very detailed and individualized. Researchers' field notes and interview transcripts can include, for example, descriptions of a person's physical appearance, biographical data about where they went to school (not just how much schooling they received), details about their employment, and so forth.

The Importance of Method Selection

Given the significant differences between qualitative and quantitative research, which methodological approach researchers choose has important implications for the questions researchers ask and the conclusions that they draw from their research. The training and experience that researchers have in a given approach can affect the questions that they pose because it can deter some researchers from asking questions that are not possible to analyze given a certain method. A quantitative researcher, for example, may not be inclined to ask questions for which it is not possible to reliably collect quantitative data on, such as which policies best reduce government corruption. It is difficult to accurately collect reliable data on the amount of government corruption due to its hidden nature.

At the same time, the training and experience researchers have in a given approach can also lead some researchers to ask questions that they otherwise would not because it broadens their ideas of what is knowable. A quantitative researcher may, for example, be likely to ask broad questions about generalizable phenomena, like what are the causes of democracy protests, or can gender quotas in politics change societal views toward women, since quantitative research is more amenable to analyzing a large number of cases than qualitative research.

A qualitative researcher, in contrast, may be more likely to develop a new hypothesis using a single case to explain an existing phenomenon, because qualitative research is better suited to analyzing a few cases in depth and is very useful for understanding the processes by which relationships unfold. A qualitative researcher, for example, might analyze the Syrian civil war to examine how foreign intervention affects the rise of terrorist groups. Alternatively, this researcher might look at the civil wars in the Balkans to understand how, if at all, foreign interventions for humanitarian purposes can encourage or prolong conflict.

The methodological approach that researchers use also affects the conclusions that they draw in their research. Quantitative researchers, for example, might overlook an important factor affecting a given phenomenon because they could not measure it numerically, or they may use a poor proxy of this factor because it is the only reliable quantitative data on this factor. Instead of measuring corruption, for example, in a study about the effectiveness of anti-corruption programs, researchers may measure perceptions of corruption. While perceptions of corruption are surely based in part on experiences with corruption, perceptions of corruption could be problematic for this study since the existence of the program itself may make people think that corruption is being reduced when it is not.

Meanwhile, qualitative researchers analyzing a few cases might conclude one thing about the causes of a given phenomenon based on what is present in the cases they examine, but which may not be true of the phenomenon more generally. Qualitative researchers, for example, examining the 1848 revolutions in Europe, the 1989 communist revolutions, the Colored Revolutions and the Arab Spring have concluded that democracy protests diffuse across countries based on the timing and rhetoric of these protests (Beissinger 2007; Bunce and Wolchik 2006; Weyland 2014). Quantitative researchers, however, examining all democracy protests since 1989 have found that protests do not diffuse because democracy protests result from domestic processes that are unaffected or undermined by the occurrence of democracy protests in other countries (Brancati and Lucardi forthcoming).

Which Methodological Approach to Choose?

Given that both quantitative and qualitative approaches have advantages and disadvantages, the question as to how to decide which approach to use naturally arises. Some questions can only be answered using either quantitative or qualitative research given the nature of the question posed or the environment in which researchers ask them. Researchers, for example, conducting research on authoritarian regimes may not be able to use quantitative methods in their research because authoritarian regimes are less likely to report government statistics, or report them accurately, than democratic regimes. In authoritarian contexts, researchers may also have to use qualitative methods, like interviews rather than surveys, to collect data on certain topics, which are either sensitive or subversive, in order to build a rapport with people so that they feel comfortable to share their views with the researchers.

Where it is possible to use either approach, researchers may choose to use the approach whose attributes they value more than others. Some researchers, for example, may use qualitative methods because they believe that the political, social, or economic phenomena that they study are too complex to be reduced to numbers, and too unique to be compared to other cases. Other researchers, meanwhile, may use quantitative methods because they believe, in contrast, that it is possible to identify basic patterns among cases even though individual cases are complex, and because they value highly the ability to develop generalizable theories based on comparisons across cases.

Researchers may also choose to use one approach over another given their skills, backgrounds, and experiences. Those who enjoy talking and have strong language and communication skills may prefer qualitative methods that involve a lot of interaction between researchers and their subjects, as in interviews, focus groups, and participant observation. Researchers, in contrast, with strong mathematical and computer skills may prefer quantitative methods. However, one should never presume that all qualitative researchers lack mathematical and technical skills, or that all quantitative researchers lack interpersonal skills.

Finally, given that qualitative and quantitative methods have advantages over each other and can offer different insights into the same issues, researchers may choose to use both approaches. Research that combines qualitative and quantitative research approaches is called mixed methods research, and is discussed in detail in the subsequent chapter. Researchers may also choose to collaborate with others who have the skills that they do not either in a single project or a series of projects.

Key Points

- There are two main approaches to research – one qualitative and the other quantitative – and a third that combines the two approaches. The former involves the collection and analysis of data based on written, verbal, and visual content. The latter involves the collection and analysis of numeric data.
- Qualitative and quantitative research have certain advantages and disadvantages over each other in terms of hypothesis building and hypothesis testing, causal inference, and generalizability. However, there is also significant variation within these approaches due to differences in specific methods and the application of these methods.
- Which approach researchers choose can depend not only on the question posed and the environment in which it is posed, but also on the personal preferences and skills of the researchers.

Further Reading

The three readings elaborate on the commonalities and differences in the approaches and applications of quantitative and qualitative research, as well as the strengths and weaknesses of these approaches.

Bartels, Larry M. 2010. 'Some Unfilled Promises of Quantitative Imperialism.' In *Rethinking Social Inquiry: Diverse Tools, Shared Standards*, edited by Henry E. Brady and David Collier, 683–88. Lanham, MD: Rowman Littlefield Publishers.

Brady, Henry E. 2010. 'Doing Good and Doing Better: How Far Does the Quantitative Template Get Us?' In *Rethinking Social Inquiry: Diverse Tools, Shared Standards*, edited by Henry E. Brady and David Collier, 67– 82. Lanham, MD: Rowman Littlefield Publishers

Goertz, Gary and James Mahoney. 2012. *A Tale of Two Cultures: Contrasting Quantitative and Qualitative Research*. Princeton: Princeton University Press.

8

Mixed Methods Research

Objectives

- develop an objectives-based typology of mixed methods research designs
- compare and contrast each of the objectives presented in this typology, namely design, concatenation, gap-filling, triangulation, and interpretation
- provide examples from academic research of each of these objectives

Mixed methods research involves collecting, analyzing, and interpreting quantitative and qualitative data in a single study or in a series of studies examining the same phenomenon. Research that combines methods within either one of these approaches, such as interviews and participant observation in the case of qualitative methods, or surveys and experiments in the case of quantitative methods, is not considered mixed methods research. The overall objective of the mixed methods approach is to combine the strengths of quantitative and qualitative research in order to build more accurate and precise theories, to construct deeper and richer analyses, and to produce greater confidence in the results of studies.

Mixed methods research designs are typologized in this chapter according the objectives of researchers in combining qualitative and quantitative research methods.[1] Five different objectives are identified herein, namely: (1) to inform the design of an analysis using another method (design); (2) to investigate different issues related to a single phenomenon (concatenation); (3) to analyze different aspects of the same issue (gap-filling); (4) to corroborate the results of a study using another method (*triangulation*); and (5) to interpret and/or explain the findings of a study based on another research method (*interpretation*). These goals, which are summarized in Table 8.1, may not represent every objective researchers have in using mixed methods design, but they do represent the principal ones.

Design

In this form of mixed methods research, qualitative and quantitative research methods are combined so that the findings from one method inform the research design of the other method. Typically, the latter includes the sample from which the data are collected, the instruments used to collect the data, and the measures that define the data. In this form of mixed methods research design, the two methods are conducted independent of each other. The method used to inform the research design of the other method is fully

Type	Purpose	Example
Design	inform the design of an analysis using the opposing method	quantitative research identifying subject pool for qualitative study
		qualitative study informing choice of data for quantitative analysis
Concatenation	analyze different components of a single phenomenon	qualitative study analyzing cause of phenomena and quantitative research analyzing outcome of it, or vice versa
Gap-filling	analyze different aspects of the same component of a given phenomenon	qualitative study evaluating alternative explanations impossible to measure in quantitative analysis
		quantitative analysis testing assumptions about human behavior made in qualitative study
Triangulation	corroborate the results of the other method	qualitative study to determine if quantitative measure correlated with an outcome predicts the outcome for the reasons ascribed to it
		qualitative research to corroborate techniques for causal inference in observational study
Interpretation	interpret and/or explain the findings of the other method	qualitative research to explain findings from quantitative analysis that are inconsistent with theoretical predictions or otherwise unexpected

Table 8.1   Mixed methods research designs

completed before any research using the other method is initiated, and is generally of lesser importance in the overall analysis than the other method.

Quantitative methods, which take this form of mixed methods research design, are most commonly used to identify the pool of subjects for a qualitative research study usually involving interviews and focus groups. Typically, in this type of mixed methods research, the pool of subjects is identified using quantitative data and a sample of participants is chosen from among this pool through one or another random sampling technique.

The types of quantitative data researchers often utilize for this purpose include data available through public records (e.g., birth, death, marriage, and divorces records) as well as voluntary registries (e.g., health and twin registries). They also include data that researchers have collected themselves through original surveys conducted on issues relevant to their work. The surveys may include demographic data as well as subjective data on individuals' values and experiences.

More often, in this form of mixed methods research design, qualitative research is used to build a theory that informs the design of a quantitative study testing this theory. Arguments generated from this approach are grounded in real cases and, thus, less likely to be based on unrealistic assumptions about human behavior than ideas generated from a deductive approach. They may also be less descriptive of the case(s) on which they are built and more theoretical because the quantitative analysis requires researchers to construct measures that are applicable to other cases. At the same time, certain nuances and complexities in the original argument are likely to be lost in the quantitative analysis because of the difficulty of constructing quantitative measures to represent certain aspects of the original arguments.

There are numerous examples of mixed methods research in which qualitative methods are used to inform the design of quantitative studies, including Leon Festinger's renowned theory of cognitive dissonance, which states that people will resolve the mental discomfort that arises from having contradictory attitudes, beliefs or values, and behaviors by their changing either their attitudes, beliefs, and values, or their behaviors. Festinger devised this theory after observing how people reacted to an earthquake in India. In Festinger's view, people who had not experienced any direct loss from the first earthquake responded irrationally to rumors that more earthquakes were imminent. Festinger developed his theory further through participant observation of an apocalyptic cult when the world did not end as the cult's leader predicted. To rationalize their belief, according to Festinger, cult members accepted their leader's explanation that the world did not end because of the actions that they took in anticipation of the world ending.

To test Festinger's theory of cognitive dissonance, Festinger and Carlsmith (1959) constructed a lab experiment in which participants performed a boring task. After completing the task, the participants were offered either $1 or $20 to tell the next participant that the task was exciting. Those who were paid $1 conveyed to the next participant that the task was more enjoyable than those who were paid $20. According to Festinger and his colleagues, this was because those who were paid $1 were forced to reduce the dissonance that they felt for lying by changing their opinion of the task, while those who were paid $20 did not, because they felt less dissonance given the higher amount of money that they received for lying.

Concatenation

In this form of mixed methods research, qualitative and quantitative research methods are used to analyze different issues related to the same phenomena. *Concatenation* allows researchers to expand the breadth or range of their research. The concatenated analyses are conducted independent of each other. Their significance in the overall research project depends on the relative importance of the issue that they are used to analyze.

Studies that use quantitative methods to analyze the effectiveness of certain policies, programs, or services in terms of the outcomes they produce in conjunction with qualitative methods to evaluate people's perceptions of these programs' effectiveness, are examples of this form of mixed methods research. In these studies, the larger phenomenon that the two methods are designed to understand is the policy, program, or service, and the two distinct aspects of the policy, program, or service that the individual methods are designed to understand are the objective outcomes associated with them and perceptions of the outcomes.

Market researchers are at the forefront of combing technology-based qualitative interviews with objective quantitative data in this way. These researchers use sales figures to evaluate the effectiveness of marketing strategies for new products, and mobile video interviews to understand the features of the new products that customers prefer and the reasons for their preferences. In the mobile video interviews, individuals respond to researchers' questions via cameras on their smart phones so that the researchers are able to observe the interviewees' facial expressions and body language in their own environments.

Concatenating research designs are not limited to program evaluations. Stokes (2001) uses a concatenating research design to understand the causes and consequences of Latin American politicians adopting neo-liberal economic policies in the late twentieth century in contrast to their campaign promises. Stokes uses a statistical analysis to demonstrate that Latin economies grew more when politicians switched their positions once in office, and that politicians who switched their positions were rewarded in subsequent elections. Stokes used interviews of politicians to understand why the politicians changed their position toward neo-liberalism once in office. Based on her interviews, she concluded that the politicians changed their positions primarily because they believed it was more important to enact policies in the interests of the people than to reflect the will of the people.

Gap-filling

Mixed methods research designs used for *gap-filling* are similar to those used for concatenation. In both, quantitative and qualitative methods are used independent of each other, either concurrently or simultaneously. However, in gap-filling designs the quantitative and quantitative methods are used to analyze the same issue, while in the latter they are used to analyze different ones.

Gap-filling mixed methods designs include studies that use qualitative analyses to investigate the relevance of potential alternative explanations for a given phenomenon that cannot be effectively measured or tested in observational studies. Ruth Ben-Artzi (2016), in her study of the lending behavior of regional development banks, uses a statistical analysis to demonstrate a correlation between various economic, political and social indicators and the amount of loans countries receive from the banks. Through interviews with high-level staff members of the banks, Ben-Artzi is able to all but rule out the possibility that the effects observed in the statistical analysis are due to certain types of countries not applying for loans because they anticipate that they will not receive them. In the interviews, the bank staff confirmed that economic, political and social factors did influence the bank's decisions regarding which countries to dispense loans to in complex and interesting ways.

They also include studies that use observational studies to establish the correlation between two factors and process tracing to establish the causal effect of one factor on the other. Lisa L. Martin (1992) uses such a design in her analysis of the conditions under which states participate in sanction regimes. Consistent with her theoretical argument, Martin finds in her statistical analysis of the Cold War period, a strong correlation between a state's willingness to participate in a sanction regime and the adoption of costly measures by the state initiating the sanctions. These measures, which signal the lead state's commitment to the sanctions, include adopting sanctions that are financially costly for the lead state and involve international institutions. Martin complements the statistical analysis with four case studies in which she uncovers qualitative evidence of the willingness of states to participate in sanction regimes in the Cold War era depending on the credible commitment of the initiating state to the sanctions. The sanctions were imposed against the Soviet Union for its intervention in neighboring states, Latin America for human rights violations, and Argentina for its invasion of the Falklands Islands.

Other gap-filling mixed methods designs include quantitative studies that use experiments to test assumptions regarding human behavior in qualitative research. Elinor Ostrom's Nobel Prize-winning research on institutions used to avoid the exploitation of common pool resources (CPRs) is an example of this form of gap-filling mixed methods research. CPRs are natural or human-made resource systems to which access can be limited only at a high cost. They include resources such as forests, fishing areas, pastures, and so forth. These resources are vulnerable to exploitation because individuals are self-interested and short-sighted and seek to obtain the most from the resources that they can for themselves without concern for how their actions might result in the depletion of the resource in the future.

The conventional view that Ostrom argues against in her research is that CPRs can only be protected through individual property rights or centralized state control. Individual property rights grant a person the exclusive authority to determine how a resource is used. Central state controls are the antithesis of individual property rights. They refer to an economic system where the government has the exclusive right to determine how a resource is used.

Ostrom (1990) argues that CPRs can be protected through self-organized systems that regulate access to and use of CPRs. Her argument is counterintuitive because these systems require individuals to be far-sighted and self-interested – a lack of which is responsible for the exploitation of the CPR in the first place. An example of a CPR is a system in which a community of fishers agrees to only fish near and from a particular harbor, and prevent and punish fishers who infringe on their location rights.

To substantiate her claims, Ostrom combines qualitative case studies of self-organized regulatory systems and experiments in a series of independent projects. Ostrom used the qualitative case studies to identify certain characteristics of CPRs that encouraged cooperation. Ostrom and others then used experiments to test some of these conditions. The experiments show that the opportunity for repeated face-to-face communication increases cooperation. In these communications, people discussed the optimal strategy to maximize yields and designed sanctioning mechanisms to punish those who did not comply with governance rules (Ostrom 1998).

Triangulation

In this form of mixed methods research, qualitative and quantitative methods are used to corroborate the results of studies using one or the other method. Ultimately, triangulating research designs may not substantiate the results of the other method, but that is their intention. In triangulating mixed methods research designs, the studies may be conducted either sequentially or concurrently. The corroborating method is always given lower importance than the method responsible for the main results.

A very good example of a mixed methods approach combining a cross-national longitudinal statistical analysis and interviews for this purpose is Nathan M. Jensen's (2006) study of the political determinants of foreign direct investment (FDI). FDI is significantly affected by how the political environment affects the risk posed or, conversely, the security of a corporation's investment. Corporations are unlikely to invest in foreign countries where they are concerned that the countries' governments will expropriate their investments in the near or short term.

Jensen contends that democracy increases FDI because property rights are typically associated with democracies and reduce the likelihood that governments will expropriate FDI. Only two of the 20 countries (or territories) in the world – Singapore and Hong Kong – with the strongest property rights are not democracies.[2] Another domestic political institution that Jensen argues reduces the risk of expropriation is federalism. In federal states, where political power is decentralized among multiple tiers of governments, Jensen claims that territories within states are likely to discipline each other because if one territory expropriates FDI it will reduce the incentive of foreigners to invest in other territories within the same state.

Jensen uses a statistical analysis to test the generalizability of his claim in which he finds, as expected, that democracy significantly increases FDI flows, and political federalism significantly decreases FDI flows. To substantiate these findings, Jensen interviews country investment agencies, location consultants and decision-makers in multinational corporations (MNCs), and political risk analysts and insurers. The interviews support Jensen's argument regarding democracy in so much as no interviewee mentioned authoritarianism as an institution conducive to investment, and at the same time, many interviewees mentioned other factors related to his argument as important, such as expropriations, instability, and restrictions on capital flows. In general, interviewees did not mention federalism as an important factor affecting investment decisions.

Interpretation

In this form of mixed methods research, qualitative, but more typically, quantitative research is used to interpret and/or explain findings resulting from the other method. Typically, these findings are ones that are inconsistent with the researchers' theoretical predictions, but they may also include findings that were simply not part of the researchers' original theory. In this form of mixed methods research, qualitative and quantitative methods are used sequentially and independent of each other. The analysis that is used to interpret the results is given lower emphasis than the analysis that produced these results.

An example of a mixed methods research design which combines surveys and interviews for this purpose is Sibyelle Artz and Diana Nicholson's (2010) study on female aggression, and in particular, their analysis of an alternative education program for high-risk girls. According to the authors' survey analysis, students in this education program felt that their teachers created an encouraging and supportive environment, but that this was not associated with a lower likelihood of high-risk girls committing violence. Through interviews with girls in the program, the authors concluded that the students' relationships with their teachers did not explain why the program reduced the girls' propensity to engage in violence, but the fact that the program encouraged pro-social behavior did. Pro-social behavior includes any behavior that is intended to benefit or help another person.

Key Points

- Mixed methods research combines qualitative and quantitative research in order to build more accurate and precise hypotheses, to construct richer analyses, and ultimately, to produce greater confidence in the results of studies.
- Qualitative and quantitative research may be combined at either the theoretical or empirical level.
- In mixed methods research, one method may be used to inform the design of a study using another method; to analyze a different issue related to the same phenomenon as another study using a different method; to fill in gaps in a study using a different method; and to corroborate or explain the findings of another method.

Further Reading

The first and third readings present different ways in which mixed methods research may be designed and the advantages and disadvantages of these designs. The second reading discusses alternative ways of defining and conceptualizing mixed method research.

Creswell, John W. and Vicki L. Plano Clark. 2017. *Designing and Conducting Mixed Methods Research*. London: Sage Publications.

Johnson, R. Burke, Anthony J. Onwuegbuzie and Lisa A. Turner. 2007. 'Toward a Definition of Mixed Methods Research.' *Journal of Mixed Methods Research* 1(2): 112–133.

Gordon, Sanford C. and Alastair Smith. 2004. 'Quantitative Leverage Through Qualitative Knowledge: Augmenting the Statistical Analysis of Complex Causes.' *Political Analysis* 12: 233–255.

EXERCISE 8.1

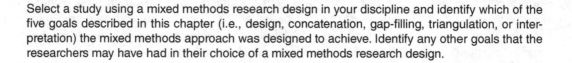

Select a study using a mixed methods research design in your discipline and identify which of the five goals described in this chapter (i.e., design, concatenation, gap-filling, triangulation, or interpretation) the mixed methods approach was designed to achieve. Identify any other goals that the researchers may have had in their choice of a mixed methods research design.

EXERCISE 8.2

Design a mixed methods research study for your own research. Identify the quantitative and qualitative techniques (e.g., interviews, surveys, and experiments) that you would use in your study and which of the five goals described in this chapter (i.e., design, concatenation, gap-filling, triangulation or interpretation) informed your choice of techniques.

9

Case Selection

Objectives

- discuss why and how the number of cases included in a study matters
- define and describe random and non-random sampling methods
- describe techniques for recruiting and retaining participants for studies
- explain selection bias and the problems that it presents for research

Prior to collecting data, either qualitative or quantitative, researchers must determine how many and which cases to include in their analyses. A *case* is an instance of a class of events (e.g., wars, protests, elections, economic crises, and so forth). In the social sciences, individuals are not generally referred to as cases as they are in the natural sciences. However, the basic techniques used to select individuals for studies in the social and natural sciences are generally the same as those used to select cases, and are discussed together for this reason.

The process of case selection, as Figure 9.1 depicts, requires no more than four basic steps. The first step involves determining the number of cases to be included in the analysis based on the goals of the study. The next step involves selecting the cases through either non-random or random sampling techniques. If the study does not include human subjects, the process of case selection ends here. For studies involving human subjects, however, the process continues with the recruitment of these subjects. If the study involves repeated measures or occurs over a long period of time, the final step in this process involves the retention of the subjects.

How Many Cases to Study?

The first step in case selection involves deciding how many cases to include in the analysis. Researchers may choose to study a single case, a mid-range number of cases, or a large number (large-N) of cases. This decision is based primarily on the researchers' goals in terms of theory building and theory testing, as well as the researchers' tolerance for limitations on the generalizability of their findings.

Single Case Studies

If the goal of the researcher is to develop a new theory to explain an existing problem, a single case study is an excellent option. Single case studies allow researchers to dig deeply into the details of a case in order to develop a rich, complex, and compelling argument.

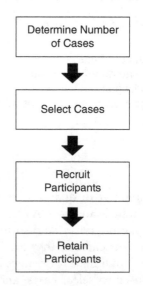

Figure 9.1 The process of case selection

However, a theory developed through a single case has a lower likelihood of being generalizable. Generalizability, of course, is of little concern if there is only one example of a certain case in the world, as in the United Nations or the European Union. It is also less of a concern if the case is unique, but very important, as in a case study of a geopolitical superpower, such as China, Russia, or the United States.

Whether an argument built on a single case is generalizable or not depends on the extent to which the argument derived from this case is theoretical as opposed to descriptive, and the extent to which it is dependent on a set of conditions particular to this case. A theory arguing that payment-by-results (PbR) contracts improve development outcomes, which is based on a case study of Botswana, is problematic for the latter reason. PbRs are a form of foreign aid in which donors distribute aid to recipients once they have achieved certain pre-agreed upon results. They are thought to eliminate the misappropriation of foreign aid because the aid is not distributed until the results are proven. PbRs may be more effective in Botswana, however, than in other aid-reliant states because government corruption is lower in Botswana than in these states, making Botswana less likely than these states to claim to achieve results that it has not.

Single case studies are much less valuable for theory testing than theory building. Single case studies can offer support to probabilistic theories, which claim that a theory is likely to result from a given factor or sets of factors, but they cannot confirm them, because the case on which the theory is tested may not be representative of many other cases. A single case study can also cast doubt on a probabilistic theory, especially if the case is one where a theory is most likely to be applied and does not. However, evidence from a single case that is inconsistent with a hypothesis cannot disconfirm this hypothesis since probabilistic theories do not claim that a given factor will always result in a certain outcome.

Single case studies also cannot confirm deterministic theories because the case is not necessarily representative of the whole universe of cases that deterministic theories claim to explain. However, single case studies can disconfirm deterministic theories under certain conditions. These cases are summarized in Table 9.1.

Single case studies can disconfirm arguments that specify necessary conditions when an outcome occurred in the absence of the necessary conditions. However, a single case study cannot disconfirm a theory if the necessary condition is present and the result does not occur, because necessary conditions are not also sufficient conditions.

Argument	Outcome
Necessary conditions	occurred in the absence of the necessary condition
Sufficient conditions	did not occur in the presence of the sufficient condition
Necessary and sufficient conditions	occurred in the absence of the necessary and sufficient condition or did not occur in the presence of the necessary and sufficient condition

Table 9.1 Single case studies that disconfirm arguments

A single case study, for example, can disprove an argument that sincere apologies are a necessary condition for corporations to rebuild their reputations after a major scandal if the case shows that a company recovered its tarnished reputation without apologizing by launching a new product or providing a new service. However, it cannot disprove this theory if the case shows that the company did not recover its reputation after apologizing because a company may also need to demonstrate that the apology is more than just lip service by changing the policy that allowed for the scandal-provoking misbehavior in the first place.

Single case studies can also disconfirm arguments about sufficient conditions when the sufficient conditions are present and the outcome is not produced. A single case study can disconfirm an argument, for example, that the depletion of non-renewable energy resources is a sufficient condition to cause oil, gas, and coal companies to invest in green energy technologies if it shows that a single company did not invest in green technologies even after its supply of non-renewable resources was extinguished because it partnered with corporations in other countries to develop new supplies of natural resources.

Finally, single case studies can disconfirm arguments that specify necessary and sufficient conditions if an outcome does not occur when the necessary and sufficient conditions are present. They can also disconfirm arguments that specify necessary and sufficient conditions when the necessary and sufficient conditions are *not* present and the outcome occurs nonetheless. For example, a single case study can disconfirm an argument that an influx of immigrants into a country is a necessary and sufficient condition to strengthen support for nationalist parties, if there is not an upsurge in support for nationalist parties when there is an influx of immigrants into a country, or if there was such an upsurge in the absence of an influx of immigrants.

Mid-range Case Studies

Mid-range case studies include more than one case and fewer cases than are needed to detect a statistically significant effect if one exists. There is no absolute number of cases needed to detect statistically significant results. This number varies, as explained in the subsequent section, based on characteristics of the analyses and expectations regarding the findings.

Mid-range case studies may be used to build hypotheses or test them. Theories developed from mid-range case studies may be more generalizable than those based on a single case because analyzing multiple cases may help researchers to develop arguments that are broader and more theoretical than specific to a case and descriptive. However, the more cases a mid-range study includes the less fully a researcher may be able to immerse themselves in any one case and develop a rich, nuanced, and compelling argument.

Mid-range case studies can also be used to test theories. However, like single case studies, mid-range case studies cannot confirm or disconfirm probabilistic theories. They can provide more compelling evidence, though, than single case studies in favor or against probabilistic theories because mid-range case studies include more incidences of an event.

However, because the number of cases in a mid-range case study is fewer than that which is needed to produce statistically significant results, mid-range case studies cannot confirm or disconfirm these theories.

Like single case studies, mid-range case studies can be used to disconfirm deterministic theories when outcomes result in the absence of necessary conditions, or do not result in the presence of sufficient ones. However, mid-range case studies cannot be used to confirm deterministic arguments. Even if the outcome is produced when the necessary condition, the sufficient condition, or the necessary and sufficient condition is present in every case analyzed, it is not known whether the outcome is produced in every case that has not been analyzed when these conditions are present. This assumes, of course, that the cases studied do not represent the whole universe of cases.

Large-N Case Studies

A large-N case study is defined herein as any study that includes the number of cases necessary to detect a statistically significant effect if one exists. Large-N studies can include, but do not have to, all cases of a particular phenomenon. It is important to note that a study can be referred to as a large-N study because it includes many observations but these observations may all belong to a single case. This is true of a survey on a single event, such as a protest or an election within a country, in which the observations that constitute the N are survey responses of individuals.

Large-N case studies are appropriate for theory testing. Using them, researchers can confirm or disconfirm probabilistic theories, as well as deterministic theories regardless of the outcome observed. Large-N case studies are analyzed using statistics. Statistics enable researchers to confirm or disconfirm theories based on whether or not the relationship observed between the explanatory factors and outcome variables is likely due to chance or not. It should be said that statistically significant results are not enough to put an end to all doubts regarding the validity of a theory. Even if the results of an analysis are significant, there is likely to still be skepticism regarding the appropriateness of the measures, data, models and estimation techniques used, among other things.

The number of cases needed to achieve statistically significant results varies across studies and can be estimated through a *power analysis*. The particular technique used to conduct the power analysis with this information depends on the type of statistical technique that will be used to analyze the data (MacCallum et al. 1996; Kadam and Bhalerao 2010). The power analysis is based on three factors: the anticipated effect size, the significance level, and the noisiness of the data.

The anticipated effect size is the minimum deviation from the null hypothesis expected. In simpler terms, it is the absolute or relative difference that a researcher might expect to observe between the value of the explanatory variable in the test condition and in the non-test or control condition. The significance level is the probability of rejecting the null hypothesis given that it is true. It is usually set at 0.05. The noisiness of the data refers to how much variation is expected in the results. It is based on the standard deviation of the relevant factor. The larger the anticipated effect size, the smaller the significance level, and the less noisy the data, the smaller is the necessary sample size.

Case Selection Methods

Researchers, unable or uninterested in analyzing every case or instance of a particular phenomenon, will analyze a subset of these cases. To identify this subset of cases, researchers may use either random or non-random sampling techniques. These techniques are relevant to both qualitative and quantitative research although random sampling techniques are more commonly used in the latter.

Random Sampling Techniques

Random sampling is the gold standard for data collection. It is necessary, but not sufficient, for constructing representative samples. In random sampling, every person or case has a known probability of being included in the sample. There are various different types of random sampling techniques, which are summarized in Table 9.2.

The most basic random sampling technique is *simple random sampling* (SRS) where every member of the target population has a known, equal, non-zero chance of being selected. The samples are chosen using this technique with either a random number chart or a computerized random number generator. Simple random sampling is appropriate when the target population from which the sample is taken is homogeneous.

Method	Procedure
Simple random sampling (SRS)	every member (or case) in the target population has a known, equal, non-zero chance of being selected.
Systematic random sampling	every k^{th} element (i.e., ratio of the sample size to the target population) of the target population is sampled. The index of the starting element is then selected within the first k elements by SRS. Multiples of k are added to the starting index to form indices for subsequent elements.
Stratified sampling	simple random samples are taken in proportion to the population from subgroups (e.g., regions, genders and religions) of the target population.
Clustered sampling	simple random samples are selected from subgroups of the target population. Samples are only taken from certain subgroups of the target population that are determined by SRS.
Over/undersampling	selection of more/fewer individuals from a sub-population of the target population known to participate at a low/higher rate to ensure that the sample is representative of the target population.

Table 9.2   Random sampling techniques

In *systematic random sampling*, every member of the target population has a known, non-zero chance of being selected, but not an equal chance of being selected. In systematic sampling, every kth element of the target population is sampled. An example of systematic sampling is airport security screening methods that stop every kth person at the gates for additional screening. This method is more efficient than SRS. Since every person or case does not have an equal chance of being selected (e.g., adjacent members could never be chosen using this method), like SRS, it is only appropriate for homogeneous populations.

Researchers also commonly use random sampling techniques that divide the population into subgroups, such as *stratified random sampling*, *clustered sampling*, and under- or more typically, *over-sampling*. All of these methods are useful when the target population is very heterogeneous and researchers want to ensure adequate representation of certain subgroups of the target population in the sample. Only over-sampling is used when *response rates* for certain subgroups are lower than for other subgroups. It is typically used to adjust surveys for lower response rates on surveys among racial and ethnic minorities, but it can be used for other populations as well.

Non-random Sampling Techniques

Non-random sampling techniques are a set of techniques in which each case or observation in the target population does not have a known, non-zero chance of being included in the analysis. The target population is the group of individuals or cases from which researchers draw their samples. Samples constructed through non-random sampling techniques are less likely to be representative of the target population than random sampling techniques.

Researchers may use non-random sampling techniques when their goal is not to make generalizable claims, but rather to gather information from a range of cases in order to develop hypotheses about human behavior. Researchers may also use non-random sampling techniques when they do not have the funds or resources to use random sampling methods, or when they are unable to identify a sampling frame, namely the target population from which to draw a random sample of participants.

It would not be possible to identify a sampling frame for a study of gender-based violence during civil wars because many women who have been raped do not report their experiences to the police or to humanitarian organizations (Meger 2016). More women report their experiences to humanitarian organizations than the police because women can often suffer repercussions from filing reports with the police, who are often responsible for the violence. Although the police may release the names of women who file reports about gender-based violence, humanitarian organizations do not release these women's names in order to protect their privacy and safety.

Where random sampling methods are not feasible or desirable, there are a number of different non-random sampling techniques that researchers may use to identify a sample of cases or individuals for analysis. These techniques are summarized in Table 9.3.

Sampling	Selection method
Convenience	respondents selected based on ease of accessibility
Purposive	respondents selected based on study objectives
Quota	respondents selected in proportion to the target population with respect to known characteristics
Snowball	respondents selected based on recommendations of prior respondents
Volunteer	respondents self-selected into survey

Table 9.3 Non-random sampling techniques

Quota sampling is similar to a random sampling method known as stratified random sampling. In quota sampling, the target population is divided in strata and the number of cases in each stratum is in proportion to the number of cases in each stratum of the target population. Unlike stratified random sampling, the cases in each stratum are not selected based on random sampling.

As a result, the people within each strata of the sample may be significantly different than those within the same strata of the target population. Quota samples have been used to understand the labor force participation of refugee communities (Bloch 1999), as well as the psychological and behavioral trauma arising from terrorist attacks (Rubin et al. 2005), among other things.

Purposive sampling is a sampling method in which researchers sample cases based either on characteristics of the cases or the objective of the study. The cases or individuals in the sample may be homogeneous in terms of certain characteristics, knowledge, or experiences (as in the example of civil war rape victims), or they may be heterogeneous so that they represent a diverse range of issues on a particular phenomenon or event. The former is a common technique used for expert surveys, while the latter is a common technique used by market researchers.

Researchers may also use purposive sampling to identify a single case instead of a set of cases although purpose sampling is not often thought of in these terms. This case may be a *typical case*. A typical case is thought to be similar to and, thus, representative of other cases. Generally, researchers choose a typical case in order to increase their odds of developing a theory that is generalizable.

Instead of a typical case, researchers may choose to study a *crucial case*. A crucial case is a case that no other theory can explain (Eckstein 1975). With good reason, many academics argue that a crucial case is a mythical case. While some cases may be less well understood than others, and while no one argument can explain everything about a case, usually, there are many arguments that can explain at least part of a case.

Alternatively, research may choose a deviant case, a most-likely case, or a least-likely case. A *deviant case* is a case that does not conform to expectations. A *most-likely case* is a type of deviant case that should fit an existing theory but does not. Researchers may also use a most-likely case in order to understand the conditions under which an existing theory holds, by identifying what is unique about this case that causes the existing theory not to apply, or they might analyze a most-likely case in order to challenge the validity of an existing theory by showing that it cannot explain a case that it should be able to explain.

Sheri Berman's (1997) analysis of the Weimar Republic is an example of a most-likely case for the latter purpose. The Weimar Republic is a case where Robert D. Putnam's (2000) argument about the essentiality of social capital to the functioning of democracy should apply because social capital was abundant in the Republic. In contrast to Putnam's predictions democracy failed in this period and the Nazis rose to power.

A *least-likely case* is also a deviant case but unlike a most-likely case, a least-likely case is a case that is unlikely to explain a theory but does. Some researchers use least-likely cases to understand what features of this particular case explain why the case fits the theory when it should not, in order to revise or refine the existing theory. Researchers also use least-likely cases to demonstrate the strength or broadness of their theory.

Arend Lijphart's (1996) analysis of consociationalism in India is an example of the latter. Lijphart argues that consociationalism – a particular constellation of political institutions involving grand coalitions, proportional representation, segmental or territorial autonomy, and minority veto powers – can explain the relative lack of conflict among hundreds, if not thousands, of ethnic, religious, and linguistic groups in India. India is a least-likely case because at the time of his writing, India lacked three of the four institutions that define consociationalism – grand coalitions, proportional representation, and minority veto powers. According to Lijphart, despite the fact that these institutions did not formally exist in India, the conflict-mitigating outcomes that he associates with them existed for other reasons, and that India supports his argument as a result. However, since these conditions existed in the absence of these institutions, India does not actually support Lijphart's argument regarding the need for the particular set of institutions that he says is necessary to prevent conflict among groups.

An alternative to purposive sampling is *convenience sampling*. Convenience sampling is a sampling method where researchers sample cases that are the easiest and less costly to recruit. When journalists stop people on the street to ask their opinion of an issue or a current event, they are using convenience samples. When market researchers conduct surveys of customers leaving stores, they are also using convenience samples. But, like other non-random sampling techniques, convenience samples may not be representative of the target population.

Volunteer sampling is where participants self-select into a study. Experiments conducted at universities are often composed of semi-volunteers. Psychological courses often require students to participate in experiments, but students can generally choose the experiments in which they want to participate. Steven D. Levitt used volunteer sampling in his study of indecisiveness in which he asked people to flip a coin to decide an important life issue, such as breaking up with a romantic partner or quitting a job, to determine if indecision itself was a source of unhappiness.

Snowball sampling is where researchers recruit participants through contacts, and their contacts' contacts, and their contacts' contacts' contacts, and so forth. This method is often used in interview-based research when it is difficult for researchers to identify people with the characteristics that they are interested in understanding. It is also used when those who possess these characteristics are hard to gain access to without someone within the group giving them the names and contact information of members of the groups, vouching for them, or helping them gain access to the group in other ways.

Selection Bias

Non-random sampling methods are more prone to selection bias than random sampling methods, but the latter are not immune to them either. *Selection bias* occurs when observations are chosen according to some rule that is correlated with the dependent variable. Selection bias may be a result of an aspect of the non-random method by which researchers select their cases, or it may be a function of nature. Selection bias is problematic for research because it results in a sample in which there are a disproportionate number of cases that are more or less likely to experience the outcome.

Democracies have won more medals on average than non-democracies in every Olympic Games since 1908, except for the 1980 Olympic Games held in Moscow, against which the United States led the largest boycott in Olympic history to protest against the Soviet invasion of Afghanistan. This is not because democracies produce better athletes than non-democracies, but because of selection bias. Throughout much of history, democracies participated in the Olympic Games more than authoritarian states. Once the greater propensity of democracies to participate in the Games is addressed, democracies do not actually outperform authoritarian states at the Olympics, although non-military based authoritarian regimes do outperform democracies (Brancati 2018).

Selection bias pervades many different issues. At higher education institutions, faculty tend to be more politically and socially liberal than the general population. While some pundits have argued that this is because higher education makes people more liberal, or rather that universities indoctrinate students into liberal ideologies, research suggests that the liberalism of higher education is at least in part a result of selection bias (Gross and Simmons 2014). One possible source of this selection bias is the fact that liberals tend to value public service over financial profit and, as a result, pursue careers in higher education in greater numbers than conservatives.

Selection bias pervades issues within the classroom as well. Learning outcomes may be lower for online or distance learning courses than traditional classrooms, not because this pedagogy is of a lower quality than more traditional ones, but because the type of student who takes online or distance learning courses is qualitatively different than those who do not take online courses (Phipps and Merisotis 1999). They may be less committed to learning. They may have less time to allocate to coursework due to employment commitments and so forth. Conversely, flipped classrooms, where students listen to lectures at home, and complete exercises in class along with the teacher, may be associated with higher learning outcomes, not because this is a more effective way to learn, but because teachers who experiment with teaching styles are more committed and effective teachers (Bishop and Verleger 2013).

Case Recruitment

Recruitment refers to the process by which researchers convince those in the target population to participate in their research. Regardless of the sampling technique used to select participants, or the research method used to study them, there are certain concerns people are likely to have about participating in any research study. These concerns, if unassuaged, can significantly reduce the numbers of those willing to participate in studies. These concerns relate to the privacy of the participants; the demand that studies place on them; the potentially negative consequences of the findings for the participants; and conversely, the payoff – financial and otherwise – for the participants. The keys to overcoming these concerns are depicted in Figure 9.2

Privacy

The sensitivity of the information shared with researchers is a primary concern of people affecting their willingness to participate in studies or to grant researchers access to those that they oversee. The more sensitive the information, the more concerned people are likely to be about their privacy and the confidence with which the information they share with researchers will be kept. In some cases, if the information that a participant shares with a researcher becomes known publicly, participants may lose their jobs, be shunned by their friends and family, and worse yet, be imprisoned, and/or killed.

Researchers may employ one of a number of strategies to allay people's concerns regarding privacy. Researchers can promise the participants anonymity. Anonymity means that the researcher will not collect any identifying information from the participants. Alternatively, the researcher may promise to keep the participants' information confidential, but not anonymous, and to explain to the participants the measures that they will use to keep the information confidential. If the data is confidential, but not anonymous, the researcher may collect identifying information from participants, but not report their names in publications or share their names with others. The researcher may use various precautions like using numeric codes to identify participants in their records and keeping the key to these codes in a separate locked or password-protected file.

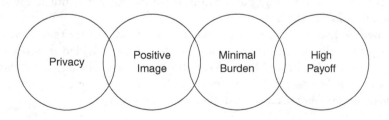

Figure 9.2   Keys to recruitment

In addition to keeping the participants' names either anonymous or confidential, researchers ought to promise participants not to report the data in such detail that their identity can be deduced from information reported about them. In qualitative research, this can entail obscuring the identity of a person quoted by describing characteristics of them in general terms. For example, in describing a person's employment, a researcher may describe a person as a high-ranking government official as opposed to an ambassador. The researcher must still provide enough detail about the person in their research, though, so that others can evaluate for themselves the authority and credibility of the source.

For quantitative data, this can involve not reporting descriptive statistics for groups with members less than a certain number of individuals. Failing to do so, can make it easy to indentify certain individuals in the data. For example, if there are only five men in a course of 20 individuals, and the course evaluations are disaggregated by gender, it is not very difficult for the course instructor to deduce the responses of each of the five men, especially if the instructor is able to triangulate the data on gender with other characteristics reported in the data, such as grade level.

Image

In deciding whether or not to agree to participate in a study, a person is also likely to be concerned about how they will personally appear in any research published based on their contribution, or how the groups that they are members of or responsible for will appear to others. For example, corporations such as Intel or Apple being interviewed about conflict-free minerals are likely to be concerned that researchers will be critical of their practices and defame them in their research. Likewise, religious communities with practices that are not widely accepted, such as Pentecostals who speak in tongues or Santeríans who practice animal sacrifice, are likely to be concerned that researchers will present their communities as naïve at best.

To alleviate these concerns, researchers should describe to potential recruits the topic of their research, but not their specific hypotheses in order not to bias the results. The researcher should explain to people that they do not have a political agenda and that they intend to portray all perspectives on an issue. Researchers should also explain how they plan to use the information they collect. People may be more willing to participate in a study if the information they share with a researcher is for an undergraduate or graduate thesis as opposed to an academic publication, since the former is not likely to receive as much public attention as the latter.

At times, people may not agree to participate in a study unless they have the right to approve any publication using information that they have provided to researchers before it may be published. Under no conditions should researchers agree to this condition because it threatens the integrity of the research. If people cannot be convinced to participate otherwise, researchers need to find alternative subjects.

Burden

Participants are often reluctant to participate in studies because they demand a lot of time from participants. Therefore, it is essential that researchers keep this burden to a minimum, and inform participants up front regarding the amount of time that the study will require of them. The amount of time will vary widely depending on the method and the subject studied. Surveys can take as little as a couple of minutes while focus groups can take as much as an hour or more. Participant observation can require even more.

To minimize the burden studies place on participants, researchers should keep any tasks that they ask of participants as simple as possible. In interviews and surveys, researchers should limit the information they request of participants by not asking them information that they are able to obtain elsewhere. They should also avoid, if possible, very taxing questions that might even require participants to peruse their records to determine, such as the exact date on which they engaged in a particular activity.

Researchers should also not ask participants for information that does not apply to them. In surveys or interviews, for example, researchers should allow participants to skip questions about married individuals if they are single, or about satisfaction with a particular service if they've never used that service before. Researchers should also not compel participants to answer questions that they do not want to answer. Poorly designed online surveys can require participants to answer questions in order to move on to the next question. Instead of compelling participants to answer questions, though, this strategy may compel participants to withdraw from surveys instead.

Payoff

Given the time commitment that studies demand of participants, it is important that researchers inform participants of the benefit to themselves in taking part in the study. The research may benefit participants personally by improving products, services, or institutions that the participant utilizes, or by addressing a problem that the person is affected by, such as the gender pay gap. Researchers must be mindful, though, not to emphasize too much the personal benefit to individuals of participating in a study as this might lead to the overrepresentation of certain groups in the data. Women, for example, who are paid much less than men may be much more likely to participate in a survey regarding the gender pay gap if this issue is given a lot of attention.

The research may also benefit participants monetarily. It is not uncommon for researchers to offer participants a chance to win a reward for participating in a survey or to compensate a participant for taking part in a focus group or survey. The possibility of winning an award is less of an incentive than a guaranteed cash payment.

While a monetary incentive is likely to increase the number of people willing to participate in a study, it can disproportionately increase the number of low-income individuals willing to take part in it. This is not problematic if the study is of low-income individuals, or if a researcher expects the number of low-income individuals willing to participate in a study without a financial incentive to be disproportionately low. Interestingly, a large financial award is likely to create less of a socio-economic imbalance among the participants since large awards may incentivize not just low-income groups, but high-income groups as well.

Sample Retention

In longitudinal studies, where there are repeated measurements of participants over time, there is tendency for participants to drop out of studies at different stages. This is particularly problematic if individuals withdraw from studies in a way that is related to the outcome. *Attrition bias* is a form of selection bias. It results when participants who withdraw from longitudinal studies differ systematically from those that remain in them, resulting in a biased sample.

Attrition bias has posed a major problem for the ongoing and widely used Michigan Panel Study on Income Dynamics (PSID).[1] The PSID study lost nearly 50 percent of the initial sample in the first 20 years of its existence. The attrition was concentrated among lower socio-economic status individuals. Attrition rates for income studies in Europe are also high. In the most recent edition of the *European Union Statistics on Income and Living Conditions* survey (2008–2011),[2] the attrition rate varied between 10 percent and 60 percent across countries, with the attrition rate lowest in the UK.

In order to reduce the likelihood of participants withdrawing from studies, researchers can employ many of the sample strategies used to recruit participants, including minimizing the burden studies place on participants, and emphasizing the benefits to participants of continuing to take part in the studies.

Another factor that can aid retention is the development of a good rapport between researchers and participants. Not only can this facilitate sample retention by making participation in the study pleasant, but it can also make participants feel obliged to continue to participate in the study to support the researcher in their research.

Sending participants reminders via postal mail, email or SMS (short message service) messages can also be very helpful. Having multiple ways to track participants that are not tied to a physical address, such as mobile phone numbers or emails, is important in order to be able to locate participants if they move.

If the attrition is significant and unavoidable, researchers may use a number of different strategies, including replacement samples, sample weights, and selection models, to adjust for biases in the sample. These techniques are discussed in subsequent chapters related to the method in which they are most commonly employed.

Key Points

- There are tradeoffs involved in the number of cases analyzed in terms of theory building and theory testing, the depth and complexity of arguments, and generalizability. Studies with few cases tend to be better for theory building than for theory testing. They also tend to be richer and more complex than studies with many cases, but tend to have a lower potential for generalizability.
- Random sampling is the gold standard for data collection because it has a higher potential to yield representative samples and is less prone to selection bias than non-random sampling. However, random sampling is not always feasible for all studies. The representativeness of samples produced from it can also be compromised by low response rates and low retention rates.
- Techniques to increase response rates include: ensuring the privacy of the participants; being sensitive to the concerns of participants about how they will be perceived; reducing the burden on participants; and providing a personal benefit to participants, including but not limited to, a financial payment.

Further Reading

The first of these readings elaborates on the concept of selection bias. The second is an edited volume presenting different views on the purpose, utility, and limitations of single case studies and the third is a comprehensive resource on sampling techniques.

Geddes, Barbara. 1990. 'How the Cases You Choose Affect the Answers You Get: Selection Bias in Comparative Politics.' *Political Analysis* 2: 131–150.

Gomm, Roger, Martyn Hammersley, and Peter Foster, eds. 2000. *Case Study Method: Key Issues, Key Text*. London/Thousand Oaks, CA: Sage Publications.

Levy, Paul S. and Stanley Lemeshow. 2009. *Sampling of Populations: Methods and Applications*. New York: John Wiley & Sons, Inc.

EXERCISE 9.1

1. Explain why a single case study can *disconfirm* an argument that specifies the following:

   - a necessary condition.
   - a sufficient condition.
   - a necessary and sufficient condition.

2. Explain why a single case study cannot *confirm* an argument that specifies the following and explain why:

    • a necessary condition.
    • a sufficient condition.

EXERCISE 9.2

Identify the potential sources of selection in each of the following research studies analyzing:

1. the psychological effects of exposure to warfare for non-combatants based on survivors' accounts after the war.
2. satisfaction with a company's products and services based on customer surveys.
3. the effectiveness of UN peacekeepers, which only intervene in states in which they are invited by governments, in preventing a return to civil war.
4. the effectiveness of a program designed to change gender norms regarding the role of women in the workplace based on a survey of women who completed the program.
5. the motivation for terrorist attacks through interviews with terrorists apprehended after they committed an attack.

IV

QUALITATIVE METHODS AND ANALYSIS

10
Interviews

Objectives

- differentiate among types of interview and interview modes
- describe the strengths and weaknesses of interviews for theory building and theory testing
- provide guidance on the nuts and bolts of the interview process
- discuss useful techniques for organizing and analyzing interview data

An *interview* is a method of collecting qualitative information from individuals through a series of questions posed to individuals either face-to-face, by phone, or through another medium, such as email. Interviews, unlike focus groups, typically involve only two people – the interviewer, who is usually the researcher, and the interviewee. Interviews provide researchers with an opportunity to collect not only factual information from individuals, but also less observable information about people's mental processes, including their cognitions, attitudes, emotions, and so forth. Typically, interviews are best suited for hypothesis building rather than hypothesis testing due to limitations in the representativeness, comparability, and objectivity of interviews, among other things.

Interview Types

There are three basic types of interviews – structured, semi-structured, and unstructured interviews. The three are distinguished from each other according to the questions asked and the order in which they are asked, and not the format of responses to them. The characteristics of each type of interview are summarized in Table 10.1.

In *structured interviews*, the researcher, using an interview guide, poses the same questions to all interviewees without altering either the wording of the questions or the order in which they are asked. The questions asked are typically close-ended. *Close-ended questions* have defined response categories (e.g., 'yes' or 'no' and 'excellent', 'very good', 'good', 'fair', or 'poor'). *Open-ended questions* do not. The rigidity of structured interviews makes responses across interviewees more comparable. Even slight alternations in the wording of questions across subjects can lead to different responses. Changes in the order of questions can also result in different responses since prior questions can influence responses to subsequent questions.

Take for example the two questions regarding same-sex marriage below:

Do you support same-sex marriage?

Do you support legalizing same-sex marriage?

In the first question, the issue of legalization is implied, but not explicit, as it is in the second question. This subtle distinction can result in different responses. Lacking an explicit reference to the legalization of same-sex marriage, the first question may be interpreted as affirmation for the practice of same-sex marriage, not the legalization of it. As a result, a

Type	Characteristics	(Dis)advantages
Structured	rigid	very high comparability
Semi-structured	flexible	medium to high comparability
		efficient due to ability to tailor questions to interviewees
		allows for follow-up questions
		high quality information due to ability to improvise and improve question wording
Unstructured	open-ended	very low comparability
		greater time investment
		high quality information

Table 10.1 Interview types

person may respond 'yes' to the second question, but not to the first question, because they believe that denying same-sex couples the legal right to marry is unconstitutional, but personally not agree with same-sex marriage because it violates their religious beliefs.

In *semi-structured interviews*, the researcher also uses an interview guide, but unlike in structured interviews, the researcher does not necessarily pose the same questions to all interviewees using the same wording or in the same order. The greater flexibility of semi-structured interviews makes it more difficult for researchers to compare the responses of interviewees to each other. It improves, however, the efficiency of the interview process as well as the quality of the information obtained. Semi-structured interviews are more efficient than structured interviews because researchers can skip questions in semi-structured interviews that are not relevant to particular interviewees. They can also alter the order of questions if an interviewee's response presents them with an opportunity to segue nicely into another question.

The flexibility of semi-structured interviews also improves the quality of the information obtained from the interviews because it allows researchers to improvise new questions in order to clarify an interviewee's responses or to probe certain responses further. It also allows researchers to alter the wording of questions if prior interviews reveal that the wording of certain questions is unclear or misleading.

Unlike with structured and semi-structured interviews, researchers do not use an interview guide when conducting *unstructured interviews*. Instead, researchers improvise the questions based on the context. Unstructured interviews typically occur in the course of participant observation where researchers embed themselves in the daily lives of the communities that they study. The much greater flexibility of unstructured interviews compared to structured and semi-structured interviews makes it all but impossible to compare the responses of interviewees. At the same time, however, the bespoke nature of these interviews enables researchers to obtain very rich information from their subjects.

How to Use Interviews

Interviews, regardless of whether they are structured, semi-structured, or unstructured, can be used either to construct hypotheses or test them. Interviews are much more effective for building hypotheses by means of inductive reasoning than they are for testing them. The advantages of interviews for hypothesis building and their disadvantages for hypothesis testing are summarized in Table 10.2.

Hypotheses Building

Interviews are very useful for hypothesis building because researchers can gain insights through them into the cognitions, perceptions, opinions, beliefs, and attitudes of individuals on the basis of which researchers may be able to construct a more general understanding of human behavior. Interviews also offer researchers an opportunity to learn information

	Hypothesis building	Hypothesis testing
Pros	open-ended questions	
	intimate environment	
	rapport	
Cons	guinea pig effect	unrepresentative samples
		non-comparable responses
		responses open to interpretation
		no rules for (dis)confirming hypotheses

Table 10.2   Utility of interviews for hypothesis building and testing

that they do not anticipate, or even know to ask. Semi-structured and unstructured interviews are better than structured interviews in this regard because they are composed primarily of open-ended rather than close-ended questions.

To understand the value of open-ended questions for hypothesis building, consider the following example about why low-income voters cast their ballots for parties that advocate policies detrimental to the poor. To understand this issue, a researcher might pose to an interviewee an open-ended question, such as:

'Why did you vote for Party X?'

A close-ended question, more typical of surveys, might ask a person instead:

'Which of the following reasons is the main reason why you voted for Party X?
a. its social values
b. its economic policies
c. its security and anti-terrorism policies
d. its leadership
e. it's better than the alternatives'

The latter close-ended question clearly limits the opportunity for researchers to learn something about why poor people vote for anti-poor parties, which researchers do not already suspect, by restricting the potential responses to the categories listed. The close-ended question also only allows respondents to provide the main reason why they voted for Party X. This is problematic since people may have had multiple reasons of equal or similar importance for voting for Party X. To improve the latter question, a researcher might include a write-in response for 'other', which would make this question more akin to an open-ended question.

Of course, interviews also have their shortcomings for hypothesis building regardless of whether they are structured, semi-structured, or unstructured. Interviewees, for one, may not be able to explain their behaviors to researchers because they are not aware of the larger processes that influence their behavior. They may also not be willing to share their views with researchers because the information solicited from them is personal, confidential, controversial, or even dangerous for them to reveal. They may also misrepresent their views or experiences in order to present themselves in the best light possible. These shortcomings are not unique, however, to interviews, but are problematic for all non-observational data, whether qualitative or quantitative in nature.

Focus groups and surveys are the methods most similar to interviews because they also involve collecting information from individuals through a series of questions posed to respondents. However, interviews differ from these other methods in important ways, which make them better in many cases than these methods for hypothesis building. Since interviews typically involve only two people, interviewees may be more inclined to share personal and confidential information with researchers in an interview environment than in a focus group, where other members of the focus group can hear what they share. A skilled interviewer can also create a very open and non-judgmental environment that makes interviewees feel comfortable to share this kind of information with the researcher.

Interviewers can do this not only through the way in which they ask questions, as is also the case with focus groups and surveys, but also through the tone of their voice, facial expressions and overall demeanor. This is also possible in focus groups and in-person surveys. However, in focus groups, even the most skilled moderator does not have complete control over how other members of the focus group behave. Other members of the group may behave in ways that are hostile, critical, and judgmental of other people's comments and that discourage others from sharing information in the group.

A skilled interviewer may also develop a rapport with the interviewee in the course of the interview, or across multiple interviews of the same person, which is less likely in a focus group and in-person survey. If such a rapport develops, the interviewee may let their guard down and share more information with the researcher than they would otherwise. The interviewee may even share information in this context with the interviewer because they want to help make the interviewer's research successful. While some individuals may be more inclined to share personal information with researchers in an anonymous survey, in an anonymous survey, the respondent is not likely to feel any obligation to the researcher to share this information.

Hypothesis Testing

Interviews, in contrast, are not very useful for testing hypotheses for a number of reasons. First, interviews are generally not representative of the larger population from which they are drawn because they are usually chosen through non-random sampling techniques, including most commonly, convenience sampling or snowball sampling. The use of non-random sampling techniques is made further problematic by the typically small number of interviews that researchers are able to conduct for their research. Researchers are usually also only able to interview a limited number of people (far fewer than in the case of surveys and focus groups) for their research, because interviews are very time-consuming for the researchers as well as the interviewees. This not only limits the number of interviews that researchers can complete in a given amount of time, but it also reduces the number of people willing to be interviewed.

The consequences of research based on unrepresentative or biased samples can be very significant. A 2003 study on conversion therapy, which is a treatment designed to change a person's sexual orientation from homosexual or bisexual to heterosexual is a case in point (Spitzer 2003). The publication of this study and the international recognition it received convinced many homosexuals who were uncomfortable with their sexual orientation to try to become heterosexual. Anti-gay activists also used the study as a tool to oppose political and civil rights for homosexuals. Ironically, the study was conducted by Robert Spitzer, who was influential in removing homosexuality from the American Psychological Association's *Diagnostic and Statistical Manual (DSM) of Mental Disorders* in 1973.

Spitzer's study concluded that conversion therapy was successful in transforming homosexuals and bisexuals who wanted to change their sexual orientation into heterosexuals based on interviews of 200 men and women. Spitzer recruited these men and women from centers performing conversion therapy. The interviews were unrepresentative of homosexuals and bisexuals in general because the people Spitzer interviewed were already enrolled in conversion therapy centers and were largely people who wanted the conversion therapy to work, and, thus, very susceptible to the placebo effect. These people may also have misrepresented the effectiveness of the treatment to Spitzer because they were ashamed of their behavior, and did not want to admit that they still had homosexual desires. In 2012, Spitzer recanted his research and apologized to the gay community for the detrimental effects that his research had on their lives.[1]

Second, interviews are not well suited for hypothesis testing because, except for structured interviews, the interviewees' responses are not easily comparable. In structured interviews the responses are comparable because researchers ask the same questions of every interviewee and restrict the interviewees' responses to a given set of options. In semi-structured and unstructured interviews, researchers do neither. Not only can slight differences in the wording of questions lead to different responses, but also the responses to open-ended questions can be difficult to interpret and compare.

Consider for example the response below of Pope Francis to an interview question regarding homosexuality, a practice that the Catholic Church does not condone. In the interview, Pope Francis said. ...

A person once asked me, in a provocative manner, if I approved of homosexuality. I replied with another question: 'Tell me: when God looks at a gay person, does he endorse the existence of this person with love, or reject and condemn this person?' We must always consider the person.[2]

Pope Francis's response is terribly ambiguous. Not only does he answer a question with a question, but he also answers the question in terms of whether God endorses the existence of a homosexual person, not in terms of whether he personally approves of homosexuality. The ambiguity of Pope Francis's response in this interview and in other comments, sparked much speculation about his views regarding homosexuality and whether the Church would change its position on homosexuality, and even gay marriage. At present, the Church has not changed its position and Pope Francis's personal view remains obfuscated.

Interviews, including structured ones, are also comparable because they are generally held under different conditions. Not only are interviews usually held in different locations, but they are also often conducted by different means (e.g., in-person, telephone or email). Different individuals can also conduct the interviews. This is problematic in the case of in-person interviews because certain characteristics of the interviewer (e.g., gender, ethnicity, age, and their socio-economic status), as well as certain characteristics of the interviewee can affect the responses that the latter provides the former.

Women, for example, interviewed about workplace sexual harassment may be more forthcoming if they are interviewed in a café than in a university setting, which is less relaxed and resembles more of a workplace environment. Women interviewed on this topic are also likely to be more forthcoming if a woman interviews them while men are less likely to be forthcoming if a woman interviews them.

Third, interview data is not well suited for theory testing because the data is largely subjective and open for interpretation. A researcher based on his or her knowledge, experiences, and biases might understand an interviewee's response as consistent with his or her expectations, while another researcher based on his or her knowledge, experiences, and biases might not. Those, for example, who are supportive of gay marriage are more likely to have interpreted Pope Francis's comments about homosexuality as more broadly supportive of gay rights than those who were not. This phenomenon, whereby researchers are more likely than other researchers to conclude that the results of their research are consistent with their argument, values, and beliefs, is known as *confirmation bias.*

Fourth, as in the case of hypothesis building, the information that interviewees provide researchers may not be honest, accurate or forthcoming. Fifth, and finally, there are also no clear-cut and established rules against which to evaluate interview data. There is no standard, for example, about how many people need to make a statement in an interview confirming a researcher's hypotheses for these hypotheses to be accepted. Nor is there any standard about how many people need to not make a statement in support of a researcher's hypotheses for these hypotheses to be rejected. Moreover, the fact that interviewees do not provide researchers with information that is consistent with their hypotheses does not necessarily mean that the researcher's hypotheses are incorrect. A person might not be unwilling to share certain information with the interviewer and might not be aware of the larger processes that influence their behavior.

The Interview Process

The interview process consists of five main steps depicted in Figure 10.1. The first step involves identifying the target population. The target population is the pool of potential interview candidates. The pool depends entirely on the research question and the objective of the interview. In the aforementioned study on the effectiveness of conversion therapy, the target population was homosexuals. The target population of a study on societal attitudes toward homosexuality would include, however, heterosexuals as well as homosexuals. For a given research question, there may be more than one pool of candidates recruited for different purposes.

The second step involves designing the interview. The four major design elements of any interview involve: the structure of the interview (i.e., structured, semi-structured, or unstructured); the format of the questions (i.e., open-ended or closed-ended); the wording and order of the questions; and the interview mode (i.e., in-person, telephone, or email). The first two issues have already been discussed at length in this chapter. The last two issues are addressed in the subsequent two sections of this chapter.

The third step involves recruiting the participants. Researchers may try to interview everyone within the target population if they are able to identify all the members of the target population, and if the number of members is manageable. If this number is not manageable, researchers may use random sampling techniques to identify potential

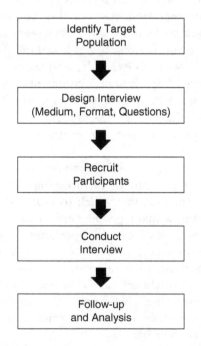

Figure 10.1   The interview process

recruits. If researchers cannot identify all the members of the target population, they may use non-random sampling techniques instead. Different types of random and non-random sampling techniques are discussed in detail in Chapter 9.

Box 10.1   What to Wear to the Interview

A researcher's attire can make interviewees feel at ease, or it may heighten their awareness of being studied and sharpen the hierarchy between the interviewer and interviewee. To make the interviewee feel at ease, the researcher should dress similarly in terms of formality and style to the interviewee. The researcher should avoid attire that is too casual, though, even if the interviewee is likely to dress very casually, because it may be perceived as disrespectful to the interviewee.

If researchers are using the interviews for hypothesis testing and plan to use random sampling techniques to identify their interview sample, they should perform a power analysis, also described in Chapter 9, to determine the number of people they need to interview in order to detect a statistically significant effect if one exists. If researchers cannot use random sampling techniques to identify their sample, they may still conduct a power analysis, but it bears repeating that the sample is unlikely to be representative of the target population.

If researchers are using the interviews for hypothesis building instead of hypothesis testing, there are no hard and fast rules regarding the number of people a researcher ought to interview. A good rule-of-thumb, though, is for the researchers to stop interviewing people when they are not learning anything new from each successive interview (i.e., saturation point). The more homogeneous the target population, the faster the researcher is likely to reach the saturation point.

The fourth step involves conducting the interviews. Prior to asking the first question, researchers may need to obtain a signed consent form from the person that they are interviewing that indicates whether the data will be kept confidential or anonymous. Generally, researchers conduct the interviews themselves, especially when using semi-structured interviews so that they can control which questions are asked, the wording of the questions, and their order. In some circumstances, though, as when the research involves a large number of interviewees, researchers may hire assistants to do the interviews. This may also be the case if certain characteristics of the researcher, such as their gender or ethnicity, might inhibit interviewees or bias their responses.

In the course of the interview, researchers may document the conversation by taking handwritten notes or by recording the interview using voice and/or video equipment with the permission of the interviewee. If researchers intend to record the interview, they should nonetheless be prepared to take handwritten notes in case the interviewee does not consent to be recorded or revokes their consent in the course of the interview, and in case the recorder breaks in the course of the interview.

Recording the interview allows the researcher to concentrate on the conversation, quote verbatim from the interview, and analyze the interview data systematically. Recording the interview also enhances the flow of the conversation and allows the researcher more time for questions. Pausing the conversation to jot down notes can consume valuable interview time.

Recording the interview, though, can make some people guarded in their responses. To reduce this likelihood, researchers should not video record the conversation, even though it allows researchers to capture non-verbal means of communication. They should also keep the voice recorder in a discrete location so that the interviewee is not constantly reminded of being recorded.

The fifth and final step pertains to the post-interview follow-up and data analysis. After every interview, researchers ought to give the interviewees their business card if they have not already done so, so that the interviewees can contact them if they have any questions afterwards. Researchers should keep their interview notes and recordings in a secure location for replication purposes. However, if researchers have promised to keep these materials confidential or anonymous, they may not be able to share them with others. Researchers may provide their interviewees with copies of any publications they produce based on the interviews, but they should not give their interviewees the right to approve their research before it can be published. Doing so can obviously distort and undermine the credibility of their research.

Interview Guides

Both structured and semi-structured interviews utilize interview guides. An interview guide is simply a written document containing the questions that researchers intend to ask interviewees in the order that they intend to ask them. The guide helps ensure that researchers phrase their questions in the same way in every interview, if this is their goal, and ask them in the same order in order to enhance comparability.

Box 10.2   Practice, Practice, Practice

Before interviewing anyone, it is important to practice the interview from start to finish on others in order to clarify questions, ensure the tone of the interview is right, and rid oneself of any nervousness regarding the interview process.

Researchers should always begin every interview with general questions to ease the respondent into the interview process, and then build up to questions that require more thought or that address sensitive issues. Researchers should close every interview by asking the interviewee if there is anything that they want to add to the conversation, in case the interviewee believes that a particular issue has not been fully or properly addressed.

If researchers are recruiting participants through non-random snowball sampling, at the end of each interview, they should ask the interviewees if they can suggest anyone that they think the researchers should also interview. Researchers should denote the questions that are most important for their research in the interview guide by highlighting them or putting a symbol next to them. This allows researchers to quickly identify the questions that are most important for their research in case they do not have sufficient time to ask their interviewees every question that they would like.

Writing good interview questions and determining the best way to order the questions, requires much skill and practice. The principals of writing good interview questions are the same as writing good survey questions, which are addressed in detail in Chapter 18. One important difference, though, between interview and survey questions, besides the fact that most interview questions are open-ended while most survey questions are close-ended, is that unlike in surveys, in telephone and in-person interviews, researchers have an opportunity to ask follow-up questions. Researchers can use follow-up questions to solicit more information from an interviewee if the interviewees' responses are vague or not very thoughtful, or if the interviewees' responses raise an issue that the researcher had not considered and wants to probe further.

Researchers may also use the opportunity to ask follow-up questions to try to obscure the focus of their research or the intent behind a question. Researchers can do this by first asking broad questions and then asking narrower, more specific questions if the interviewees' responses to the broad questions are not informative. This strategy is also effective for gauging the issues that are most salient for the interviewee. If the interviewee does not raise a particular issue in response to a broad question, it is not likely a significant issue for them.

The two questions below exemplify this strategy:

What effects, if any, do you think that the legalization of marijuana has had on your community?

What effects, if any, do you think that the legalization of marijuana has had on the social stigma associated with the recreational use of marijuana in your community?

The first question is broad and does not mention anything about the stigma regarding the recreational use of marijuana. The second question, in contrast, is very specific and is designed to elicit the interviewee's opinion on these social norms. If the interviewee does not mention social norms in response to the first question, the researcher may assume that the effect of the law on these norms is not a very salient one for the interviewee.

Interview Modes

The three primary ways in which researchers may conduct interviews are either in-person, by phone, or by email. In-person interviews are the gold standard for interviews. However, it is not always possible to conduct interviews in-person, either because of time or physical distance or the interviewees' preferences. Thus, it is important for a researcher to be aware of the tradeoffs involved in conducting interviews through different ways. The advantages and disadvantages of in-person, telephone and email interviews are summarized in Table 10.3.

In-person and phone interviews are conducive to longer and more in-depth responses than interviews conducted via email, because it generally takes less time for a person to convey their points verbally than in writing. Both in-person and phone interviews also allow researchers to ask follow-up questions to clarify or probe certain points further. Researchers, however, may be able to build a better rapport with an interviewee in person than in a phone interview and elicit more honest, personal, and in-depth responses from interviewees as a result.

Both in-person and phone interviews also allow researchers to capture interviewees' spontaneous unguarded reactions to questions. With email, interviewees are able to think more deliberately about their responses and sanitize them. Through in-person and video-phone interviews, researchers can also observe the body language of their interviewees, which may convey information about the interviewees' thoughts and feelings. For these reasons, email is a more valuable tool in collecting factual information from interviewees than information about cognitions, attitudes and emotions.

Two other options exist for conducting interviews – computer-assisted personal interviews (CAPI) and computer-assisted self-interviewing (CASI). In the former, a computer displays the questions onscreen and the interviewer reads the questions to the interviewees and then enters the interviewees' responses directly into the computer. In the latter, the interviewees enter the responses themselves. Other than transcription, the benefits of these systems are not obvious, and neither method is commonly used in social scientific research.

Mode	(Dis)advantages	Best use
In-person	conducive to elaborate and spontaneous responses body language observable follow-up questions possible	semi-structured or unstructured interviews open-ended questions
Phone	conducive to elaborate and spontaneous responses body language observable (video phone only) follow-up questions possible	semi-structured or unstructured interviews open-ended questions
Email	encourages brief and guarded responses less costly for interviewer more convenient for interviewee no recording or transcription necessary	structured interviews collection of factual information close-ended questions

Table 10.3 Interview modes

Analyzing Interview Data

Not all researchers who conduct interviews systematically analyze their interview data. Some who do not use interviews to generate an idea for a research project or to develop arguments that they test through other methods. Others who do not use interview data to enliven or support an argument that they have already developed. These researchers may incorporate excerpts from their interviews in the write up of the research, but go no further.

Other researchers, however, analyze their interview data systematically, whether they are using the interviews to bolster an existing argument, construct a new argument, or test their argument. Researchers who analyze interview data systematically characterize the whole of the interviews and identify patterns among the responses. A systematic analysis of interview data is only possible if the interviews have been recorded and transcribed. Structured interviews are most amenable to this kind of analysis since all interviewees are asked in them the exact same questions.

Interview data can be analyzed systematically through either an inductive or deductive approach. Through the first approach, researchers peruse the transcripts of their interviews to identify common themes or analytic categories in response to each question. Using this approach, researchers may also develop a typology of the interviewees based on demographic or other characteristics that they possess. With this information, researchers can draw connections among respondents and their responses. A fully inductive approach would allow this typology to arise organically from the interviewees' comments as well.

To illustrate this approach, consider the following example of instant divorce. Instant divorce is a practice whereby a Muslim man can legally divorce his wife by stating verbally or in writing the word 'talaq' three times. Governments in increasing numbers are banning this practice, with notable cases of husbands divorcing their wives via text messages calling attention to this practice. The debate around the illegalization of this practice concerns primarily whether the practice is in accordance with religious doctrine and constitutional provisions regarding the separation of church and state and non-gender-based discrimination, as well as the harm the practice causes to women who are unable to seek alimony or other financial support through secular law as a result of it.

To analyze responses to an interview question regarding whether the practice of instant divorce should be banned using an inductive approach, a researcher would first read the transcripts of every interviewee's responses to the question posed. Then, the researcher would develop categories to describe the different types of behaviors that interviewees describe. Table 10.4 presents three analytic categories or themes that a researcher might develop based on seven different views regarding banning this practice.

Using these analytic categories, the researcher would then code each of the interviewees' responses according to the behavior mentioned. In this example depicted in Table 10.4, both views in support of and against outlawing instant divorce cited constitutional principles and religious doctrine. Those in support of banning the practice also cited the economic hardship that the practice causes women. The two views against outlawing the

Do you think the practice of 'instant divorce', whereby a Muslim man can legally divorce his wife by stating verbally or in writing the word *talaq* three times, should be outlawed? Why?

Respondent	Response	Reason	Analytic category
1	yes	contradicts national laws regarding divorce	constitutionality
2	yes	violates the right of women to equality under the law	harm to women
3	yes	prevents women from obtaining alimony from husbands	harm to women
4	yes	violates religious doctrine regarding the sanctity of marriage	religious doctrine
5	yes	is not mentioned in Quran	religious doctrine
6	no	violates constitutional principles of noninterference in religious matters	constitutionality
7	no	is consistent with religious doctrine	religious doctrine

Table 10.4 Analyzing interview data

practice also cited constitutional principles and religious doctrine. In this barebones example each interviewee only mentioned one type of behavior. In reality, individuals' responses are likely to be much more complex and multifaceted.

Alternatively, researchers can analyze interview data deductively by devising a coding scheme prior to conducting any interviews about what they expect to find in response to each question, and then after interviewing everyone, evaluate the responses against this coding scheme. To develop a set of analytic categories about instant divorce deductively, a researcher might draw on other academic literature, legal opinions, anecdotal evidence, and so forth. Using a deductive approach, researchers might also develop a priori a set of analytic categories about the types of individuals they expect to have differing views on an issue, and then code the interviewees' responses against these categories, in order to identify the types of views different categories of individuals are likely to have regarding the practice of instant divorce. Across countries, views regarding instant divorce are likely to vary based on gender, religious denomination, religiosity, socio-economic class, and education level, among other things.

Inductive and deductive approaches have certain advantages and disadvantages. An inductive approach is very sensitive to researchers' coding decisions. One researcher might develop a very different set of analytic categories than another based on the same interview responses. This is less of an issue for researchers using a deductive approach. However, researchers using a deductive approach can fail to capture information in the data that they had not anticipated. A sociology researcher might overlook, for example, the political reasons, such as a desire to curry favor with female voters and marginalize certain religious parties, why individuals might want the practice of instant divorce either upheld or banned.

Typically, researchers, in analyzing interview data, do not report how many, or what percentage of respondents, mention a particular theme, but rather simply report what themes emerged from the interviews. Reporting absolute or relative frequencies suggests, when this is unlikely to be the case, that the views expressed in the interviews are representative of the larger population. Researchers also do not usually construct quantitative indicators, as described in Chapter 17, from the interview data, regarding the number of times certain words or types of words are mentioned in interviews. Although this is possible, it would significantly simplify the information collected from the interviews.

Regardless of whether researchers use an inductive or deductive approach to analyze interview data, or a qualitative or quantitative approach, it is important that researchers document in a codebook the rules and procedures by which the data are coded. This includes the analytic categories used to code the data and the way in which differences are resolved among independent coders. Researchers should not code the data themselves so that they do not allow their biases to affect the coding. Ideally, they will have more than one person code the data for them in order to minimize errors, among other things.

Researchers should also document the coding process. For each coder, researchers should record how each response is coded using the coding rubric, as in Table 10.4, and calculate the level of agreement between coders using intercoder reliability statistics. Researchers may not be able to share the raw data with others, even if the responses are anonymized, in order to protect the interviewees' privacy. However, it is still essential that researchers follow this protocol to make sure for themselves that the data are coded carefully, consistently, and in as unbiased a manner as possible.

Key Points

- Interview research is better suited for theory building than theory testing due to a number of factors: the typically small number of persons that can be interviewed one-on-one; the likelihood that the views of the interviewees are not generalizable; the subjectivity of interpreting responses; and the lack of clear cut guidelines for (dis)confirming hypotheses using them.
- There is a tradeoff in terms of generalizability, richness, and the opportunity to learn unexpected information based on the extent to which interviews are structured. Generalizability is lower, but richness and the opportunity to learn unexpected information are greater, the less structured the interview.
- The wording and ordering of questions, the interview mode, and the environment in which an interview is conducted significantly affect the quality of the responses and should be tailored to the subject of the interview and the person interviewed.

Further Reading

The first and third readings discuss practical issues around designing, conducting and analyzing interviews, as well as epistemological and ethical issues involved in interviewing. The second reading provides a concise introduction to a non-positive, interpretive approach to interviewing.

Brinkmann, Svend and Steinar Kvale. 2014. *InterViews: Learning the Craft of Qualitative Research Interviewing*. London: Sage Publications.

Fujii, Lee Ann. 2017. *Interviewing in Social Science Research: A Relational Approach*. New York: Routledge.

Galletta, Anne and William E. Cross. 2013. *Mastering the Semi-Structured Interview and Beyond: From Research Design to Analysis and Publication*. New York: New York University Press.

EXERCISE 10.1

Read the excerpt below from an interview with Evelyn Amony. Evelyn was abducted when she was 12 years old by the Lord's Resistance Army (LRA), which perpetrated a war in Uganda for almost 30 years, and was forcibly married to Joseph Kony. The goal of this interview is to shed light on the experiences of women in war, the unique struggles women face in their communities after wars have ended, as well as the resilience and innovativeness of women in overcoming these struggles.

Read the interview below and answer the following questions.

First, did the interview achieve all its stated goals? Which goals did it achieve and why? Second, analyze the structure and order of the questions. In what ways are they effective, and in what ways could they be improved? Third, this interview was conducted via email. Discuss the tradeoffs of an in-person, phone, and email interview in this case. What interview mode do you think is best? Fourth, what research questions might you devise regarding the experiences of women in post-conflict countries based on this interview?

[Q1] Interviewer: Evelyn, tell me about what you are doing now?

[A1] Amony: I wrote a book not too long ago called, *I am Evelyn Amony: Reclaiming My Life from the Lord's Resistance Army*[3], about my experience, so that the world knows that war is bad and has very negative consequences for women and children. I also helped found the Women's Advocacy Network (WAN). It lobbies for women's issues in Uganda, trains women in leadership, and helps them heal through storytelling, poems, memory quilts, etc. Right now, I am involved in the reintegration of children born of war – to reunite children born into the LRA captivity with their families for family support and a sense of identity, a move that has proved to bring healing to the families that lost their children during the war. In most instances, these children are seen as a replacement for their parents.

[Q2] Interviewer: Can you tell me a little about how you got to where you are today? What was your first experience like when you returned home?

[A2] Amony: I was so fearful when I got back home. I could not even talk to people because Kony told me that in case I got home not to trust my own relatives because they might kill me. My real mother and my other siblings were so happy to see me back but other people stigmatized me, called me names, and said bad things about me. This started to change, though, when we founded WAN and started engaging with the communities through dialogues and radio to sensitize and make them realise that we were just victims of the war.

[Q3] Interviewer: How is it that you were able to return home?

[A3] Amony: We escaped. I made the first attempt to escape when I was just 3 months in abduction. The person we attempted to escape with was a friend to my uncle. Unfortunately, we were caught. After confessing that he wanted to help take me home, he was killed. I was beaten terribly. After that, I really didn't want to escape anymore for the sake of the safety of my entire family. If you escaped, the LRA would retaliate against your entire family clan as revenge against your escape. Eventually, though, I escaped again but entered a UPDF ambush at a place called Palabek, where I was caught by the UPDF, then lifted to the Fourth Division barrack in Gulu district. From there, I was taken to GUSCO rehabilitation center. Considering my health condition and the baby I had I was first hospitalised for about two weeks and then taken back to GUSCO where I stayed for about eight months before I was released to come home.

[Q4] Interviewer: Do women face different struggles than men when they return to their communities?

[A4] Amony: Yes. Definitely.

[Q5] Interviewer: In what way?

[A5] Amony: Many women returned from the war with children and had to find a way to pay for school fees, food, medication, etc. for them. I returned with two children, but the third disappeared and I'm still looking for that child today. If women remarry, the men would often leave them because of the children. Those who returned with many children also find difficulties in getting a house to rent. Men who returned, such as commanders, were taken back to school by the government. Women who returned have not been allowed the opportunity to go back to school. Women also face more stigma in the community because of children.

[Q6] Interviewer: What stigmas do they face?

[A6] Amony: People think we wanted to kill, that we didn't want to return from the war, but we couldn't escape because we'd be beaten or killed. They say we are unworthy of marriage, that we are dangerous and that our kids are violent because their fathers were rebels. The stigma makes you remember the past. And that takes away the possibility of peace in your life.

[Q7] Interviewer: What's next for you?

[A7] Amony: I am going to keep advocating for women. I don't want to be seen as a victim. I want to be known as a Human Rights Defender! I am also working tirelessly to ensure that we get funding support for these vulnerable women to empower them to be self-reliant.

EXERCISE 10.2

Design a semi-structured interview based on your own research. First, identify the target population(s). Then, in 2–3 sentences indicate the type of information that you want to collect from each population. Next, compose 8–10 questions designed to elicit this information from your subjects. (If your research involves more than one target population answer this question for only one of them.) Arrange the questions in the order that you intend to ask them. Finally, discuss in 2–3 sentences why you have chosen this order and any concerns that you have about prior questions influencing responses to subsequent questions. You may consult Chapter 18 and the section on question wording ('Survey Questionnaire Design') to complete this exercise.

EXERCISE 10.3

Analyze the interview with Evelyn Amony in Exercise 10.1. First, identify at least 2–3 analytic categories or themes that emerge from the interview. Then, code each response of Evelyn Amony denoting the theme(s) that each contains. Organize this information into a two-column table similar to the table below. The first column should represent the analytic categories or themes you have identified and the second column should contain an excerpt from the interview that fits the analytic category.

Analytic category	Interview excerpt
category 1	excerpt 1
category 1	excerpt 2
category 2	excerpt 3
category 2	excerpt 4
category 3	excerpt 5

11

Focus Groups

Objectives

- discuss the utility of focus groups for hypothesis building and hypothesis testing
- describe the (dis)advantages of focus groups vis-à-vis interviews and surveys for building and testing hypotheses
- provide information on practical issues about how to conduct focus groups, such as recruitment, compensation, location, and so forth
- outline different approaches for analyzing focus group data

Focus groups are perhaps best known as a tool in marketing research responsible for helping corporations to tailor their products and services to the needs of their customers and develop effective branding strategies with which to pitch them. Focus groups, however, are an essential tool of academic research as well. In fact, focus groups were first developed by academics commissioned by the US government during the Second World War in order to study the impact of military propaganda films on the public (Featherstone 2018).

Formally, a *focus group* is a semi-structured group interview designed to elicit information from participants on a defined topic of interest. It is a group interview because the views of more than one person are solicited at a single time, and is semi-structured because the moderator leading the focus group uses an interview guide to prompt the discussion, but does not adhere strictly to this guide, instead allowing the flow of the conversation to determine the questions asked and the time allocated to individual questions.

Focus groups share much in common with one-on-one interviews and surveys. Like these other methods, focus groups provide researchers with an opportunity to gain direct insight into the preferences, opinions, emotions, attitudes, and so forth that motivate human behavior. Yet, focus groups are also quite distinct due to the group nature by which they are defined. Focus groups are preferable to these other methods for understanding human behavior when the group environment by which focus groups are defined is more likely to elicit honest and full responses than these methods, or when the interaction among individuals in the focus group is important to understanding the phenomenon in question.

How to Use Focus Groups

Focus groups can be utilized to either build theories or test theories but they are much better suited to the latter than the former. Focus groups are not very useful for theory testing because focus group participants tend to be unrepresentative of the population from which they are drawn; their responses are subjective and non-comparable; and no clear-cut standards exist for confirming or disconfirming hypotheses based on them. The advantages and disadvantages of focus groups for building and testing hypotheses are summarized in Table 11.1.

	Hypothesis building	Hypothesis testing
Pros	open-ended questions	more respondents than interviews
	group dynamic	
Cons	guinea pig effect	unrepresentative samples
		non-comparable responses
		responses open to interpretation
		no rules for (dis)confirming hypotheses

Table 11.1 Utility of focus groups for hypothesis building and testing

Hypothesis Building

Focus groups, like interviews and surveys, present researchers with an opportunity to understand the cognitions, attitudes, and emotions that drive human behavior. The open-ended nature of focus groups, like one-on-one interviews, lends itself well to generating hypotheses. Since focus group moderators generally pose questions to participants, which do not have defined response categories like surveys, and vary their questions in response to the participants' answers, focus groups give researchers an important opportunity to learn things from participants that they had not expected.

The group environment of focus groups can also be helpful in this regard, as a comment by one person may spark an idea in another person, which may spark an idea in still another participant, and so on and so forth. If the goal of the researcher is to identify only those issues that are most important for participants, this dynamic would be counterproductive because it would lead participants to recall issues that are not necessarily salient for them. However, if the goal of the researcher is to collect all relevant ideas and perspectives on a given issue this dynamic can prove very useful.

Hypothesis Testing

While focus groups are helpful for generating hypotheses by means of inductive reasoning, they are not useful for testing hypotheses. Researchers are generally able to solicit the opinion of more people in the same amount of time using focus groups than one-on-one interviews. However, focus group participants are still unlikely to be representative of the population from which they are drawn because, like interviews, focus group participants are generally chosen through non-probability sampling techniques. Moreover, since focus groups require a significant time investment from participants, those who participate in them may be highly invested in the issues studied and have stronger opinions on the issues discussed than those who do not participate in focus groups.

Focus groups are also not very useful for hypothesis testing because the responses of focus group participants are not comparable. They are not comparable because focus groups are semi-structured. In other words, moderators do not pose the same questions to all participants in every focus group. Given the flow of the conversation, moderators may not have sufficient time to ask the same questions of every focus group. Moderators may change the wording of certain questions if the responses of participants in prior focus groups suggested that the original wording was unclear, imprecise, misleading, or problematic in another way. Or, they may pose new questions to probe ideas that previous focus groups sparked in them. The responses of focus group participants are also not comparable because they are influenced by the comments of other members of their particular focus group.

Finally, focus groups are not very valuable for hypothesis testing because there are no clear-cut rules regarding how many respondents in a focus group need to express a certain idea in order to confirm a hypothesis, or how many respondents in a focus group must not express a certain idea in order to disconfirm a hypothesis. Further complicating the matter is the subjectivity of the participants' comments, and the tendency of researchers to interpret new evidence as confirmation of their existing beliefs or theories.

When to Use Focus Groups

As the previous discussion makes apparent, focus groups have much in common with one-on-one interviews, but are also strikingly different due to their group nature. Often focus groups are used over interviews in order to save time and money. Focus groups should not be used for expediency, however, but only when the group environment, which distinguishes focus groups from both one-on-one interviews and surveys, is likely to elicit more honest and complete responses than either of these methods, or when the interaction among individuals in focus groups is important to understanding the phenomena in question.

Greater Openness through Others

While focus groups are best used when individuals are more likely to share intimate and honest information with researchers in the presence of others than on their own, in most cases, the group nature of focus groups is likely to result in less open, honest, and complete responses than one-on-one-interviews and even potentially surveys. In focus groups, individuals may be reluctant to share their opinions on issues or to admit to certain behaviors in front of others due to concerns about their privacy. This is especially likely to be the case when the issues discussed are very personal or controversial, or when the participants' opinions or behaviors run counter to social norms, or are illegal, as in the case of homosexuality or sexual relations outside of marriage in some countries.

One-on-one interviews offer individuals much more privacy in this regard than focus groups since the responses of interviewees are not heard by anyone other than the interviewer. Interviewers may also create a safe, comfortable, non-judgmental environment that encourages respondents to reveal private information, which is harder to do in focus groups since moderators cannot control how other members of the group respond to questions or interact with others. Surveys can provide individuals with even more privacy than one-on-one interviews since they can be anonymous. In surveys, though, people are less likely to feel any responsibility to share private or intimate information with researchers than in focus groups or interviews because survey respondents generally lack a personal connection to researchers.

Individuals might also provide inaccurate information to researchers in focus groups due to social pressures to conform, even on non-sensitive and non-controversial issues, as the Asch conformity experiments demonstrate. In the first Asch conformity experiment (1951), participants were asked to identify out loud which line on a card was the same as

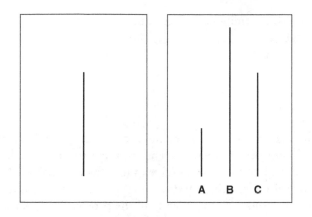

Figure 11.1 Asch conformity experiment

the line on another card, as in Figure 11.1. Participants in the study gave their response only after listening to the responses of others in the room, who unbeknownst to the participants were part of the experiment. Even on such a simple task, where the correct answer was obvious, about a third of the participants in the study incorrectly identified the wrong pair of lines when everyone in the room prior to them gave an incorrect answer. In interviews after the experiments, the participants gave distinct reasons for why they conformed, including lack of confidence, adherence to social norms, and perceived confusion over the objective of the task.

Focus group participants may also provide inaccurate information to moderators in order to project a certain image in front of other participants. Men, for example, among other men might exaggerate their sexual prowess, while a woman in the presence of other women might downplay their sexual experiences. Similarly, in some contexts, a person may deny being given special favors due to personal connections or bribes, while in other contexts, where both are seen as attributes of personal success and wealth, a person may not.

While in general focus groups are likely to result in less open, honest, and complete responses than one-on-one interviews and possibly even surveys, in certain circumstances, participants may feel more comfortable and more willing to share private information in a group environment than in either interviews or surveys. This may be the case when focus groups bring together people that have something in common with each other, but that do not otherwise have an opportunity to interact with each other. The awareness of others like them, as well as their shared experiences, may make these individuals more willing to share information with others than they might otherwise would, especially if the experiences that they have in common are rebuked or stigmatized by the communities in which they live, as in the case of women who have experienced dowry-related violence or men who have been raped (Christian et al. 2011). Focus groups of men who were sexually abused during civil wars have proven remarkably revealing. In these groups, men have said that they had not told their families about the abuse because they feared being stigmatized by society, of no longer being seen as a man, and of being abandoned by their wives for being too weak to protect them.

Group Dynamics Matter

Focus groups should also be used when the interaction among individuals is important to understanding the phenomena in question. That is, focus groups should be used when the researcher seeks to understand how group dynamics affect individuals' perceptions, information processing, decision-making, and so forth. In sociology and psychology, focus groups have been used in this way to understand the process by which collective identities are formed (Munday 2006) and how people develop empathy for others when others reveal complex thinking for a policy opinion that they do not share. In political science, they have also been used in this way to study theories of deliberative democracy, which posit that laws derive their legitimacy through group discussion (Hibbing and Theiss-Morse 2002; Fishkin 2011).

They are particularly well suited to studying the concept of deliberative democracy because focus groups allow researchers to observe how people resolve uncertainties, and whether they do so, as some theorists posit, by emphasizing areas of mutual agreement. Focus groups also allow researchers to determine whether or not deliberative democracy builds a sense of community among individuals and enhances people's perceptions of the fairness and rationality of outcomes, among other things, often associated with deliberative democracy.

Focus groups are also very useful where social pressures to conform or the desire to project a certain image to others is the subject of the study. In a study on deference to authority in post-conflict Rwanda, Elizabeth Levy Paluck and Donald P. Green (2009) used focus groups for this purpose. The researchers sought to understand if listening to a radio program that depicted scenarios in which the actors challenged authority would lead people to voice their opposition to, and refuse to comply with, opinions and behaviors that they opposed. In Green and Paluck's view, insufficient deference allows leaders to orchestrate the kind of mass violence Rwanda experienced in 1994, when as many as 800,000 people died in a single year of fighting.

In the study, Rwandans were divided into two groups – one group listened to this radio show and another group listened to a radio show on the human immunodeficiency virus (HIV). While HIV rates have declined in Rwanda over the last two decades, HIV remains a significant problem in Rwanda as in much of Africa. After the experiment was completed, the researchers asked individuals in one-on-one interviews and in focus groups, whether there was mistrust in their communities. Compared to the one-on-one interviews, denials of mistrust were much more frequent in the focus groups, as we would expect given the pressure to conform to the group environment. But, this was only the case among those who listened to the HIV radio show. This suggests that it is possible for people to learn to challenge authority through non-deferential behavior modeled in radio programs.

Conducting Focus Groups

There are five major steps involved in conducting a focus group. These steps are depicted in Figure 11.2 and described below.

The first step involves *identifying the target population*. Focus groups are typically composed of individuals that share a common knowledge or experience related to the research subject under investigation. These people may be professors, teachers, students, lawyers, judges, businessmen, customers, and so forth. Although focus group participants are homogeneous in relation to the subject under investigation, they are generally diverse along other dimensions, such as gender, age, income, and so forth, in order to capture a range of opinions and experiences on this subject.

How researchers go about identifying their target population depends on their particular research questions and subjects. Researchers might seek out the names of organizations that their target groups are likely to be members of, including professional organizations, labor unions, universities, and so forth. Alternatively, they might identify magazines, newspapers, or journals that target groups are likely to subscribe to and try to purchase their member lists.

The second step involves *designing the focus group*. There are many issues researchers need to consider in designing a focus group. Foremost among them is the size and number of focus groups to hold. Typically, focus groups include between 6–12 participants.

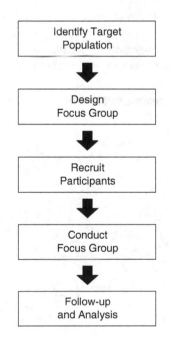

Figure 11.2 Focus group steps

In groups smaller than 6, a voluble person is more likely to dominate the conversation. In groups larger than 12, everyone may not be able to contribute fully to the conversation. The optimal number of participants also depends on the complexity of the issue, with complex issues better dealt with by focus groups including fewer participants.

If researchers are using focus groups to test a theory, researchers ought to conduct a power analysis, as described in Chapter 9, in order to determine the total number of participants and/or groups needed to identify a statistically significant effect if one exists. Otherwise, there are no hard and fast rules regarding how many focus groups researchers need to hold in order to generate hypotheses regarding any given subject. As in the case of interviews, it is advisable for researchers to stop holding focus groups once they have reached a saturation point – the point at which they have stopped learning anything new from the discussions.

In designing the focus group, researchers must also consider where to hold the focus group so that it is not difficult and costly for participants to attend. They should also consider the implications for their study of holding the focus groups in an academic versus non-academic setting, as well as the conditions of the room in which the focus group is held. The room, regardless of where it is located, should be quiet and free of distractions. All the seats within this room should be arranged in a non-hierarchical way so that no one person's opinion is seen as more important than another.

Focus groups can last from anywhere between one hour – if the subject of the focus group is simple and the number of participants is small – to two hours – if the subject is more complex and the number of participants is large. Beyond two hours, the number of people willing to participate in a focus group and the quality of the participants' responses are likely to diminish.

It is best to audio record the conversation because it is all but impossible for a moderator to effectively manage the conversation while taking notes. If it is not possible to record

"Looks like we've got an out-of-focus group."

Cartoon 11.1

the conversation because of objections from the participants or another reason, someone other than the moderator needs to be present to take notes. Video recording a focus group is generally not advisable. Even though it can capture the physiognomy of the participants, it can also inhibit the conversation.

The third step involves *recruiting the participants*. Researchers may use either random or non-random sampling techniques to select participants from among the target population that they have identified. Both techniques are discussed in detail in Chapter 9. Whether researchers use random or non-random sampling techniques depends on the target population, their access to the target population, and the purpose of the focus group. While random sampling techniques are necessary for researchers to make generalizations about target populations, they are not sufficient in the case of focus groups for this purpose due to the non-comparability of responses across focus groups.

Given the significant time commitment that focus groups demand of participants, it is not uncommon for researchers to compensate participants in some way for their time. Cash generally provides people with a greater incentive to participate in focus groups than other forms of compensation because the reward may not be equally appealing to all potential participants. Offering any form of financial compensation, though, can result in the over-representation of low-income individuals in the focus group. Whatever form of compensation the researchers choose to provide participants, researchers should distribute it prior to the start of the focus group. Otherwise, participants may feel compelled to remain in the group, or respond in a certain way during the conversation, in order to receive their compensation.

The fourth step is to *conduct the focus group*. Before conducting the first focus group, researchers should do a trial run of the focus group, substituting friends and colleagues for the participants, and making adjustments to the procedures and questionnaire as needed. Often researchers will hire another person, who is more experienced than them, to run the focus groups. This person should also participate in the trial run.

The person who conducts the focus group is known as a moderator. An effective moderator is able to skillfully draw out responses from less vocal participants without pressuring them to participate; to redirect the discussion when it runs adrift; to rein in participants who try to dominate the conversation without offending them; to deescalate potential conflicts among participants; and to create an open and safe environment in which people feel comfortable to share their views.

Box 11.1   Sample Focus Group Introduction

Good evening. My name is _____ and I will be the moderator of this evening's discussion. I am a professor/student/researcher at _____ and this discussion is part of the research that I am conducting on _____. This discussion is an important part of my research and I appreciate you taking the time to participate in it and to share your views with me.

(Continued)

(Continued)

Before we begin, let me establish some ground rules for the discussion. I'd appreciate it if everyone would please share his or her views openly and frankly. There are no right or wrong answers to any questions that I pose, only differing points of view. I'd also ask that you respect the opinions of others even if their views differ from yours, and to please not interrupt others while they are speaking.

So that I do not miss anyone's comments, I am recording tonight's discussion. Everything you share tonight is confidential. I will not use your real names in any written work that results from tonight's conversation.

If at any one point, you don't feel comfortable participating in the discussion, please raise your hand and let me know, and you may leave if you would like. In front of you, you will find a consent form that explains what I just said. Please sign the form if you agree to these conditions, and once I have collected everyone's consent forms, we will begin.

Usually, the moderator begins a focus group by introducing themselves, explaining the purpose of the study, and describing what the focus group entails. An example of an introductory speech is provided in Box 11.1. After the introductory speech, the moderator may ask the participants in the group to introduce themselves, but only to provide their first name to ensure confidentiality. Participants should be given the option to use a pseudonym if they desire, and everyone, including the moderator, should wear a nametag so that people can refer to each other by name. The latter helps foster a more familiar and comfortable environment that is conducive to conversation.

Typically, the moderator will begin the discussion with a general question and then ask more specific and complex questions that require more reflection as the discussion proceeds. It is important, though, for moderators to ask those questions that are most important for the study sufficiently early on in the discussion to ensure that the group has an opportunity to consider these questions fully before time runs out in the session.

In the course of the focus group, moderators may ask probing questions. Probing questions are used to keep the conversation flowing, to clarify comments, to draw out fuller responses from participants, and to encourage less vocal participants to share their views. The following are all examples of probing questions:

Could you explain further?

Could you elaborate?

Could you give an example of what you mean?

Would anyone in the group like to add to what _____ said?

Does anyone have any other thoughts?

Moderators must not only phrase their questions carefully, but they must also be mindful of any non-verbal messages that they send participants. Moderators nodding their heads, for example, to acknowledge a comment might suggest agreement with a point of view, and dissuade others from raising a differing opinion.

At the end of the focus group, moderators ought to close the discussion by offering participants an opportunity to raise any final points that they would like to make, and by reiterating their thanks for everyone's participation in the focus group.

The fifth and final step concerns the *post-focus group period*. After the focus group, researchers should give every member of the group, if they have not already, a business card so that the members of the group can contact the researchers if they have any questions afterwards. Researchers may also share with the members of the focus group copies of the publications they produce from the discussion, but under no circumstances should they give members of the focus group the right to approve their research before it can be published since this can distort and undermine the credibility of the research.

Analyzing Focus Group Data

The procedures involved in analyzing focus group data have much in common with those involved in analyzing interview data. The one difference between the two is that with focus group data, researchers have the opportunity not only to analyze the conversation that takes place during the focus group, but also to analyze the interactions among the participants. Researchers may approach analyzing these interactions either inductively or deductively. Using a deductive approach, researchers may categorize the interactions they observe among participants in their focus groups based on an existing framework for understanding small group dynamics, such as the Emotional Group Culture Categorization System (EGCCS). The EGCCS classifies group interactions based on whether they demonstrate compliance with or independence from the group; criticism or supportiveness; and intimacy or evasiveness, among other things (Rothwell 2010). Using an inductive approach, researchers may instead develop their own coding scheme, which is tailored to the subject of their research and the behaviors that they observe among the members of their focus groups.

Key Points

- Focus groups are better suited to building theories than testing theories due to the following factors: the relatively small number of persons interviewed using focus groups; the likelihood that the views of the interviewees are not generalizable; the non-comparability of responses across focus groups; the subjectivity of interpreting the responses; and the lack of clear cut guidelines for (dis)confirming hypotheses using focus groups.

(Continued)

(Continued)

- Focus groups are best used over one-on-one interviews or surveys when the group environment by which focus groups are defined is more likely to elicit honest and full responses than these methods, or when the interaction among individuals in the focus group is important to understanding the phenomenon in question.
- Analyzing focus group data offers an opportunity to categorize the statements of individuals as well as the types of interactions among participants.

Further Reading

All three readings discuss the applications, advantages, and limitations of focus groups and practical issues around designing, conducting, and analyzing focus groups.

Krueger, Richard A. and Mary Anne Casey. 2014. *Focus Groups: A Practical Guide for Applied Research*. London: Sage Publications.
Morgan, David L. 2015. *Focus Groups as Qualitative Research*. London: Sage Publications.
Stewart, David W. and Prem N. Shamdasani. 2014. *Focus Groups: Theory and Practice*. London: Sage Publications.

EXERCISE 11.1

Discuss the advantages and disadvantages of using focus groups to understand one of the issues below (involving the groups indicated), and how the focus group could be designed to minimize any potential disadvantages. Also, discuss whether one-on-one interviews or surveys would be more useful for researching the topics identified below than focus groups.

- Public opinion regarding a new government policy among voters supporting different political parties.
- Policies needed to create family-friendly work environments including men and women of equivalent employment ranks.
- Attitudes toward police of young men and women whose friends were killed by police under different circumstances.
- Motivations of pro-democracy activists in authoritarian regimes with pro-democracy activists within the same country but representing different organizations.
- Societal perceptions of women who work outside the home in patriarchal societies, including only women employed outside the home in the same patriarchal society but from different socio-economic strata.
- Attitudes towards child soldiers in the communities in which they are to be reintegrated after a civil war, involving only non-combatants.

EXERCISE 11.2

Find a video of a focus group published online, or one that your instructor has chosen for you, and evaluate: (1) the effectiveness of the moderator in terms of his/her ability to extract full responses from participants and to prevent members of the group from shutting down and preventing others in the group from participating in the discussion; and (2) the quality of the discussion in terms of the depth of the responses given and the effect of members' comments on the responses of others in the group. Make two recommendations regarding how the focus group could be changed to improve the discussion, and explain how these changes would do so.

Participant Observation

Objectives

- identify types of participant observation (i.e., active vs. passive and overt vs. covert)
- discuss the utility of participant observation for hypothesis building and hypothesis testing
- provide practical information about conducting participant observation (e.g., case selection, access, building rapport, and recording observations)
- describe the process of analyzing and presenting information collected through participant observation

Participant observation is commonly associated with ethnographic research in anthropology, but is increasingly used today in other fields, including education, criminology, sociology, and even business and marketing.[1] *Participant observation* is a form of qualitative data collection that involves the immersion of researchers into the environment of their subjects for an extended period of time. The reasoning behind participant observation is, as Harper Lee wrote in *To Kill a Mockingbird*, that '[y]ou cannot really understand a person until you consider things from his point of view ... until you climb into his skin and walk around in it.'[2] Through immersion, researchers are able to observe the daily lives of people – their exchanges with each other, their formal and informal conversations, activities, habits, and so forth. Immersion provides researchers with an opportunity to collect candid and intimate information about people. This information, though, is filtered through the perspective of the researchers who, in using this method, are at risk of losing their objectivity and of altering the behavior of the groups that they study through their presence.

Features of Participant Observation

While participant observation by definition involves the immersion of a researcher into the environment of their subjects, there are two dimensions that distinguish different forms of participant observation from each other. They are the extent to which the researchers interact with their subjects (i.e., active versus passive observation), and whether the observation is concealed or not (i.e., overt versus convert observation). Table 12.1 summarizes the advantages and disadvantages of these different forms of participant observation.

Active versus Passive Observation

In the passive form of participant observation, researchers observe and record the behaviors of their subjects in their own environment without conversing or interacting with their subjects in any way. Many studies using this form of participant observation are studies in which researchers observe the behavior and communications of people in public places, such as restaurants, cafés, transportation hubs, and even the internet. Examples of the

	Active	Covert
Advantages	better access to certain activities of subjects	subjects do not alter behavior in response to researcher's presence (no guinea pig effect)
	experience activities as subjects would experience them	
Disadvantages	researcher's presence may alter behavior of subjects	potentially violates privacy of subjects and denies subjects right to consent to be studied
	practices that researcher participates in may be dangerous or illegal	
	greater risk of losing objectivity	

Table 12.1   (Dis)advantage of types of participant observation

latter include studies of support groups for people with medical or psychological disorders (Sharf 1997; Brotsky and Giles 2007) and chat rooms of extremist or hate groups (Awan 2017; Bloom et al. 2017).

In the active form of participant observation, in contrast, researchers converse with their subjects and take part in the daily life of the groups that they study, including their activities, customs, rituals, routines, and so forth. The extent to which researchers engage with these groups varies. Some researchers limit their interactions to interviews while others engage in every aspect of their subjects' lives. Examples of this form of participant observation include studies where researchers lived for long periods of time among different ethnic, cultural, or religious communities (Mead 1928; Geertz 1973; Goffman 2014), resided in prisons or in gang-run communities (Wacquant 2002), and checked into medical and/or psychiatric facilities as patients (Rosenhan 1973).

An important advantage of the passive form of participant observation is that researchers are unlikely to significantly change the behavior of the groups that they study by only observing, as opposed to interacting with, groups. This provides researchers with a more natural or accurate representation of the groups that they analyze.

At the same time, though, researchers may not be able to observe as many activities of the group as they would be able to through a more active form of participant observation because some activities may only be observable to someone who participates in them.

Moreover, unless researchers participate in the daily lives of their subjects, they cannot experience events in the same way as members of the group. For example, unless researchers wear a hijab or other religious garments, they cannot experience what it feels like for passersby on the street to look at them as if they were an outcast or threat to their community.

Although researchers may have better access to a group, and may be able to experience things as a member of a group would in the active form of participant observation, researchers are at a greater risk in this form of participant observation of losing their objectivity through such close interactions with members of the group. If researchers experience contentious interactions with members of the group, they may overlook sympathetic characteristics about the group's behaviors. Conversely, if researchers experience positive interactions, they may perceive the group's behaviors in an overly compassionate light.

Researchers, for example, after spending months in refugee camps, may come to deeply empathize with the plight of the refugees, and overlook, as a result, information about the negative behaviors of refugees, including crimes they commit against other refugees, which might undermine the willingness of governments to accept further refugees into their countries. If researchers, however, are victims of the crimes themselves, they may emphasize or exaggerate in their research the potential threat refugees pose to local communities.

Finally, in the active form of participant observation, researchers can be asked to participate in dangerous or illegal acts perpetrated by the groups they observe. These acts may entail minor infractions, such as unpermitted protests, or major violations, such as illegal drug deals and theft. In these situations, researchers face a moral dilemma as to whether or not to participate in the activity, to violate the confidence of the group to stop the wrongful act, and to report the perpetrators to authorities. Researchers may also be asked to participate in acts that are not dangerous or illegal but that are odds with their views, which can be equally disconcerting for researchers in many cases.

Overt versus Covert Observation

Participant observation also varies in terms of the extent to which the observation is covert or overt. In the case of covert participant observation, researchers do not make their presence known to their subjects and, if they do, they do not identify themselves as researchers, while in the case of overt participant observation they do both. But, even when the research is overt, researchers do not generally inform people that they encounter in the course of their research about the specific purpose of their research, or inform everyone that they meet that they are researchers since this could needlessly disrupt the conversations and events being observed.

Examples of covert participant observation include studies in which researchers observe and even interact with people in public places, such as restaurants, transportation hubs, stores, and online chat rooms, but do not introduce themselves as researchers or inform people that they are being studied (Sharf 1997; Brotsky and Giles 2007; Awan 2017; Bloom et al. 2017). They also include studies in which researchers have gone undercover as patients in psychiatric hospitals (Rosenhan 1973; Smithers 1977), alcoholics at Alcoholic Anonymous meetings (Lofland and Lejeune 1960; Rudy 1986), and adherents of religious sects with unconventional practices (Homan 1978).

The primary benefit of covert observation is that since participants do not know that they are being observed, they cannot change their behavior (the guinea pig effect) in response to the presence of the researcher. If participants knew they were being studied, they might try to hide particular behaviors from the researcher or frame events to put themselves in the most positive light possible. They might even fabricate or contrive events for the benefit of the researcher. A police department, for example, that knows it is being observed by a researcher in light of recent cases of police brutality, might inundate this researcher with stories of blatantly falsified brutality charges, or hold anti-bias training programs that it otherwise would not.

Another benefit of covert participant observation is that researchers may be able to observe a group through covert observation that they otherwise would not be given permission to observe. Such was the case in a study conducted by Leon Festinger and colleagues (1956) about an apocalyptic cult. Festinger and his colleagues did not seek permission of the cult leaders to observe the group, expecting to be denied permission if they did. They gained access to the cult by pretending instead to believe in the cult's predictions. In the study, Festinger and colleagues sought to observe how cult members reacted when the world did not end on the day the cult expected.

When it did not, cult members accepted their leader's explanation that God spared the world because they had spread light in the world by sitting outside all night long in anticipation of the world's end. The cult members' behavior was consistent with Festinger's theory of cognitive dissonance because they rationalized the situation in a way that maintained their self-esteem. Festinger's theory of cognitive dissonance states that when people hold contradictory beliefs, ideas, and values, they will either change their behavior or cognitions to resolve the contradiction or ignore or deny any information that conflicts with their existing beliefs.

This justification for covert observation is controversial and would not be permissible under many human subject standards today. Critics argue that researchers do not have the right to observe a group that does not give its consent to being observed. Others argue that at least in certain circumstances, as in the case of research on extremist groups that pose a threat to society (Awan 2017; Bloom et al. 2017), the benefit of the research outweighs the privacy concerns of the group. Still others argue that researchers should not have to ask the permission of a group to observe it if anyone who was not a researcher or a member of the group could observe the group's behaviors.

Types of Participant Observation

The combination of these two dimensions – active versus passive observation and overt versus covert observation – results in four different types of participant observation with their own unique advantages and disadvantages, as depicted in Figure 12.1.

Covert and Active Participant Observation

There are several advantages to covert and active participant observation. In this type of participant observation, researchers may have access to a group that they may not otherwise have an opportunity to observe, and they may experience the practices of the group as members of the group would experience them. Researchers, though, may alter the behavior of the group through their presence. However, in this form of participant

	Overt	**Covert**
Passive	overt and passive	covert and passive
Active	overt and active	covert and active

Figure 12.1 Types of participant observation

observation, groups would not knowingly change their behavior in response to the presence of the researcher because in this form of participant observation, groups would not be aware of being observed (the guinea pig effect).

Festinger et al.'s (1956) study of the Seekers' cult is an example of covert and active participant observation. The observation was covert since the researchers gained access to the group by pretending to be followers of the cult and professing stories about dreams and prophecies consistent with the group's beliefs. It was active since the researchers not only observed the cult's activities, but also led group meetings and participated in mediums. While the researchers tried to limit their participation so as not to change the group's behavior, the researchers did admittedly reinforce the apocalyptic cult's beliefs by participating in its activities.

Covert and Passive Participant Observation

Unlike in the case of overt and passive participant observation, researchers are not likely to alter the behaviors of their subjects in the case of covert and passive participant observation, because researchers do not actively engage with their subjects in this form of participant observation, and because their subjects are also unaware that they are being observed. However, since the observation is passive in this form of participant observation, researchers do not have the opportunity to experience the lives of their subjects for themselves. Examples of covert and passive participant observation include studies in which researchers observe people in public places without making their identity known and without interacting with their subjects in any way (Sharf 1997; Brotsky and Giles 2007; Awan 2017; Bloom et al. 2017).

Overt and Active Participant Observation

If participant observation is both overt and active, people may participate in the activities of their subjects and experience them as their subjects would, but they run the risk of both changing the behavior of their subjects through their interactions with them, and their subjects changing their behavior on their own knowing that they are being studied. Examples of this form of participant observation include studies of different ethnic, cultural, or religious communities (Mead 1928; Geertz 1973; Goffman 2014).

Overt and Passive Participant Observation

As in the case of covert and passive participant observation, researchers do not run the risk of their presence altering the behavior of the groups that they study through their interactions with them in the case of overt and passive participant observation. However, the guinea pig effect is an issue for this form of participant observation unlike in the case of covert and passive participant observation, because participants are aware of being studied in this form of participant observation. Researchers are also unable to experience the world as their subjects would experience it in this form of participant observation.

An example of overt and passive participant observation is Zachariah Mampilly's (2011) study of rebel governance structures. In it, he examines why certain rebel groups and not others provide public goods (e.g., security, justice, education, and health care) to communities under their control. His research was overt because Mampilly identified himself as a researcher to the local communities he observed. It was passive because Mampilly did not personally receive any of the public goods that the rebel groups distributed or engage with the communities he observed in other ways. On the basis of his research, Mampilly concluded that only rebel groups with unified command structures provide public goods to communities and only when they can co-opt international aid agencies and existing government institutions for this purpose.

The Utility of Participant Observation

While participant observation is excellent for hypothesis building, it is not very useful for hypothesis testing. The single-case design, the subjectivity of the data derived from participant observation, and lack of clear guidelines regarding the conditions under which data collected from participant observation can confirm or disconfirm an argument, make this method of limited utility for hypothesis testing. The fact that participant observation can alter the behavior of those observed if it is overt and active is a problem for both building and testing hypotheses.

Table 12.2 summarizes the advantages and disadvantages of participant observation for both hypothesis building and hypothesis testing.

	Hypothesis building	Hypothesis testing
Pros	direct, close, and prolonged observation of subjects	
Cons	potential observer bias (except covert observation)	single case study
		generalizability uncertain
	potential guinea pig effect (except covert observation)	conclusions open to interpretation
		no replicability
		potential observer bias (except covert observation)
		potential guinea pig effect (except covert observation)

Table 12.2   Utility of participant observation

Hypothesis Building

Participant observation is very useful for building hypotheses through inductive reasoning because it gives researchers an opportunity to obtain an in-depth and candid view of their subjects in their own environment. The extent to which it does both of these things depends on the form of participant observation and the duration of the observation. The view is less candid if the observation is overt, and less in-depth if the observation is passive and short-lived.

However, even when the observation is overt, researchers are likely to get a more candid view of the groups that they observe than with other methods, such as interviews, focus groups, and surveys, because the observation takes place in the subjects' own environment and because these other methods are subject to the same biases. In their own environment, people are not continually reminded that they are part of a research study and are likely to be less guarded in their conversations with researchers as a result. By contrast, the formal environment of an interview or focus group makes people very much aware that they are being studied, and the likelihood that their responses will be guarded even higher as a result.

By observing people in their own environments, researchers are also able to observe people's spontaneous reactions to unexpected events, such as the death of a close relative or a natural disaster. Through participant observation, researchers may also be able to detect patterns in people's behaviors that people themselves are not consciously aware of and, therefore, cannot share with researchers in an interview, focus group, or survey.

Take for example a consumer preferences study commissioned by the Swedish alcohol brand, Absolut Vodka. In order to learn why people buy liquors for at-home parties, Absolut Vodka hired a firm, which observed guests at these parties across the US.[3] At these parties, researchers noticed that guests often told humorous anecdotes related to their experiences with a particular liquor, like going to a bar on the wrong night for a birthday party. From this observation, the researchers deduced that individuals purchased liquors for at-home parties due to a personal attachment with the liquor. On the basis of this, the researchers recommended that Absolut Vodka adopt a marketing strategy that emphasized conversation, storytelling, and humor rather than the quality of the liquor, in order to capture the at-home market.

Although most participant observation today still involves the immersion of a researcher into the real-world environment of their subjects, new technologies have recently been developed that allow for virtual participant observation. In virtual participant observation, subjects permit researchers to observe their environments via so-called video surveys. So far, this technology is used primarily by businesses that want to observe how customers use their products. In these video surveys, subjects use their mobile phones to not only show researchers their surroundings, but also to answer questions, and/or undertake tasks asked of them. The technology does not provide researchers with the same experience as in-person participant observation since the observation is limited in time and content, but it does enable researchers to have a broader, more elaborate understanding of certain issues.

Hypothesis Testing

Participant observation is not very useful for testing hypotheses, in contrast, and not commonly used for this purpose either. In addition to the fact that the act of observation itself can alter the behavior of subjects if it is overt and active (also a problem for hypothesis building), participant observation is not useful for hypothesis testing because studies using it are generally based on a single case, and the data derived from these cases are subjective and non-transparent.

Studies using participant observation are generally based on a single case because of the prolonged and involved nature of research using this method. Single case studies, as discussed in Chapter 9, cannot confirm or disconfirm probabilistic theories, which are the vast majority of theories in the social sciences. Single case studies cannot confirm probabilistic theories because the one case analyzed is not necessarily representative of other cases. They cannot disconfirm them either because probabilistic theories do not claim that a given factor always results in a certain outcome.

Single case studies cannot confirm deterministic theories either because even if the outcomes resulted in the presence of necessary conditions or sufficient conditions (or necessary and sufficient conditions), there may be other cases in which the result occurred in the absence of these conditions. Single case studies can disconfirm deterministic theories, but only when outcomes consistent with a theory resulted in the absence of the necessary conditions, or did not result in the presence of sufficient ones.

Data collected through participant observation is also not useful for theory testing because it is subjective and non-transparent and, therefore, not replicable as well. The data are subjective in so much as researchers can interpret the same observations collected through participant observation very differently based on their own backgrounds and experiences. As in the case of interview and focus group data, which are also subjective, there are no clear-cut guidelines against which to evaluate whether the conclusions that researchers draw based on data collected through participant observation confirm or disconfirm their hypotheses.

Data collected through participant observation are often non-transparent as well. Typically, researchers cannot share the raw data that they collect through participant observation in order to protect the confidentiality of their subjects. Even if researchers redacted the names of their subjects from their field notes, due to the specificity and uniqueness of the information that researchers typically gather through participant observation, others may be able to deduce the identities of people described in these notes.

At times, researchers using participant observation have gone to great lengths to protect the confidentiality of their subjects, as in the infamous case of Mario Brajuha (Brajuha and Hallowell 1986). Brajuha refused to comply with a subpoena for his field notes when the

New York City restaurant that he was observing as a waiter burned down in an arson incident. Brajuha faced jail time for refusing to hand over his notes and death threats against him and his family if he did. The death threats stopped when the two arson suspects died for reasons unrelated to the case. In the end, a judge rejected the subpoena, deciding that academics' notes, like those of journalists, are entitled to protection against unwarranted scrutiny in legal proceedings.

Conducting Participant Observation

Participant observation requires first selecting the case to observe and second, gaining access to this group. Once researchers have access to this group, they can then set about establishing a rapport with members of the group while observing, interacting with, and recording the behaviors of members of the group, and then, ultimately, interpreting the information they collect. With the exception of the first two steps, these steps are not sequential but continuous throughout the entire observation period, as reflected in the illustration in Figure 12.2.

Selecting the Case

The first step in conducting an analysis using participation observation is to identify the case for analysis. If the researcher is using the case to build an argument, a researcher may select a case that they believe is typical of other cases. Many times researchers are unable to determine if a case is typical or not because they lack information about the whole universe of cases. In this situation, the researcher may instead choose a case that is prominent or that is convenient for the researcher to explore due to a personal connection to the group or another reason. The hypotheses researchers build may not be generalizable in this case, however.

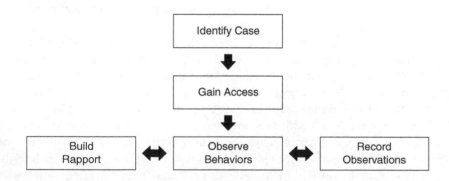

Figure 12.2 Steps involved in participant observation

If researchers are using a case to disconfirm a deterministic hypothesis (the ideal situation for a single-case study design), researchers ought to choose a case where they suspect that the necessary condition (or the necessary and sufficient condition) is absent and where the hypothesized outcome occurred anyway, or where the sufficient condition (or the necessary and sufficient condition) is present and the hypothesized outcome did not result. If researchers are using participant observation to test a probabilistic theory (or to confirm a deterministic theory), they should try to select a representative case if at all possible.

Gaining Access

The next step involves acquiring permission to observe the group. If the research is covert, this step is not necessary. The person or persons responsible for granting researchers access to a group depends on the subject of the study. These individuals may be political, community, or religious leaders, military or police officials, union heads, bureaucrats, managers of online chat rooms, and so forth.

In order for researchers to convince this person to grant them permission to observe the group, researchers ought to furnish this person with a letter of introduction explaining the general purpose of their research and how long they would like to observe the group, and also proof of their affiliation and funding sources. In the letter of introduction, researchers should also explain in detail the procedures they have put in place to maintain the confidentiality and/or anonymity of the group they want to study, and the way that they intend to use the information they collect.

Once researchers have permission to study a group, they may still need the help of a gatekeeper to introduce them to individuals within the group. The gatekeeper should be someone who has many associates within the group and who will not alienate researchers from any subset of members within the group. The gatekeeper should not be someone who will cause members of the group to suspect that researchers have a certain agenda in their work due to their association with this person.

If, for example, the researcher is observing prison life, the gatekeeper should not be a member of a gang, who will alienate the gatekeeper from rival gang members. Likewise, if a researcher is analyzing the organizational cultures of firms that permit sexual harassment, the gatekeeper should not to be a person within the organization who has been vocal about gender-related issues.

Building Rapport

Gatekeepers only introduce researchers to members of the group. In order for researchers to convince individuals within the group to share information with them, researchers need to develop a rapport with them. Rapport is built over time. To develop a rapport with members of the group, researchers need to listen attentively to what individuals share with them without passing judgment on it, show respect for the group's language, customs and traditions,

*"I seem to be having a little difficulty getting
past your gatekeepers..."*

Cartoon 12.1

and demonstrate their ability to maintain the confidentiality of the information shared with them. The researcher must be mindful that their efforts do not come across to members of the group as fake or manipulative. Spending a significant amount of time with a group can also help to build rapport by demonstrating the genuineness of the researcher's interest in the group.

Observe Behaviors

When in the field, researchers will invariably have to make choices about whom to observe and what to observe about whom since they cannot observe every member of a group or every event. These choices can affect the conclusions that researchers draw from their research. Another researcher observing the same group, but a different set of people and events, might reach different conclusions. In order to produce the most complete representation of a group possible, researchers ought to observe as many different types of people within the group as possible.

Ideally, to do this, a researcher would use a nested sampling frame to select individuals to observe, choosing people randomly among categories of individuals and settings. However, this is not realistic. Many of the interactions researchers have with people in the field occur by chance, or through snowball sampling – that is, with individuals, including the gatekeeper, introducing the researcher to one person, who introduces the researcher to another person, and so on and so forth.

In participant observation, not just whom the researcher observes is important, but what the researcher observes about whom. Researchers should take notes not only of what is said between individuals, but what is not said between them, and what events do not occur. They should also pay heed to how things are said – the tone of voice used, as well as the emotions, facial expressions and body language conveyed.

Body language can provide researchers with important insights into people's unconscious thoughts. In order to interpret it properly, though, researchers must be very familiar with the culture of the group that they are studying since the meaning behind certain mannerisms can differ significantly across groups. Bulgarians, for example, nod their head up and down to indicate 'no', while in the rest of Europe and North America, people nod their head up and down to indicate 'yes'.

Researchers should also take note of the physical appearance of individuals, including their dress, and the physical environment in which activities occur. The latter may include the number of people present at an event, the location and time that an event or conversation occurs, and the condition of the location. If appropriate, the researcher may take photographs or videos of the location.

Recording Observations

Participant observation requires that researchers take copious notes. Taking notes openly and continuously in certain circumstances can be obtrusive and can trigger the guinea pig effect by reminding people that they are being studied. Openly recording a conversation or event can be equally problematic. In these circumstances, the best researchers can do is take brief notes in the moment, if possible, and write down in detail what they can recall in their field notes afterwards.

Typically, at first, researchers write down notes on everything they observe. Eventually, however, researchers tend to take notes more selectively as it becomes apparent to them what is important to record. It is important that in doing so, researchers do not ignore or neglect to record information that does not fit with any patterns that they think are already emerging from the data.

In addition to taking notes about what they observe, researchers should also take notes about what they think of what they observe. That is, researchers should record their impressions, opinions, and thoughts about the conversations and events that they witness, clearly distinguishing their empirical observations from their interpretation of them. This commentary will prove helpful in constructing the final analysis.

Prior to analyzing the data, some researchers ask their subjects whether or not their field notes accurately describe their beliefs and behaviors. This technique, referred to as 'respondent validity,' is controversial, and for good reason, because it allows respondents to change how events or conversations really occurred in order to fit with how they would like them to be seen in the world.

Analyzing Participant Observation Data

Ideally, researchers will not leave the field until they have reached a saturation point and are learning little, if anything, new from their observations. Once they do, they can begin in full their analysis of the data. The process of analyzing data from participant observation is very similar to the process of analyzing data collected from interviews and focus groups. The first step involves developing analytic categories with which to organize the researchers' observations. Since the goal of participant observation is usually to generate hypotheses, not to test hypotheses, these categories are typically developed inductively based on the researchers' field notes. These categories should include not only conversational data, as in the case of interviews and focus groups, but data on events as well. What these analytic categories are depends on the data. They may include types of events, interactions, reactions, attitudes, and so forth.

After researchers have defined these categories, and coded their data accordingly, researchers can begin to identify more systematically patterns or recurrent themes in the data. The final step is to interpret and explain these patterns. In the write up of the analysis, it is important that researchers, if they promised to keep the information that they collected confidential and/or anonymous, only describe people and places in general terms and use pseudonyms where necessary. In this process, researchers must be careful not to provide false or misleading information, either intentionally or unintentionally, as sociologist Alice Goffman learned the hard way in her first book, *On the Run: Fugitive Life in an American City*. In this book, Goffman describes how policing tactics in one low-income neighborhood in Philadelphia, known as '6th Street', created a climate of fear, distrust, and paranoia among African-American men in the neighborhood.

Unfortunately, inconsistencies in her account of 6th Street overshadowed the story of this neighborhood. Goffman claims that the inconsistencies arose from her efforts to protect the identities of her sources, while Goffman's critics claim that they are evidence that Goffman fabricated aspects of her account. In one such inconsistency a person named Chuck drove a family member to a court hearing despite having died two years earlier. Since Goffman promised members of 6th Street anonymity and destroyed her field notes to do so, doubts will always remain regarding the integrity of this work.

Key Points

- Participant observation lends itself well to hypothesis building because it allows researchers to observe their subjects in their own environment for a prolonged period of time.
- Participant observation is not suitable for hypothesis testing due to its single-case study design; the subjectivity of the interpretation of data collected through it; the lack of replicability; and the potential for researchers to change their subjects' behavior through it. The latter is also problematic for hypothesis building.
- The active versus passive and covert versus overt forms of participant observation have tradeoffs related to the depth and accuracy of the information acquired, and the subjects' right to privacy.

Further Reading

The first and third readings provide introductions to the method of participation observation and discuss practical issues and ethical concerns involved in it. The second and fourth readings discuss issues specific to marketing research and women.

Angrosino, Michael. 2008. *Doing Ethnographic and Observational Research*. London: Sage Publications.

Belk, Russell, Eileen Fischer, and Robert V. Kozinets. 2013. *Qualitative Consumer and Marketing Research*. London: Sage Publications.

Jorgensen, Danny L. 1989. *Participant Observation: A Methodology of Human Studies*. London: Sage Publications.

Mazzei, Julie and Erin E. O'Brien. 2009. 'You Got It, So When Do You Flaunt It? Building Rapport, Intersectionality, and the Strategic Deployment of Gender in the Field.' *Journal of Contemporary Ethnography* 38(3): 358–383.

EXERCISE 12.1

For one of the scenarios depicted below, design a study using participant observation. First, decide what it is you want to study, and second, what type of participant observation you will use (i.e., overt or covert and active or passive). Justify your decision based on what it is you want to learn from your study and what ethical concerns you have about any potential harm to your subjects and their right to privacy.

- An extremist organization's (encrypted) Telegram group.
- Customers in a trendy London coffee shop.
- LinkedIn accounts accessible to you because the account owners are members of the same LinkedIn Group that you joined using a fake account.
- Psychological support groups in which the rules for membership do not explicitly prohibit research but indicate that the forum is for mutual support and information sharing only.
- Facebook pages accessible to you as a friend of a friend.

EXERCISE 12.2

Compose your own field notes. Visit a public place for 15 minutes where you can both see and hear the activity that is taking place. Record the conversations you hear using your phone or an audio recorder, but do not write down anything while in the field. Then, leave the location, and immediately write down (without referring to your audio recording) what you observed about the environment and the conversations you heard, as well as your impressions of the conversations. Then, listen to the recording. How much of the conversations did you recall in your notes?

Now, return to the location, how well did your notes depict the physical environment of the place you visited? Identify the reasons why you think you did not document certain things in your field notes about the environment and the conversations you heard, and why you did others. Consider how you might improve your observation skills.

13

Process Tracing

Objectives

- describe the procedures and techniques involved in process tracing
- identify the standards used to evaluate the quality of evidence derived from process tracing
- discuss the limitations of process tracing for hypothesis testing

Process tracing is a qualitative research method used to evaluate causal processes within individual cases. In other words, it is a method used to test whether or not a certain explanatory factor produced a given outcome in a particular case. Process tracing is academic sleuthing. In a criminal investigation, an investigator specifies a priori the types of evidence that they expect to find if a person has committed a crime regarding a motivation for the crime and the opportunity and means to commit a crime, and then sets about looking for evidence of them. Process tracing works the same way.

In process tracing, researchers articulate hypotheses regarding phenomena likely to be observable if the relationship between two factors is causal, and then marshal evidence, which is largely historical in nature, to evaluate the validity of these hypotheses. They further evaluate alternative explanations through the same process of hypothesis generation and testing using this technique. While process tracing is used primarily to test existing theories, the failure to confirm theories can give rise to new explanations. Understanding the standards by which arguments are tested through this method also provides insight into how to construct arguments that can withstand similar scrutiny.

Process Tracing Techniques

Process tracing is used to evaluate causal processes in so-called *on-the-regression-line cases*. These are cases that are consistent with theoretical expectations. In other words, they are cases where the explanatory factor hypothesized to cause a given outcome is present and the outcome is produced. In these cases, researchers investigate the intervening processes by which the explanatory factor is argued to produce the outcome in order to determine if these processes unfolded in ways consistent with the argument. A theory may be evaluated against a single case or more than one case using process tracing. If it is evaluated against more than one case, the process tracing is carried out separately for each case.

The steps involved in process tracing are illustrated in Figure 13.1. The first step involves the researcher deriving hypotheses about what is likely to be true and observable if the explanatory variable caused the outcome variable as theorized. Typically, these hypotheses take the form of counterfactuals. *Counterfactuals* are conditional statements about the past in which an event is supposed (or imagined) to have occurred when it did not (or vice versa), and about what would have occurred in the past as a result. They take the form of 'If X had (not) occurred, then Y would (not) have occurred.'

'If Adolf Hitler had been accepted into the Academy of Fine Arts in Vienna, then the Second World War would not have occurred,' is an example of counterfactual. The statement theorizes about whether a past event – the Second World War – would have occurred had another event – Hitler being accepted into art school – that did not occur, happened. Hitler applied twice to the Academy of Fine Arts but was rejected each time.

Counterfactuals are distinct from hypothetical statements. *Hypotheticals* are statements about present conditions that do not exist and conjectures about the consequences that would result from them in the future if they did. Hypotheticals often take the form of 'What if' statements – such as 'What if X were to occur, then Y would not occur either'.

For example, 'What if Kim Jong-un were removed from power through a military coup d'état, would North Korea's nuclear weapons program slow down or cease to exist?' is an example of a hypothetical. It is a hypothetical, as opposed to a counterfactual,

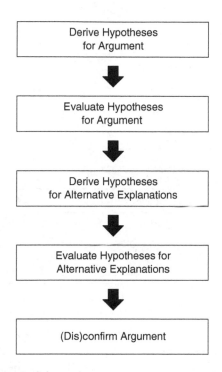

Figure 13.1 Steps in process training

since the event – the removal of Kim Jong-un from power – refers to a present condition that does not exist, and the effect of this condition on the future of nuclear weapons in North Korea.

In general, the purpose of counterfactuals is to understand the relative importance of a given factor in producing an outcome. The counterfactual above regarding Hitler is used to evaluate the pivotalness of Hitler and, more specifically, his rejection from art school to the Second World War. His rejection from art school is believed to have affected Hitler's personal psychology and his career path. However, as many scholars have pointed out, the Second World War would likely have occurred even if Hitler had been accepted into art school, because Hitler still would have been exposed to currents in German nationalism and anti-Semitism at the time, which contributed to his political ideologies and goals.

In process tracing, the purpose of counterfactuals is different. Their purpose is to identify phenomena likely to be evident in a particular case if an explanatory factor caused a given outcome as theorized. Table 13.1 illustrates in abstract terms the format and purpose of counterfactuals in process tracing.

If the explanatory factor *caused* the outcome variable then …

Hypothesis	Observation	Conclusion
X_1 would occur	X_1 occurred	support
Y_1 would occur	Y_1 occurred	support
Z_1 would not occur	Z_1 occurred	no support

If the explanatory factor *did not cause* the outcome variable then …

Hypothesis	Observation	Conclusion
X_2 would occur	X_2 did not occur	support
Y_2 would occur	Y_2 did not occur	support
Z_2 would not occur	Z_2 did not occur	no support

Table 13.1   Process tracing example

The top table depicts three hypotheses regarding what should have occurred if the explanatory variable *caused* the outcome variable. Two of these hypotheses (X_1 and Y_1) are about phenomena that should have occurred if the explanatory variable caused the outcome variable, and one of these hypotheses (Z_1) is about a phenomenon that should not have occurred if the explanatory variable caused the outcome variable. In the case of X_1 and Y_1, there is evidence that the associated phenomenon occurred in support of the argument, and in the case of Z_1, there is evidence that Z_1 occurred when it should not have occurred in contrast to the argument. Thus, only two of the hypotheses in the top panel support the argument.

The bottom table depicts three hypotheses regarding what to expect if the explanatory variable *did not* cause the outcome variable. X_2 and Y_2 are about phenomena that should have occurred if the explanatory variable did not cause the outcome variable, while Z_2 is about a phenomenon that should not have occurred if the explanatory variable did not cause the outcome variable. There is no evidence to suggest that X_2 and Y_2 occurred, so these two hypotheses support the argument that the explanatory variable caused the outcome variable. However, there is evidence to suggest that Z_2 did not occur and that the explanatory variable, therefore, did not cause the outcome variable. As in the top panel, two hypotheses in the bottom panel support the original argument and one does not.

After deriving hypotheses to test the argument, the next step in process tracing is to evaluate these hypotheses against the available evidence. Researchers may draw on many different types of qualitative or quantitative data to evaluate these hypotheses, including data derived from interviews, focus groups, documents, surveys, and so forth. The strengths and weaknesses of data derived from these methods are discussed in separate chapters. For some hypotheses, there may not be any data to support it. The absence of evidence, though, is not evidence of absence. In other words, the fact the researchers do not find evidence in support of a hypothesis does not mean that the hypothesis is not valid. The evidence to test this hypothesis may simply not exist or may not be available to the researcher.

After evaluating these hypotheses, the next step in process tracing involves deriving hypotheses to evaluate potential alternative explanations. (Note that researchers may choose to derive hypotheses for both their argument and the alternative explanations before evaluating either against the available data.) Alternative explanations imply that a given outcome was produced by a factor other than the one theorized, not that another factor contributed to (or caused) the outcome. The fact that another factor may have contributed to an outcome does not mean that the explanatory factor hypothesized to produce the outcome did not. In other words, an outcome may be produced by more than one factor or combination of factors, a phenomenon known as *equifinality*. Thus, only alternative explanations cast doubt on the validity of arguments.

In order to rigorously test an argument, researchers must consider the full range of plausible alternative explanations and openly and honestly evaluate their validity. Researchers ought not to interrogate alternative explanations more rigorously than they interrogate their own. That said researchers do not have to consider every possible alternative explanation for an argument, only those that are reasonable and/or prominent in the academic literature.

After deriving hypotheses to test the alternatives, the next step in process tracing is to evaluate these hypotheses against the available evidence. The final step in process tracing requires researchers to weigh the evidence for all of the hypotheses, including those for the argument and its alternatives, in order to draw an overall conclusion regarding the strength of the evidence in favor of the argument. This process is inherently subjective. In rendering their conclusion, researchers must consider not only the strength of the evidence in support of the hypotheses, but also the quality of the hypotheses. Researchers ought to give less weight in their conclusions to strong evidence in favor of weak hypotheses and weak evidence in favor of strong hypotheses, than strong evidence in favor of strong hypotheses.

Standards for the Evaluation of Evidence

Developing hypotheses to test causal processes is difficult, and not all hypotheses that researchers devise for this purpose are equally useful. Two criteria against which the quality of these hypotheses are evaluated are: their validity and their discriminatory power.[1] The two criteria are distinct. A hypothesis may have high validity and low discriminatory power, or vice versa. Validity and discriminatory power are two of the same criteria on which quantitative measures, which are discussed in Chapter 15, are evaluated.

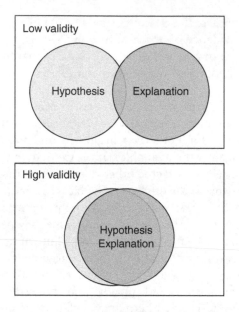

Figure 13.2   Hypothesis validity

Validity, in this context, refers to the extent to which a hypothesis is a good test of the relationship between the explanatory and outcome variables. It indicates how likely it is that if a hypothesis is true, that the explanatory variable caused the outcome variable. The concept of hypothesis validity is depicted in Figure 13.2. The hypothesis at the top has low validity because it only overlaps the explanation to a small extent, while the hypothesis at the bottom has high validity as it overlaps the explanation to a large extent. Hypotheses with high validity are more useful for evaluating causal arguments than hypotheses with low validity.

Discriminatory power refers to the extent to which a hypothesis distinguishes among competing (or alternative) explanations for a phenomenon. Hypotheses with higher discriminatory power are more useful for evaluating causal arguments than arguments with low discriminatory power. The concept of discriminatory power is depicted in Figure 13.3. The hypothesis depicted in the image on the top has low discriminatory power as it overlaps two explanations – the one theorized to affect the outcome and an alternative explanation for the outcome, while the image on the bottom has high discriminatory power as it only overlaps the explanation. In this illustration, the hypothesis with high discriminatory power favors the explanation, but it is possible for a hypothesis with high discriminatory power to favor the alternative explanation instead.

Process Tracing in Practice

To further elucidate the technique of process tracing and the concepts of validity and discriminatory power using a real-world example, the two concepts are applied below to an analysis of why no bankers in the United States were imprisoned for their behaviors leading

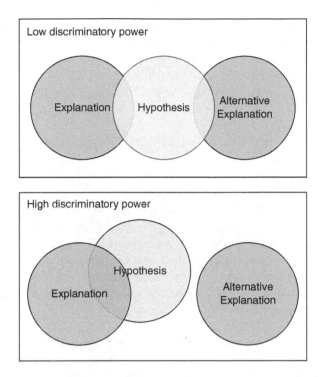

Figure 13.3 Hypothesis discriminatory power

to the global financial crisis. The United States is not alone in its failure to put its bankers behind bars. In fact, Iceland and Ireland are the only countries to have jailed bankers in relation to the financial crisis. The explanation for this puzzle, which is evaluated below through process tracing, is the following:

> There are no bankers imprisoned in the US for actions resulting in the global financial crisis, because the US government feared that bringing charges against the bankers would have a further negative impact on the global economy.

There are many hypotheses that one might derive that are consistent with this argument. Below are four hypotheses that vary in the extent to which they are high in validity and discriminatory power. If no bankers were imprisoned in the US for the reason hypothesized above, then ...

Hypothesis 1: ... US bankers would have made reckless and unwise investment decisions that caused the global financial crisis.

Hypothesis 1 has low validity and low discriminatory power because it does not indicate that the bankers' actions were illegal and prosecutable in court, or that the government had any intentions about prosecuting the bankers that were not based on the illegality of the bankers' actions and their likely conviction in court. In the US, for the bankers' actions to have been illegal, the bankers had to have had an intention to deceive. This makes it difficult to prosecute them under US criminal law. An important alternative explanation for the lack of bankers jailed in the US is the difficulty of prosecuting them under US law.

> **Hypothesis 2:** ... the government would not have brought charges against any bankers.

Hypothesis 2 has medium-to-high validity because it must be true that the government did not bring charges against the bankers (and not that the government brought charges against the bankers but failed to successfully prosecute them), for the prosecutors to have been motivated by fears of the economic repercussions of prosecuting them. The prosecutors' fears related to bringing cases against the bankers, not to putting them in jail. Hypothesis 2 has low discriminatory power because there are many reasons, including the prosecutors' expectations of not winning the cases, which can explain why the government did not bring charges against any bankers in court.

> **Hypothesis 3:** ... any written or verbal communications by those in the government with the authority to prosecute the bankers should indicate that they had concerns about the economic repercussions of bringing cases against the bankers.

Hypothesis 3 only has medium validity because any communications indicating that the government had concerns about the economic repercussions of prosecuting the bankers does not indicate that these concerns were factors that they considered when deciding whether or not to prosecute the bankers. Government officials may also have had such concerns, and these concerns may have driven the government's decision not to prosecute the bankers, but they may not have voiced them. Hypothesis 3 has high discriminatory power because concerns regarding the economy are not consistent with any other alternative explanations for why there are no US bankers in jail for their role in the global financial crisis.

> **Hypothesis 4:** ... any written or verbal communications by those with the authority to prosecute the bankers, should indicate that they had concerns about the economic repercussions of bringing cases against the bankers, and that despite what they believe was sufficient evidence to successfully prosecute the bankers, they were not going to pursue charges against the bankers because they feared that the economy would suffer further as a result.

Hypothesis 4 has high discriminatory power since concerns regarding the economy are not consistent with any other alternative explanations for the lack of bankers incarcerated in the United States. Hypothesis 4 also has high validity because, unlike Hypothesis 3, the communications indicate that the officials were motivated by these concerns.

Each of these hypotheses focuses on the main argument regarding the economic motivations of government officials for not prosecuting bankers for the global financial crisis, and what one would expect to observe if this argument is true. A fuller account of how process tracing works would also include hypotheses about what one expects not to see evidence of if the original argument is true. It would also include a rigorous interrogation of alternative explanations, such as the high bar that US law requires of evidence regarding intent to have successfully prosecuted the bankers.

Another example of how process tracing works is presented in Box 13.1. It does not test any alternative explanations for the outcome either, but it does discuss the availability of evidence for each of the hypotheses, which the previous example did not.

Box 13.1   Process Tracing Example: Taking Responsibility for Cyberattacks

Governments are increasingly using cyberattacks, trolls, and internet propaganda to achieve their international political goals. On 24–25 May 2017, the Al Jazeera Media Network was hacked. In information released from the hack, the Emir of Qatar described 'tensions' with President Trump, recommended a friendship with Iran, praised Hamas, and attested to his own 'good' relations with Israel. The US Federal Bureau of Investigation (FBI) concluded that the leaked information was false and that private Russian hackers were responsible for the hack on Al Jazeera's network. The Emir of Qatar claimed that Saudi Arabia and the United Arab Emirates (UAE) most likely commissioned the hack to discredit him. Following the hack, the UAE, Saudi Arabia, and a number of other countries severed diplomatic and trade ties with Qatar.

If Saudi Arabia and the UAE were responsible for the hack, then …

Hypothesis 1: … the leaked information ought to have been seen as representative of the Qatari government.

Hypothesis 1 has low validity because although it is true that for the hacked information to justify action against all of Qatar, the hacked information would have to have been attributed to the government, the hypothesis does not include information about the content of the hacked information, and whether it could justify a negative reaction from Saudi Arabia and the UAE. Hypothesis 1 has low discriminatory power as well because the hypothesis cannot rule out alternative arguments that other countries, or private hackers within Saudi Arabia and the UAE, engineered the hack in order to increase tensions between the countries. Nonetheless, there is clear evidence for this hypothesis since the Emir is the supreme authority of Qatar and the hacked information was attributed to him.

Hypothesis 2: … there ought to have been tensions between Qatar and Saudi Arabia and the UAE in order for Saudi Arabia and the UAE to have had a motivation to harm Qatar.

(Continued)

(Continued)

Hypothesis 2 has high validity because Saudi Arabia and the UAE have no other reason to have requisitioned the hack. Hypothesis 2 has low discriminatory power, however, because it also cannot rule out alternative arguments that other countries, or private hackers within Saudi Arabia and the UAE, engineered the hack in order to increase tensions between the countries. There is strong evidence in support of this hypothesis. Qatar and Saudi Arabia were on opposing sides in the conflicts in Egypt, Libya, and Syria, and Qatar had friendly ties at the time with Saudi Arabia's regional foe, Iran. The UAE also wanted news outlets seen as critical of the Gulf monarchies, such as the Qatari funded Al Jazeera, to be closed down.

Hypothesis 3: … the issues that Saudi Arabia and the UAE had with Qatar ought to have been advanced through information released in the hack, and/or through the punishment that Saudi Arabia and the UAE imposed on Qatar as a result of the hacked information.

Hypothesis 3 has high validity because it gives Saudi Arabia and the UAE a strong motivation for the hack. Hypothesis 3 has low discriminatory power, however, because it cannot rule out the possibility that other countries, or private hackers, engineered the hack to increase tensions between the countries. There is only partial evidence in support of this hypothesis. The UAE and Saudi Arabia made the blockade contingent on changes in Qatar's behavior that are consistent with differences among the countries and are unrelated in some cases to the hacked information. Among other things, the UAE wanted Qatar to sever its ties with Egypt's Muslim Brotherhood, Hamas, and Iran. The hacked information did not mention Egypt or the Muslim Brotherhood.

Hypothesis 4: … there ought to be direct evidence linking the government of Saudi Arabia and the UAE to the Russian hackers, such as a bank transfer or an admission by the hackers of who hired them.

Hypothesis 4 has high validity and high discriminatory power. It has high validity because it would directly tie Saudi Arabia and the UAE to the hack. Hypothesis 4 has high discriminatory power as well since it would rule out arguments that other countries or private individuals were responsible for the hack. Evidence for this hypothesis is weak. Qatar only reported having evidence of the mobile telephones used in the hack linked to Saudi Arabia and the UAE, but not to the government.

Hypothesis 5: … the hack should have allowed Saudi Arabia and the UAE to achieve certain political goals unique to them.

Hypothesis 5 has medium-to-high validity because it provides a motivation for the attack. Hypothesis 5 also has medium-to-high discriminatory power since it makes it less likely that other countries engineered the hacks, but not private hackers within these countries. The evidence for this hypothesis is modest. The hacked information was consistent with the political goals of the UAE and Saudi Arabia of driving a wedge between Qatar and the US and between Qatar and Hamas, and these goals were arguably specific to the UAE and/or

Saudi Arabia at the time. However, the hack did not clearly offer Saudi Arabia and the UAE support from other countries for these goals, which they would not have had anyway had they imposed the blockade without the pretext of the hack.

Hypothesis 6: … there should be information that the hack was only a pretext, not the real motivation for the blockade.

Hypothesis 6 has medium-to-high validity because it explains why Saudi Arabia and the UAE would have wanted to engineer the hack. Hypothesis 6 has low-to-medium discriminatory power because, although it explains the potential motivation of the UAE and Saudi Arabia for the hack, the UAE and Saudi Arabia may have used the hack as a pretext to punish Qatar but were not responsible for the hack themselves. Evidence in support of this hypothesis is strong. Even after the FBI confirmed that the hacked information was fake, Saudi Arabia and the UAE kept the blockade in place.

Conclusion: It is very likely that Saudi Arabia and the UAE were responsible for the hack against Al Jazeera.

Limitations of Process Tracing

Process tracing is limited in its ability to confirm or disconfirm a theory by its subjectivity and single case study design. Process tracing provides clear metrics regarding how to evaluate the quality of a hypothesis in terms of its validity and discriminatory power. However, the extent to which hypotheses meet these criteria, and the extent to which evidence is deemed to support a given hypothesis or not, is open to interpretation. One researcher using his or her own judgment may consider a hypothesis to be a strong test of a theory and the evidence in support of it to be equally strong, while another researcher, using his or her own judgment, may not.

Consider Hypothesis 5 in Box 13.1. It is rated as medium-to-high in terms of its validity and discriminatory power. Another researcher might consider this hypothesis to have high validity and high discriminatory power because this hypothesis requires the political goals of Saudi Arabia and the UAE to be unique to them. Another researcher might also see the evidence in support of Hypothesis 5 as moderately strong, rather than weak, because this researcher thinks that Saudi Arabia and the UAE might not have had the support of other countries for a blockade had they not had a pretext for it.

Process tracing also lacks clear metrics about how to reach an ultimate conclusion regarding an argument based on all the hypotheses and all of the alterative explanations tested in the analysis. Is it sufficient to conclude that there is strong support for an argument if nearly all of the hypotheses related to the argument support it and nearly all of the hypotheses related to the alternative explanation do not support it, even if all the hypotheses only have low-to-medium validity? What if only half of the hypotheses for the argument support the argument, but they all have high validity?

There are also no rules in process tracing regarding how researchers ought to deal with the absence of evidence in the conclusions that they draw, although this is also not a problem unique to process tracing. Information may not exist in support of a hypothesis because the hypothesis is not valid, or because the information needed to substantiate the hypothesis is simply not observable. This information may be unobservable because it has not been documented, or because it is confidential, as in the case of communications regarding whether or not to prosecute US bankers for crimes leading to the global financial crisis.

Consider again the example in Box 13.1. Half of all the hypotheses in this example have strong evidence in support of them, but only two of these hypotheses have high validity and none have high discriminatory power. Based on this information, is it fair to conclude, as the example does, that it is 'very likely' that Saudi Arabia and the UAE engineered the attacks? Or, would 'likely' as opposed to 'very likely' be a more appropriate characterization?

Reaching an overall conclusion regarding the validity of an argument in process tracing is made all the more difficult by the fact that researchers have discretion over how many hypotheses to test in the first place, and may intentionally or unintentionally fail to consider hypotheses that are likely to cast doubt on their argument, and more likely to derive hypotheses that are likely to substantiate their argument. (This issue is not unique to process tracing, however. In observational studies, for example, researchers may not include variables in a model that they expect to suppress results supporting their argument.) Researchers using process tracing may also derive more hypotheses when they do not find evidence in support of their initial hypotheses, and fewer hypotheses when they do, so that in the end, there are more hypotheses that support their argument than there are hypotheses that do not.

Even if process tracing were to provide incontrovertible evidence in support of an argument, the conclusions that one can draw about a theory in general are limited by the single case design of process tracing. Process tracing can only speak to the validity of an argument in a single case. It cannot speak to the validity of this argument more generally because the one case evaluated using this method is not necessarily representative of other cases. A single case study, as discussed in Chapter 9, can only disconfirm a deterministic theory specifying necessary conditions or sufficient conditions (or necessary and sufficient conditions), and only when outcomes consistent with this theory resulted in the absence of the necessary conditions, or did not result in the presence of sufficient ones.

Key Points

- Process tracing facilitates the identification of causal mechanisms through the development and evaluation of counterfactuals about phenomena likely to be true if a given factor caused another.
- Counterfactuals are useful to the extent that they are likely to be true if the explanatory variable caused the outcome variable and can discriminate among alternative explanations.

- The absence of evidence in support of a counterfactual does not mean a counterfactual is not true. The evidence may simply not be available.
- Process tracing is limited in its ability to (dis)confirm theories due to its subjectivity and single case study design.

Further Reading

The first and second readings provide comprehensive introductions to the technique of process tracing, discuss its limitations and applications, and provide concrete and practical information regarding how to conduct process tracing. The third reading outlines the attributes of useful counterfactuals.

Beach, Derek. 2013. *Process-tracing Methods: Foundations and Guidelines*. Ann Arbor: University of Michigan Press.
Bennett, Andrew and Jeffrey T. Checkel, eds. 2015. *Process Tracing: From Metaphor to Analytic Too*. New York: Cambridge University Press.
Fearon, James D. 1991. 'Counterfactuals and Hypothesis Testing in Political Science.' *World Politics* 43(2): 169–195.

EXERCISE 13.1

Use process tracing to test the validity of one of the following arguments below. For each example, identify at least three to four hypotheses that must be true (or must be false) if the argument is true; indicate the level of validity and discriminatory power of each hypothesis; and assess the evidence in favor of the hypothesis. For each example, repeat the process for the main alternative explanation provided. Then, make a judgment as to whether the argument or the alternative explanation provides a more compelling explanation for the outcome, and explain why. Finally, discuss the limitations of using process tracing to evaluate the validity of the argument and its alternative.

1. Brexit

    Argument: The primary reason that the British voted in 2016 to leave the European Union was Prime Minister David Cameron's misplaced confidence in the likelihood of the British electorate voting to remain within the European Union and his failure, as a result, to spearhead a vigorous campaign to remain within the Union.

    Alternative: The primary reason the British voted to leave the European Union was the British people's strong and enduring sense of nationalism.

2. Marketing Brand Extension

    Argument: High-end luxury brands profit when they extend their brands to adjacent product categories (e.g., from jewelry to watches) because the premium degree of the brand (i.e., the extent to which customers perceive a brand as offering more quality than comparable offerings and are willing to pay a premium price for it) transfers undiminished to adjacent product categories.

    Alternative: High-end luxury brands profit when they extend their brands into adjacent categories, not because consumers believe that the new product offers them more quality than comparable offerings, but because adjacent brands are also luxury items with a reputation of elitism and exclusivity.

3. North Korea Military Program

    Argument: In recent years, displays of North Korea's military power, including parades, nuclear tests, and ballistic missile launches, are indicative of Kim Jong-un's fear of a coup d'état, and not his aggressive intentions towards neighboring states.

    Alternative: Recent displays of North Korea's military power are motivated by international, not domestic, geo-political goals that are furthered by a demonstration of North Korea's military strength abroad.

4. Education and Course Evaluations

    Argument: The publication of course evaluations online results in higher course evaluations because it increases the pressure on faculty to use information from the evaluations to improve their courses, and incentivizes competition among faculty to earn the highest evaluations in their department.

    Alternative: The publication of course evaluations online results in higher course evaluations because students use the evaluations to sort themselves into courses for which they are likely to be most satisfied.

EXERCISE 13.2

Follow the instructions in Exercise 13.1 to conduct process tracing on your own research, or an example of research of your own choosing within your academic discipline.

Comparative Case Method

Objectives

- define and describe different comparative case study methods
- present the advantages and disadvantages of Mill's method of difference and method of agreement for hypothesis building and hypothesis testing
- discuss the advancements that nested-case designs and qualitative comparative analysis (QCA) offer over Mill's methods

The *comparative case method* is an umbrella term that refers to a set of qualitative research techniques used for both theory building and theory testing involving comparisons between and among classes of events, otherwise known as cases. These techniques include the two workhorses of the comparative case method – the method of difference and the method of agreement – as well as two others – nested case designs and qualitative comparative analysis (QCA). The approach shared by these techniques involves isolating either similarities or differences between or among cases in order to construct or validate theories about generalizable phenomena. The latter two methods overcome some of the shortcomings of the method of difference and method of agreement – namely their inability to identify complex and multi-causal relationships, their high potential for omitted variable bias, and their limited generalizability, but like all comparative case methods, they are limited to deterministic relationships.

Method of Difference

The method of difference, which was developed in the nineteenth century by John Stuart Mill along with its counterpart the method of agreement, identifies causal relationships by isolating similarities across cases to explain divergent outcomes. To be more specific, in the *method of difference*, cases are compared in which the outcome is different. The cases are alike in terms of all factors, except for one, that may potentially explain the different outcomes. The factor that is different between the two is the one, according to this method, responsible for the divergent outcomes.

The method of difference is illustrated in Table 14.1. In this example, two cases are compared in terms of three different factors that are potentially related to the outcome. Only one factor, Factor A, varies between the two cases, and therefore, is the only factor that could be related to the divergent outcome.

Table 14.2 illustrates the method of difference using the occurrence of transnational terrorist attacks in Europe in the first 15 years following the 2001 World Trade Center attacks. Transnational terrorist attacks are defined as acts of violence perpetrated against civilians in one country by governments or non-state actors of another country or acts committed in their name. These attacks marked the beginning of a new age of global

Case	Factor A	Factor B	Factor C	Outcome
Case 1	present	present	present	result
Case 2	absent	present	present	no result

Table 14.1 Method of difference

Case	Counterterrorism strategies	Region	Afghanistan and Iraq invasions	Transnational terrorism
UK	moderate	Europe	military support	attacks
Italy	strong	Europe	military support	no attacks

Table 14.2 Method of difference example

terrorism. In this example, Italy is compared to the UK. The UK experienced a number of attacks in this period, while Italy did not experience any despite the presence of terrorist cells in the country. One of the terrorists responsible for the 2016 London Bridge bombings was even an Italian national.

Two factors that make countries likely to experience transnational terrorist attacks are geography and international involvement in other countries (Pape 2003; Savun and Phillips 2009). Both Italy and the UK are located in Europe, which is in close proximity to the Middle East and North Africa (MENA), where most transnational terrorist activity has originated in the post-9/11 period. Both the UK and Italy also supported the US invasion of Afghanistan in 2001 and the US invasion of Iraq less than two years later. The invasions have provided a focal point around which terrorist actors in MENA have recruited supporters. The fact that the UK and Italy are alike in terms of these two factors eliminates them as explanations for the variation in transnational terrorist acts in the two states.

One difference between the two cases that can explain this variation is the strength of the countries' counterterrorism programs. Typically, democracies are more vulnerable to transnational terrorism due to their strong civil and political rights protections (Eubank and Weinberg 1994; Li 2005). Italy, however, is much less constrained than the UK in this regard. The Italian government has robust and wide-ranging counterterrorism powers arising from its history of combating the mafia.[1] They include broad powers to coordinate intelligence and law enforcement forces, to intercept communications, and to convince suspected terrorists to break ranks and cooperate with Italian authorities through the use of residency permits and other incentives.

The larger theory, which the comparison of these two cases suggests, is that weak counterinsurgency efforts are the reason for transnational terrorist attacks in countries (Art and Richardson 2007). The case comparison further suggests that counterterrorism measures that do not curtail political and civil rights, but that emphasize intelligence gathering, cooperation and coordination are effective in combating terrorism (Kydd and Walter 2006; Lum et al. 2006). Experience with the mafia is the specific reason why Italy adopted certain counterinsurgency tactics, but is not the theory itself, because it is too narrow. There may be many reasons besides organized crime that countries have this type of counterterrorist strategy, and many countries that have problems with organized crime do not necessarily have these strategies.

As is quickly apparent through this example, a significant weakness of the method of difference is that it assumes that the relationship between the explanatory factor and outcome is deterministic. According to the method of difference, in a two-case comparison where the outcome is produced in one case and not the other, the explanatory factor that is present where the outcome is produced (and not present where the outcome is not produced) is deemed sufficient to produce the outcome. This factor may also be necessary but this cannot be discerned from this two-case comparison, because it cannot be observed whether or not the outcome is only produced when this explanatory factor is present. The other variables in the comparison may also be necessary to produce the outcome, but not be sufficient. However, this too cannot be discerned from this comparison. It is further possible that the explanatory factor is not sufficient to produce the outcome, but simply makes the outcome more likely to occur because it cannot be observed from this two-case comparison if the outcome is always produced when the explanatory variable is present.

In this example, since Italy did not experience a terrorist attack while the UK did, robust counterinsurgency measures are considered sufficient to prevent transnational terrorism. However, a comparison with Greece indicates that these tactics are not necessary to prevent a terrorist attack, since Greece had poor counterterrorism strategies, as explained further below, and ones different from Italy's, and yet did not experience an attack. Moreover, a comparison with Spain suggests that they are also not sufficient, but only make transnational terrorism less likely. Spain has fairly similar counterterrorism measures as Italy at the time but experienced a massive terrorist attack in Barcelona in 2017.

The method of difference cannot handle complex relationships among variables either, as when one variable only causes an outcome conditional on other variables. Strong counterinsurgency tactics, for example, or particular types of counterinsurgency tactics, may be necessary to prevent terrorist tactics in the post-9/11 period, but only in countries where the threat of transnational terrorism is high due to a country's proximity to the Middle East and North Africa, where most transnational terrorist attacks originated in this period, or foreign intervention in the region. In a country like Chile, which is not located near MENA and which did not participate in the invasions of Afghanistan and Iraq, these tactics were not necessary to prevent a transnational terrorist attack in this period because the threat of an attack was low in the first place.

The comparison of the UK and Italy also makes apparent the difficulty of matching cases on all relevant factors and the potential for omitted variable bias in the method of difference. There are a number of other factors that were different between Italy and the UK in this period that could have made one or the other country more likely to have experienced a transnational terrorist attack. Only those factors that made the UK more likely to experience transnational terrorist attacks, though, pose a challenge to the theory identified above. One such factor is the size of the UK's second-generation MENA immigrant population. It is larger than Italy's and provides a base of potential recruits for transnational terrorist groups (Leiken 2012).

Whether or not cases match on any given dimension is also subjective and controvertible. Both Italy and the UK supported the invasions of Afghanistan and Iraq. However, the UK's commitment was greater than Italy's commitment. Italy initially opposed the invasion of Iraq and pulled its troops out of Iraq years earlier than the UK. As a result, the UK's engagement in Afghanistan and Iraq may have been more likely to incite a terrorist attack as a result.

Another shortcoming of the method of difference is its sensitivity to case selection. A comparison of another set of cases could yield a different conclusion. This problem is illustrated in Table 14.3.

Greece is compared to the UK using the method of difference in Table 14.3. The comparison of Greece to the UK indicates that Italy's counterterrorism strategy is neither a necessary nor a sufficient condition for countries to avoid transnational terrorist attacks, although it might have made them less likely. Greece, like Italy and unlike the UK, did not

Case	Counterterrorism strategies	Region	Afghanistan and Iraq invasions	Transnational terrorism
UK	moderate	Europe	military support	attacks
Greece	poor	Europe	no or limited military support	no attacks

Table 14.3 Sensitivity of method of difference to case selection

experience a transnational terrorist attack in the first 15 years of the War on Terrorism. Instead, it served as a major transit hub in this period for those who committed terrorist acts in other European countries.

In this example, there are two dimensions in which Greece and the UK do not match and, thus, two viable explanations for the difference between the two cases – the countries' counterterrorism strategies and their military support for the invasions of Afghanistan and Iraq. Greece had very poor counterterrorism abilities in the first 15 years after 9/11, and offered only limited support for the Iraq and Afghanistan invasions. While Greece deployed troops to Afghanistan, it outwardly opposed the US invasion of Iraq in 2003. It also did not directly participate militarily in the NATO and US-led coalition against the Islamic State in the Middle East and North Africa, which was active in these two countries.

The fact that the cases do not match on more than one dimension is not problematic in this example of the method of difference because Greece's weaker counterterrorist strategies made it more likely to have experienced a counterterrorist attack, and yet, it did not. The comparison between Greece and the UK suggests that countries' foreign intervention in the domestic politics of other states in the MENA region explains why some states were more vulnerable to transnational terrorist attacks in the early post-9/11 period than others.

Method of Agreement

In contrast to the method of difference, in the *method of agreement*, the outcome is the same in the cases compared, while the explanatory variables are different across cases, except for the one factor believed to cause the outcome. The method of agreement is illustrated in Table 14.4. In this example, the two cases are compared in terms of three

Case	Factor A	Factor B	Factor C	Outcome
Case 1	present	absent	present	result
Case 2	present	present	absent	result

Table 14.4 Method of agreement

Case	Unemployment	Protest culture	Confidence in government	Protest
Romania	5.3%	moderate	<25%	protest
South Korea	3–4%	high	<25%	protest

Table 14.5   Method of agreement example

different factors. Only one factor, Factor A, is the same between the two cases, and therefore, is the only factor that could be related to the outcome.

Table 14.5 illustrates the method of agreement using the example of the massive anti-government corruption protests that occurred in South Korea and Romania in the second decade of this century. These protests were the largest mass demonstrations either country experienced since they democratized decades earlier, with estimates of protesters numbering in the hundreds of thousands daily.

The two countries differ from each other in terms of a number of factors that are hypothesized to affect the likelihood of protests. In South Korea, protests are much more common than in Romania, and almost a way of life in the country, according to experts.[2] The protests in the two countries were also triggered by different events. In Romania, the protests were precipitated by an emergency ordinance that decriminalized offenses for damages below 44,000 euros. At the time, hundreds of Romanian politicians were in prison for government corruption and thousands were still under investigation. The protesters demanded that the law be rescinded, and it was following the protests.

The South Korean protests occurred, meanwhile, in response to incontrovertible media reports that President Park Geun-hye shared confidential government documents with her close friend, the daughter of a religious cult leader. These documents allowed the friend to extort large sums of money from Korean business conglomerates. The protesters demanded that the president step down. Geun-hye refused but South Korea's National Assembly ultimately impeached her and removed her from power.

The socio-economic context in which these triggering events occurred was also different. At the time, Romania had a higher unemployment rate than South Korea. Employment, and youth unemployment in particular, is associated with a higher likelihood of protests because the unemployed are more aggrieved, and because young people are socially more active (Reiss and Perry 2011; Brancati 2016). In South Korea, in the months prior to the protests, the overall unemployment rate ranged between 3–4 percent and youth unemployment was approximately 8–9 percent (25–29 year olds), according to KOSTAT.[3] In Romania, in the months prior to the protests, the overall unemployment rate was higher, ranging between 5–6 percent, according to EUROSTAT.[4] The youth unemployment rate was still higher. It was over 20 percent (15–24 year olds).

Although the two countries are different in terms of their protest cultures and unemployment rates, South Korea and Romania are similar to each other in terms of their long-standing distrust of their national governments, which extends far beyond the issue of corruption. According to the Gallup World Poll, in South Korea, only about quarter of the population in the five years leading up to the protests had 'confidence in the national government', while in Romania less than a quarter of the population did in the five years leading up to the protests in this country.[5] The comparison of these two countries, thus, suggests that a widespread lack of confidence (of which corruption is only one component) in national political institutions provides the basis for anti-corruption protests.

Like the method of difference, the method of agreement assumes that the relationship between the explanatory and outcome variables is deterministic. According to the method of agreement, in a two-case comparison where the outcome is produced in both cases, the explanatory factor that takes on the same value in both cases is deemed necessary to produce the outcome. This factor may also be sufficient but this cannot be discerned from this two-case comparison, because it cannot be observed from it whether there are cases in which the outcome is not produced and the necessary condition is present. The other variable in the comparison may also be sufficient to produce the outcome, but not necessary since the outcome is produced in the absence of them. However, this too cannot be discerned from this comparison.

It is further possible that the explanatory factor is not necessary to produce the outcome, but only makes the outcome more likely to occur because it cannot be observed from this two-case comparison if the outcome is produced when the explanatory variable is not present. In this example, since protests occurred in both Romania and South Korea, a lack of confidence in the government is considered necessary for anti-corruption protests to occur. However, a comparison of either country to Russia, where anti-corruption protests occurred in the same year but where confidence in the government was high, as explained further below, makes apparent that it is not necessary for protests to occur, but perhaps only makes them more likely to occur.

The method of agreement also cannot handle complex relationships among variables, such as interaction effects, where one variable only causes an outcome conditional on other variables. It is possible, for example, that a lack of confidence in the government would not result in protests if there were not also at least a moderate culture of protest, as in Romania and South Korea, or a moderate or high level of democracy in these countries, which permits people to organize collectively.

The method of agreement also faces the same challenges as the method of difference regarding matching cases on all the relevant theoretical dimensions. Another factor not considered in this example is the history of corruption in Romania and South Korea. Both countries have long histories of corruption and for years prior to the protests, they ranked very similarly on Transparency International's Corruption Perceptions Index.[6] The emergency ordinance in the case of Romania and the breach in confidentiality in the case of South Korea may have been the immediate causes of the protests, but these countries' long histories of corruption are likely to be the underlying cause of the protests.

Not only is it difficult to match cases on all theoretically relevant variables, but what constitutes a match is not incontrovertible. It is not obvious, for example, whether South Korea and Romania are sufficiently different in terms of unemployment to rule out this explanation for the protests. In Romania, the overall unemployment rate is higher than in South Korea, but it is calculated slightly differently than in South Korea, and youth unemployment is based

Case	Unemployment	Protest culture	Confidence in government	Democracy (0–10)	Protest
Romania	5.3%	moderate	<25%	9	protest
Russia	5.7%	weak	≥60%	4	protest

Table 14.6   Sensitivity of method of agreement to case selection

on a different age range. The natural rate of unemployment is also different for the two states since South Korea is much more economically advanced than Romania.

The method of agreement is also sensitive to case selection like the method of difference. Comparing the Romanian protests to anti-corruption protests that occurred in Russia only a few months after the Romanian protests illustrates this shortcoming. Table 14.6 depicts the comparison between the Romanian and Russian protests.

In this example, Romania and Russia are different in terms of their protest culture, public confidence in the government, and levels of democracy. Russia is not a democracy like Romania and severely restricted public demonstrations after the 2011–12 democracy protests. The protest culture was also arguably weaker in Russia than Romania. The 2017 anti-corruption protests were the first major protests in Russia since the 2011–12 anti-electoral fraud protests. Public confidence in the government was also much higher in Russia than in Romania. Thus, according to the method of agreement, neither of these factors can explain why both countries experienced anti-corruption protests in 2017.

The comparison of Russia and Romania suggests that unemployment is the cause of anti-corruption protests rather than a lack of public confidence in the government. Both Russia and Romania have very similar unemployment rates and both experienced protests. However, this conclusion is likely an artifact of the particular cases compared. An unemployment rate of 5–6 percent is modest.[7] The youth unemployment rate in Russia was even lower than in Romania prior to the protests. It was approximately 15 percent (15–24 year olds). Moreover, further research into the individual cases finds no evidence to suggest that unemployment was related to the anti-corruption protests in either country.[8]

Nested Case Designs

A nested case design offers one potential solution to the challenge of matching cases along all relevant dimensions and reducing the likelihood of omitted variable bias in the method of difference. A *nested case design*, as the name suggests, involves the analysis of two or more cases that are categories of another case. The cases may be different events (e.g., protests, wars, or elections) that occur within the same country, for example, or different members of the same organization (e.g., corporation, government, school, or organization).

A nested case design can help address issues regarding matching cases and omitted variable bias because the cases compared are subject to many of the same conditions present in the larger case to which they belong. Events, for example, that occur within the same countries are exposed to the same type of political regime, while members of the same organization are subject to the same organizational norms and policies. Since these factors are exactly the same across cases, they cannot explain why the outcome varies across cases using the method of difference. A nested case design is only appropriate for the method of difference because it holds variables constant across cases. The method of agreement requires all factors, except the causal one, to vary instead across cases.

The previous example of transnational terrorism is an example of a nested case design. All three countries analyzed – the UK, Italy, and Greece – are countries nested within Europe. Due to their geographic proximity to the Middle East and North Africa, where many post-9/11 terrorist groups are active, all three states are similarly vulnerable to terrorist attacks. The UK is located further from MENA than Italy and Greece. However, the UK experienced terrorist attacks in the first 15 years after 9/11 while Italy and Greece did not, ruling geographic proximity out as an explanation for transnational terrorism in this period.

A nested case design may also reduce the likelihood that unknown or unobserved heterogeneity will confound the results. Researchers may not be aware of all the factors that might be causally related to the outcome. However, if the cases compared are categories of another larger case, they may be similar along these other factors as well, ruling them out as potential explanations for the outcome. Another factor that the UK, Italy, and Greece are similar in terms of and that may be related to the incidence of terrorism, but that is controlled for in a nested case design, is the counterterrorism strategies of the European Union.

While nested case designs provide traction on one issue, they lose ground on another. Nested research designs are potentially less generalizable than non-nested designs because the cases compared are categories of another case, which may not be representative of other cases. Consider again the example of post-9/11 transnational terrorism. The conclusion drawn from the comparison of the UK and Greece was that foreign intervention in the MENA region sparks transnational terrorism. Foreign intervention may not provoke terrorism in general, however, but only the type of intervention that the UK engaged in along with the US and its allies in Afghanistan and Iraq. The Afghan and Iraq invasions eviscerated these countries' states and created political vacuums where weak and fractionalized insurgents vied for power and sought support for their goals through transnational terrorism.

Qualitative Comparative Analysis (QCA)

Qualitative Comparative Analysis (QCA), and the many variants of it (e.g., csQCA, MvQCA, fsQCA, and fuzzy sets), offer a number of advantages over Mill's methods of difference and agreement, which are different from that which nested case designs offer (Ragin 1987).

The findings from QCA are more likely to be generalizable than those produced from either approach because the number of cases included in QCA analyses is much greater. QCA also allows researchers to identify complex relationships among explanatory factors and multiple paths to the same outcome (Mahoney 2010). Several standalone programs, as well as various tools within major software packages, exist to conduct QCA where the number of cases is large and the combinations of variables across cases is complex.

In order to demonstrate the advantages of QCA, the steps and procedures involved in QCA are outlined below and summarized in Figure 14.1.

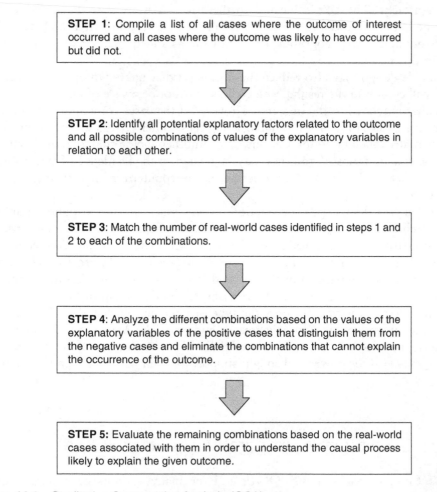

STEP 1: Compile a list of all cases where the outcome of interest occurred and all cases where the outcome was likely to have occurred but did not.

STEP 2: Identify all potential explanatory factors related to the outcome and all possible combinations of values of the explanatory variables in relation to each other.

STEP 3: Match the number of real-world cases identified in steps 1 and 2 to each of the combinations.

STEP 4: Analyze the different combinations based on the values of the explanatory variables of the positive cases that distinguish them from the negative cases and eliminate the combinations that cannot explain the occurrence of the outcome.

STEP 5: Evaluate the remaining combinations based on the real-world cases associated with them in order to understand the causal process likely to explain the given outcome.

Figure 14.1   Qualitative Comparative Analysis (QCA)

For the sake of simplicity, the most basic version of QCA is described and illustrated using the previous example of anti-corruption protests. The first step in the process involves identifying a complete list of cases that exhibit the outcome of interest, which in this example, is anti-corruption protests.

After constructing a list of cases that exhibit the outcome of interest, the researcher then identifies a list of negative cases. These are cases that have the potential to exhibit the outcome, but do not. In constructing a list of negative cases, researchers ought to cast as wide a net as possible. To compile a list of negative cases on anti-corruption protests, researchers could include countries that score above a certain level on corruption indices published by investment groups and non-government organizations, such as Transparency International's Corruption Perceptions Index.

After compiling a list of positive and negative cases, the next step is for researchers to identify the major explanatory factors that are likely to be relevant to the outcome, and all possible combinations of the values of these explanatory variables. In the example of anti-corruption protests, there are three explanatory variables – unemployment, protest culture, and confidence in the national government. The most basic form of QCA requires dichotomizing these variables.

For the purposes of this example, unemployment is dichotomized in terms of whether an unemployment rate is above or below the world average. Protest culture is dichotomized based on whether or not three or more protests (with a thousand or more participants) occurred in a country in a year. Lastly, confidence in the national government is dichotomized according to whether or not a majority of the population has confidence in the national government. These are obviously rather crude measures.

With three dichotomous explanatory variables, there are eight unique possible combinations of the explanatory variables. They are displayed below in what is known as a 'truth table'.

Unique combinations	Unemployment world average	Protest culture	Confidence in government	No protest	Yes protest
1	above	yes	majority	2	0
2	above	yes	no majority	0	6
3	above	no	majority	4	0
4	above	no	no majority	0	4
5	below	yes	majority	1	1
6	below	yes	no majority	0	4
7	below	no	majorlty	2	2
8	below	no	no majority	0	1

Table 14.7 QCA truth table

After constructing the truth table, the next step is for researchers to match the number of real-world cases from the list of positive and negative cases of anti-corruption protests that they compiled to the combinations of explanatory variables in the truth table, and then assess each of the combinations for consistency.

An outcome is consistent if all the real-world cases for a particular combination of explanatory variables either display the outcome or do not display the outcome. An outcome is inconsistent if there are real-world cases in which the outcome occurred and real-world cases in which it did not occur for a particular combination of explanatory variables.

In Table 14.7, the column 'yes protest' represents the number of real-world cases where anti-corruption protests occurred that match the particular combination of explanatory variables in a given row. The column 'no protest' represents the number of real-world cases where anti-corruption protests did not occur that match the particular combination of explanatory variables in a given row.

In Table 14.7, there are four consistent combinations where the outcome was produced (i.e., #2, #4, #6, and #8); two consistent combinations where the outcome was not produced (i.e., #1 and #3); and two inconsistent combinations (i.e., #5 and #7). There are no combinations for which there are no real-world cases (known as residual cases).

In the penultimate stage of this process, the researcher simplifies the list of cases based on the features of the positive cases that distinguish them from the negative cases. This involves comparing the consistent cases in pairs where the outcome variable is the same and only one of the explanatory variables between the two pairs differs and, therefore, cannot explain the outcome. The pairwise combination for which the explanatory variable cannot explain the outcome is eliminated from the truth table. Remainder cases are also used in this simplification process.

Consider, for example, combinations #1 and #3. In this pairwise combination, the outcome is the same – no protests. The explanatory variables are the same for unemployment and confidence in the government, but not for protest culture. Since the outcome is not produced when there is a culture of protest, the presence of a culture of protests cannot explain why anti-corruption protests occur. The first combination, the one that differs, is eliminated from the truth table as a result.

This process continues until the table cannot be simplified any further. In the example of anti-corruption protests, this process culminates in three combinations – two in which anti-corruption protests occurred and one in which they do not – which are depicted in Table 14.8.

Unique combinations	Unemployment world average	Protest culture	Confidence in government	No protest	Yes protest
3	above	no	no majority	4	0
4	above	no	majority	0	4
8	below	no	no majority	0	1

Table 14.8 QCA truth table, consistent outcomes

Finally, the researcher analyzes the real-world cases that remain in order to identify the causal process likely to explain the given outcome. Researchers may use process tracing for each case to substantiate their claims. An analysis of the real-world cases of anti-corruption protests remaining in Table 14.8 yields a result consistent with the conclusion reached in the analysis of Romania and South Korea regarding confidence in the government.

In the anti-corruption protest example, a majority of the public did not have confidence in the government (unemployment varies across combinations) in the two combinations in which protests occurred (i.e., #3 and #8). In the one combination in which anti-corruption protests did not occur (i.e., #4), a majority of the public had confidence in the government. This suggests that a lack of confidence in the national government is a necessary and sufficient condition for an anti-corruption protest to occur.

Although QCA offers a number of advantages over the standard Mill's approach to case comparisons, QCA has a number of limitations. First, QCA requires a lot of information that may not be available to researchers in order to identify the initial list of positive and negative cases to be analyzed. The prior example of anti-corruption protests benefitted from existing corruption indices, but relevant data such as this might not be available for other subjects.

Second, the procedure may not capitalize on the knowledge, skills, and experience of researchers because the cases included in the final analysis are outside the researchers' expertise. A researcher might be an expert on Russia, for example, and yet Russia might not be included in the analysis.

Third, QCA inferences are deterministic, not probabilistic. According to several statistical studies, the findings produced from QCA are fragile as a result, and likely to result in Type I errors (i.e., true hypothesis being rejected as false) (Hug 2013; Braumoeller 2015; Krogslund et al. 2015).

Researchers have modified QCA to address some of these issues. Fuzzy sets include probabilistic assumptions, but it is still only appropriate for the analysis of necessary and sufficient conditions, where different degrees of necessary or sufficient causation are considered (Ragin 2008). Fuzzy sets also eliminate the crude measurement decisions that QCA entails in terms of the dichotomization of measures that take on a much wider range of values.

Key Points

- The comparative case method has a higher potential for generalizability than single case studies but is sensitive to case selection.
- The comparative case study method is limited by its inability to handle non-deterministic relationships and to identify complex relationships among variables as well as multiple paths to the same outcome, and in its high potential for omitted variable bias.

Further Reading

The first reading presents a through introduction to the strengths and weakness of the single case studies. The second book is the original source of the comparative method and the third book offers a comprehensive guide to qualitative comparative analysis (QCA).

Gerring, John. 2017. *Case Study Research: Principles and Practices*. Cambridge: Cambridge University Press.

Mill, John Stuart. 1874. *A System of Logic*. New York: Harper & Brothers.

Ragin, Charles C. 2014. *The Comparative Method: Moving Beyond Qualitative and Quantitative Strategies*. Oakland, CA: University of California Press.

EXERCISE 14.1

Foreign Direct Investment (FDI) is a controversial issue and foreign corporations are not always welcome in the communities in which they invest. However, polls indicate that African communities have had a generally positive view of the Chinese corporations that have invested in them.

1. According to the example of the method of difference below, producing quality goods and services is the reason why Chinese corporations are viewed positively by a majority of Africans in the communities in which these corporations invest. Explain how this conclusion is reached from the information provided in the table. Also, explain why the other explanatory factors (i.e., creating jobs for locals; maintaining safe work environments; and supporting local activities) are still potentially necessary conditions (albeit not sufficient conditions) for the majority of Africans to have a positive perception of Chinese foreign direct investment in their communities.

Method of difference

Case	Create jobs for locals	Maintain safe work environment	Support local community activities	Produce high quality goods and services	Majority positive view of Chinese FDI
Corporation 1	yes	yes	yes	yes	yes
Corporation 2	yes	yes	yes	no	no

2. According to the example below of the method of agreement, producing quality goods and services is also the reason why Chinese corporations are viewed positively by a majority of Africans in the communities in which these corporations invest. Based on this example, explain why the other explanatory factors (i.e., creating jobs for locals; maintaining a safe work environment; and support for local community activities) are not necessary, but may be sufficient, for a majority of Africans to have a positive perception of Chinese FDI in their communities,

Method of agreement

Case	Create jobs for locals	Maintain safe work environment	Support local community activities	Produce high quality goods and services	Majority positive view of Chinese FDI
Corporation 1	yes	yes	yes	yes	yes
Corporation 4	no	no	no	yes	yes

EXERCISE 14.2

Using either your own research or existing research in your discipline, construct two examples of comparative case study designs – one using the method of difference and one using the method of agreement. Construct tables to depict these examples as in Table 14.1 (method of difference) and Table 14.4 (method of agreement). What are the conclusions from these analyses about the explanatory factors associated with the outcomes studied? Discuss any problems that you had in constructing the tables for your analyses, and any shortcomings of the method for understanding the question you have chosen. Which method is preferable, if either, for this question?

V

QUANTITATIVE METHODS AND ANALYSIS

Quantitative Measures

Objectives

- identify different types of measures according to their response categories
- describe the criteria most commonly used to evaluate measurement quality
- define random and systematic measurement error and the problems each presents for research
- explain the ecological inference problem

Measures are quantitative representations of concepts used as a basis or standard of comparison. As such, measures are the linchpin between the theoretical and empirical components of any research project. The importance of measurement cannot be overstated. '[N]early all the grandest discoveries of science have been but the rewards of accurate measurement,' as Lord Kelvin once stated.[1] Early in his career Kelvin developed an alternative measure for temperature known as the Kelvin scale, which begins at zero – the point where the gas has no kinetic energy. Today, it is the standard unit of measurement used in the physical and natural sciences and the basis for numerous scientific discoveries. In order for great discoveries to be made, however, much consideration must be given to the structure, appropriateness, and quality of the measures used to represent concepts.

Types of Measures

The key aspect by which measures are distinguished from each other is their level of measurement. There are four basic levels of measurement: nominal, ordinal, interval, and ratio. See Table 15.1.

Nominal Measures

Nominal level measures are *discrete measures* in which there is no order or hierarchy among categories. Discrete means that the data can only take on certain values and that there are clear boundaries among those values. In the case of nominal variables, the categories are mutually exclusive and exhaustive. The former indicates that no observation belongs to more than one category, while the latter specifies that all observations belong to one of the categories. Nominal measures can be dichotomous or multichotomous.

Nationality, ethnicity, race, religion, and gender are all examples of nominal measures. Ethnicity, race, and religion are generally multichotomous. Typically, gender is a dichotomous measure defined by two categories 'male' and 'female', but today, gender is increasingly a multichotomous measure. Multichotomous measures of gender evolved to accommodate people who do not identify themselves as either male or female.

Nepal was the first country in the world to use a multichotomous measure of gender on its census, allowing people who do not identify themselves as either male or female to identify as 'other'. Australia also allows individuals to identify as 'other' on its censuses while a handful of other countries, including Bangladesh, India, Germany, and New Zealand, allow individuals to identify as something besides male or female on other official documents, such as passports and voter registration cards.

Level	Characteristics	Examples
Nominal	discrete	gender; ethnicity; religion
Ordinal	discrete	Likert scales; democracy indices
Interval	continuous	age; income categories
Ratio	continuous	numbers of events

Table 15.1 Measurement level

Ordinal Measures

Ordinal measures are discrete measures in which there is, as the name suggests, an order among the categories of this measure, but in which the distance between categories is not necessarily equal. As in the case of nominal measures, the categories are mutually exclusive and exhaustive.

Attitudinal measures using Likert scales about the degree to which an individual shares a certain opinion, such as 'strongly agree', 'agree', 'neither agree nor disagree', 'disagree', or 'strongly disagree' are all examples of ordinal variables. The differences between categories of this measure are not necessarily equal, as it cannot be said that the difference in the intensity of opinion between 'neither agree nor disagree' and 'disagree' is the same as that between 'disagree' and 'strongly disagree.'

Ordinal measures can also be dichotomous. But, unlike dichotomous nominal measures, the two categories of a dichotomous ordinal measure are ordered in some way, as in the case of a dichotomous measure of 'yes' or 'no'. The categories of this variable are ordered in terms of their level of agreement.

Ordinal level measures are not limited to Likert scales. Other common examples of ordinal measures include indicators of degrees of democracy (e.g., Polity Index), political and civil rights (e.g., Freedom in the World), human rights protections (e.g., Universal Human Rights Index), militarized inter-state disputes (e.g., MIDs dataset), territorial autonomy (e.g., Regional Authority Index) and judicial independence (e.g., Rule of Law Index), among other things.[2]

Ordinal measures, as these examples suggest, are commonly constructed from multiple sub-measures. The Polity Index, for example, is based on measures of five separate factors related to the independence of executive authority, the openness of executive recruitment, the competitiveness of executive recruitment, the regulation of participation and the competitiveness of participation. The Freedom House Index is currently based on 20 indicators of political rights and civil liberties.

A significant challenge in constructing these measures is how to weigh each of the composite measures in the construction of the index. All the factors may be weighed equally, as in the Freedom House Index, or certain factors may be weighed more heavily than others in order to emphasize their importance, as in the Polity Index. The way in which the weights are assigned can have a significant impact on how particular observations fall on an index.

In 2000, the World Health Organization (WHO) released an index ranking 191 countries' health care systems according to five factors (i.e., the overall level of health of the population; the distribution of health in the population; the degree of responsiveness; the distribution of responsiveness; and the distribution of financial contributions to health).[3] France scored the highest on the index followed by Italy, San Marino, Andorra and Oman. Australia, the United Kingdom, and the United States came in 18th, 32nd, and 37th, respectively. The ranking was highly criticized for, among other things, the weight it assigned to the five factors, which critics argued was responsible for the high ranking of very small countries. For example, fairness of contribution, a measure of cost sharing between governments and individuals, comprised 25 percent of an individual country's score, the same as disability-adjusted life expectancy. Due to the worldwide controversy that the ranking sparked, the WHO discontinued the index after its first issuance.

The way in which composite measures are weighed in indices also affects which countries are the least corrupt; which universities are deemed the best; which law firms are considered the most prestigious; which pharmaceutical companies are seen as providing poor countries with the most access to medicine, and so forth. The consequences of these rankings for those ranked can be significant. As a result, many governments, organizations, and groups invest a great deal financially to raise their rankings. Often, however, they only make minor or superficial changes in their activities to improve scores. Sometimes they even lobby the groups that have compiled the indices for higher scores (Cooley and Snyder 2015).

Interval Measures

Unlike both nominal and ordinal measures, *interval measures* are continuous measures. *Continuous measures* can take on any value or any value within a range of values. Interval measures are a particular type of continuous measure in which the distance between units is known and equal. Examples of interval-level measures include: age; days per week spent engaged in an activity; and rainfall amounts (millimeters) per year. Income, which is a very common social scientific measure, could be an interval-level variable, but because of the categories by which it is defined, it generally is not.

In the following example, income is not an interval-level measure. Although the income categories are ordered, the distance between categories is not equal. The income categories are: less than €24.000; €24.000 to under €48.000; €48.000 to under €80.000; €80.000 to under €120.000; and €120.000 or more. The difference in income categories, excluding the maximum category, which is unbounded, ranges between just under €24.000 at the lower end of the measure to just under €40.000 at the higher end of the measure.

Ratio Measures

Ratio measures are similar to interval measures. Ratio-level measures are continuous measures in which the distance between units is known and equal. However, unlike in interval-level measures, there is an absolute zero value that is meaningful in ratio-level measures. As a result, a fraction or ratio can be constructed from a ratio-level measure. The number of terrorist acts, reported rapes, or deaths from a particular disease in a year are all examples of ratio-level variables.

Measurement Quality

The process by which concepts are transformed into measures is known as *operationalization*. The commonly heard phrase, 'How is that operationalized?', means how is a concept measured. In practice, it is not always possible to measure well important concepts. There are two standard metrics used to evaluate the quality of measures, namely, validity and reliability. To these two, I would add a third, which I refer to as discriminatory power. These three criteria are summarized in Table 15.2.

Validity

Validity refers to the extent to which a measure captures the concept it is intended to represent. Validity is a matter of degrees with some measures exhibiting a higher degree of validity than others. Figure 15.1 illustrates the concept of validity. The figure on the top depicts a measure with a low level of validity. The overlap between the concept and the measure is small. The figure in the middle depicts a measure with a moderate level of validity, while the figure at the bottom represents one with a high level of validity, as demonstrated by the large overlap between the concept and the measure.

To better understand validity, consider the example of civic engagement. Civic engagement refers to the ways in which citizens participate in the life of their community either to improve the conditions of others or to help shape their community's future. A common measure of civic engagement is voting (Putnam 2000). Voting in local elections can be a way in which people participate in the life of their community and voting in local elections can shape the future of that community depending on the outcome.

However, when people vote, it is questionable whether they are voting for the party that they think will improve the lives of others in their community, or really voting for the party that they think will most improve their own conditions. Much academic research suggests that self-interest is the primary motivation for voting (Downs 1957; Riker and Ordeshook 1968). These benefits include the ability to influence policy to one's own advantage, but are limited to them. They also include psychological benefits, such as a sense of empowerment, wellbeing, and self-satisfaction. Research also finds that people vote for normative reasons and habit (Gerber et al. 2008).

Criterion	Definition
Validity	extent to which a measure captures the concept it is intended to represent
Reliability	extent to which a measure produces consistent and dependable results
Discriminatory power	extent to which a measure is able to distinguish between two concepts

Table 15.2 Criteria for measurement quality

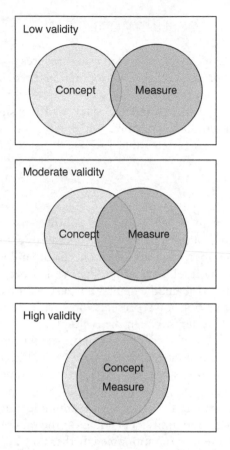

Figure 15.1 Validity of measures

Volunteering in one's local community and donating to local groups and causes are arguably more valid measures of civic mindedness than voting. Survey research shows that community-mindedness is a significant reason why people volunteer and donate to causes (Unger 1991; Clary et al. 1996). However, neither volunteering nor donating are perfectly valid measures of civic mindedness either since people engage in both activities for reasons other than a desire to improve the lives of others (Anderson and Moore 1978; Clary et al. 1996). These motivations include a desire to look like a good person, self-actualization, loneliness, skill acquisition, and so forth.

Reliability

Reliability refers to the degree to which a measure produces consistent and dependable results. A reliable measure yields the same data each time that it is used. Validity and reliability are independent of each other. Measures may have high validity and low reliability, or vice versa.

A very reliable measure is a count of the number of times certain words are repeated in a written text using computerized content analysis. Unless the computer program has a bug in it, or if the person running the program makes an error using it, the program will produce the same estimates every time it is used. Content analysis is used in this way to estimate the importance of certain issues in a text – the more often a word is repeated, the more important it is considered to be according to this method.

A person hand-counting the number of times certain words are repeated in a text will be less reliable than a computer, especially for longer texts, but still rather reliable. In the case of hand-coding context analysis, the coding process is repeated by different people to assure that the results are correct. The term *intercoder reliability* refers to the degree to which the coding of data by two or more individuals using the same measure or coding scheme produces the same results.

A much less reliable measure is an open-ended question of what people think is important in a written text. Two individuals reading the same text may not agree about which issues are most important because certain issues may resonate more with them based on their own interests. Even the same individual re-reading the same text may not draw the same conclusions the next time s/he reads it. The next time they read it the individual may take into consideration different things, such as the author's diction or where in the text an author discusses an issue, assuming that an issue mentioned earlier in a text is more important than one mentioned later.

Discriminatory Power

Although validity and reliability are the primary standards used to evaluate the quality of measures, what I refer to here as discriminatory power is also very important. *Discriminatory power* pertains to the degree to which a measure is able to distinguish between two different concepts. It is important because a high degree of discriminatory power enables researchers to differentiate not only between two concepts, but also between two competing theories. Discriminatory power is distinct from validity – that is, two measures may represent equally well or equally poorly a concept, and in both cases, they may be unable to discriminate between competing theories.

Figure 15.2 illustrates the principle of discriminatory power. In the image on the top, the measure has low discriminatory power as it overlaps two competing concepts. In the image at the bottom, the measure has high discriminatory power as it overlaps only one of the two concepts.

Gross domestic product (GDP) per capita is an example of a measure that has a poor ability to discriminate between competing explanations for civil war. GDP per capita is strongly correlated with the likelihood of civil wars to occur, with a higher GDP per capita associated with a lower likelihood of civil wars. GDP per capita has been used to measure at least three different concepts theorized to be related to civil wars, namely state strength, economic grievances, and rebel recruitment. Not only is GDP per capita unable to discriminate well among these different concepts, but it is also only a modestly valid measure of each of them.

Low discriminatory power

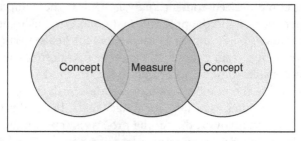

High discriminatory power

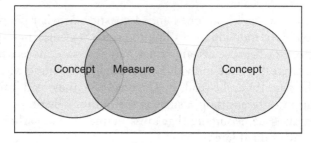

Figure 15.2   Discriminatory power of measures

GDP per capita is theorized to be associated with strong states because a higher GDP per capita provides governments with more revenue with which to build a strong military and police force (Fearon and Laitin 2003). GDP per capita is not a very valid measure of state strength. There are many countries that have low GDPs per capita, such as North Korea, and strong military and police forces because they have allocated a large portion of their government budget to security. At the same time, there are countries with high GDPs per capita that lack strong military and police forces. Iceland, for example, has a high GDP per capita, approximately five times the current world average, and yet has no standing army.

GDP per capita may also be associated with economic grievances, which inspire individuals to rebel against governments and/or support rebel groups that may have formed for other reasons. The effect of GDP per capita on economic grievances depends on the level of income inequality in countries (Cederman et al. 2013). Inequality causes lower income groups to perceive their economic state as unjust, and the government as responsible for this injustice, through intergroup comparisons (Gamson 1992). Where economic development is low and income inequality is high, grievances among lower income groups are likely to be greater than when economic development is high and income inequality is low.

GDP per capita is also associated with rebel recruitment. In poor countries, where people are only able to make a pittance each day, the poor have an incentive to join rebel movements, which can offer them shelter, food, and a salary that is much higher than they could earn otherwise. In some provinces in Afghanistan, the Taliban has been rumored to pay recruits hundreds of US dollars a month, where the average Afghanistan survives on only a dollar or two per day. However, there can be large segments of the population that are poor in countries where GDP per capita is high due to high levels of income inequality in these countries.

There are other measures of these concepts that would discriminate among these concepts much better, but systematic data on most of them would either be impossible to collect, and/or inaccurate. The size of a country's police or military forces, for example, would represent state strength better than GDP per capita, and would not be conflated with economic grievances or rebel recruitment, but authoritarian states are unlikely to accurately report these figures publicly. North Korea has been known to doctor (and not very well) photos of its military to make it appear stronger than it is. In one widely distributed photo, North Korea doctored a photo of hovercrafts landing on a beach in which several of the hovercrafts were obvious clones of other hovercrafts in the photo.[4]

Public opinion polls on economic grievances would also allow researchers to distinguish economic grievances from state strength very well, but not from rebel recruitment since economic grievances are correlated with poverty.[5] Public opinion polls on economic grievances would also be a more valid measure of grievances than GDP per capita, although people in very authoritarian states may be reluctant to honestly report their grievances to pollsters (Coffey and Horne 2011). Finally, unemployment rates would be preferable to GDP per capita to measure rebel recruitment, and it would distinguish rebel recruitment well from state strength, but not economic grievances. Unemployment rates are available for a large number of countries from the World Bank and International Labour Organization, although there are likely to be some reporting issues with these figures as well, especially for authoritarian states.[6]

Measurement Error

In addition to the aforementioned criterion of validity, reliability and discriminatory power, another factor important in evaluating the quality of measures is the amount of error incurred in the measurement process. *Measurement error* is the difference between the true value of an object and the observed value. The greater the difference between the two values, the greater the amount of measurement error.

There are two types of measurement error, which are summarized in Table 15.3. One is more problematic than the other. *Random measurement error* is measurement error that is unrelated to the real value being measured. Random error is unlikely to bias the results. An example of random measurement error are inaccuracies in the number of times words related to the economy are used in 'above the scroll' news accounts of immigration due to

Error type	Definition
Random	unrelated to the real value being measured
Systematic	related to problems in the test setup

Table 15.3　Measurement error

a few spelling errors. Misspellings of this kind are an example of random measurement error because they are not systematically related to the subject of the researchers' study.

Systematic measurement error is much more problematic. It is a result of imperfections in the test setup and has a much greater potential than random measurement error to bias the results. It can also be harder to identify and correct. Examples of errors in the setup that result in systematic measurement error include: only collecting data on events from online news sources that are likely to cater to particular audiences (i.e., younger and wealthier individuals); the failure to conduct double-blind experiments; characteristics of the researchers or participants, such as the difficulty of older participants to recall issues and the reticence of minority respondents to share certain information when interviewed by non-minority researchers; and glitches in the measurement tools.

Systematic measurement error resulting from glitches in the measurement tools has had catastrophic consequences for a large number of studies using functional magnetic resonance imaging (fMRI). FMRIs measure and map brain activity by detecting changes in blood flow associated with changes in neural activity. In the social sciences, fMRI studies have been used to identity patterns in people's decisions to vote and for whom they vote; the likelihood of people to commit certain crimes; romantic attraction; the ways atheists and non-atheists evaluate statements of fact; the effects of healthy relationships on reactions to negative stimuli, and so forth.

This systematic measurement error in the fMRI studies is a result of a software glitch identified by Eklund et al. (2016) in the most commonly used software packages for fMRI analysis. According to the researchers, the glitch can result in false-positive rates of up to 70 percent. The glitch resulted from the programs not adequately taking into account multiple comparisons among voxels or clusters of voxels (i.e., crudely defined as units in which three-dimensional objects are divided). A few years earlier, Craig Bennett et al. (2009) conducted a study demonstrating the need for correcting for multiple comparisons. The study showed significantly more neural activity in a dead salmon when the dead salmon was asked to identify the emotions of people it pictures it was shown than when the dead salmon was not shown any pictures.

Ecological Inference Problem

The types of problems that can arise in the measurement process do not end with measurement error. Ecological inference problems also pose major challenges for academic research. Ecological inference problems arise when researchers, unable to collect data directly on their subjects, make inferences about individuals based on characteristics of the group to which these subjects belong.

People make ecological inference errors in their everyday lives all the time. They make these errors when people assume that an Asian person is strong in math and science because Asian countries top most world rankings in academic achievement in these areas; that a person from Singapore is rich because Singapore has one of the highest GDPs in the world; and that a Dutch man is tall because Dutch men are on average the tallest in the world.

Drawing inferences about individual-level behavior from aggregate-level data can lead to wrong conclusions about individuals for obvious reasons. While Hong Kong, Singapore, South Korea and Japan rank highly in the world in math and science, Thailand and Indonesia do not. A particular person from any one of these countries may not excel in math and science, especially a person from Thailand or Indonesia, where the academic training in these subjects is not as strong as in other countries in East Asia. Similarly, while Singapore has a high GDP, income inequality is also significant, so that a particular Singaporean may not be well-off at all. And, of course, it goes without saying that while Dutch men today may be on average the tallest in the world, not every Dutch man is. Olympic champion Dutch speed skater, Sjinkie Knegt, is only 1.75m (5' 9" tall) and popular television personality, Martijn Joop Krabbé, is only 1.65m (5' 5").

Ecological inference errors have resulted in wrong conclusions in academic research as well. On the basis of aggregate economic data, it has been widely assumed that the Nazi Party drew its support primarily from economically distressed individuals within Germany's lower and middle classes. However, statistical regression models designed to deal with ecological inference problems suggest that the picture is more complicated. According to these models, unemployed people supported the Nazi Party less than the national average in the Reichstag elections, which brought the Nazi Party to power in 1932, the same year unemployment was near its peak (Hamilton 1982).

Key Points

- Concepts can be measured at different levels: nominal, ordinal, interval, and ratio.
- Measures are useful to the extent that they capture the concept that they are intended to represent (validity); produce consistent and dependable measures (reliability); and are able to discriminate among objects (discriminatory power).
- Systematic measurement error, which refers to imperfections in the test setup, is problematic for research. Random error, which is unrelated to the real value being measured, is not.
- Making inferences about individuals based on characteristics of the group to which they belong is problematic since individuals may not possess the characteristics of the group (ecological inference problem).

Further Reading

The first and second readings elaborate on the standards for good measurement. The third book is an edited volume discussing the shortcomings of measures used to rank countries in terms of certain social, economic, political, health, and environmental conditions.

Adcock, Robert and David Collier. 2001. 'Measurement Validity: A Shared Standard for Qualitative and Quantitative Research.' *American Political Science Review* 95(3): 529–546.

Jackman, Simon. 2008. 'Measurement.' In *The Oxford Handbook of Political Methodology*, edited by Janet M. Box-Steffensmeier, Henry E. Brady, and David Collier, 119–151. Oxford: Oxford University Press.

Snyder, Jack and Alexander Cooley, eds. 2015. *Ranking the World: Grading States as a Tool of Global Governance*. Cambridge: Cambridge University Press.

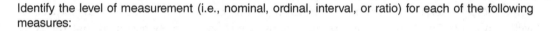

EXERCISE 15.1

Identify the level of measurement (i.e., nominal, ordinal, interval, or ratio) for each of the following measures:

1. gross domestic product (GDP) (current local currency).
2. population (total persons).
3. satisfaction with the state of the economy (i.e., very satisfied; satisfied; neither satisfied or unsatisfied; unsatisfied; very unsatisfied) .
4. sexual orientation (e.g., heterosexual; homosexual; bi-sexual; asexual transgendered; questioning; other).
5. government policies regarding refugees (i.e., temporary labor visas; non-immigrant visas for purposes other than work; visas for permanent residence; and political asylum).

EXERCISE 15.2

Construct interval- and ratio-level measures for the issues below. Discuss the tradeoffs between measuring these issues at the two different levels, and decide which is preferable.

1. terrorist incidents.
2. European Commission decisions on infringements of labor laws.
3. daily use of social media.
4. caloric intake as a measure of nutrition.

EXERCISE 15.3

Evaluate the extent to which the following measures are valid and reliable measures of the associated concepts.

1. **Concept:** poverty
   Measure: ratio of metal versus thatched roofed houses in Uganda according to satellite imagery

2. **Concept:** electoral fraud
   Measure: anonymous SMS text messages reporting fraud observed by voters at polling stations

3. **Concept:** number of outward migrants in conflict zones
   Measure: number of geocoded cell phone tower pings

4. **Concept:** public engagement on the issue of global climate change
   Measure: volume and content of tweets about climate change in English, French and Spanish

5. **Concept:** political ideology of judges
   Measure: ideology of clerks hired by judges based on the clerks' political donations

EXERCISE 15.4

Indicate whether the following measures exhibit random or systematic measurement error (or neither) and explain why.

1. Number of rape cases based on reports of rapes in post-civil war countries in a study of the factors influencing the likelihood of rape during civil wars.
2. Election results reported online by national election commissions in order to understand the effects of different electoral rules on the number of parties in an election.
3. Income inequality based on income data reported to the World Bank by countries in order to understand the effect of income inequality on democratization.
4. Failure to administer computer-based graduate school entrance exams due to problems with certain platforms on both PC and Macintosh-based systems in order to understand how socio-economic factors affect exam performance.

EXERCISE 15.5

The following are all examples of ecological inference problems. Choose two of the following examples and explain what aspect of each example the ecological inference problem is and discuss what types of incorrect conclusions might be drawn about the subject in question as a result of it.

1. propensity for a baby born today to be incarcerated in their lifetime based on the current lifetime incarceration rate of someone of the same gender, racial or ethnic group, and socio-economic status as the baby.
2. vote choice of a minority voter based on the past choice of all minority voters in the district in which this voter resides.
3. performance of a child on a national achievement exam based on the average exam scores of two schools that merged to form the school where the child is a student.
4. gender of a chief executive officer (CEO) based on the percentage of female CEOs in Fortune Global 500 companies.
5. demographic characteristics of all protesters based on the demographic characteristics of protesters arrested by police for vandalism.

Quantitative Data

Objectives

- compare and contrast observational and non-observational data
- provide criteria with which to evaluate data quality and present techniques for identifying high quality data
- identify different types of data distributions and techniques for analyzing data consistent with these distributions

The adage 'In God we Trust, all others bring data' is a fitting description of our time.[1] Hardly any decisions, it seems, are made today without data. Everything from how to pitch an electoral campaign, to where to eat and whom to date is based on data. Datasets are the products of measurement. *Quantitative data* is any type of data that is numeric in form. Quantitative data are not limited to obvious forms of numeric data measured in terms of frequency, weights, lengths, amounts, and so forth. But, rather include any data assigned numeric values to distinguish one component of the data from another.

Quantitative data vary along a number of different dimensions, including their type (i.e., observation versus non-observational), structure (i.e., continuous versus discrete), and quality (i.e., accuracy, validity, precision, consistency, and completeness). These dimensions affect not only the insight researchers have into subjects, but also the techniques researchers use to analyze datasets as well as the credibility of claims they make based on them.

Data Types and Sources

Quantitative data consists of two basic types – observational data and non-observational data – that are distinguished from each other by the process through which the data are collected. The former are collected without researchers interacting with their subjects or intervening in their subjects' environments, while the latter are collected through one or both of these means. The two types of data have their distinct advantages and disadvantages. The choice of which type of data researchers collect depends less on the advantages and disadvantages of each, and more on the measures that researchers employ to test their hypotheses.

Observational Data

The defining feature of *observational data* is that it is collected without researchers interacting with their subjects or their environments. Observational data addresses an endless array of issues that are both objective and subjective in nature. Table 16.1 provides some examples of observational data that are commonly used in the social sciences, and that are objective in nature.

Socio-economic data are perhaps the most common form of observational data. Typically, these data are compiled by governments or by international agencies to which governments report their data. However, due to advancements in technology, it is also possible today for researchers to collect these data using digital technologies, such as

Issue	Data
Demography	population; religion; ethnicity
Economics	gross domestic product per capita; income; income inequality; unemployment; balance of trade
Crime	homicide rates; drug tracking offenses; conviction and incarceration rates; prison occupancy rates; police officers per person
Education	literacy; years in school completed; government education spending
Health	immunization rates; life expectancy; infant mortality; HIV prevalence; underweight children

Table 16.1   Objective observational data

satellite images, mobile phone records and SMS (short message service) messages. These technologies allow researchers to circumvent governments that may not only lack the bureaucratic and financial capacity to collect these data themselves, but that may also have an incentive to report their data inaccurately for political or other reasons.

Researchers, for example, are able to collect data on population density from satellite images of light intensity (Mellander et al. 2015). They are also able to use satellites images to collect data on economic development based on the presence of disorganized street grids, the small size of buildings, and the use of thatched or other nondurable roofs. Transactional data, such as mobile phone usages, purchases, and money transfers, also provides useful information on economic development. Economic data are especially difficult to collect in developing countries without these technologies due to the frequent lack of government censuses and tax returns in these countries, as well as the remoteness of some communities, among other things.

Other examples of objective forms of observational data include data on the occurrence of events at the international level (e.g., wars, treaties, and trade disputes), the national level (e.g., elections, civil wars, and protests), and the individual level (e.g., purchases, meeting attendance, and dislocations). Typically, researchers compile such data from newspapers, government reports, legal documents, and so forth. Today, however, researchers are able to use digital technologies to collect these data as well.

Using satellite images, researchers are able to collect data on intrastate violence based on visible signs of destruction to buildings, infrastructures, forests and so forth. Researchers are also able to use SMS messages and crowdsourcing tools, such as Ushahidi, to amass data on intrastate violence, as well as other events, based on witnesses' reports of these events. Researchers are even able to compile data on events like these from what is referred to as 'data exhaust'.

Data exhaust is passively collected transactional data acquired from people's use of digital services. Researchers are not alone in collecting information in this way. Both for-profit businesses and non-profit universities do as well. Businesses collect transactional data based on purchases to assess the effectiveness of advertisement campaigns, while universities collect data about their students from ID card swipes at campus activities, libraries, programs and centers. Universities use these data in order to monitor campus engagement and to predict drop-out rates, among other things.[2]

Observational data that is subjective in nature is more often derived from content analysis of written, spoken, and visual material. Much of these data today are based on web content, including blogs and social media websites. From these sources, researchers are able to identify information about people's attitudes toward and opinions of political policies and news events; their intentions and motivations for participation in certain activities; and their prejudices and biases towards certain groups, among other things.

Observation data, by virtue of the way in which it is collected, have certain advantages over non-observation data. Observational data are generally not subject to human subjects' protocols because researchers collect these data without interacting with individuals or manipulating their environments in any way. Observational data are also generally not subject to either observer bias or the guinea pig effect. Observer bias results from researchers unwittingly influencing the responses of their subjects through their actions, while the guinea pig effect results from subjects changing their behavior independent of any particular behaviors of the researchers, but simply because they are being observed.

They are not susceptible to the former because observational data by definition do not involve the interaction of researchers with their subjects. They are not typically subject to the latter either because subjects are often not aware that data is being collected about them when it is observational in nature. Since observational data are not typically subject to either of these biases, and depict real-world phenomena, observational data are all but immune to the criticism leveled at experimental data that it does not represent real human behavior well.

Observational data also have the potential to be much larger in size than non-observational data. Most data today referred to as 'big data' are observational in nature. Big data owes its name to its volume and its bulkiness, which is particularly evident in the case of satellite images, fMRIs, and videos. There are no specific parameters as to how large data must be in order for it to be defined as 'big data' but, in general, big data requires terabytes, petabytes and even exabytes of storage space. (The storage space on your average laptop is only about .0002 terabytes in size.) While big data offers new and interesting research possibilities, it also requires high-end computer infrastructures to which many researchers lack access.

Non-observational Data

Non-observational data, in contrast, is collected through researchers either interacting with their subjects or intervening in their subjects' environments. Survey data are non-observational in nature for the first of these two reasons. Survey data are collected through a series of questions posed to individuals, which even if not in the presence of the researcher or an associate, constitute a means of interaction with another person.

Experiments, with the exception of natural experiments, which are described in Chapter 20, are non-observational in nature for the latter reason. Experiments require participants to complete particular tasks either in a laboratory or real-world setting. In lab, lab-in-the-field, and survey experiments, these tasks generally involve playing a game, reading a vignette, looking at images, or watching a video. In field experiments, the experimental manipulations are much less artificial. They generally involve a change in or the adoption of a new policy or program in the real world.

Experimental data is often criticized for not representing the real world well. In certain cases, however, not representing the real world can be an advantage, as researchers may use experiments to explore outcomes associated with certain policies, rules, or practices that do not exist in the real world, such as approval voting systems (Brams and Fishburn 2007). At present, no country in the world uses approval voting in national elections. In these systems, which are believed to increase voter turnout, people approve of as many candidates as they like in multicandidate elections, and the candidates with the highest approval votes win. In a similar vein, non-observational data can also raise the awareness of study participants about their own behaviors, which they would not otherwise be cognizant of through interviews, focus groups, or survey questions, and not document, as a result, in diaries, letters, memoirs, and so forth.

Data Quality Standards

The attributes of high quality data are the same regardless of whether the data are observational or non-observational data. These attributes relate to the accuracy, validity, precision, consistency, and completeness of the data, as summarized in Table 16.2.

Accuracy

Accuracy refers to the extent to which the values of the data are correct. A dataset on coups d'état is accurate to the extent that the number of coups d'état per year reported in the dataset is the same as the number of coups d'état that actually occurred each year. Likewise, data on the percentage of startups (or small business) that fail each year is accurate to the extent the percentage of startups that close (or go out of business) each year in the data matches the percentage of startups that close each year in the real world.

Validity

Validity describes the extent to which data depicts the measures they claim to represent. The term validity was mentioned in prior chapters regarding the degree to which a measure represents a concept, and the degree to which a concept represents an idea. The term applies equally to the degree to which data represent measures. Figure 16.1 illustrates the different usages of the term validity.

Attribute	Definition
Accuracy	correctness of the values
Completeness	extent to which the values represent the whole universe of cases
Consistency	uniformity of the data across observations
Precision	specificity of the data
Validity	extent to which the data represents the measures

Table 16.2 Criteria for evaluating data quality

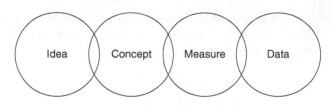

Figure 16.1 Types of validity

In order to explain the concept of data validity and demonstrate how it is similar to but also distinct from other forms of validity, consider the example of prison overcrowding. A valid measure of prison overcrowding is prison density – the amount of space each prisoner has in a cell measured in terms of square meters/feet. Prisons are overcrowded to the extent that they exceed a certain square meters/feet per prisoner. Norway's Halden prison is likely one of the most spacious and luxurious prisons in the world.[3] Each cell in the prison is 10 square meters (110 square feet) and is equipped with a flat-screen television, desk, mini-fridge, and private toilet.

Data on prison density is not widely available across countries, making research on the relationship between prison density and recidivism, among other things, difficult. In lieu of data on this metric, researchers, activists, and policy-makers often use data on prison occupancy rates. However, prison occupancy rates are not valid measures of either overcrowding or prison density. A prison may not be overcrowded, even if it has a large prison population, if the prison is large in terms of physical space. Likewise, a prison may be overcrowded, even if it has a relatively small prison population, if the prison is small in terms of physical space.

Box 16.1   Off-the-Shelf Data

Off-the-shelf data are data that researchers have not collected themselves. Data validity issues seem to arise more often when researchers use off-the-shelf data rather than original data, because off-the-shelf data are not tailored to the researchers' specific questions. To avoid issues of data validity from arising with off-the-shelf data, researchers frequently tailor their measures to match the available data. To avoid issues of validity from arising with original data, researchers often define their measures in terms of data that are feasible to collect.

Precision

Precision refers to the specificity of the data. Data are more precise the smaller the units and intervals in which they are measured. Data, for example, on yearly income is more precise than data on income ranges (e.g., less than €24.000; €24.000 to under €80.000;

Cartoon 16.1

€80.000 to under €120.000; and €120.000 or more). Likewise, data on the total votes that parties receive within a country in an election is less precise than data on the number of votes that parties receive within a district or a polling station in that election.

Box 16.2   Is the Most Precise Level of Measurement Always the Best?

While more precise data contains more information, it is not always best to measure a concept and collect data for this measure at the most precise level possible for at least two reasons.

More precise data can be less accurate. It is not possible to precisely identify certain information, such as the number of individuals present at a protest, the number of deaths in an international or civil war, or the number of hours spent per week engaged in a particular activity, especially if this activity occurred in the distant past. In this case, it is preferable to use ordinal measures rather than continuous measures in which the data are reported in ranges such as 0–1000 persons; 1001–5000 persons; 5001–10000 persons, or 0–1 hours, 2–3 hours, 4–5 hours, and so forth. These data are less precise but more likely to be accurate.

Measuring certain data at a less precise level may also increase people's willingness to share certain data. People may be very reluctant to share certain information at a precise level, such as how much money they spent gambling in the last year, or how much weight they gained, but they may be willing to provide this information in ranges.

Completeness

Completeness is the extent to which data includes values for the whole universe of relevant cases. Datasets may be incomplete because they only include a subset of all relevant cases, or because a large number of values for certain variables are missing. A dataset would be incomplete for the first of these two reasons if, for example, it only included certain regions of the world, top-tier universities, or fast-growing firms, when the theories for which the data were collected applied to all regions, universities, or firms. Data that are incomplete for this reason are more limited in terms of their generalizability.

A dataset may also be incomplete even if it includes the whole universe of relevant cases, if there are a lot of missing data for certain measures. A dataset may include every country of the world, but still be incomplete, for example, because it is missing a lot of data on economic, social, or political indicators for different countries. Missingness is especially problematic when the data are not 'missing at random' because any analysis of it may be biased as a result. Missing at random means that there are no patterns in the cases for which the data are missing. Data, for example, on prison density are likely to be missing for countries where prison density is high and prison conditions are poor more generally. Thus, any analysis of what conditions contribute to prison overcrowding, or what effects prison overcrowding has on various outcomes, is likely to be biased.

Consistency

Consistency refers to the absence of contradictions in the data. Data may be inconsistent because the data for all cases are not coded according to the same rules and procedures, or because the data are not collected using the same types of sources.

Official Development Assistance (ODA) data from the Organisation for Economic Co-operation and Development (OECD) are not consistent across countries or over time for the first of these reasons.[4] The ODA data are based on data reported to the OECD by member states. Initially, the OECD did not provide member states with detailed rules regarding what constitutes ODA. As a result, the member states interpreted the meaning of ODA differently and included different forms of economic assistance in their ODA data. Over time, the OECD provided more detailed instructions to countries regarding what to count and not count as ODA. As a result, the data are more consistent now across countries, but are still inconsistent over time. Due to the new instructions, many countries do not include certain types of data that they had included previously, and include other types of data that they had not.

Event data from the GDELT Project is inconsistent for the latter reason.[5] GDELT extracts event data from international print, broadcast, and online news sources from 1979 to the present. However, it does not use the same sources over time since online sources have only become widely available at the turn of the twenty-first century. As a result, there are more incidents of all types of events in the GDELT data today than earlier in the past, making it seem that events, such as natural disasters, are occurring with increasing frequency today when they are not.

Data Quality Evaluation Techniques

Whether or not the data meet these standards cannot be judged solely on the basis of the data itself for certain cases. Researchers can observe the precision of the data by the units in which the data are measured, and the completeness of the data in terms of the amount of missing values they contain. However, it is much harder for researchers to determine the accuracy and consistency of the data based on the data itself. Fortunately, there are several strategies that researchers can employ to evaluate the data along these dimensions.

Box 16.3   Strategies for Evaluating Data Quality

- Search for any obvious biases in the sources of the data.
- Inspect the data by checking if values for familiar cases conform to expectations.
- Observe the level of detail and precision of the coding rules in the codebook.
- Verify that intercoder reliability statistics are high.
- Graph the data and calculate the central tendencies of the data.
- Triangulate the data by comparing values in the dataset to other values in the dataset.
- Compare the dataset to another similar dataset.

Source Bias

In order to evaluate the accuracy of the data, researchers ought to consider whether there are any potential biases in the sources used to collect the data. If the data is collected by, or using sources from, any government, organization, or individual that may personally, professionally, or financially benefit from, or be harmed by, its publication, there is a potential for the data to be biased. Those who have a direct and immediate stake in how the data are perceived also have an incentive to misconstrue this data.

China is well known to misreport national statistics that may undermine the legitimacy of its regime, threaten its political or financial stability, and undercut its reputation and/or bargaining power in the international arena. For years, for example, it has dramatically underreported the amount of coal it consumes each year.[6] In underreporting its coal consumption, China – one of the biggest consumers of coal worldwide – is able to avoid cutting its consumption in real terms to meet international commitments. In recent years, it is also believed to have underreported its capital outflows to avoid panicked selling of its currency – the yuan – greater purchasing of Bitcoin, and even more capital outflows.

Potential sources of biases are not always quite so obvious. Internet trolls are a potential source of hidden bias. Governments, especially those of Russia and China, are known to use trolls to plant information on the internet to flatter their countries' governments and discredit their opponents. China reportedly employs up to two million trolls, referred to as the 50 Cent Party. The name originates from the amount of money that the Chinese government is believed to have initially paid these trolls for each post they made.[7]

Coding Procedures

An examination of the coding procedures researchers use is also important in assessing the accuracy and consistency of the data. Coding procedures are the rules used to assign quantitative values to observations. They are typically provided in a codebook available directly from the researcher or an online data repository. Data are more likely to be accurate and consistent the more detailed are the coding procedures that researchers use. A high level of detail reduces ambiguity regarding how a particular observation ought to be coded.

When multiple coders are used to score the data, the codebook may contain information regarding the intercoder reliability. There are various measures of intercoder reliability besides the most obvious metric of percent agreement, which does not account for the possibility that individuals agree on the codings by chance. Regardless of the metric used to calculate it, low intercoder reliability suggests that the data are not accurate because of the large number of disagreements among coders regarding the correct value to assign to an observation.

The manner in which information regarding the coding procedures and data is described is itself also a sign of the care with which the data has been collected. The failure of researchers to describe in detail this information suggests that the researchers did not put sufficient care into the coding of the data and potentially other aspects of their research, but this is not always the case. Researchers may not be very transparent about their data and coding procedures if they constructed the data for commercial use, because doing so would enable others to collect the same data without purchasing theirs.

Inspecting the Data

In order to evaluate the accuracy and consistency of the data, it is also necessary to inspect the data. To inspect the data means to check if the values for individual cases conform with your expectations as to how these observations should be coded if the data were coded according to the rules and procedures outlined in the codebook.

In a dataset, for example, on political institutions, is Chile coded as a democracy in 1990, the year Augusto Pinochet lost power, and as a non-democracy the years that Pinochet was in power? Has the number of startups in India grown exponentially in the last decade as multinational corporations, like Google and Microsoft, have established funds to finance startups in the country? Do students from China, followed by India, constitute the largest number of international students in the US and Europe in the last decade?

To verify the accuracy of the data in this way, it is best to focus on the observations for which you have the most familiarity. After checking if the data conforms to your expectations based on the coding rules set out in the codebook, it is also useful to check if the values for individual cases conform to your expectations of how these cases should be coded regardless of the rules and procedures by which the data are said to be coded. The failure of the cases to conform to your expectations may suggest that the measure is not a valid measure of the underlying concept.

In addition to verifying the values for individual observations, it is important to triangulate the data internally. This means to check the data against itself. Add up the rows and the columns and make sure that they add up to the numbers that they should. If the figures are percentages, do they add up to 100 percent? Also, check if the values for different variables are consistent with each other. For example, do the dates on which requests are made or applications filed occur before the dates on which the requests were fulfilled or the applications accepted? If not, then there has to be an error in one of these dates.

At this juncture, it is also useful to graph and calculate the central tendencies of the data. Central tendencies are single values that describe a set of data by identifying the central position within that set of data. They include the *mean*, *median*, and *mode* of the data, as defined in Table 16.3.

From these central tendencies, researchers can judge whether or not the values of the data seem reasonable and conform to their expectations at the aggregate level. For example, is the average for world trade increasing over time? Is the median value for democracy higher in Europe than in Africa and Asia?

Researchers can also use this information to detect outliers. *Outliers* are any values that are far from the other values in the data. Outliers may represent true values, but they may also represent errors in the data. Their presence, regardless, can significantly affect the results of an analysis.

Central tendencies also allow researchers to preliminarily detect trends in the data consistent with their hypotheses, and to help identify the distribution of data. The distribution of the data determines the types of statistical techniques researchers need to analyze the data, as explained in the subsequent section.

Measure	Definition
Mean	average of a set of numbers (e.g., 4, 5, 5, 5 = 4.75)
Median	middle value of an odd number of numbers listed in numeric order or the average of the two middle values of an even number of numbers listed in numeric order (e.g., 4, 5, 5, 5 = 5)
Mode	value that appears most often in a set of numbers (e.g., 4, 5, 5, 5 = 5)

Table 16.3 Measures of central tendencies

Triangulating the Data

It is important for researchers not only to triangulate the data internally, but to also triangulate it externally by comparing the data to similar datasets. In this comparison, researchers ought to assess the extent to which the data matches where it is expected to match, and does not match where it is not expected to match. For example, if researchers triangulated data on democracy protests with another dataset on protests against electoral fraud, we would expect democracy protests to include all cases of protests against electoral fraud.

The success of this technique hinges on the quality of the comparison dataset and the appropriateness of the comparison. If the comparison dataset is not accurate, there may be many discrepancies between the two datasets that are not due to errors in the original dataset, but to errors in the comparison dataset. In order to determine the reason for the discrepancies, researchers must investigate each divergent case individually.

For this technique to be effective, the datasets must also be very similar in terms of the measures compared. If they are not, there may be discrepancies between the datasets as a result of differences in the measures, not errors in the original data. However, the comparison does not need to be exact, and in most cases is unlikely to be so if the differences between the datasets can be isolated.

These differences can be isolated if the measures compared have certain components in common. A dataset, for example, which measures democracy in terms of 'open and competitive elections', and another dataset, which measures democracy in terms of 'open and competitive elections' and 'political and civil rights', can be usefully compared along the electoral component that they have in common.

They can also be isolated if one measure is a subset of another. A dataset on democracy protests, for example, can be usefully compared to a dataset on all protests since democracy protests constitute a subset of all protests. If the dataset on democracy protests is accurate, then the number of democracy protests that occur each year in a country should be equal to or less than the number of all protests that occur in a country each year.

Data Distributions

In statistics, the appropriate estimation technique used to analyze data once it has been collected is based on the distribution of the data of the outcome variable. The distribution of the data is a listing or function of all possible values of the data, and is a function in large part on the measurement level of the data. Table 16.4 summarizes the main distributions for continuous and discrete data and the estimation techniques commonly used to analyze them.

Data	Measurement	Distribution	Estimation technique
Continuous	interval	normal	ordinary least square regression
			probit, ordered probit and multinomial probit models
	interval	Weibull	duration models
Discrete	nominal	logistic	logistic regression
	nominal	categorical	multinomial logistic regression
	ordinal	logistic	ordered logistic regression
	ratio	Poisson	Poisson models
			zero-inflated Poisson models
	ratio	negative binomial	negative binomial models
			zero-inflated negative binomial models

Table 16.4 Statistical models for different types of data

Continuous Data Distributions

For continuous data, the most common distributions are the uniform distribution, normal distribution, t-distribution, Chi-square distribution, and F-distribution. In the uniform distribution, there is a finite number of values that are equally likely to be observed. For this reason, the uniform distribution is commonly used to draw a simple random sample.

The normal distribution is perhaps the most well-known distribution that is easily identifiable by its bell-shape. In the normal distribution, the mean, medium, and mode of the data are equal, and the data is symmetrical around the mean. Normal data are typically analyzed using ordinary linear regression (OLS). Probit models, ordered probit models, and multinomial probit models are also based on a normal distribution.

The t-distribution is similar to the normal distribution but it has heavier tails, meaning that the distribution decays at a speed that is less than exponential. The t-distribution is used in a comparison of means tests.

The Chi-square distribution is the sum of the squares of k independent standard normal random variables. It is used in 'goodness of fit' tests, such as Chi-square tests. A Chi-square test measures how well the observed distribution of data fits with the distribution that is expected if the variables are independent.

The F-distribution is the ratio of two chi-squares, each divided by its degrees of freedom (i.e., the number of observations minus the number of parameter estimates). Analysis of variance (ANOVA) tests are based on the F-distribution, as are many test statistics.

ANOVAs are used for categorical data where a comparison of means test is not appropriate.

The Weibull distribution is much less common than these distributions. It is used in regression techniques to evaluate the effects of explanatory variables on outcomes that are measured in terms of the time until an event occurs, such as the number of months that have passed before a civil war recurs, an unemployed person finds a new job, or a divorcee remarries.

Discrete Data Distributions

For discrete data, the most commonly used distributions are the logistic distribution, categorical distribution, Poisson distribution, and negative binomial distribution. The logistic distribution has only two outcomes that represent either the success or failure of an outcome. Dichotomous data indicating whether or not an event, such as a crime, election, or cyberthreat, occurred in a given time period follows a logistic distribution. Data that is consistent with this distribution are typically analyzed using logistic regression. Ordinal data are also associated with a logistic distribution but is analyzed using an ordered logistic regression.

The categorical distribution is associated with multinomial data. Like ordinal data, this data has multiple outcomes, but unlike ordinal data, these outcomes are not ordered in any way. Data that are consistent with a categorical distribution are modeled using multinomial logistic regression.

Lastly, a Poisson distribution is a discrete distribution depicting the number of events that occur per unit of time. This data is generally analyzed using either Poisson models or zero-inflated Poisson models (when the proportion of non-events in the data is high). The negative binomial distribution is an alternative to the Poisson distribution. It describes count data that are overdispersed (i.e., data where the sample variance exceeds the sample mean) and is analyzed using either negative binomial regression models or zero-inflated binomial models.

Key Points

- Observational data, which is collected without researchers interacting with their subjects or their environments, are generally not subject to human subjects' protocols, observer bias, or the guinea pig effect, and can be more realistic than non-observational data, including survey and experimental data.
- Higher quality data are accurate, valid, precise, consistent and complete.
- Data with different distributions requires different estimation techniques.

Further Reading

The first reading discusses the factors that make collecting high quality data in practice difficult and suggests ways to overcome them. The second reading is a popular book that uses examples to illustrate misleading presentations of data. The third reading discusses the potentials of big data as well as technical issues and ethical concerns around its use.

Herrera, Yoshiko M. and Devesh Kapur. 2007. 'Improving Data Quality: Actors, Incentives and Capabilities.' *Political Analysis* 15(4): 365–386.

Huff, Darrell. 1993. *How to Lie with Statistics*. New York: W. W. Norton & Company.

Kitchin, Rob. 2014. *The Data Revolution: Big Data, Open Data, Data Infrastructures and their Consequences*. London: Sage Publications.

EXERCISE 16.1

Choose four to five variables from a commonly used dataset in your discipline and assess their quality according to the following attributes: accuracy, precision, validity, consistency and completeness. If the dataset does not provide sufficient information to evaluate an attribute fully, state this and explain why. Below are a few datasets that you may consider using for this exercise:

- Human Development Index (HDI), United Nations Development Program, http://hdr.undp.org/en/data
- The World Health Report, 2000, www.who.int/whr/2000/en/whr00_en.pdf
- Gender Inequality Index (GII), United Nations Development Program, http://hdr.undp.org/en/content/gender-Inequality-index-gii
- International Development Statistics (IDS), Organization for Economic Co-operation and Development, http://stats.oecd.org/qwids/
- UCDP/PRIO Armed Conflict Dataset, Uppsala Conflict Data Program and Peace Research Institute Oslo, http://ucdp.uu.se/downloads/
- Freedom in the World, Freedom House, https://freedomhouse.org/report-types/freedom-world
- World Values Survey (WVS), World Values Survey Association, www.worldvaluessurvey.org/WVSContents.jsp

---

17

Content Analysis

Objectives

- describe potential sources of data for content analysis and common problems associated with them
- identify types of measures commonly derived from these sources
- present the types of information often derived from these measures
- discuss the advantages and disadvantages of human-coded versus computerized content analysis

One of the strengths of quantitative data is their ability to provide objective, consistent, and comparable information across individuals or cases. However, as William Bruce Cameron once said, 'not everything that can be counted counts, and not everything that counts can be counted'.[1] Much of what counts and that is hard to count is qualitative data, including interviews, newspapers, blogs, tweets, and so forth. Qualitative data can provide interesting, nuanced, and unique insights into issues, but as previous chapters have highlighted, subjective and not necessarily consistent and comparable across individuals or cases. Content analysis is intended to rectify these issues.

Content analysis is a research method used to construct quantitative data from written, spoken, and visual materials. The quantitative data are derived from different aspects of the words and objects contained with these materials, including their number, location, and similarity to other words and objects. While the quantitative data derived from content analysis provide consistent and objective measures of the information contained within qualitative data, the meaning derived from the measures is still largely subjective and open to interpretation.

Source Materials

Researchers utilize many different types of written, oral, and visual materials in content analysis. These materials include both primary and secondary sources, as well as traditional and newer forms of internet-based and electronic communications. Examples of some of these materials are summarized in Table 17.1.

Written Materials

The most common type of written materials, either in print or online, that researchers use for context analysis are newspapers. Newspapers are generally used to determine whether or not and how many times an event, such as an election, natural disaster, coup d'état, and so forth, has occurred. Newspapers allow researchers to study events far back in history across the globe.

Written	Verbal	Visual
blog posts	films	comic books
books	music lyrics	commercials
email messages	public statements	films
letters	radio programs	music videos
magazines	speeches	photographs
newspapers	television shows	television program
textbooks		video games
Twitter messages		
web searches		

Table 17.1 Common source materials for content analysis

However, event counts derived from newspapers can underrepresent events in authoritarian states because governments can censor newspaper coverage of events that they anticipate might threaten the stability of the regime. They can also underrepresent small, internationally marginal countries because events in these countries are less likely to have repercussions for and be of interest to newspaper readers outside them, as well as developing countries where newspaper readership is typically low.

Other text-based materials that researchers commonly use for content analysis include popular magazines and textbooks. These resources are not used so much to identify historical events like newspapers, but rather to characterize the political, social, and cultural values they exhibit, especially in regard to stereotypes and biases towards ethnic, religious, gender, and sexual minorities (Al-Olayan and Karande 2000; Evans and Davies 2000; Baker 2005). A recent content analysis of 10,000 book reviews in the *New York Times Book Review* (NYTRB) found that men wrote two-thirds of the books reviewed, and that the reviews of female-authored books tended to reflect gender stereotypes.[2]

Today, electronic media and online content, such as emails, Twitter messages, and blog posts, are commonly used in content analysis as well. These resources, unlike newspapers, magazines, and textbooks, provide insight directly into individuals' views on events, issues, policies and so forth. From these sources, researchers have culled information about people's awareness of and interest in particular events, including environmental disasters and epidemics (Chew and Eysenbach 2010), their opinions on political, social and economic issues, their attitudes towards national leaders (Tumasjan et al. 2010), and their satisfaction with commercial products and services (Hornikx and Hendriks 2015), among many other things.

Even web searches are an opportunity for content analysis. In 2008, Google developed a flu tracker to identify flu outbreaks based on the number of Google searches for the word 'flu' and related terms. Initially, the predictions of Google Flu Trends were as accurate as those of the US Center for Disease Control (CDC). However, with continued use, it became apparent that the tracker overpredicted flu outbreaks. The inflated results were due in large part to people who did not have the flu but had flu-like symptoms searching for the word flu. Google has discontinued the tracker as a result.

These internet-based and electronic forms of communication are used as a source of public opinion. However, they are not representative of the general population. These resources tend to underrepresent the views of groups who do not often use computers, namely the elderly, the poor, and the less educated. They also tend to underrepresent people who live in authoritarian states where government censorship of these modes of communications is high.

The information amassed from these sources may not even accurately depict those who do use them because people may not reveal or misrepresent their real views online. Trolls can also distort information on the web. Trolls are individuals who assume the identities of others in order to plant, often false, information on the internet. Trolls have interfered with election campaigns in France, Kenya, the UK, and the US, among others.[3] They have also discredited countries, businesses, and individuals, while defending and glorifying others (King et al. 2017).[4]

Verbal Materials

No single resource dominates the landscape of verbal or spoken materials used in content analysis. Among the many different kinds of spoken materials that researchers content analyze are: music lyrics, dialogue in films, television, and radios programs, as well as speeches and other public statements. The information that researchers amass from these materials is as varied as the sources themselves.

Researchers have used content analysis of music lyrics, films, as well television and radio programs in order to characterize the political, social, and cultural values they portray, as in the case of magazines and textbooks. DeWall et al. (2011), for example, content analyzed the lyrics of chart-topping songs in order to measure the level of narcissism in these songs over time. Primack et al. (2008) also content analyzed popular songs, but they did so in order to determine the prevalence of substance abuse in them. About a third of all chart-toppers they analyzed included lyrics about substance abuse. This figure was highest for rap songs. Three-quarters of the rap songs analyzed included lyrics about substance abuse.

Researchers have also content analyzed speeches, announcements, and public statements in order to determine the speakers' values, ideologies, positions, and personality traits, among other things (Coffey 2005; Neuman et al. 2015). Using YouTube and other video sources, Elise Giuliano (2018) analyzes the statements made by activists at demonstrations in the Ukraine in order to understand what motivated their support for Russian-backed separatists in Donbas. The statements emphasized concerns about Ukraine's membership in the European Union, the Ukrainian government's condemnation of the special police, and its policies toward the Russian language and the nationalist far-right.

Visual Materials

A multitude of different visual materials are used for content analysis as well. These materials include television programs, commercials, films, music videos, comic books, video games, and Instagram photographs, among other things. Like content analyses of written and spoken forms of media, content analyses of visual forms of media are typically used to characterize the political, social and cultural values portrayed in them. Unlike content analyses of written and spoken media, though, content analyses of visual content are based not on what individuals say, or what is said about them, but the appearance of individuals. This includes whether or not certain groups appear in visual content, their actions and activities, as well as their physiognomy, among other things.

Consistent with analyses of print and spoken media, much research on visual media indicates that women and minorities appear less frequently in advertisements and entertainment media than men and non-minorities, and are often portrayed in traditional and stereotypical roles (Rudy et al. 2010, 2011). PepsiCo produced such a commercial in 2013 to great controversy. In the soft drink commercial, a woman who had been assaulted is depicted viewing a police line-up in which all the suspects were Black men, except for a goat, who taunted the woman with phrases like 'snitches get stiches.'[5] PepsiCo pulled the ad, which was soundly criticized for depicting Black men, and only Black men, as criminals, aggressors, and animals, shortly after it first aired.

Content analyses of video games reach similar conclusions about stereotypes and discrimination. These analyses find that minority males are not only underrepresented in magazines and covers for top-selling video games, but they are also often portrayed in them in stereotypical roles, as either athletes or aggressive and violent thugs (Burgess et al. 2011). In the video games themselves, men and women are also often portrayed with idealized bodies in terms of strength in the case of men, and thinness in the case of women (Martins et al. 2009, 2011).

Measures and Applications

Using content analysis, researchers have constructed a number of different types of quantitative measures from qualitative materials. The most common types of these measures and the meanings researchers ascribed to them are discussed below and summarized in Table 17.2. The shortcomings of these measures and examples of their use are also presented in this section.

Size

The most basic type of information that researchers derive from content analysis is the size of the written, spoken, and visual material. For a written or spoken text, size is measured in terms of the length of a text or, more specifically, the total number of words used in it.

Size	Counts	Location	Similarity
importance	events	events	influence
interest	intensity	importance	
discretion			
effort			
quality			

Table 17.2 Common measures and their meanings

For a visual image, size is measured in terms of the dimensions of the object. Researchers have inferred a number of things about the attributes of and intentions behind the size of a text or image.

Meaning of the Measure

Typically, researchers take the size of a written or spoken text or image to represent the importance of, or interest in, an issue, either in terms of the producer of the content or the intended audience. More words and larger images are understood to signify greater importance and interest in a text or image. A cursory inspection of print and broadcast media supports this assumption. In these media, longer articles and broadcasts are devoted to topics that editors want to emphasize, deem important, and expect to be of greater interest to their audiences.

Some researchers have suggested that the length of a text is also indicative of its quality. Length, according to Joshua Blumenstock (2008), is a good measure of quality in terms of Wikipedia entries, because it is indicative of the authors' interest in a subject and, thus, their motivation to write a high quality entry. Consistent with his expectations, Blumenstock finds that the number of words contained in a Wikipedia entry is strongly correlated with its quality. Quality is assessed in terms of whether or not an entry is a 'feature article'. The Wikipedia editors designate entries as feature articles based on their assessment of the entries' accuracy, neutrality, completeness, and style.

The motivation that John Huber and Charles Shipan (2002) associate with length does not arise from interest in a subject, but rather a desire of legislators to limit the discretion of bureaucrats. This motivation is greater, according to the researchers, when issues are complex and when the preferences of bureaucrats are not aligned with those of the legislators. Statutes are longer, according to Huber and Shipan, because they are more detailed, and include more policy-specific language about what bureaucrats ought to do as opposed to procedural language about how to do it. Their argument is supported by a content analysis of Medicare legislation in the United States, and legislation on gender discrimination in 19 other countries.

Validity of the Measure

The size of a written or spoken text and image is a largely valid measure of the importance of, or interest in, the content contained within a text or image. Of course, that is not to say that it is a perfect measure of the importance. In written and spoken texts, length is determined in part by style. Some people are very concise and to the point in their writing and conversation, while others are verbose and desultory. Length can also reflect differences in language. Fewer words, for example, are needed to express ideas in German than in other languages because independent words can be combined in German to convey new ideas. German is not alone in having rather lengthy words. Apparently, Mongolian and Greek have some of the longest words of any written language.

While the size of a written or spoken text or an image is a largely valid measure of importance or interest, it is not, in general, a valid measure of quality of a written or spoken text – whether this text is a book, thesis, news or magazine article, speech, and so forth. Length is not indicative of the originality of an idea, the quality of an argument, the appropriateness of the evidence provided in support of an argument, and so forth. Length may be a good predictor of quality in the case of Wikipedia entries because these entries are factual in content and completeness is a criterion of quality, but not otherwise.

Written and spoken texts, as well as images, can also be multifaceted, making it difficult to attribute the size of a text or image to one subject. Political speeches, for example, delivered by candidates running for office, leaders already in power, as well as those stepping down from power, are likely to address many topics related to their countries' current and future states of affairs. Likewise, legislation, known as omnibus legislation, contains measures on many different subjects. For this reason, many researchers use counts of specific elements of texts and images instead of the overall size of a text or image to measure the importance of, and interest in, certain issues, among other things.

Counts

The number of times certain words or images appear in a text is perhaps the most common type of quantitative data that researchers extract from qualitative materials using content analysis. These counts are often expressed as a percentage of the total words used in a text to account for variation in the size of texts. Researchers also count, although less commonly, the number of times certain types of words (e.g., non-specific words, slang, and vulgarities) and non-words (e.g., exclamation marks or emoticons) appear in texts.

Meaning of the Measure

Counts of types of words and non-words are frequently used to characterize the overall tone or sentiment of a text as either positive or negative. Sociologists Scott Golder and Michael Macy (2011) have used the number of positive versus negative words and emoticons in Twitter posts to identify changes in moods. Positive moods, the researchers find, tend to peak mid-morning and late evening, including weekends, suggesting, according to the researchers, that moods are driven, at least in part, by an underlying biological rhythm that transcends culture and environment.

Political scientists have used the number of negative words in political campaign advertisements to ascertain the effects of mudslinging on the willingness of voters to cast ballots for candidates using them (Kahn and Kenney 1999). Researchers across disciplines have also used counts of the number of positive and negative words in a text to characterize public sentiment towards goods and services (Qu et al. 2008; López et al. 2012), political, social, and economic issues, as well as political candidates and world leaders (Jensen and Anstead 2013; Ceron et al. 2015).

Counts of specific words or objects are used for different purposes. Counts of specific words are used instead to identify the number of times an event, such as an election, natural disaster, or terrorist attack, occurs based on reports of these events in newspapers. They are also used to enumerate the representation of particular groups, typically women and minorities, in different texts and images, as well as their behaviors.

Counts of specific words or objects are further used, as in the case of size, to measure the importance of and interest in a specific issue either from the perspective of the producer of the text or its intended audience. The *Comparative Manifesto Project*, for example, measures the importance or salience of an issue for political parties based on the number of times an issue or item is mentioned in a party platform (as a share of all coded issues or items).[6] Using this information, researchers have estimated parties' left–right positions (Laver and Garry 2000), and analyzed why particular issues are salient for certain parties and not others (Netjes and Binnema 2007).

Validity of the Measure

Word counts overcome several of the problems with using measures of the overall size or length of a text or image. Word counts are not dependent on stylistic or linguistic differences among writers because they are based on specific words or sets of words. They are also not affected for this reason by unrelated or extraneous content in a text or image, as in the case of omnibus legislation.

However, count measures are not without their own shortcomings. Measures of the number of times positive versus negative words (or non-words) are used in a written text only provide a superficial account of attitudes, and cannot recognize sarcasm or other playful uses of language.

Meanwhile, counts of specific words or objects are often hard to interpret and to accurately infer meaning from. The word 'beat', for example, may mean to physically harm someone or it may mean to outperform another person in a competition. Likewise, the word 'protest' may mean to object to something or it may refer to a mass street demonstration.

Word counts of single words are especially problematic because the meaning of particular words can vary based on the words that precede or follow them. The word 'depression', for example, represents an emotional state but 'economic depression' represents a financial state. Similarly, the word 'security' can refer to the military defense of a nation, the physical security of an individual, or an economic assistance program, depending on whether it is preceded by the word 'national', 'personal', or 'social'.

This particular problem with word counts can be resolved by analyzing sets of consecutive words. However, it is still difficult to understand the meaning behind the use of either single or consecutive words out of context. A valuable example in this regard is the DeWall et al. (2011) study of narcissism in American culture. To measure narcissism, the authors calculated the difference in the number of times the first-person singular (i.e., 'I' and 'me') and the first-person plural (i.e., 'we' and 'us') were used in the most popular songs in the United States between 1980–2007. Based on an increase in the use of the first-person singular relative to the first-person plural, the researchers concluded that narcissism rose sharply in the United States in this period.

The use of the first-person singular versus the first-person plural does not necessarily characterize well the degree of narcissism within songs (nor is narcissism in popular songs indicative of narcissism among Americans in general). For example, in 'Rise Up' a song by Andra Day, considered an anthem of courage and resilience in the face of adversary, the word 'I' is used 22 times and the word 'we' is used 16. This is a mildly narcissistic song based on the differences in the usage of 'I' and 'we' in it. However, the word 'I' is not used narcissistically in the song, as this refrain demonstrates: 'And I'll rise up. I'll rise like the day. I'll rise up. I'll rise unafraid. I'll rise up. And I'll do it a thousand times again. For you. For you. For you. For you.' In this refrain, the word 'I' is used to refer to an action undertaken on behalf of another person.

Location

In addition to the number of times a word or object is used, researchers use content analysis to identify the location of words or objects. For words, the location is defined in terms of where the words appear within a sentence or within an entire text. For objects, the location is defined in terms of where the objects appear within an image, and where this image is located within certain textual or visual content.

Meaning of the Measure

The location of a word within a sentence is used to ascertain information not only about whether or not an event occurred, but also about who were the initiators and recipients of the action. The location of a word within a sentence indicates whether the word is the subject (initiator), verb, or object (recipient) in a sentence. (This technique is only used on lead sentences in news articles because they typically follow a standard format.) Consider the following sentence: 'Israel launched an air strike today at Hamas-held positions in Gaza in response to rockets that it claims the group launched at Israel last week.' In this example, Israel is the initiator of the action and Hamas-held positions are the object of the action.

Information about where words are located in a sentence, as in this example, provides a much richer understanding of an issue. A simple word count of an air strike or a missile launch would only indicate whether or not a launch occurred, while information about who is the initiator and recipient of the action based on the location of a word in a sentence would reveal who launched the missile against whom. The identity of the initiator and recipient of the action can seriously change the significance of the event. In this example, the significance of the event would be quite different if Hamas launched an attack against Israel rather than vice versa.

Knowing the location of a word in a sentence in some cases can also help clarify the meaning of some words. It could help resolve, for example, the ambiguity around the use of the word protest and other words whose meaning varies depending on whether it is a noun or verb in a sentence. If the word protest is used as a noun in a sentence than it is more likely to refer to a mass demonstration than an objection. Likewise, the word attribute refers to a characteristic of an object when it is used as a noun and it means to credit or blame someone for something if it is used as a verb.

The location of a word or image within an entire text is also used as a measure of the interest in, or importance of, an issue, from the perspective of either the producer of the content or its intended audience. The location of words is coded in terms of whether the words appear at the beginning, middle, or end of a written or verbal communication. Words that appear either at the beginning of a written or spoken text or at the end are generally considered to be more important than those that appear in the middle of a text.

The location of an object is coded in terms of whether the object is in the center or on the sides of the text. Images in the center are generally more important than those on the sides of the text. Which side is more important depends on the language. For languages that are read from left to right, such as Latin-based and Germanic languages, images that are on the left are potentially more important, while for languages, such as Arabic, Hebrew, and Urdu, which are read right to left, images that are on the right are arguably more important. For online content, words or images that appear 'above the scroll' are considered more important, and of greater interest to others, than those that appear 'below the scroll'. Content that is 'above the scroll' can be viewed without paging down. This term is equivalent to the term 'above the fold' for broadcast sheet newspapers, where words and images that appear 'above the fold' are considered more important, and of greater interest to readers, than those that appear 'below the fold.'

Validity of the Measure

Knowing the location of a word(s) and object(s) provides researchers with additional information with which to refine their measurement of events and to estimate the importance of, or interest in, a subject. As a measure of importance of, and interest in, a subject, this measure has certain shortcomings. Like the previous measures of importance and interest, this measure captures two distinct motivations, namely what producers of the content think is important and interesting, and what producers of the content think consumers of the content will find interesting and important.

A potentially more valuable measure that better distinguishes between the two might be the number of times a user clicks on an article or image. Clicks would directly measure the interest of viewers in a subject. However, where an item is located on a page can also influence the number of times it is clicked on.

There are also practical difficulties in using the location of a text or image as a measure of importance of, and interest in, a subject. For online media, it can be difficult to identify the location of items on a website because publishers, especially publishers of newspapers and magazines, often change the location of their online content throughout the day, so that a story or an image that is 'above the scroll' one moment, may be 'below the scroll' the next.

Similarities

Lastly, researchers also use content analysis to construct measures of the similarity of words or images used in different written, oral, and visual sources. The extent to which two texts are similar depends on the number of words or images that they have in common.

Meaning of the Measure

The similarity of texts in terms of the use of words or images is used to identify influence. In educational settings, it has been used to identify cheating (a perverse of influence), based on similarities in students' assignments using computerized software. In communications research, it has been used to demonstrate the influence of news media, and their choices of which stories to publish, on each other (Denham 2014).

Conversely, the lack of similarity in texts and images has been used to demonstrate a lack of or decline in influence. Using content analysis to compare commonalities between the US Constitution and other countries' constitutions, David S. Law and Mila Versteeg (2012), for example, find that the United States' influence on the human rights components of other countries' constitutions has declined in recent decades. Meanwhile Himelboim et al. (2013), analyzing the political opinions of individuals expressed on social media outlets, find that individuals have little influence over the political opinions of others in their social media networks because people in the same networks are already ideologically similar to each other.

Validity of the Measure

Commonalities in words and objects provide a rather compelling measure of influence, but they cannot definitively demonstrate influence because the similarity in two or more texts or objects may be due to the influence of another unidentified source. Two papers, for example, may be very similar to each other, not because the students copied each other's work, but because they both independently bought the same paper from a service selling term papers. Analyses based on commonalities are compelling to the extent that researchers can eliminate other potential sources of influence.

They also cannot identify negative influence. That is, where the example of one case discourages a similar outcome in another. If, for example, a newspaper receives a lot of criticism for publishing a certain story, and another newspaper decided not to publish the same story as a result, the absence of the story in other news outlets would suggest that the original newspaper did not influence the other newspapers when it did.

Techniques and Tools

Content analysis can be conducted using either human-coders or computer programs depending on the measure and the material analyzed. Spoken materials can only be content analyzed using computers through written transcripts, and visual materials can only be content analyzed by human-coders. Computers also cannot be used to identify the location of an object, whether it is written, verbal, or visual, with a larger text, such as a newspaper or magazine, but it can be used to identify the locations of words within a sentence. Computerized content analysis is also not completely independent of humans. In order to analyze data with a computer, researchers have to first clean the data by correcting spelling and transcription errors, and in many cases, compose dictionaries to instruct the computer regarding which words to code in the text.

Advantages and Disadvantages of Different Techniques

Computerized content analysis has several advantages over hand-coded content analysis. It allows researchers to analyze many more materials than human-coders at a greater speed and lower cost. Computer programs also provide more reliable estimates because they are not subject to human errors, like miscounting, but they are sensitive to misspellings.

The coding of terms is also less subjective in computerized content analysis than in human-coded content analysis as it is based simply on the appearance and location of words or sets of words, and not on any interpretations of their meanings. The objectivity of these measures, though, is also a shortcoming of computerized content analysis vis-à-vis human coding because the meaning of a word in many cases cannot be distilled from a word or set of words, and can be different, as the previous examples have shown, depending on the context in which it is used. Computers are not able to discern meaning from words, as can human-coders.

A computer cannot, for example, understand the meaning or the importance of the use of the acronym, Daesh versus ISIL, to refer to the Islamic State of Iraq and the Levant (ISIL). In Arabic, ISIL is known as al-Dawla al-Islamiyafi al-Iraqwa al-Sham. Daesh is an acronym for the Arabic name of the group. Many leaders, analysts, commenters, and so forth use the term Daesh instead of ISIL to delegitimize the group. The group vehemently objects to the use of Daesh to describe it, and has threatened to cut out the tongues of anyone using it, because the acronym is similar to two derogatory Arabic words – 'Daes', which means 'one who crushes something underfoot', and 'Dahes', which means 'one who sows discord'.

The How-tos of Different Techniques

The first step involved in hand-coding texts or images requires the development of a clear and detailed coding rubric. A rubric explains what needs to be coded and what must be true for a given observation to be coded one way versus another. Prior to beginning their analysis, researchers ought to test the rubric against examples that will not be used in the analysis and refined as needed. After the rubric has been developed, researchers must train the human coders on how to use it. This process may help to further clarify and refine the coding rubric. In training the coders, researchers should assign the coders a few pre-coded examples against which they can compare the trainees' work, to ensure that the coders understand the rubric fully and are diligent in their work.

During the coding process, researchers may randomly assign coders examples of pre-coded texts in order to ensure that the quality of the coders' work is high and consistent. Researchers may also inform the coders that their work will be periodically checked against pre-coded texts to further encourage careful and thorough work. Ideally, two people should code each case with a third expert coder resolving any discrepancies between the two. Researchers should also record the potential reasons for these discrepancies and calculate intercoder reliability statistics (e.g., Krippendorff's Alpha and Cohen's Kappa). Low intercoder reliability will cast serious doubt on the quality of the analysis.

The process of computerized content analysis is quite different. The first step in computerized content analysis is for researchers to clean the materials to be analyzed by eliminating misspelling and transcription errors. While human coders can ignore these issues, computers are very sensitive to them. The next step, depending on the type of computerized content analysis performed, is for researchers to construct a dictionary. A dictionary informs the computer about which words or sets of words to identify. This step is not necessary if the researcher is only interested in a total word count or is coding every word in a text. The final step is to run the program.

There are various programs and tools for computerized content analysis, many of which are free and open-source. The best program for a given project depends, in part, on the structure and language of the original materials and the types of measures to be extracted from them. For simple measures involving counts of words and sets of words, there are many user-friendly programs with point-and-click interfaces, such as Atlas.ti, SAS Text Miner, Text Analyzer, and WordStat. Some of these programs have built-in dictionaries to categorize words into positive and negative sentiments. For more complex analyses identifying sets of consecutive words or the function of a word in a sentence, researchers will likely need to write their own code using programs, such as Python.

Further Reading

The first reading discusses the use of content analysis for analyzing the effects of the media. The second and third readings provide comprehensive guides to collecting and analyzing data using content analysis.

Key Points

- Content analysis allows massive amounts of qualitative data to be compared systematically through the transformation of this data into quantitative measures.
- There are tradeoffs involved in transforming qualitative data into quantitative measures and data. The qualitative data is richer, more nuanced, and complex than the quantitative data, but the quantitative measures are objective, comparable, consistent, and reliable.
- Measures constructed through content analysis are evaluated based on the same criteria all quantitative measures are evaluated against, namely their validity, reliability and discriminatory power.
- There are tradeoffs involved in hand-coded and computer-coded content analysis. Hand-coded content analysis is more subjective and sensitive to the context and less reliable than computer-coded qualitative materials.

Jerit, Jennifer and Jason Barabas. 2011. 'Exposure Measures and Content Analysis in Media Effects Studies.' In *The Oxford Handbook of American Political Opinion*, edited by George C. Edwards III, Lawrence R. Jacobs, and Robert Y. Shapiro, 139–155. Oxford: Oxford University Press.

Krippendorff, Klaus. 2018. *Content Analysis: An Introduction to its Methodology*. Thousand Oaks, CA: Sage Publications.

Schreier, Margrit. 2012. *Qualitative Content Analysis in Practice*. London: Sage Publications.

EXERCISE 17.1

For each of the examples below, discuss how well the measures derived from content analysis represent the associated concepts. For each measure, identify at least one or two virtues of the measures and at least one or two shortcomings of the measure.

1. importance of security versus other issues for a political party in a given election based on the number of times the word terrorist or terrorism is mentioned in all campaign commercials produced by the party.
2. number of earthquakes that occur each year based on the number of times that an earthquake is mentioned in newspapers with the largest circulation on each continent (i.e., *Yomiuri Shimbun* (Asia); *Bild* (Europe); *Clarín* (Latin America), *Al-Ahram* (Middle East and North Africa); *The Wall Street Journal* (North America); *Mail & Guardian Online* (Sub-Saharan Africa). (Duplicates events are not counted.)
3. satisfaction with a product or service based on the number of positive versus negative words used in reviews of the product or service on Yelp or another similar service.
4. support for a policy based on the number of 'likes' a Twitter message extolling this policy receives.

EXERCISE 17.2

Design a study using content analysis to examine one of the issues below or an issue of your own choosing. Your study should include all of the following:

* a list of the sources you will use and a discussion of any potential problems that may arise with the quality of these sources.
* a description of the measures you will derive from these sources.
* an explanation of the link between these measures and the extent to which they are valid measures of the given concept.
* a discussion of whether a computer program or human-coders will be used and why.

Examples:

1. use of 'frank' or 'honest' speak in electoral campaigns.
2. portrayal of homosexuals in product advertisements.
3. gender bias in undergraduate textbooks.
4. public opinion regarding a specific government corruption scandal based on Twitter comments.
5. attribution of blame for terrorist attacks based on the comments by readers posted online beneath front-page news articles covering the attacks.

18
Surveys

Objectives

- identify the different types of surveys used in social science research
- discuss the strengths and weaknesses of surveys vis-à-vis other research methods
- provide guidance on designing survey questionnaires
- identify types of survey modes and their appropriateness for certain respondents
- explain how to calculate formulas relevant to the analysis of surveys

Of all the quantitative methods used in the social sciences, surveys are probably the method that is best known to the greatest number of people. It seems almost impossible today to do anything without being asked to complete a survey – from flying across country to purchasing a ticket for an artistic performance to even attending a religious ceremony. Formally, a *survey* is a method for collecting information from a sample of individuals in order to construct quantitative descriptors of attributes of the larger population from which this sample is drawn. Therefore, almost by definition the strength of surveys is their ability to produce comparable and generalizable data. However, the strength of surveys in terms of comparability is a double-edged sword. While the close-ended nature of most survey questions enhances the comparability of survey responses, it also simplifies a person's experiences and limits the utility of surveys for theory building. The extent to which researchers are able to maximize the advantages of surveys, while minimizing their shortcomings, depends on many different aspects of survey research, beginning with the selection of the participants and ending with the administration of the survey itself.

Types of Surveys

There are different ways to typologize surveys. Surveys can be categorized by the mode in which they are distributed (e.g., paper, telephone, in-person, and online), by their breadth or scope (e.g., longitudinal versus cross-sectional), or by the population that they survey (e.g., expert and non-expert). The latter typology is used here because differentiating surveys from each other by their population also distinguishes them in certain respects in terms of their purpose and content as well.

Expert Surveys

Expert surveys are surveys of individuals with a specialized knowledge on a particular subject related to the theme of the survey. These experts may include academics, researchers, and professionals, such as lawyers, judges, curators, businessmen, government officials, and so forth. These experts, as such, are not chosen through random sampling, but rather through non-random, purposive sampling.

Expert surveys can take one of two forms. In the first, the opinion of the experts is the quantity of interest. That is, the purpose of the survey is to collect information about the sample of experts questioned. Examples of this kind of expert survey include: the TRIP Snap Polls of IR Scholars[1] and the Academic Reputation Survey.[2] The TRIP polls survey international relations scholars about their opinion of global events to provide policymakers guidance on these issues. The Academic Reputation Survey, instead, asks academics to identify what they think are the world's top-performing institutions for research and teaching in order to ascertain information not captured by commercial ranking systems.

In the second, the opinion of the experts is not the quantity of interest. The quantity of interest is the thing about which their expert opinion is solicited. These expert surveys are not surveys in the sense described in the introduction because they do not seek to generalize about the experts, but to use information acquired from the experts to characterize something else. The difference between the two is subtle but important.

There are various expert surveys on parties' political positions (Laver and Hunt 1992; Huber and Ingelhart 1995; Benoit and Laver 2007). These surveys ask academics to identify the positions of political parties on key political, economic, and social issues, as well as their overall left–right ideology. The Electoral Integrity Project (EIP) is another example of this kind of expert survey. The EIP asks country experts a battery of questions to assess the quality of elections along a number of different dimentions.[3]

Non-expert Surveys

Non-expert surveys, in contrast, are surveys of individuals that do not have a specialized knowledge on a particular subject. Non-expert surveys are much more common than expert surveys, and are the type of survey that most people think of when they think of surveys. Respondents for non-expert surveys may be chosen through either non-random or random techniques. Only the latter, however, are likely to yield survey samples that are representative of the population from which they are drawn.

Using non-expert surveys, researchers can collect an array of information. They can collect subjective information on people's opinions, attitudes, perceptions, desires, and so forth, as well as objective information on people's age, income, education, religion, and ethnicity. In some cases, surveys are the only way to obtain the latter information because this information is not collected on government censuses. France does not collect census data on race or ethnic origins, for example, reportedly because it is reminiscent of the Nazis' branding of Jews and other minorities during the Second World War. Rwanda does not collect census data on ethnicity either as a result of the 1994 Rwandan genocide in which as many as a million Hutus and Tutsis died in a single year of fighting.

The Utility of Surveys

Surveys are unparalleled in their ability to provide objective, comparable, and generalizable data about the cognitions, emotions, and behaviors of individuals. The extent to which surveys are able to achieve these ends depends on many different aspects of survey design, including the selection and recruitment of participants, the wording of the questions and response categories, as well as the administration of the survey.

Comparability

Surveys facilitate comparisons across individuals for two reasons: first, every respondent to a survey is asked the same question. Although the wording of the questions is the same across respondents, not every person may be asked every question if the question is not relevant to them. For example, a person may not have to answer a question in a survey about how long they have been unemployed if the person indicated on a prior question that s/he was employed.

Second, most survey questions are close-ended. Close-ended questions are questions with defined response categories. These categories may be discrete (e.g., 'male' and 'female') or continuous (e.g., age and years of schooling), dichotomous or multichotomous. Close-ended questions facilitate comparisons across respondents by standardizing the respondents' answers.

Techniques for close-ended questions, such as *anchoring vignettes* (King et al. 2004), can further facilitate comparisons across responses. This innovative technique standardizes respondents' answers to survey questions using vignettes to determine whether their answers tend to run high or low compared to other respondents. This technique is challenging to implement in certain contexts because it can be difficult for researchers to construct effective vignettes, and because the vignettes themselves are time-consuming and mentally taxing for respondents to complete. Standardizing responses may also not always be necessary or helpful given the research subject.

Although close-ended questions facilitate comparisons across responses, close-ended questions also simplify individuals' experiences because they do not allow respondents to explain why they answered a question the way that they did. As a result, two people may provide the same response to a question for very different reasons. One person, for example, may be 'somewhat satisfied' with the outcome of an election because they believe that their candidate should have won by a larger margin of victory than s/he did, while another person may be 'somewhat satisfied' with the outcome of an election because their candidate lost, but their second most preferred candidate won.

Since close-ended questions do not allow respondents to explain why they answered a question the way that they did, a close-ended question, in and of itself, cannot be used to generate new hypotheses if the respondents' answers to this question are inconsistent with the researcher's expectations. Researchers, though, may be able to deduce why certain questions do not confirm their hypotheses from respondents' answers to other questions.

For example, a researcher lacking an open-ended question asking participants who said that they do not support democracy promotion abroad why they do not, might deduce from other questions about national spending, as well as the feasibility and utility of installing democratic regimes in other countries, that the cost of democracy promotion is an important reason why they do not (Brancati 2014a). This would be the case if a majority of those who said that they do not support democracy promotion abroad also said that they thought it was possible to install democratic regimes in other countries, and that it was in their country's national interest if other countries were democracies, but also allocated no money to foreign aid in response to another survey question about national spending.

Generalizability

Surveys have a high potential to yield generalizable results because surveys are amendable to random sampling and large-N designs. A large-N design increases the likelihood that a survey will be representative of the larger population that it claims to represent because when the number of observations in a study is large, there is a greater potential for a range of views representing this population to be captured than when it is small. The chances are greater that if a researcher surveys 500 people rather 50 people from a group that the researcher is interested in characterizing, that the survey will be indicative of the whole of the group's views in the case of the former than the latter. Random sampling techniques, which are discussed in Chapter 9, also facilitate generalizability because they reduce the odds that the survey participants are systematically different in some way from the larger population from which they are drawn and are purported to represent.

Of course, neither random sampling nor large-N designs guarantee that surveys are fully representative of the larger population that they are intended to represent. Low response rates, survey attrition, observer bias, and the guinea pig effect can all threaten the generalizability of surveys.

There are a number of strategies that researchers can utilize in order to maximize response rates and minimize attrition (i.e., participants dropping out of longitudinal surveys after successive rounds). These strategies are summarized in Table 18.1. There are a number of themes that unify the individual strategies summarized in this table. They relate to reducing the burden that surveys place on participants; ensuring that participants perceive a personal benefit in completing the survey; protecting the privacy of the participants; and sending reminders.

Stage	Strategy
Pre-survey	distribute survey in non-busy time periods (if known) and avoid holidays
	send invitation letter and reminder emails
	describe survey's importance and how information from it will be used
	inform potential participants of the time estimated to complete the survey
	explain to potential participants the personal benefit from participation, such as improved services
	promise to keep participants' identities anonymous or confidential
	alleviate concerns that participation will result in contact information being sold to commercial mailing lists
	offer payment or a chance to win a reward
Survey	distribute survey via means (e.g., internet, phone, or in-person) easiest for person to complete
	keep number of questions to minimum
	use simple, straightforward language
	ask non-time intensive questions
	do not require responses to questions
	allow respondents to skip questions not relevant to them

Table 18.1 Strategies to maximize response and complete rates

Observer bias, where the researchers unintentionally influence the results of the survey through their presence is not common, since researchers rarely administer surveys themselves. With in-person surveys, the enumerator (or interviewer) could influence the participants' responses and, therefore, should not know what the researcher is testing in the survey. However, it is impossible to avoid the guinea pig effect in the case of a survey. To reduce the likelihood of participants providing responses that do not represent their views but which they think are socially more desirable, researchers should not ask leading questions or use judgmental language that might suggest that one answer is more desirable than another.

The publication of survey results can also make it appear as if a survey is not representative of the population it claims to represent when it was at the time the survey was administered. This is because the results themselves can change public opinion on issues, especially for those who have a weak opinion on an issue. Individuals who have a weak opinion, or are undecided, may upon seeing the results of a survey change their opinion to be consistent with the majority opinion. Not only can the results change people's opinion on issues, but they also can alter their behaviors. If, for example, an election poll indicates that a particular candidate is winning an election by a small margin, supporters of the opposing candidate may turn out in large numbers to vote for their preferred candidate, tipping the scales in favor of their candidate. Polls taken on political policies ahead of referendums to decide these policies can have similar effects.

Survey Questionnaire Design

Designing survey questionnaires is as challenging as it is important to the success of a survey. The survey design affects not only the comparability and generalizability of the survey responses, but their accuracy and completeness as well. Thus, researchers must put a great deal of thought into the construction of the questionnaire. Prior to putting the survey in the field, researchers should also always solicit feedback from friends, family members, and colleagues on the survey design, and pre-test the survey among a small group of individuals who ideally resemble those who will ultimately take the survey.

Table 18.2 summarizes a number of rules to facilitate researchers in writing effective surveys.

Question wordings

- do not ask leading questions to encourage responses consistent with theoretical expectations
- use simple everyday language
- use unambiguous and precise language
- define terminology where its use is unavoidable
- avoid double-barreled questions
- do not assume familiarity or knowledge with an issue

Question wordings

- use consistent wording and terminology across questions
- avoid judgmental and pejorative words or terms
- avoid double negatives and other convoluted language
- do not put high demand on recall in terms of details or past events

---

Response categories

- eliminate redundant words by including words common to all response categories in question
- ensure response categories flow directly from the question wording
- do not put high demand on recall by requiring detailed information
- include a neutral category that may be a true representation of people's views
- do not use numerical scales (e.g., 1–5) without words
- include 'other' categories (with write-in spaces) where response categories are not necessarily exhaustive of all possible answers
- use open-ended questions only where uncertain of how people might respond to questions and where respondents' answers may be very broad
- include a 'do not know' category apart from a 'no response' category since respondents may not answer a question for reasons besides 'not knowing' the answer

---

Question order

- begin survey with a general, neutral, and welcoming question
- ask less important questions, including demographic questions (e.g., gender, age, education, income) at the end
- ask open-ended questions towards the end of the survey

Table 18.2 Questionnaire design

Clarity

Clarity is the most important rule for writing effective survey questions from which many other rules follow. Survey questions have to be very clear so that the respondents interpret the questions in the way the researcher intended them and provide accurate answers to the questions as a result. The questions also need to be clear so that the respondents interpret the questions in the same way as each other. If they do not, their responses will not be comparable. If the respondents do not think that the questions are clear, they may also skip them entirely.

To ensure that the questions are clear, researchers ought to use ordinary, but precise language, as well as simple and straightforward sentence constructions. Researchers should also avoid double negatives (e.g., 'Please identify which of the following statements is not inaccurate'), as well as double-barreled questions. Double-barreled questions ask two questions in one (e.g., 'Do you support increased spending on education and health?'). This question is double-barreled because it asks respondents about both education and health in a single question. Respondents should be asked about these issues in separate questions because although education and health are both forms of public spending, respondents may support increased spending on one of these issues and not the other.

Not only should the question wording be clear, but the response categories should also be clear. For this reason, it is important that researchers do not use numerical scales (e.g., 1–5) without words, since respondents may interpret the meaning of the numbers differently. Using words does not rule out the possibility that respondents will have different ideas of what constitutes 'very good' or 'excellent', but it does reduce the range of their interpretations. See Figure 18.1.

DON'T	1	2	3	4	5
	1	2	3	4	5
DO	Excellent	Very Good	Good	Fair	Poor

Figure 18.1 Numerical scales

Terminology

Clarity demands that researchers define their terms. Researchers must define the terms that they use because participants may not be familiar with them, or understand them in the same way as either the researcher or other respondents. While democracy, for example, is a widely familiar term, it means different things to different people. Western countries define democracy in terms of open and competitive elections, as well as strong political and civil liberties. However, Singaporeans associate democracy with good governance (e.g., employment and social welfare). As a result, Singaporeans rate the level of democracy in Singapore very highly in surveys even though Singapore does not have open and competitive elections or strong political and civil rights.[4]

Sometimes, it is best to avoid using a term entirely. Instead, for example, of asking participants how democratic they think their country is, researchers may ask respondents 'To what extent do laws in their country make it difficult for parties to get on the ballot?', or 'How likely is it that a person who publicly criticizes the government will be jailed for expressing his/her view?' This strategy is especially useful when a concept, like democracy, has many different components to it so that it is difficult to define the term clearly and concisely.

Conciseness

In striving to make questions clear and precise, researchers can unintentionally make questions long and verbose. Verbosity can deter respondents from answering questions. To avoid it, researchers should eliminate redundant and unnecessary words or phrases from their questions. Researchers may also make use of pictures for this purpose. In the Middle

East Values Study (MEVS), instead of using terms that respondents might not be familiar with, or using a lot of words to describe different types of religious attire, researchers showed respondents pictures of the attire and asked them to indicate what style of head covering they thought was most appropriate for women in public.[5] See Figure 18.2.

Conciseness is important not only for individual questions, but also for surveys overall. In order to reduce the burden that surveys place on respondents, researchers should ask the fewest number of questions, and the fewest number of open-ended questions, possible. Open-ended questions require more elaborate responses and tend to have lower response rates as a result. Too many open-ended questions, especially in a row, can cause people to stop filling out a survey. For this reason, open-ended questions are best placed either at the end of the survey or dispersed throughout it.

Demand

Surveys should not only be concise, but they should also not place high demands on respondents in terms of their time or knowledge. A high demand on either will reduce the likelihood that respondents will answer a question. A high demand on the latter can also reduce the accuracy of their responses. Open-ended questions are only one way in which

'Which one of these women is dressed most appropriately for public places?'

% of women saying garment is most appropriate for public places

	1	2	3	4	5	6
Tunisia	1	2	3	57	23	15
Egypt	1	9	20	52	13	4
Turkey	0	2	2	46	17	32
Iraq	4	8	32	44	10	3
Lebanon	2	1	3	32	12	49
Pakistan	3	32	31	24	8	2
Saudi Arabia	11	63	8	10	5	3

Figure 18.2 Survey using pictures for response categories

Source: Mansoor Moaddel, 'A Report: The Birthplace of the Arab Spring: Values and Perceptions of Tunisians and a Comparative Assessment of Egyptian, Iraqi, Lebanese, Pakistani, Saudi, Tunisian, and Turkish Publics,' University of Michigan Political Studies Center. 15 December 2013.

surveys can place a high demand on respondents' time. Another thing that places a high burden on respondents' time and knowledge is to ask respondents' questions requiring very specific responses.

A survey question asking respondents to recall how many hours they spend each day on particular social media websites (e.g., Facebook, Twitter, YouTube, and Instagram) requires much more specific information of respondents than a question asking them to estimate how many hours they spend each day using any form of social media. The former places a much higher burden on respondents' time and knowledge. For many respondents, the second question may still place too high a demand on their recall. A better question may be to ask respondents: 'How much time do you spend using social media websites (e.g., Facebook, Twitter, YouTube, and Instagram) each week?' using the following response categories: 'a lot'; 'a fair bit'; 'very little'; and 'none at all.'

Efficiency

Streamlining questions can also make them less taxing for respondents. Eliminating extraneous words (e.g., 'a', 'an', and 'the'), as well as redundant language (e.g., 'added bonus', 'close proximity', and 'foreign imports') is important in this regard.

Another important strategy for streamlining survey questions is to make sure that the response categories follow a common syntax and include in the text of the question any words common to all response categories. One way, but not the only way, to accomplish this is by using an ellipsis, which is preceded by the word that is common to all the response categories. For example: 'I use social media websites for ...' (1) 'business purposes primarily'; (2) 'social purposes primarily'; (3) 'business and social purposes about equally'; (4) 'neither business nor social purposes'; (5) 'don't know'.

Another important way to streamline survey questions is to make sure that the response categories follow directly from the question wordings. This is not the case in the following example: 'On average, how often do you use the internet every day?' '0–1 hours'; '1–2 hours'; '3–5 hours'; '5–8 hours'; '8–12 hours'; '12 or more hours'. The response categories do not follow directly from the question in this example because the question asks 'how often' a person uses the internet, not 'how many hours per day' they use it. To make the question and response categories consistent, the response categories could be changed to denote frequency as in: 'very often'; 'fairly often'; 'occasionally'; 'rarely'; and 'never'. Alternatively, the question could be rewritten as: 'On average, how many hours per day do you spend using the internet?'

Sensitive Issues

Survey questions on sensitive issues present a particular challenge for researchers. Respondents may provide inaccurate responses to these questions because they are embarrassed, or worried that if their responses become known their physical safety or livelihood could be harmed. Or, the respondents may simply be so offended by the questions that they refuse to answer them or complete the survey.

There are several strategies researchers can use to elicit honest responses to sensitive questions. These strategies are summarized in Table 18.3.

Desensitize the Environment

First and foremost, researchers ought to desensitize the environment in which these questions are asked. This means that researchers should extend anonymity, not just confidentiality, to respondents. Anonymity means that researchers do not collect any identifying information from the respondents, while confidentiality means that researchers only disclose identifying information under mutually agreed upon terms.

For in-person surveys, researchers should also create a safe, comfortable, and nonjudgmental environment for the respondents. This may be achieved through the interviewers' tone, facial expression, and body language. It may also be achieved by matching the demographic characteristics of the person administering the survey to those of the respondent. This could entail, for example, having female enumerators (i.e., persons conducting the survey interviews) interview female respondents for surveys on domestic abuse; minority enumerators interview minority respondents on surveys about racial bias among police officers; and secular enumerators interview secular respondents regarding laws about the banning of veils worn for religious reasons in public places.

Desensitize the Questions

Desensitizing the question wording is equally important. To accomplish this, researchers must avoid judgmental and pejorative language. Researchers should do this for all questions, though, regardless of whether they address sensitive issues or not. Researchers can also desensitize questions by phrasing them and their response categories in broad terms. For this strategy to succeed, the question wording and response categories should be no

Stage	Strategy
Pre-survey	promise respondents anonymity, not just confidentiality
Administration	create safe, comfortable, and nonjudgmental interview environment
	match interviewer and respondent demographics
Questions	de-sensitive question wordings and response categories
	list experiments
	randomized response techniques

Table 18.3 Strategies for sensitive questions

more specific than is necessary for researchers to obtain the information they need for their research.

Consider the example of voting. In some countries, especially weakly democratic states, information about which party someone voted for is a very sensitive issue. In some countries, individuals can be denied educational opportunities, employment, economic and health services if they did not vote for the 'right' candidate. In these countries, instead of asking respondents whom they voted for in the last election, a researcher might instead ask respondents how satisfied they were with the outcome of the last election.

This question is less sensitive than the first because it does not ask respondents outright what party they voted for in the election. It still captures this information indirectly, though, because a person is less likely to be satisfied with the outcome of an election if the party they voted for did not win the election. However, it is not as precise as the first question because there may be different reasons why someone was not satisfied with the outcome of the election. A person may not be fully satisfied with an election because their preferred party did not win, or because their preferred party did not win by as many seats or by as wide a margin as the person believes they should have won. Depending on the subject of the research, though, a researcher might not need to know anything more than how satisfied a person was with the outcome regardless of the specific reason why they were not.

The same strategy may be applied to the response categories. For example, in questions regarding income, researchers provide very wide response categories for income, such as '€50–100K' instead of '€50–75K' and '€75–100K'. Similarly, for questions regarding gambling or addictive behaviors, rather than asking a person how much they lost gambling or how many hours they spend gambling per week, a researcher may ask respondents if they lost more or less than a given threshold (e.g., 'Did you lose more or less than X gambling in the last month?'), or how often they gamble (e.g., 'Which of the following best describes how often you gamble? … never; several times a year; several times a month; several times a week; and almost every day.').

If, researchers are unable to desensitize the question and response categories in this way, they may ask respondents questions indirectly about sensitive issues by asking them about related behavior or traits, which are likely to be true if the person engaged in the sensitive act. Of course, this is not as useful as having honest answers to direct questions, but it is preferable to having dishonest answers to direct questions.

If, for example, a researcher wants to know the motivations of former combatants for joining a civil war, they may not receive honest answers if they asked the respondents this question directly (Humphreys and Weinstein 2008). Many former combatants may claim to have been abducted and forced to fight because it is often socially more acceptable to have been abducted than to have volunteered to fight because of shared ideals or money. It can also be safer if the former combatants are on the losing side to the conflict.

Therefore, researchers might ask former combatants indirect questions that give them a sense of these motivations instead. Researchers might ask, for example, 'What did you know about the political goals of the group at the time you joined?' or 'Did the group offer you a cash payment if you joined?' If the respondent did not know very much about the groups' goals, or was not offered material incentives to join, then the researcher may get a sense that neither ideology nor financial gain were important in the combatants' decision to join the war.

List Experiments

In addition to de-sensitizing questions, there are two other commonly used strategies for gathering information on sensitive issues – list experiments and randomized response techniques (Blair, Imai, Zhou 2015). In a *list experiment*, the survey sample is split into two groups. Both groups are asked to identify 'the number' of statements (not which ones) on a list that are true of them. All but one of these statements is the same across the two groups. The one that is different is related to the sensitive issue. In order for the researcher to determine the frequency of the sensitive behavior from differences in the number of statements that people in the sensitive and non-sensitive groups say are true of them, all of the non-sensitive statements must be statements that everyone in both groups would agree are true.

Figure 18.3 depicts a list experiment designed to determine if foreign students cheated on their college entrance exams. Cheating poses a major challenge for many universities as foreign students who have cheated on their exams often lack the competence to undertake their studies once accepted. In China, firms exist through which students can hire high-performing proxies to take entrance exams for them. A list experiment is appropriate to understand this issue because students are unlikely to honestly answer this question directly, since they could be expelled from their universities or have their degrees revoked if it is known that they cheated on their entrance exams.

As this example illustrates, there are a number of shortcomings to list experiments. First, the instructions are not easy to understand for enumerators (i.e., the person administering the survey) or survey respondents. Often, respondents do not understand that they only need to indicate 'how many' statements are true of them, not which ones.

Second, everyone in both the sensitive and non-sensitive groups must agree with all of the non-sensitive statements. However, it can be difficult for researchers to come up with

We are interested in learning about the experiences of Chinese students studying abroad. Can you please tell me HOW MANY of the following things are true of you? We are not interested in knowing WHICH ONES are true of you, only HOW MANY?

Non-sensitive group	Sensitive group
1. I can communicate proficiently in either Mandarin or Cantonese	1. I can communicate proficiently in either Mandarin or Cantonese
2. I attended middle and high middle school in China.	2. I attended middle and high middle school in China.
3. I know at least a little English.	3. I know at least a little English.
	4. Someone took the SAT or ACT exam for me.

Figure 18.3 List experiment

questions that every respondent would agree are true. Almost everyone is likely to respond in the affirmative to the first and third question in the survey experiment depicted in Figure 18.3. There may be a sizeable number of students, though, who do not agree to the second question because parents in China are increasingly sending their children abroad for secondary school to increase their likelihood of being accepted into foreign colleges and universities.

Third, since everyone in both the sensitive and non-sensitive groups must agree with all of the non-sensitive statements, the sensitive statement is quite conspicuous. As a result, many respondents are unlikely to admit to the sensitive behavior. In the cheating example, the fourth statement is obviously different from the other three, and not something a student who fears losing their college degree would likely admit.

Randomized Response Techniques

A randomized response technique offers an alternative means to solicit information on sensitive issues. Using a randomized response technique, the respondent is asked to toss a coin when the back of the enumerator is turned, so that the enumerator does not know if the coin landed on heads or tails.[6] The enumerator then tells the respondent that if the coin lands heads to respond 'yes' to the question, and if the coins lands tails to tell the enumerator the truth. Once everyone's responses have been collected, the probability of person's correct response being 'yes' is calculated using the following formula: $P(yes) = P(yes|heads)P(heads) + P(yes|tails)P(tails)$

In this equation, $P(yes)$ is the probability that a respondent answers 'yes' to the question. It is equal to the proportion of respondents who responded 'yes' to the question in the survey. $P(yes|heads)$ is the conditional probability that a respondent says 'yes' when the coin lands on heads. This probability equals 1 because a participant is instructed to always respond 'yes' in this case. $P(yes|tails)$ is the conditional probability of saying 'yes' to tails, and $P(heads)$ and $P(tails)$ are the probabilities of obtaining heads and tails, respectively. Both are equal to 1. Letting $P(yes|tails) = P$ in the above formula and solving for P gives: $P = 2P(yes)-1$.

To see how this is calculated, consider the following example regarding foreign students cheating on their college entrance exams. In this example, 75 of 100 students surveyed said 'yes' to the following question: 'Did you cheat on your college entrance exam?' This includes some students who cheated on their exams and some who did not. Using the above formula to calculate the percentage of 'yes' responses that are true of the respondents, you get: $P = 2P(75) - 1$. Thus, in this example, 50 percent of the survey respondents cheated on their college entrance exam.

Like list experiments, *randomized response techniques* are not easy for respondents to grasp. Often, respondents do not understand how the setup of the technique prevents researchers from knowing whether they engaged in the sensitive behavior or not, and even those that do, may deny the behavior regardless. As a result, when the coin lands on heads, many people are not likely to say 'yes' as instructed, especially those who did not engage in the sensitive behavior. Likewise, when the coin lands on tails, and the person is supposed to tell the truth, many respondents are unlikely to admit to the sensitive behavior.

Survey Administration

The *survey mode* is the means by which the survey is administered. Surveys may be administered either in person, on paper, by telephone, or via the internet. In deciding how to administer their surveys, researchers need to consider three major issues – the cost, the response rate, and the potential for selection bias.

Online is generally the least expensive means by which to administer a survey, while in-person is the most expensive. In an in-person survey, an enumerator reads each question to the respondent and marks down their response. The costs of in-person surveys are much greater than other survey modes because they involve hiring an interviewer to travel to people's homes generally and to read each question to the respondent.

The costs of online surveys are minimal because they only involve designing the survey and paying a service to distribute the survey via email. Telephone surveys are less expensive than in-person surveys but generally more expensive than internet surveys. Although researchers need to pay enumerators to call respondents and to pay for the phone calls, calling respondents is less time consuming than travelling house-to-house to interview them. The costs involved in paper surveys generally fall somewhere in between in-person and telephone surveys, but this really depends on the country and the costs involved in printing and mailing surveys.

In deciding how to administer the survey, researchers must balance their concerns about the costs of running the survey against their concerns regarding the response rate. To maximize the response rate, researchers ought to administer the survey according to the method that is easiest for the greatest number of participants in the sample. In developing countries, where literacy rates are low, postal systems are unreliable, and access to the internet is limited, this is likely to be an in-person survey. In advanced economies, where the opposite is true, paper or online surveys are more appropriate.

The final issue of concern for researchers in deciding how to administer surveys is the potential for selection bias to arise from the mode of administration. Even if the response rate is high certain groups may be excluded from the sample. Older and poorer people may be underrepresented from online surveys, while younger people and wealthier people may be underrepresented in paper, telephone, or in-person surveys. To avoid this predicament, sometimes researchers may use more than one mode of administration, or as discussed in the next section, they may use statistical techniques to adjust the sample afterwards.

Analyzing Survey Results

Many issues relevant to analyzing surveys are also relevant to other quantitative methods and are discussed in other chapters. This section focuses instead on several analytic issues specific to surveys, namely response rates, samples, and margins of sampling error.

Response Rates

A high response rate is necessary for a survey to be representative of the population from which the survey sample is drawn. The response rate is calculated as: the number of respondents/the number of persons contacted*100. Calculations of the response rate differ based on who is included among the 'respondents' and 'persons contacted'.

Some researchers calculate response rates taking a 'respondent' to be anyone who answered at least one question on the survey, while others only consider a 'respondent' to be a person who answered every question on a survey. For the latter the response rate is equivalent to the *completion rate* (i.e., the percentage of individuals who 'completed' the survey).

The 'number of persons contacted' varies as well. Some researchers include in this figure everyone who they attempted to contact, while other researchers only include those who they were able to contact. Some researchers also exclude from this group those who they were able to contact, but upon contacting them, learned that they were mistakenly included in the original sample. This would be the case if men with gender-neutral names ended up in a sample for a survey of women, or if children ended up in a sample for a public opinion survey of likely voters.

Regardless of who is included among these groups, it is good practice to calculate the response rate using different definitions of respondents and persons contacted, and to report any significant discrepancies among the results.

Weights

Sample weights are used to create more representative samples, which can occur when response rates are low. Sample weights adjust for the over-, or more typically, the under-representation of certain groups of individuals by altering the weight assigned to each observation in the sample. There is a general consensus that sample weights should be used for descriptive statistics, but there is no such consensus regarding regression analyses and multivariate analyses since sample weights result in less precise and more variable estimates.

There are two types of sample weights – design weights and post-stratification (or non-response) weights. *Design weights* are used to compensate for over- or under-sampling of specific observations or for disproportionate stratification. Design weights are easily calculated for each case as 1/(sampling fraction). The sampling fraction is the ratio of the sample size to population size. If, for example, we oversample minorities at a rate four times higher than non-minorities, the design weight would be ¼ for minorities and 1 for non-minorities.

Post-stratification weights are used after the sample has been selected and used to compensate for the fact that persons with certain characteristics are less likely to respond to surveys than others. Calculating post-stratification weights is much more complicated than calculating design weights. It involves an iterative process in which the weight is first calculated for a certain demographic characteristic and then successively re-calculated for each demographic characteristic included in the weight.

Replacement samples, multi-imputation, and selection models offer alternative means for creating representative sample weights. Replacement samples are used in longitudinal surveys. A replacement sample is a sample of new respondents added to the original sample to replace respondents that withdrew from a longitudinal survey after having participated in at least the first round of the survey. Multi-imputation does not alter the respondent sample, but rather assigns values to missing data based on characteristics of the observed data.

Unlike replacement samples and multi-imputation, selection models, such as propensity score matching and Heckman selection models, adjust for the potential differences between individuals that remain in the sample and those that do not. However, there is much skepticism as to the ability of these techniques (which are discussed in greater depth in Chapter 20) to correctly identify the reasons why participants withdraw from surveys.

Margin of Sampling Error

The *margin of sampling error* indicates how much the results of a survey question may differ due to chance compared to what would have been found if the entire population was surveyed. The smaller the margin of sampling error the better. The margin of sampling error is based on the sample size (not the total size of the population) and is generally smaller for larger samples. The margin of sampling error is a percentage and usually reported alongside the response to a particular question. A margin of sampling error of +/–3 or +/–5 percent is common.

The margin of sampling error is calculated as follows:

$$z^* \sqrt{\frac{\hat{p}(1-\hat{p})}{n}}$$

where $\hat{p}$ is the sample proportion, n is the sample size, and z^* is the appropriate z^*-value for the desired level of confidence (1.96 for a 95 percent confidence interval). Both $n\hat{p}$ and $n(1-\hat{p})$ must be at least 10 in order to use a z^*-value in the formula for the margin of error for a sample proportion.

Below is an example of how the margin of the sampling error is calculated for the following question: 'Do you approve or disapprove of the way the president/prime minister is handling his/her job?' In this example, the number of people in the 1000-person sample who said that they approved of the job the prime minister/president was doing is 480.

The margin of sampling error for this question, therefore, is:

$$z^* \sqrt{\frac{\hat{p}(1-\hat{p})}{n}} = 1.96 \sqrt{\frac{(0.48)(0.52)}{1000}} = (1.96)(0.0158) = 0.031, \text{ or } +/-3.1 \text{ percent}$$

Key Points

- Surveys can be used to collect objective data as well as subjective data on a variety of topics and issues.
- Surveys, through the use of random sampling and consistent measures across subjects, are able to produce comparable and generalizable data, but can simplify subjects' experiences compared to interviews or other forms of qualitative data.
- The wording and ordering of questions, the survey mode, and the environment in which surveys are conducted can significantly affect the quality of responses and should be tailored to the subject of the survey and the person surveyed in order to encourage honest and complete responses.

Further Reading

The first four readings provide guidance on designing survey questions. The fifth reading provides information not only on designing survey questions, but also on issues related to data quality, data collection, and survey administration.

Fowler, Floyd J. 1995. *Improving Survey Questions: Design and Evaluation.* Thousand Oaks: Sage.

Iarrosi, Giuseppe. 2006. *The Power of Survey Design.* Washington, DC: World Bank.

Krosnick, Jon A. and Lee R. Fabrigar. 2006. *The Handbook of Questionnaire Design.* New York: Oxford University Press.

Tourangeau, Roger and Ting Yan. 2007. 'Sensitive Questions in Surveys.' *Psychological Bulletin* 133(5): 859–883.

Wolf, Christof, Dominique Joye, Tom E.C. Smith and Yang-chih Fu. 2016. *The SAGE Handbook of Survey Methodology.* London: Sage Publications.

EXERCISE 18.1

Re-write three of the poorly worded survey questions below in order to encourage people to respond honestly regarding the sensitive information solicited in these questions. Explain why you worded the questions as you did; how well the questions get at (or capture) the sensitive information; to what extent you think the questions are still sensitive; and how many people (e.g., most, some, or barely anyone) do you think will answer your revised questions.

- Have you ever bribed someone in exchange for a favor?
- Do you use illegal drugs for recreation use?
- Are you a racist?
- Are you sexist?
- Have you ever snooped on your partner?
- Have you ever seriously considered committing suicide?

- Have you ever lied on a job application?
- How much do you donate to charity every year?
- Have you ever been arrested?

EXERCISE 18.2

For one of the sensitive issues that you wrote desensitized questions on in Exercise 18.1, write a list experiment. Compare the desensitized questions and the list experiment in terms of the extent to which each gets at (or captures) the sensitive information, and the likely effectiveness of each in soliciting honest responses regarding the sensitive issues.

19

Experiments

Objectives

- identify the different types of experiments used in social science research and compare and contrast their advantages and disadvantages
- discuss the strengths and weaknesses of experiments vis-à-vis other quantitative research methods
- present the criteria commonly used to evaluate the quality of experiments
- explain the basic estimation techniques used in the analysis of experiments

Experiments are a type of quantitative method in which researchers randomly assign individuals to experimental conditions (i.e., a treatment condition where the explanatory factor is present and a control condition where it is not) in order to test causal arguments. Experiments are most commonly associated with the natural sciences, but are used widely across the social sciences to study various subjects, including cognitive biases, political preferences, social programs, learning outcomes, and so forth. The types of experiments, though, commonly used in the social sciences are more diverse than those used in the natural sciences where laboratory experiments are predominant. In the social sciences, field experiments and natural experiments are also common.

Experiments, regardless of their type, are considered the gold standard in quantitative methods for causal inference. The random assignment of individuals to experimental conditions, and the variation of only the explanatory variable across these conditions, isolates the effect of the explanatory variable and helps to eliminate alternative explanations for the outcome of interest. Although the goal standard for causal inference, experiments are not always feasible or appropriate for many interesting and important questions in the social sciences, and are not necessarily representative of the real world.

Types of Experiments

There are three basic types of experiments: laboratory experiments, field experiments and natural experiments, as well as a number of sub-types, such as lab-in-the-field experiments and survey experiments. The experiments are distinguished from each other by the location in which they are conducted, the medium through which the experiments are administered, and the process by which the random assignment is achieved. As experiments, they all have an advantage over other methods in terms of causal inference. At the same time, however, they have a number of strengths and weaknesses vis-à-vis each other due to their differences.

Lab Experiments

Laboratory experiments are experiments that are conducted in a common location in which the researcher has full control over the environment in which the experiment is conducted. Although one typically thinks of laboratories in terms of university settings, a lab may be any location in which all study participants complete the experiment. Regardless of the location, the lab is typically a sterile environment with minimal decorations to distract participants.

In laboratory experiments, these tasks generally involve participants playing a game, reading a vignette, looking at images, or watching a video. Participants' responses to these stimuli can be measured in terms of the outcome of the game, the participants' behaviors in subsequent tasks, and their responses to survey questions, among other things. Lab experiments are especially useful when experimental manipulations do not exist in the real world, as in the case of a particular voting system, and cannot be studied through observational approaches as a result.

Laboratory experiments have been used to understand human behavior on a wide range of subjects. In political science, they are commonly used to understand voting decisions under different electoral rules. In business and economics, instead of voting decisions, laboratory experiments are commonly used to understand financial decisions under different incentive structures. In psychology, meanwhile, laboratory experiments are often used to understand attitudes and bias, and in education, they are frequently used to understand learning outcomes and the psychological factors involved in them.

Laboratory experiments have a number of advantages over other types of experiments. With lab experiments, researchers are better able to ensure that the experiment is administered properly than with other types of experiments. In lab experiments, researchers are more capable of ensuring that individuals are fully randomized to treatment and control groups, that every individual in the explanatory condition receives the same treatment and complies with it, that individuals in the control condition do not inadvertently receive the treatment, and so forth.

The high degree of discretion that researchers enjoy in laboratory experiments also allows researchers to analyze more variation in experimental conditions than is often possible in field experiments. In a laboratory experiment on investment, for example, researchers could test the effectiveness of multiple different types of financial programs that encourage people to invest more and spend less simply by having subjects play different games for each type of inventive structure. In a field experiment, to do the same study, researchers would have to convince multiple governments, banks, or development agencies to adopt different programs with a range of investment incentives, and to accept the financial risk of doing so should the programs fail.

Despite, or perhaps because of these virtues, laboratory experiments have a number of shortcomings that limit the generalizability and validity of the experiments. First, lab experiments may not represent well real-world effects because the experimental manipulations and environments in which the experiments are conducted are artificial. Lab experiments, which use computerized games to understand foreign policy decision-making, for example, do not capture well the gravity and pressure leaders face regarding the financial and human costs of these decisions in the real world.

The effects observed in lab experiments may also be exaggerated because distractions common in the real world are eliminated in lab experiments in order to rule out confounders and to ensure that participants engage in the experiments fully. They may also be exaggerated because laboratory experiments do not assess the long-term behaviors of subjects. A lab experiment would be unlikely to detect what Uri Gneezy and John A. List (2006) found through field experiments regarding employee bonuses for the latter reason. In two field experiments involving real employees, Gneezy and List found that employees work harder when they are given a bonus for their work, but that the effect of the bonus dissipates within only a few hours of work.

The effects of lab experiments may also be inflated because in the real world people generally make decisions based on multiple considerations over a long period of time rather than in response to a single and immediate stimulus. Laboratory experiments, which ask participants how likely they are to vote for a candidate based on a single consideration, such as the physiognomy of the candidates (Todorov et al. 2005) or even a scandal (Funk 1996) exemplify this issue. In the real world, people cast their ballots based on multiple factors that they weigh against each other over a prolonged period of time.

Second, the findings from lab experiments may not be representative of the population at large or the specific population that the experiments purport to represent because they are often conducted on non-representative populations. In the social sciences, lab experiments are often conducted on university students, who are younger, more educated, and wealthier than the general population. In some experiments, like the voting experiments mentioned above, this may not be particularly problematic since it is not obvious that young, educated, and upper-income individuals would be affected differently by the treatment than others. However, in other experiments, such as those on savings and investment, they are. Much research shows that young people and those in low-income brackets make different savings and investments decisions from those of their counterparts (Noussair et al. 2014; Filiz-Ozbay et al. 2015).

Students are not only different from the general population, but they also tend to be homogeneous. As a result, researchers are unable in lab experiments to identify heterogeneous treatment effects – that is, effects that vary depending on characteristics of individuals, such as age, education, wealth and so forth. For some experiments, the effects may not vary across demographic groups, but in others, as in the case of experiments on savings and investments, there is likely to be significant variation among demographic groups.

Lab-in-the-Field Experiments

To address the concern that laboratory experiments are conducted on non-representative populations, researchers will often use lab-in-the-field experiments instead. *Lab-in-the-field experiments* (LITFE, also known as artefactual field experiments) are laboratory experiments that are conducted on theoretically relevant populations.

LITFEs are lab experiments because they are conducted in a common location over which the researcher exerts full control, although this location may be unconventional, such as a judge's chamber, an empty jail in a police station or prison, or a tent in a rural setting. The kinds of tasks that participants complete in these locations are the same as in laboratory experiments. Participants may be asked to play a game, read a vignette, look at images, watch a video and so forth.

LITFEs differ from standard lab experiments in that the participants in LIFTEs are theoretically relevant. The participants in a LITFE on the influence of racial bias, for example, might be police officers, while the participants in a LIFTE on transitional justice might be former combatants in civil wars. For many, though, the distinction between laboratory and lab-in-the-field experiments is unnecessary, because the population on which the experiments are conducted is not a defining feature of laboratory experiments.

Field Experiments

Field experiments, in contrast, are experiments in which researchers do not have control over the environment in which the experiment is conducted beyond the experimental manipulation. Field experiments include survey experiments, which are discussed in the next section, and non-survey based field experiments. Non-survey based field experiments involve changing an aspect of the real world and measuring the effect of this change. That change often involves a revision or modification of an existing policy, program, or institution, or the adoption of a new one.

Field experiments like these have been used to understand many different issues. They have been used to analyze the effectiveness of rehabilitation programs in reducing recidivism among ex-convicts and former wartime combatants (Blattman and Annan 2016; Köbach 2016); the ability of cash transfer programs to alleviate poverty (World Bank 2016; Hadna et al. 2017); the utility of electoral monitors in reducing electoral fraud (Hyde 2007; Ichino and Schündeln 2012; Brancati 2014b; Bush and Prather 2017); and the impact of empowerment programs on rates of child marriage (Sandøy et al. 2016), among many other things. In these studies, the participants are randomly assigned to be subjected to a given program or policy, or not. The effectiveness of the program or policy is then assessed through a comparison of those who participated in the program or policy and those who did not, in terms of certain outcomes related to the purpose of the program or policy.

Since field experiments are conducted outside the laboratory, they are generally more realistic or true to life than laboratory experiments. By virtue of the same fact, however, researchers are also less capable of ensuring that an experiment is administered properly in the case of field experiments than in the case of lab experiments. In field experiments, there is a greater chance than in lab experiments that the randomization will not be complete, that participants will not comply with the treatment, and that the treatment and control conditions will be cross-contaminated, among other things. In field experiments, for example, the randomization may not be complete because agencies require certain politically important or at-risk groups receive the treatment. Participants may not comply fully with the treatment in field experiments by not attending all the meetings of a program, while persons in the control condition may be treated in field experiments because persons in the treatment condition share information learned through the treatment with them.

With non-survey based field experiments researchers also often do not have full control over the research design because they have to work in collaboration with governments and organizations, which have their own priorities and concerns, in order to conduct the experiments. Often, these collaborations can make it difficult for researchers to fully randomize treatment assignment and to change only one aspect of a policy or program across treatment and control conditions. It can also result in shorter treatment periods than desirable due to the collaborator's funding prerogatives.

Survey Experiments

A *survey experiment* is a type of field experiment in which the experimental manipulation is executed via a survey. Survey experiments are a type of field experiment because the researcher does not have full control over the environment in which the survey is completed.

However, the experimental manipulation in a survey experiment is abstract and artificial, as in the case of laboratory experiments.

Typically, in survey experiments, the experimental manipulation or treatment is a vignette, but it can also be an image or video. In these experiments, participants are asked to read the vignette, view an image, or watch a video and then answer questions related to their outcome of interest. Only one aspect of the treatment – either the vignette, image, or video – is different between the treatment and control conditions so that it is possible for researchers to evaluate the effect of this one aspect on the given outcome.

An example of a basic survey experiment about the effect of CEO apologies on the reputations of corporations is presented in Box 19.1.

Box 19.1   Survey Experiment on Corporate Apologies

In the experiment, the participants, who are divided equally into two groups, read one of the following vignettes:

> Vignette 1: After a video of a CEO – who heads a major corporation whose products and services you use and like – surfaced in which the CEO made sexual comments about the appearance of one of his female employees, the CEO immediately issued a public statement saying that he regretted the incident.

> Vignette 2: After a video of a CEO – who heads a major corporation whose products and services you use and like – surfaced in which the CEO made sexual comments about the appearance of one of his female employees, the CEO immediately issued a public statement saying that he regretted the incident, and made a lengthy and thoughtful apology for his behavior.

After reading the vignette, the respondents are asked the following questions:

[Vignettes 1 and 2]: How, if at all, does the CEO's sexual comments about his employee affect your opinion of the corporation?

1.   lowers it a lot
2.   lowers it somewhat
3.   has no effect on it at all
4.   raises it somewhat
5.   raises it a lot
6.   do not know

[Vignettes 1 and 2]: How, if at all, does the CEO's comments affect your willingness to use the company's products and services?

1.   reduces it a lot
2.   reduces it somewhat

3. no effect on it at all
4. increases it somewhat
5. increases it a lot
6. do not know

[Vignette 2 only]: How sincere, if at all, do you believe the CEO's apology was?

1. very sincere
2. somewhat sincere
3. neither sincere or insincere
4. somewhat insincere
5. very insincere
6. do not know

[Vignette 1 and 2]: What do you think the CEO meant when he said that he regretted the incident? [open-ended response]

This example illustrates the strengths of survey experiments in terms of their generalizability and their weaknesses in terms of realism. The example is potentially generalizable because it does not depict a specific corporation, CEO, or incident of sexual harassment in the real world (although a person might be thinking of a particular incident in their mind when answering the question). The action that provoked the apology is specific to sexual harassment, however, and may not have changed people's perception about the corporation much in the first place because it did not directly relate to the corporation's products and services.

While the fact that the vignette does not depict a specific corporation, CEO, or event is an advantage in terms of generalizability, it is a disadvantage in terms of the realism of the experiment. The survey experiment is not very realistic not only because the vignette does not depict a specific company, CEO, or incident, but because the vignette also lacks details about the CEO's sexual comments and subsequent apology. Without these details, the incident described in the vignette may not provoke the same kind of emotional response that an incident of sexual harassment would in the real world, and might either exaggerate or underestimate the effect of corporate apologies as a result.

Natural Experiments

Finally, the last type of experiment is a *natural experiment*, which was discussed in the previous chapter on observational studies. It is arguable whether natural experiments should be classified as experiments or not because some definitions of experiments, like the one provided at the outset of this chapter, specify that subjects are randomized to treatment and control groups specifically as a result of the actions of a researcher. In natural experiments the treatment assignment is random, but not as a result of the researcher. In natural experiments, the treatment is exogenous to the outcome as a function of the real world. Natural experiments are discussed instead for this reason in Chapter 20.

Evaluating Experiment Quality

Three basic criteria are used to evaluate the quality of experiments. They are: construct validity; internal validity; and external validity. Various factors affect the extent to which experiments satisfy these criteria, and some types of experiments are better positioned to meet these criteria than others. Table 19.1 summarizes the forthcoming discussion and the potential for different types of experiments to meet these criteria (with the exception of natural experiments for which many of these criteria are not relevant). As is apparent from this table, there is a significant tradeoff between internal and external validity – with the potential for internal validity greatest for laboratory and LITFE experiments and the potential for external validity greatest for non-survey- and survey-based field experiments.

Construct Validity

Construct validity refers to the degree to which inferences from an experiment are relevant to a theory. A construct is the measure of the explanatory condition in an experiment (e.g.,

	Laboratory experiment	Lab-in-the-field experiment	Non-survey field experiment	Survey experiment
Construct validity	low-medium-high	low-medium-high	low-medium-high	low-medium-high
Internal validity				
Researcher bias	low	low	low	low
Non-compliance	low	low	low-medium-high	low-medium-high
SUTVA	low	low	low-medium-high	low-medium-high
External validity				
Unrepresentative sample	high	low-medium	low-medium	low-medium
Attrition bias	low-medium-high	low-medium-high	low-medium-high	low-medium-high
Guinea pig effect	high	high	low-medium	high

Table 19.1 Validity of experiments

Note: The evaluations presented in this table (i.e., low, medium, and high) are subjective, and the extent to which an experiment meets a given criterion depends not only on the type of the experiment, but also on the quality of a particular experiment. To capture the range in the quality of different types of experiments to meet each criterion, multiple labels are used as appropriate.

survey vignette, dictators game, and job training program). Construct validity is similar to measurement validity, which is discussed in Chapter 15. Measurement validity refers to the degree to which a measure captures the concept it purports to represent, while construct validity refers to the degree to which an experimental setup tests the theory it claims to represent.

Construct validity is very specific to the particular experiment. No particular type of experiment – whether it is a laboratory, LITFE, or non-survey- or survey-based field experiment – is better positioned to satisfy this criterion than another.

To better understand the concept of construct validity, consider the example of laboratory-based voting experiments. Voting experiments in which people are asked to cast ballots for hypothetical candidates under different electoral rules in order to understand these rules' effects on vote choice have very high construct validity. They have high construct validity because the rules under which participants are asked to cast their ballots can be constructed to perfectly match the rules that the researchers have theorized.

A construct that has lower validity is the use of 'Black sounding-names' as a measure of race. Numerous field experiments have been conducted in which researchers have used Black-sounding names as a proxy for race. The experiments are designed to understand the extent of racism in society, and its effect, in particular, on people's willingness to hire candidates for jobs (Bertrand and Mullainathan 2003); the inclination of landlords to rent apartments to people on Airbnb (Edelman et al. 2017); and the predisposition of teachers to perceive certain students as trouble makers (Okonofua and Eberhardt 2015), among other things. Black-sounding names, such as Lakisha and Jamal, has low-medium construct validity because Black-sounding names may signify more than just race. For many people, they also connote certain cultural attributes (e.g., dress, language, and tastes) and socio-economic status. Therefore, experiments analyzing the effects of racial discrimination using Black-sounding names may be identifying racism towards Blacks who exhibit particular cultural and economic characteristics, not Blacks in general.

Internal Validity

Internal validity refers to the degree to which the relationship between the explanatory variable and the outcome variable is causal. The internal validity of a study may be compromised by a number of conditions including the failure of researchers to fully randomize subjects to treatment and control groups, non-compliance with the treatment, observer or researcher bias, violations of the stable unit treatment value assumption (SUTVA), and so forth.

The failure to fully randomize subjects to treatment and control groups can compromise the internal validity of an experiment because it can result in systematic differences in the types of participants in the treatment and control conditions. This is especially problematic if these differences make the participants more or less likely to be responsive to the experimental treatment. Experiments in which the randomization is not full are referred to as 'quasi experiments'.

The French weather and courtship study is one such example (Guéguen 2013). In this experiment, five 20 year old men who were part of the study approached 500 women walking on the street in two towns in western France, and asked these women for their phone numbers after telling them that they thought they were very pretty. In the study, the women were significantly more likely to give the man who approached them their phone number on sunny days than on cloudy days. The randomization was not full in this experiment since the researchers could not randomize the type of women likely to be on the street on sunny versus cloudy days. It is possible that more women, who are less open to being flirted with and sharing their phone numbers with men regardless of the weather, are on the streets in greater numbers on cloudy days than on sunny days, because they are more serious, work-driven, less social, and so forth.

In general, in laboratory experiments and non-survey-based field experiments, researchers face fewer difficulties randomly assigning subjects to treatment and control groups than in field experiments. In laboratory experiments and non-survey-based field experiments, when researchers are unable to fully randomize the assignment to treatment and control conditions, it is typically because the explanatory factor in the experiment is an innate characteristic of the person, such as gender or personality. It is obviously impossible to randomly assign a person to a gender, for example, in order to determine if women are more or less likely than men to make certain types of policy and legal decisions (Boyd, Epstein, Martin 2010).

In field experiments, it is even more difficult to fully randomize treatment assignments due to the ethical, political, and programmatic concerns of the collaborating agency. In a field experiment, for example, evaluating a post-civil war reintegration program, Blattman and Annan (2016) were unable to fully randomize the treatment assignment because the program sponsors required that all top military commanders be included in the treatment condition since they posed the greatest threat to society. The inclusion of these leaders in the study may have resulted in the effectiveness of the program being underestimated because commanders are less likely to be receptive to the program than lower ranked combatants, and more likely to engage in renewed violence.

Non-compliance with the treatment also poses a threat to the internal validity of the experiment. Treatment non-compliance occurs when participants in an experiment do not undertake the task asked of them, whether it is to play a game, read a vignette, or adhere to the rules required of a program, and so forth. If a large number of participants fail to comply with the treatment, the experiment might result in a weak or null effect, not because the treatment is ineffective, but because the participants did not fully take part in the experiment.

In general, non-compliance is less of a concern for laboratory experiments than for field experiments because in the lab, participants do not have any distractions and the researcher (or their assistant) is in the same room with the participants when they complete the experiment, serving as a reminder, if not pressure, to undertake the experiment fully. In field experiments neither is the case. In field experiments, participants may discard a flyer mailed to them as part of an experiment without reading it. They might not read carefully the vignettes or questions in a survey experiment when completing the experiment at home, or they may not adhere to the requirements of a program due to other obligations, and so forth.

Box 19.2   Manipulation Check

A *manipulation check* is a test included in an experiment to determine if the participants received the treatment. Participants might not have received the treatment for many different reasons, including not reading the vignette in a survey experiment, discarding a flyer in a survey-based field experiment, not listening to the discussions in a group therapy session, and so forth. A manipulation check generally asks participants a factual question regarding the treatment. A manipulation check in the case of the survey experiment in Box 19.1, might consist of a question asking the respondents, after reading the vignette, to describe the actions of the CEO. Researchers may exclude the responses of participants who did not pass the manipulation test from their analysis as long as the researchers report having done so in the description of their results.

While participants not being observed can lead to non-compliance with the treatment, being observed can result in other effects that compromise the internal validity of the study through a phenomenon known as observer bias. *Observer bias* (or experimenter bias) occurs when the researcher unintentionally affects the outcome of a study through their presence. Researchers may do so through verbal or non-verbal clues, such as facial expressions and gestures, which influence the behavior or choices of the participants. The paradigmatic example of observer or experimenter bias is Clever Hans, a horse whose trainer claimed he could do mathematics.

When asked basic math problems, this turn-of-the-century fair horse tapped the correct answer with his hoof. While Clever Hans may have been clever, his mathematics ability was due to observer bias. His trainer unintentionally gave away the correct answer through his body language, which was discovered when the horse was asked to do calculations in different experimental conditions in which the horse could not observe his trainer. It turns out that as Clever Hans approached the right answer, his trainer's posture and facial expression changed in ways that were consistent with an increase in tension. When the horse tapped the right answer, the trainer's expression changed again in ways indicative of a release of tension, indicating to Hans that he had tapped his hoof a sufficient number of times.

The likelihood of observer bias arising can be minimized through double-blind experiments. A double-blind experiment is an experiment in which neither the person running the experiment nor the participants know whether the participants are in the treatment or control group. If the person running the experiment is unaware of which participants are in the treatment condition and which participants are in the control condition, this person cannot unintentionally behave in ways that are likely to lead to differences between the two groups.

Violations in the *stable unit treatment value assumption* (SUTVA) also compromise the internal validity of an experiment. SUTVA is violated under two conditions. The first is when the treatment is not the same across subjects, and the second is when there is cross-contamination between the treatment and control groups. Both compromise the internal validity of an experiment because they can mask the true effect of the experimental treatment.

The first SUTVA violation is often a function of poor design. If 100 people are given the same vaccine in communities of different sizes, so that 10 percent of one community is treated and 100 percent of another is treated, the treatment is not the same, because the percentage of people treated in the communities is not the same. As a result, the people in the first community are more likely to get the disease than those in the second, because they are more likely to interact with others who have not been given the vaccine.

The second type of SUTVA violation may also result from poor design or execution, as when researchers or their assistants mistakenly give the treatment to individuals in the control group. It is more likely to result, though, due to the actions of the participants and the researchers' lack of full control over the environment in which the experiment is conducted, as in the case of field experiments. A researcher, for example, may select communities that are far apart in distance so that members of one community – all of whom are in the treatment group – do not interact with people from another community – all of whom are in a control group. However, weather or other conditions, such as drought or localized conflict, might force people to leave their communities so that people in the treatment and control conditions ultimately interact with each other.

External Validity

External validity refers to the extent to which inferences from an experiment are generalizable. Threats to an experiment's external validity can arise from a number of issues, including the representativeness of the population, the time period in which the experiment is conducted, the experimental construct, and differences in people's behavior in and out of experiments.

The representativeness of the population, as already discussed, is essential to the external validity of the experiment. If the experimental population is not representative of a theoretically relevant population, then the effect observed (or not observed) may not be indicative of the effect that the experimental treatment would produce in the real world. As previously mentioned, the representativeness of the population on which the experiment is conducted tends to be more of an issue for lab experiments, which are typically conducted on students in the social sciences, than for lab-in-the-field experiments or field experiments.

For longitudinal experiments of any kind, the representativeness of the experimental population may decrease over time if large numbers of participants drop out of the study.

This is especially problematic if the participants drop out of the study in ways related to the outcome – a phenomenon known as attrition bias. This can occur if, for example, a large number of people who withdraw from a program, which is being evaluated through a field experiment, quit the program because it does not work. This would be the case if women participating in an empowerment program to reduce child marriage rates drop out of the program in order to get married.

Experiments may also have limited external validity because the time period in which the experiment takes place is unrepresentative given the particular social or political climate present in a country at the time. A survey experiment, for example, about public support for international democracy promotion may yield very different results if conducted after the second Persian Gulf War than after the 1999 war in Kosovo (Brancati 2014a). While the US intervention in Iraq and subsequent attempts to build democracy in the country destabilized the region and were only partially successful in democratizing Iraq, the US intervention in Kosovo stabilized the Balkans and effectively helped democratize Kosovo.

Another threat to the external validity of an experiment is not in terms of the representativeness of the population or the time period, but the representativeness of the construct. The constructs in lab experiments, LITFEs, and survey-based field experiments tend to be abstract and, thus, unrealistic, while the constructs in non-survey-based field experiments tend to be realistic, but specific. The lack of realism in the former and the specifity of the latter both limit the external validity of these experiments.

A field experiment, for example, about the effectiveness of electoral monitors in reducing electoral fraud may be very specific to the particular organization that conducted the monitoring, the size of the mission, the receptivity of the government that they observed to their work, and so forth (Hyde 2007; Ichino and Schündeln 2012; Brancati 2014b; Bush and Prather 2017). Similarly, conclusions drawn from a field experiment regarding psychological counseling in post-civil war societies are likely to depend on the type of counseling provided, the frequency of the counseling sessions, the duration of the treatment program, and so forth (Köbach 2016).

The guinea pig effect is also an issue for all types of experiments, except some field experiments. The guinea pig effect is a threat to the external validity of experiments because it says that the effect observed within an experiment is not the same as that which would be observed outside it, because people behave differently in experiments, knowing that they are being studied, than they do in the real world.

In some field experiments, the guinea pig effect is not an issue because participants do not know that they are in a study. In the above example of electoral fraud, voters at polling stations are unlikely to know that a researcher is studying whether or not electoral monitors reduce fraud by randomizing the presence of electoral monitors at polling stations throughout a country, and measuring whether indications of fraud are lower in stations where monitors are present than where they are not. And, even if they were, the study is not likely to change the voters' behavior any more than the presence of the monitors themselves.

"I think the guinea pig knows we're watching him."

Cartoon 19.1

Analyzing the Results of Experiments

Analyzing experiments has become much more technically advanced in recent decades, keeping pace with the increasing complexity of experiments. Now, more than ever, it requires much more training than that which can be provided in this discussion. Herein only basic information regarding the types of analyses that are necessary for different experimental designs are described in order to make researchers aware of what types of techniques are appropriate to address different issues, and when and where researchers ought to pursue further statistical training.

The appropriate technique for analyzing experimental data depends on a number of considerations, including: the structure of the data; whether the same or different individuals participate in each condition of the explanatory variable; whether it is necessary or not to control for factors that might not be randomly distributed across experimental conditions; the researchers' interest in explaining heterogeneous treatment effects; and the researchers' adherence to a Bayesian or non-Bayesian philosophy.

The most basic techniques used in the statistical analysis of experiments involve comparisons of the means or variance between or among experimental conditions. These techniques do not control for factors that might not be randomly distributed across experimental conditions, and cannot be used to understand heterogeneous treatment effects. Basic and commonly used techniques to compare the means or variance between or among experimental conditions include: t-tests, chi-square tests, and ANOVAs.

A t-test is a comparison of means test and is appropriate where the outcome variable is continuous and there is only one dichotomous explanatory factor. A paired sample t-test is needed when the same participants are compared with each other, as when values for the participants are compared before and after the experiment. A regular t-test can be used otherwise. A chi-square test is needed when the outcome variable is categorical. Like a t-test, a chi-square test is only appropriate when there is one dichotomous explanatory factor.

When there is more than one explanatory factor, which is not necessarily dichotomous, an analysis of variance (ANOVA) can be used, but the dependent variable must also be continuous. ANOVAs indicate whether or not there are significant differences between the means of three or more groups. They cannot identify which specific groups were significantly different from each other, only that at least two groups were different. A post-hoc test, such as the Tukey Test and the Games Howell Test, is needed to determine which specific groups differed from each other. ANOVAs assume that the population variances in each group are also zero, which should be tested for using either the Bartlett's Test, Levene Test, or the Brown-Forsythe Test. A repeated measures ANOVA is needed when the same participants are compared with each other. A one-way or two-way ANOVA may be used otherwise.

When the structure of the outcome variable does not permit the use of these methods, or when it is necessary or important to control for certain variables, the researcher will need to use regression analysis. As discussed in previous chapters, the structure of the dependent variable – whether it is continuous, categorical, interval, or ratio – determines what types of regression techniques are necessary and/or appropriate to analyze the data. Bayesian techniques may also be used in order to incorporate prior knowledge on the model parameters and to account for uncertainties in the observations.

Key Points

- Experiments are the gold standard for causal inference due to the random assignment of subjects to treatment and control groups. Causal inferences can be compromised, however, by a loss of control over the experimental environment.
- Laboratory and field experiments entail tradeoffs in terms of control over the experimental environment and realism. In general, control is greatest and realism is lowest in laboratory experiments, while control is least and realism is greatest in field experiments.
- Generalizability is compromised in all experiments by poor constructs, non-representative populations, observer bias, and the guinea pig effect.

Further Reading

The first, third and fourth readings provide guidance on the design and analysis of field experiments, laboratory experiments, and survey experiments respectively. The second reading provides an in-depth discussion of internal and external validity in experiments across social science disciplines.

Gerber, Alan S. and Donald P. Green. 2012. *Field Experiments: Design, Analysis, and Interpretation*. New York: W.W. Norton.

McDermott, Rose. 2011. 'Internal and External Validity.' In *The Cambridge Handbook of Experimental Political Science*, edited by James N. Druckman, Donald P. Green, James H. Kuklinski, and Arthur Lupia, 27–40. Cambridge: Cambridge University Press.

Mutz, Diana C. 2011. *Population-based Survey Experiments*. Princeton: Princeton University Press.

Webster, Murray and Jane Sell, eds. 2014. *Laboratory Experiments in the Social Sciences*. London: Elsevier Inc.

EXERCISE 19.1

Design a laboratory experiment (or LITFE experiment) and a non-survey field experiment (or survey experiment) to analyze one of the questions below. If you prefer, you may use your own question instead. Identify three to five advantages of using a laboratory experiment (or LITFE experiment) to analyze the question over the non-survey field experiment (or survey experiment). Then, identify three to five advantages of using a non-survey field experiment (or survey experiment) to analyze the question over the laboratory experiment (or LITFE experiment). Use your discretion to interpret the questions as needed in order to design the experiments.

- Are government strategies to discredit anti-government protests by claiming that the protests have been engineered by foreign countries and do not represent local sentiment effective?
- Are women influential in policy-making when women are elected to legislative bodies where quotas require female representation?
- Does the wearing of body cameras by police officers reduce police brutality?
- How effective, if at all, are cash transfers in convincing young men engaged in illicit activities (e.g. selling drugs or guns) to forgo this activity in favor of legal employment?

EXERCISE 19.2

Evaluate the following field experiments in terms of their construct validity, internal validity, and external validity. Provide at least two reasons for your evaluation of each criterion. If you cannot provide two reasons for each criterion because you do not have sufficient information to make a judgment, state this, explain why, and describe the type of information you would need to make this judgment.

- Airtime credit purchases (a.k.a. pre-paid minutes) for mobile phones in Nepal as a measure of socio-economic status in localities identified according to the area codes of mobile phone numbers.
- Incidence rate of Zika based on the number of internet searches for 'Zika' (and similar spellings) geolocated using IP addresses.

- Incidence of electoral violence based on crowdsourcing software that allows people to report information on observed cases of electoral violence via text messages, phone calls, and emails in Burundi.
- International postal flows (i.e., the total number of letter post items for international service per year) for 200 countries based on data reported by these countries to the Universal Postal Union (UPU) as a measure of a country's level of socio-economic development, with greater postal flows indicating a higher level of development.

Observational Studies

Objectives

- define the key features of observational studies
- present the advantages and disadvantages of observational studies vis-à-vis other research methods
- discuss the difficulty of causal inference in observational studies and the techniques available to address it

An *observational study* is a quantitative research method for testing arguments in which researchers do not randomly assign subjects to treatment and control conditions as in an experiment. The term 'observational' refers to the fact that researchers do not interact with their research subjects or manipulate their environment using this method as in an experiment. Despite their name, observational studies are not related to the qualitative research method of participant observation, which typically involves researchers interacting with their subjects. Studies of the association between terrorism and regime strength; international laws and human rights abuses; immigration and crime; patents and research investment; as well as teaching evaluations and learning outcomes are all examples of observational studies.

Often, observational studies are referred to as large-N studies or statistical analyses. Observational studies are large-N studies and are analyzed using statistics. However, this terminology does not differentiate observational studies from experiments and surveys, which may also be described in these terms but which involve researchers' interacting with their subjects and/or manipulating their subjects' environments in some way. Since researchers do not randomly assign subjects to treatment and control groups in observational studies, causal inference is a significant challenge for observational studies with the exception of natural experiments.

The Strengths of Observational Studies

Observational studies offer researchers a number of advantages over other research methods. Some of these advantages are the same as other quantitative methods although the ways in which observational studies arrive at them are different. Others are entirely unique to this method due to the fact that observational data are collected without researchers interacting with their subjects or intervening in their environment in any way. The advantages as well as the disadvantages of observational studies, which are discussed in the subsequent section, are summarized in Table 20.1.

Advantages

- allow for probabilistic relationships
- encourage clear exposition of hypotheses
- facilitate rigorous tests of hypotheses
- allow for complex relationships among explanatory factors
- permit the examination of multiple predictors at one time
- provide estimates of the size and significance of effects
- facilitate cumulative knowledge building
- possesses high potential for generalizability
- offer high potential for replicability
- present little or no human subjects concerns

Disadvantages

- measurement can simplify concepts and relationships
- causal inference is difficult

Table 20.1   Observational studies

Observation Only

Observational studies do not generally pose ethical issues regarding the use of human subjects since researchers using them do not engage with or intervene in the lives of their subjects. Most observational data are collected through secondary accounts of events, such as journalistic reports, censuses, and non-governmental or governmental documents. These data are also often based on aggregate human behaviors, such as economic crises, protests, wars, and so forth.

Newer forms of observational data are collected through the by-products of individual behaviors referred to as 'data exhaust', such as data cell phone calls, grocery store purchases, university ID card swipes, or web content scrapped from internet blog posts, Twitter feeds, and resume hosting websites. These newer forms of observation data measure individual behaviors, but still do not involve the interaction of researchers with their subjects.

As a result, researchers using observational studies are able to comply more easily with ethical standards regarding the use of human subjects than researchers using other methods, either qualitative or quantitative, which involve researchers interacting with their subjects. Since researchers do not interact with their subjects, observational research does not raise concerns regarding the potential physical or psychological harm that it will inflict on participants. Privacy concerns are still an issue, however, even in some cases for information derived from online web content. Although these data are public, the producers of the content did not consent to their communications being used for research. Information collected from online content, as well as data exhaust, can contain identifying information about individuals, so that researchers need to exercise care in keeping the names of individuals confidential and/or anonymous depending on the requirements of their institutions.

Since researchers do not interact with or intervene in the lives of others in order to collect observational data, observational studies are more realistic than qualitative and quantitative studies in certain respects. Since researchers do not interact with the subjects, researchers cannot unintentionally influence their behavior of their subjects – a phenomenon known as observer bias. For example, since researchers conducting observational studies of Twitter feeds only analyze the existing content and do not post Twitter messages themselves on these feeds, they cannot change the discussions on these feeds.

Likewise, since subjects in observational studies typically are not aware that data are being collected on them for research purposes, the guinea pig effect is also not an issue. People who do not know that their cell phone pings are being used to measure population movements, or students who are unaware that their university is collecting information on the times of the day that they use the library based on ID swipes to determine peak usage times, are not going to change their phone call behavior or library usage as a result.

Quantitative Approach

The quantitative nature of observational studies, like other quantitative methods, such as surveys and experiments, allows for the systematic and rigorous comparison of observations. These observations may be countries, events, such as wars, protests, coups d'état, individuals, and so forth. The comparisons are systematic because they are based on the same measures for all observations and isolate the effect of the explanatory variable from other factors that may also affect the outcome.

In an observational study, for example, examining the relationship between laws prohibiting dowries and the number of reported cases of domestic abuse against women in countries each year, each observation would be compared in terms of whether or not a law banning dowries existed in a country in a given year and the number of reported cases of violence perpetrated against women by their husbands in that country in that year. To isolate the effect of this law from other factors, the analysis may also measure and analyze the effect of the level of economic development in the country in a given year, the majority religion in the country, and so forth.

Observational studies can be rigorous, because if done well, they involve subjecting this data to many different types of statistical models and tests to determine the robustness of the relationships detected. The conclusions that are drawn from observational studies are also objective because they are based on clear-cut and established rules in statistics about when to reject or accept hypotheses. In statistics, a relationship is 'significant' if it is not attributable to chance. Normally, researchers base their conclusions about the significance of an explanatory factor on a 95 percent confidence interval (for which there is a 5 percent chance that a result is not true).

While these comparisons are rigorous, systematic, and objective, they can unfortunately simplify the conditions within countries in two respects. First, the measures used to compare cases can be broad due to a lack of available quantitative data and the need to construct quantitative measures that are the same across observations. Reliable cross-national data on dowry-related violence, for example, does not exist – not only due to underreporting, but also due to different definitions of dowry-related violence, the difficulty of linking violence against women to dowries per se, and the multiplicity of issues involved in violence against women. Therefore, researchers who want to conduct an observational study of this issue, may have to measure domestic violence against women instead. However, domestic violence against women can include violence unrelated to dowries, and does not include violence perpetrated by in-laws, former spouses, or fiancés against women regarding dowries.

Second, factors that may be relevant to an outcome may not be tested due to the inability to construct quantitative measures to represent them, across countries. For example, in the example of dowry-related deaths, a measure of whether or not a law exists in a country banning dowries does not capture whether or not the law is enforced in practice. If the law is not enforced, it is unlikely to serve as a deterrent against domestic violence.

Large-N Design

The large-N nature of observational studies also provides researchers with significant analytic leverage. It allows researchers to identify and estimate probabilistic relationships, unlike comparative case methods, which only allow researchers to identify deterministic relationships. Since probabilistic relationships do not claim that an explanatory variable always causes a given outcome, a large number of cases is needed to determine if a given explanatory factor is associated with a given outcome by more than just chance.

The large-N nature of observational studies also enables researchers to identify complex relationships, such as interaction effects, among variables. A large number of cases is needed in order to be able to observe the outcome variable under all possible combinations of the explanatory and intervening variables. At least 24 observations would be needed, for example, to observe all possible combinations of an explanatory factor that takes on four values, an intervening variable that takes on three values, and an outcome variable that takes on two values. Of course, in order to establish a significant pattern in the outcome as a result of the interaction effect, the data would need to include more than just one incident of every combination.

Not only is it possible to identify probabilistic relationships in observational studies, but it is also possible through statistical analysis to estimate the size of the explanatory factor's effect on the outcome variable vis-à-vis other factors that may also affect it. That is, a statistical analysis of an observational study can indicate how much of a change in the outcome variable results from a given change in the explanatory factor, and whether this change is substantively greater or smaller than other variables in the statistical analysis.

The large-N design of observational studies makes it possible to isolate the relationship between the explanatory factor and the outcome variable from other factors that may also influence the outcome. However, this is not possible because the explanatory factor may be strongly correlated with other factors in the analysis. When factors are strongly correlated with each other their estimates are unreliable, and the likelihood of incorrectly concluding that a result is not significant is high. Two factors or variables may be strongly correlated with each other in an analysis because they are measuring the same underlying concept, as in the case of education and literacy, or because there is limited variation in them in either the dataset or the real world.

The latter is illustrated in the example presented in Table 20.2 regarding democracy, Islam, and oil production. The rarity of democracy in the Middle East and North Africa (MENA) has been attributed to both oil and Islam in academic and policy-related research. Oil-rich states, it has been argued, are less likely to be democracies because they do not need to tax citizens to raise revenue, appease their citizens through high public spending on employment, health, and education, and maintain strong repressive apparatuses (Ross 2001). Islam has also been associated with a lack of democracy due to its tenets regarding divine law and women, and its use by autocratic, religious, and non-state actors to acquire and maintain power, among other things (Fish 2002; Ali 2007; Tessler et al. 2014).

However, it is difficult to separate out the effects of oil and Islam on democracy in analyses of the MENA region, because there is only one country in this region for which Islam is not the majority religion, and because most states in MENA produce oil (with half of them producing tens to hundreds of thousands of barrels each day).[1] Looking outside this region provides some, but not much, additional variation. Outside MENA, there are six Muslim majority democracies – Albania, Comoros, Indonesia, Kosovo, Malaysia and Senegal – only two of which – Indonesia and Malaysia – produce tens of thousands of barrels of crude oil per day.

Finally, a very important effect of the large-N design of observational studies is their high potential for generalizability. The greater number of observations these studies

Country	Democracy	Muslim majority	Crude oil production (bbl/d/1k)
Algeria	0	1	1091
Bahrain	0	1	43
Djibouti	0	1	0.0
Egypt	0	1	490
Iran	0	1	3920
Iraq	0	1	4630
Jordan	0	1	0.0
Kuwait	0	1	2710
Lebanon	1	1	0.0
Libya	0	1	678
Morocco	0	1	0.2
Oman	0	1	966
Qatar	0	1	615
Saudi Arabia	0	1	9748
Syrian Arab Republic	0	1	14
Tunisia	1	1	51
United Arab Emirates	0	1	3060
Yemen	0	1	12
Israel	1	0	0.4
West Bank and Gaza	NA	1	0.0

Table 20.2   Indeterminate research design

Note: Countries are defined as part of the Middle East and North Africa based on the World Bank taxonomy. (See: www.worldbank.org/en/region/mena. Accessed: 17 July 2017.) The data on crude oil production are based on the amount of crude oil production in each country in January 2017. BBL/D/1K= thousands of barrels per day. (See: http://tradingeconomics.com/. Accessed: 17 July 2017.) The designation of a country as a democracy or not is based on the 21-point polity index, which ranges from –10 to +10. Democracies are defined as countries scoring a 5 or above on the polity index (2015). Information on the religious makeup is derived from the *Global Religious Landscape*, December 2012, produced by the Pew Research Center Forum on Religion and Public Life.

NA = not applicable; 0 = no; 1 = yes

contain makes it more likely that findings from them are characteristic or typical of the larger population that they claim to represent. That said, every observation in an observational study may be related to a single case, as in a study analyzing incidences of electoral violence across districts of a single country. In this example, there is only one case – an election within a particular country – but many observations — the individual districts of the country. When every observation is related to a single case, the results are only generalizable to that case. In other observational studies, the observations may represent distinct cases, as in a study of electoral violence where each observation represents an election in a different country. In this example, the results may be generalizable to all elections.

Causal Inference

A few of the shortcomings of observational studies were mentioned in the previous section regarding their simplification of relationships due to broad measures and inability to measure all theoretically relevant factors. However, the primary shortcoming of observational studies is the difficulty they present for causal inference. Most observational studies, with the exception of natural experiments, can only effectively establish a correlation between an explanatory variable and outcome variable, a fact which has given rise to the well-known mantra that '[c]orrelation does not make causation.'

Cartoon 20.1

Source: https://xkcd.com/552/

In a statistical analysis of an observational study, a causal effect can never be observed directly due to the *fundamental problem of causal inference*, which states that for any given observation, it is impossible to observe the outcome under both treatment and control conditions. For example, it is impossible to know if the UK would have voted to leave the European Union in 2016 were it not for the European refugee crises, because one cannot observe how Brits would have voted in the referendum were there no refugee crises. Similarly, it is impossible to know if a jury would convict someone based on the same evidence if this person were of a different race or ethnicity, because it is impossible to observe the exact same jury trial with only the race or ethnicity of the person different.

Although in a statistical analysis it is not possible to observe the same observation under both the treatment and control conditions, it is possible to compare observations that experienced the treatment with those that did not, and to control for other potential differences between the two that might also affect the outcome in order to isolate the effect of the explanatory factor on the outcome variable.

In an observational study, for example, a researcher interested in understanding the effect of immigration on support for European integration, could compare support for EU membership within member states across years, given the level of immigration into the EU each year, and controlling for other factors that might also affect support for EU membership. Likewise, a researcher interested in understanding the effect of race or ethnicity on judicial decisions could compare criminal convictions, where the race of the defendant was different, but the weight of the evidence was similar (e.g., DNA evidence; fingerprint evidence; corroborating witnesses).

In most cases, it is difficult to establish the causal effect of the explanatory factor on the outcome variable in observational studies for a number of reasons. As mentioned in the previous section, it is often difficult to identify, measure, and control for all factors that might affect the outcome of interest. In the case of the Brexit example above, it is difficult to measure nationalist sentiment within the UK independent of people's attitudes toward European integration. At the same time, in the example of racism evident in criminal convictions, it may be difficult to measure the quality of the lawyers. The failure to control for all factors that influence the outcome variable is known as omitted variable bias. If a variable that is related to the outcome is not included in the analysis, an explanatory factor may be significant when it should be insignificant (or vice versa), or substantively stronger when it should be substantively weaker (or vice versa).

Also problematic for causal inference, is the fact that there may also be systematic differences in covariates across the treatment and control conditions that could affect the outcome of interest because the treatment assignment is not random. These differences can result from selection bias which, as discussed in Chapter 9, occurs when observations are chosen according to some rule that is correlated with the dependent variable. The relationship between economic growth and shoplifting illustrates the problem that selection bias poses for causal inference in observational studies.

Economic growth has been associated with a decline in shoplifting.[2] One explanation for this is that people shoplift out of necessity and that growth reduces this necessity. However, it is also plausible that people steal for psychological reasons, including impulse-control and addiction problems (Lamontagne et al. 2000; Blanco et al. 2008). In periods of economic decline, there are likely to be more people with untreated mental illnesses due to the inability of people to pay for psychological counseling in these periods. As a result, economic growth may be associated with a decline in shoplifting, not because people have less financial need to shoplift in periods of economic growth, but because there are fewer people in these periods of growth with untreated mental conditions that dispose them to shoplift.

Due to the fundamental problem of causal inference, *simultaneous causation*, which is one form of endogeneity, and reverse correlation are also serious concerns for most observational studies.[3] As explained in Chapter 6, simultaneous causation refers to a situation where the explanatory variable influences the outcome variable and the outcome variable influences the explanatory variable. Reverse causation refers, instead, to a situation where the explanatory variable does not cause the outcome variable, but the outcome variable causes the explanatory variable.

In fact, there is practically no observational study, with the exception of true natural experiments, which is not vulnerable to accusations of either simultaneous or reverse causation. Nevertheless, not all accusations of simultaneous and reverse causation are as plausible as others. A strong argument for reverse correlation can be made regarding the association between video games and violent behavior among young men. While some argue that playing video games causes young men to behave violently, it is equally plausible that young boys who are violent are more likely to play violent video games in the first place.

A strong argument for reverse correlation can also be made in terms of the association between home security systems and home burglaries. While burglaries are likely to lead homeowners to purchase home security systems, home security systems can also increase home burglaries, because the lawn signs and stickers that home owners post indicating that their property is protected by a security system, also signal to would-be burglars that there are valuables inside a home worth stealing.

However, a strong argument for reverse correlation cannot be made regarding the effectiveness of programs for pregnant teenagers. Teen pregnant rates are higher where these programs exist than where they do not. However, it is unlikely that these programs cause teenagers to become pregnant. Knowing that support programs exist if they become pregnant, teenagers could act more recklessly sexually, but this is not likely the case. Research suggests that teen pregnancy is generally due to alcohol and drug use, peer pressure, dysfunctional family environments, and so forth (Kirby 2001).

Natural Experiments

Natural experiments are observational studies in which the assignment to treatment and control groups is random or 'as if' random. In other words, they are observational studies in which the explanatory variable is exogenous to the outcome. The random assignment is a function of the real world, not the researcher, as in the case of laboratory and field experiments. Natural experiments are valuable for causal inference because, in any experiment where the assignment is random, the difference in the outcome between the explanatory conditions is unlikely to be due to covariates that vary systematically across the explanatory conditions.

Studies of the effects of certain weather events, such as earthquakes or rainfall, on intra-state violence are examples of natural experiments (Miguel et al. 2004; Brancati 2007). Whether or not an earthquake occurs, or how much rain falls, in a country is not a function of whether or not there is an internal conflict within a country. Earthquakes occur as a result of shifts in tectonic plates in the earth's lithosphere while rainfall results from the condensation of moisture trapped in the earth's atmosphere. Yet, natural disasters, such as earthquakes and rainfall, can fuel intrastate conflict through different channels. Natural disasters can increase poverty and homelessness, generate competition for scarce resources, stoke grievances against governments, and divert government resources away from fighting ongoing conflicts, among other things.

Not all weather events, though, are natural experiments. A flood, for example, is not a natural experiment even though rainfall is a natural experiment. A flood occurs when there is an overflow of water on otherwise dry land. It results not only from rainfall, but also from human engineering. A foot of rain may constitute a flood in one country, but not in another, due to the absence of technologies, such as floodwalls, sewer systems, canals, green spaces, and so forth. These technologies may, in turn, be related to the outcome of interest, as in the previous example regarding intrastate conflict. Floods, for example, are more likely to arise in response to a given amount of rainfall in countries where intrastate conflict occurs, because these conflicts destroy infrastructures needed to protect against floods and make investment in them less likely in the first place.

Not only are all weather-related events not natural experiments, but weather-related events are not the only examples of natural experiments. Identical or monozygotic twins, which have been raised in different households, are a natural experiment because each twin in a set of twins has the same genetic makeup as the other. Identical twins that have been reared separately for various reasons have been used to study the effect of the environment on psychological, behavioral, and health-related attributes in the never-ending debate regarding nature versus nature (Tellegen et al. 1988; Plomin et al. 1994; Boomsma et al. 2002).

Lottery earnings are another commonly used natural experiment. Imbens et al. (2001) use lottery winnings to understand the effects of unearned income on labor earnings. Specifically, the researchers sought to understand whether or not unearned income reduced labor output in order to inform the seemingly never-ending debate regarding the potentially negative effects of welfare assistance (a form of unearned income) on the economy. The researchers do not use playing the lottery, but rather lottery earnings, as the natural experiment since low-income individuals play the lottery at a much higher rate than high-income individuals. In their study, the researchers find that unearned income reduces labor earnings, especially for those nearing retirement. Whether or not welfare payments are similar to lottery payments is a matter for another debate.

Although lottery earnings are commonly used as a natural experiment, it is not clear that lottery earnings constitute a natural experiment, either in general or in this study in particular. In the United States, where the study was conducted, and elsewhere, there are different types of lottery tickets. These tickets cost different amounts to purchase and have different jackpots associated with them. It is possible, even likely, that low-income individuals prefer certain lotteries to others. Low-income individuals may prefer less costly lotteries to more costly ones, even if the payout is smaller, because they can afford these lotteries more easily, and because the odds of winning them are also greater.

As this example suggests, a significant concern for natural experiments is the extent to which the explanatory factor presented as the natural experiment is actually random. Some researchers claim that 'virtual twins' constitute a natural experiment (Segal et al. 2012; Segal 2013). Virtual twins are same-age, unrelated siblings who have been raised together since infancy. Often one or both of the twins have been adopted.

Virtual twins, despite claims to the contrary, are not natural experiments. Virtual twins are different from each other in terms of their biological traits and experience their environments differently as a result. Societies, for example, treat girls differently than boys, thin children differently than obese children, pretty children differently than less attractive children, and so on and so forth. Even the families of virtual twins may treat each twin differently. Family members might, for example, treat the child who is the biological offspring of one or more of the parents and a biological relative of theirs, better than the adopted child.

Estimation Techniques for Causal Inference

If an observational study is not a natural experiment, researchers may use different estimation techniques to address problems of causal inference in observational studies. These include Heckman selection models (Heckman 1979), propensity score matching (PSM) methods (Rosenbaum and Rubin 1983), and instrumental variable (IV) regression (Stock and Trebbi 2003). Both Heckman selection models and PSM methods address issues of selection bias, but they are appropriate in different circumstances. Instrumental variable regression addresses issues of simultaneity bias, and other forms of endogeneity in linear models where the explanatory variable and error term are correlated. These techniques do not exist for all data distributions, and in practice, rarely eliminate doubts about causal claims.

Heckman models address selection bias issues related to unobservable factors. They are only appropriate if the first-stage selection model is analyzed as a probit model, if the second-stage outcome model is analyzed as a linear regression model, and if the unobservable factors are binormally distributed. The Heckman selection model is a two-stage model. In the first stage, researchers estimate a model predicting the explanatory factor. In the second stage, researchers estimate the effect of the explanatory variable on the outcome of interest. Researchers correct for selection bias by incorporating a transformation of the predicted probabilities from the first-stage model as an explanatory variable in the second-stage model. The bias correction is in the form of an inverse Mills ratio (i.e., a ratio of the standard normal probability density function over the standard normal cumulative distribution function).

Propensity score matching is also a two-stage process. In contrast to Heckman selection models, PSM addresses issues of selection bias related to observables only. The term 'observables' refers to any measureable characteristic of the data that affects selection into the treatment. In the first stage, researchers estimate a model predicting the explanatory factor. Unlike Heckman models, PSM allows for continuous treatments in the first stage. In the second stage, researchers estimate the effect of the explanatory variable on the outcome of interest. Prior to the second stage, researchers match each observation in the dataset to one or more other observations in the dataset based on their propensity score, dropping any unmatched observations from the data. Researchers may use one of a number of different techniques to match the observations. The propensity score, which is estimated from the first-stage model, is the probability of treatment assignment conditional on the observed baseline characteristics.

A common criticism of applications of Heckman and PSM models in practice is that the first-stage models are not fully specified. The success of both techniques hinges on these models being fully specified. Models that are fully specified include all the variables that predict selection into the treatment. For matching, there are tests to determine if the balance in the covariates between the treatment and control conditions is better as a result of the PSM, as well as sensitivity tests, such as Rosenbaum bounds. However, doubts nearly always remain in practice regarding the specification of the first-stage models in both Heckman and PSM models.

Instrumental variable regression, in contrast, is used to address concerns regarding endogeneity in linear models. *Endogeneity* arises when the explanatory variable and the error term are correlated. This occurs when there is simultaneous or reverse causation, measurement error, or omitted variables. IV regression produces consistent, but biased estimates. (The former refers to the fact that the estimates converge in probability to the true value, while the latter refers to the fact that there is a difference between the expected and true values of the estimated parameters.)

Like the previous techniques, IV regression is a two-stage model. In the first stage, the endogenous explanatory variable is regressed on the excluded instrument(s) and all other exogenous variables. Instruments are variables that are highly correlated with the explanatory variable and not with the outcome variable. In the second stage, the outcome of interest is regressed on the predicted values from the first-stage regression model and all other covariates hypothesized to affect the outcome.

A common criticism of applications of IV regressions in practice is that the instruments used in the analyses are weak. The consequences of weak instruments are arguably worse than no instruments at all (Staiger and Stock 1994; Bound et al. 1995). There are indirect tests of the quality of the instruments when there is more than one instrument for each endogenous regressor, but there are no direct tests (Stock and Yogo 2002). Nor are there any tests for when the number of instruments is the same as the number of endogenous regressors.

A well-known example of a strong instrument is the use of school enrollment cut-off dates (i.e., the dates by which children must be of a certain age in order to enter school) as an instrument for education (Angrist and Krueger 1991). The cut-off dates affect the length of schooling children receive by allowing children who start school earlier to drop out of school with less schooling than children who start school later. In their research, Angrist and Krueger use school enrollment cut-off dates to analyze the effect of education on earnings. Cut-off dates are unlikely to affect earnings through any other process than years of schooling, because, as the researchers argue, they are unlikely to be related to innate ability, motivation, family connections, and so forth.

In general, however, it is very difficult to identify variables that are correlated with the explanatory factor and not with the outcome of interest other than through the explanatory factor. The results of poor instruments can have major consequences for research findings and serious real-world implications. In their work studying the effect of child abuse on homosexuality, Roberts et al. (2013) use four instruments for childhood abuse: the presence of a stepparent, poverty, parental alcohol abuse, and parental mental illness. All four of these factors have been shown in other research to be strongly associated with child abuse. Their analysis using these instruments yielded very controversial findings showing a strong correlation between childhood abuse and homosexuality. The results are controversial because they imply that homosexuality is a dysfunction.

A number of scholars have questioned the validity of these instruments because, they argue, the instruments are a function of people's genes, which are related to homosexuality (Bailey and Bailey 2013; Rind 2013). Independent research has shown a strong correlation between people's biology and alcohol abuse and mental illness, but there is no equally strong research regarding the genetic basis for the remaining instruments. New research has also shown preliminary evidence that there is also a genetic basis for homosexuality in addition to environmental and social factors (Sanders et al. 2015; Gómez et al. 2017). Roberts et al. (2013) conclude in their study that child sexual abuse, especially among males, is causally related to homosexual behavior.

Key Points

- Due to their quantitative nature, observational studies allow for systematic, objective, and rigorous comparisons; generalizable conclusions; and the identification and estimation of complex and probabilistic relationships.
- Since researchers do not interact with or intervene in the lives of others in order to collect observational data, ethical concerns regarding the use of human subjects, observer bias, and the guinea pig effect are not issues in observational studies.
- However, since researchers do not randomly assign subjects to treatment and control groups in observational studies, causal inference is a significant challenge for observational studies with the exception of natural experiments.
- Natural experiments are observational studies in which the assignment to treatment and control groups is random or 'as if' random. Many studies are mischaracterized as natural experiments because the treatment assignment is not fully random.
- Estimation techniques exist to facilitate causal inference in observational studies (excluding natural experiments), but in practice are rarely fully convincing.

Further Reading

The three readings all address issues related to causal inference in observational studies. The first and third readings focus specifically on the challenges and shortcomings of instrumental variable regression and natural experiments respectively.

Angrist, Joshua D. and Alan B. Krueger. 2001. 'Instrumental Variables and the Search for Identification: From Supply and Demand to Natural Experiments.' *Journal of Economic Perspectives* 15(4): 69–85.
Rosenbaum, Paul R. 2010. *Design of Observational Studies.* New York: Springer.
Sekhon, Jasjeet. S. 2012. 'When Natural Experiments are Neither Natural nor Experiments.' *American Political Science Review* 106(1): 35–57.

EXERCISE 20.1

Discuss the extent to which any two of the following examples of research constitute natural experiments:

1. Variation in exposure to racist propaganda which was disseminated by the Hutu-led government against Tutsis through Radio Tele Libre Mille Collines (RTLM) in the 1994 Rwandan genocide, as a natural experiment to understand the effect of propaganda on intergroup violence (Yanagizawa-Drott 2014). Exposure to racist propaganda is a natural experiment, according to the author, because the hilly topography of Rwanda and the distance to radio transmitters determined access to radio transmissions. Consistent with expectations, Yanagizawa-Drott found that greater exposure to propaganda results in higher intergroup violence

2. The division of Germany after the Second World War and the reunification of East and West Germany in 1990 as a natural experiment to understand the importance of market access for economic development (Redding and Sturm 2008). The East–West German border, the authors claim, is a natural experiment because it was based on military considerations and the need to allocate roughly equal-sized occupation zones to American, British and Russian forces. The authors theorize that West German cities close to the border should have experienced a disproportionate loss of market access relative to other West German cities, and found results consistent with this effect.

3. Redistricting in the United States as a natural experiment to study the effect of the personal vote – the vote based on candidates' attributes rather than those of their parties (Ansolabehere et al. 2000). Mandatory redistricting occurs every ten years in the United States, and although rules and procedures regarding redistricting vary by state, all state rules and procedures must comply with federal regulations regarding equal population and racial fairness. As a result of redistricting, an incumbent's district includes people who voted for the incumbent in the last election and voters who did not have the opportunity to vote for or against the incumbent. The researchers expect and find that the personal vote is greater among the former set of voters than the latter.

4. State borders in Africa, and in particular those borders between Kenya and Tanzania, as a natural experiment to study how local nation-building policies among ethnic groups affect public good spending (Miguel 2004). International borders in Africa, the author claims, constitute a natural experiment because the colonial powers created them without reference to the location of ethnic groups, dividing these ethnic groups across state borders. Consistent with his expectations, Miguel finds that Tanzania's nation-building policy, which has been more aggressive than Kenya's, has resulted in higher public spending by encouraging collective action. Tanzania's nation-building policy aggressively promoted the use of Swahili over English, emphasized Tanzanian history, culture and values in school curricula, and overhauled the country's political institutions to replace colonial-era institutions.

VI

CONCLUSION

Social Scientific Writing

Objectives

- provide advice regarding titles and subtitles
- explain the purpose and contents of effective abstracts
- describe the content of the different sections of a written research project
- provide helpful hints regarding writing academic research

Writing in the social sciences shares much in common with the natural sciences both in content and tone given the fields' shared orientation around the scientific method. Since the purpose of social scientific research is to inform rather than to persuade, social scientific writing is generally formal, objective, and analytic. Ideas are conveyed through the use of clear, plain, but precise, vocabulary and a syntax that is simple and straightforward. The discussion in this chapter focuses on writing an article-length research paper in the social sciences, but differences between article- and book-length studies (e.g., monographs, theses, and dissertations) are noted throughout the discussion, as are differences among disciplines.

Box 21.1   Watch Your Language

- Avoid jargon. It can impede comprehension and appear pedantic.
- Unless specifying necessary and sufficient conditions, avoid deterministic and unconditional language, such as 'always' and '(dis)proves'. Instead, use probabilistic language, such as 'more likely' or 'less likely' since relationships in the social sciences are rarely absolute.
- Avoid the passive voice because it adds verbiage and obfuscates the meaning of sentences.

Front Matter

The front matter of an academic article consists of the title, acknowledgements and abstract, the basic contents of which are described herein. In a book-length project, including a thesis or dissertation, the front matter typically also includes a preface, dedication page, and the table of contents.

Titles

The purpose of any title in academic research is to convince others to read the work. For titles to attract readers in academic research, unlike in other genres, they must be informative and fully disclose the purpose of the research. An informative title concisely encapsulates the key question that the research study addresses, and may even divulge the conclusions of the findings.

A useful strategy for devising an effective title is to compose a list of key words (and their cognates) related to your research, and then to explore different combinations of these words to identify an arrangement of words that accurately, precisely, and succinctly captures your research question. The final title should be more than a list of these key terms, however. A title comprised of only key terms is unlikely to sufficiently define the research question posed and to differentiate it from other questions. For example, 'What's Behind Iran's Nuclear Ambitions?' is a much more effective title than 'Iran and Nuclear Weapons'. The former explains exactly which aspect of Iran's nuclear program the project addresses, while the latter does not. The latter is so broad that it could apply equally to a paper on the geopolitical reasons that Iran has pursued a costly nuclear program just as much as a paper on international sanctions against Iran's nuclear programs.

In addition to defining the research question, the title can also help frame the research question posed within the broader literature. This titling strategy can expand the audience for the project. However, if the title is too broad and uninformative as a result, it can have the opposite effect. For example, 'Can Realism Explain the Twenty-first Century Security Strategies of the Middle East?' is a title that would situate the question of Iran's nuclear weapons program within the larger international relations literature on security, but it is too broad. It does not identify nuclear weapons as the strategy analyzed. It also implies that the study addresses more than one security strategy and discusses them within all of the Middle East, as opposed to just Iran.

In framing the research question in the larger literature, it is important to avoid jargon as jargon can obfuscate the purpose of the research. The previous title regarding security strategies in the Middle East is further problematic because it includes the term 'realism' in it. For an audience of only international relations scholars, this term is not problematic since all international relations scholars should be familiar with this term. But, if the intended audience is wider, and includes people who might not be familiar with this term, such as historians or scientists studying nuclear weapons, this title can potentially deter readers.

Box 21.2   100 percent Proofread

Be sure to carefully proofread your paper or have another person proofread it for you, especially if English is not your first language. Too many grammatical and typographical errors will lead readers to question the quality and care with which the research behind the writing was conducted, and in some cases, can be very costly. In 2010, Penguin Australia had to recall and reprint thousands of copies of *The Pasta Bible*, when instead of listing the ingredient black pepper for one recipe, it called for 'freshly ground black people'.[1] And, more recently in 2017, a missing Oxford comma cost a Maine company millions of US dollars due to confusion that the comma, or rather the lack thereof, caused regarding the conditions under which laborers were owed overtime.[2]

Another strategy researchers use to increase their readership is creative puns and twists on well-known sayings or popular culture references. While entertaining, these titles, like jargon, can obscure the purpose of the research and diminish its readership. Some titles, though, hit the right note exactly and are both clever and clear, such as *When States Come Out: Europe's Sexual Minorities and the Politics of Visibility* (Ayoub 2016) and *Dam Politics: Restoring America's Rivers* (Lowry 2003). The titles are attention getting, but also perfectly descriptive of the studies – the legal recognition of lesbian, gay, bisexual, and transgender minorities in the case of the former and the political circumstances affecting the restoration of rivers in the case of the latter.

Social sciences titles, as in these examples, often include subtitles, which are separated from the main title using a colon. The information following the colon can serve a number of different purposes. It may clarify or provide more specific information about the goal of the research project, or it may define the project's temporal or geographic scope. *When States Come Out* and *Dam Politics* do both. Subtitles can also identify the methodology used in the paper, as in 'The Resource Curse: A Bayesian Meta-Analysis' or as in 'Environment Social Movements: A Review Essay.' This strategy is most useful when the methodology is the primary contribution of the study to the existing literature.

Section titles serve a significantly different purpose than project titles. They do not solicit readers, but summarize the objective of each section. Introductory sections, though, do not typically have section titles. Section titles also give readers a breather and an opportunity to reflect on what they just read before moving on to the next section. They further help readers skim research quickly to familiarize themselves with its contents. While section titles have a different purpose than titles, they should generally follow the same rules as those for titles. They should be clear, informative, and precise. They should also be concise and no longer than a single line of text. The rules for section titles do differ from those for titles in one respect, however. Section titles should not have subtitles that are separated from the main part of the title by colons. This elongates the section title and reduces its crispness.

Acknowledgements

In the acknowledgements, researchers express their thanks to those who contributed to the research in some way, but whose contribution does not warrant co-authorship. These people may have read or offered comments on the paper but did not conduct any of the research. The acknowledgements are also an opportunity for researchers to mention any institutions or conferences where they presented earlier versions of the research, or agencies that helped fund the research. In an article, the acknowledgements usually consist of footnotes linked to the title. In a book-length project, researchers typically thank individuals and institutions that contributed to the project in the preface, where they may also relate the historical development of the project, among other things.

Abstract

After the title, a reader's next engagement with a research project is the abstract. The abstract is not like a movie trailer. A movie trailer teases viewers. It gives them a sense of the movie's plot line, as well as the excitement or drama surrounding it, but it does not give away the ending. An abstract, in contrast, is a summary of the most important components of a research project – one of which is the conclusion. Unlike a movie trailer, it is important to report the results of the project in the abstract since the abstract may be the only thing a person reads of the research.

The abstract should dedicate one or two sentences to each of the following five aspects of the research project: the research question or puzzle; the importance and/or contribution of the project to the existing literature; the argument offered to explain the research question or puzzle; the method used to analyze it; and the results of the analysis. The abstract is typically about 150 words in length. Below is an example of an effective abstract regarding child marriage. Each of the aforementioned research components is identified in parentheses.

Despite international agreements and national laws banning child marriage, the rate of child marriage across the globe is still very high. Over one-third of girls in developing countries are married before they are eighteen due to poverty, as well as cultures and traditions that devalue women. These girls suffer major long-term psychological and physical trauma as a result (importance). Yet, despite high levels of poverty and patriarchal traditions, the rate of child marriage in Algeria is less than 5 percent (puzzle). Algeria's child marriage rate, we argue, is much lower than other developing countries due to the involvement of France in Algeria's traditional family law system during the colonial period (argument). Our argument, which examines the flip side of child marriage rates (contribution), is supported through an analysis of historical documents from the colonial period, as well as interviews with judges, legal scholars, and human rights organizations currently active in the country (method). This analysis links the rate of child marriage in Algeria today to the country's family law system and the family law system, in turn, to the colonial legacy of France (findings).

Body

Any written presentation of research in the social sciences consists of six basic components. They are (in order): the introduction; literature review; argument; methodology; analysis or results; and conclusion. However, not all research questions will necessarily conform neatly to this particular mold. There may also be differences across and within disciplines and especially depending on the research methodology used. The best way, and perhaps only way, to determine the most effective presentation of your own research is through the writing process, and more importantly the re-writing process.

Introduction

The introduction should be organized around the same five issues identified in the abstract – the research question or puzzle, the importance of the question, the argument, the contribution of the research, the method and the findings. Instead of dedicating a single sentence to each issue, though, as in the abstract, the introduction should devote a paragraph or two to each.

There are various ways in which to include this information in the introduction. One obvious way to organize this information is to begin the introduction with the research question or puzzle, in order to draw in readers, and then move on to discuss the argument offered to explain the research question or puzzle. After establishing the theoretical groundwork for the project, researchers may move on to discuss the method used to test their argument, and the results of the analysis.

An example introduction is presented in Box 21.3.

Box 21.3   Example Introduction

Below is an abbreviated example of an introduction from a study on the international diffusion of democracy protests. References have been excluded to conserve space.

Democracy exists in both geographic and temporal clusters. At the beginning of the twentieth century, democracy was isolated to a few countries in North America and Western Europe. After World War II, however, it expanded to Latin America and Asia, toppling military regimes and colonial powers in the process. Shortly after the end of the Cold War, democracy moved into East Central Europe, where it dislodged deep-rooted communist regimes, and made significant inroads into Africa. One of the primary international factors proposed to explain this geographic and temporal clustering of democracy is the diffusion of democracy protests.

Democracy protests, which are public demonstrations in which participants demand countries adopt or uphold open and competitive elections, are thought to diffuse primarily through a demonstration effect and secondarily, through transnational activists. According to the former, protests in one country precipitate protests in another based on the positive information that they convey about the likelihood of successful protests elsewhere, while according to the latter, they diffuse through the direct actions of activists, who provide material, training, and financial support to activists in other countries. As evidence of these processes, scholars point to the large number of countries that have experienced protests at any one time, and to the fact that where protests are believed to have diffused, protesters were aware of earlier protests, made reference to these protests, and adopted similar strategies, tactics, and goals.

In contrast to these expectations, we argue that, in general, democracy protests are not likely to diffuse across countries because the motivation for and the outcome of democracy protests results primarily from domestic processes that are either unaffected or undermined by the occurrence of democracy protests in other countries. Democracy protests arise when strong public sentiment against governments is triggered by internal events, such as elections and economic crises, which facilitate collective action against governments by making individuals cognizant of their shared opposition to regimes. In general, the occurrence of democracy protests in neighboring countries does not raise this level of discontent, nor does it facilitate collective action on behalf of it. In fact, most democracy protests in neighboring countries are poor models for protests elsewhere and can lead governments to undertake measures to block protests from occurring in their own countries.

To evaluate our argument, we conduct the first cross-national and longitudinal statistical analysis of the diffusion of democracy protests. Existing studies on the diffusion of democracy show a strong statistical correlation between the presence of democracy in one country and the presence of democracy in neighboring countries and/or the world, but they are unable to distinguish empirically among the different mechanisms through which democracy might diffuse. To understand these mechanisms, it is essential to examine the diffusion of democracy protests apart from the diffusion of democracy, because although protests themselves might diffuse, their political successes might not. The protest diffusion literature, in contrast, shows the influence of democracy protests on each other, but its conclusions are not necessarily generalizable since they are based on qualitative descriptions of the most prominent waves of democracy protests.

Our statistical analysis supports our argument. Using daily data on the onset of democracy protests around the world between 1989 and 2011, we found that in this period, democracy protests were not significantly more likely to occur in countries when democracy protests occurred in neighboring countries, regardless of the number or size of these protests. Democracy protests were also not more likely to occur in this period in ways consistent with diffusion arguments. That is, democracy protests were not significantly more likely to occur in this period in countries when protests in neighboring countries were not repressed or were able to extract political concessions from governments. Nor, were they more likely to occur when neighboring protests occurred in influential countries or politically and socio-economically similar countries. Therefore, if democracy does diffuse to other countries, it is not likely a result of democracy protests.

Source: Dawn Brancati and Adrián Lucardi. 'Why Democracy Protests Do Not Diffuse,' forthcoming.

The first part of the introduction may be devoted to identifying the research question or puzzle and describing what about the research question posed is interesting, important, or surprising. If the puzzle or the argument requires certain terminology or concepts, it is important to briefly define them in the introduction, ideally with a single clause the first time that the term is used, saving a more elaborate definition of the term for later.

The next section may briefly summarize the argument offered to explain the research question, and if appropriate, distinguish how this argument is different from existing explanations. Ideally, the argument should be encapsulated in a single sentence, commonly known as the thesis statement, and structure the entire argument section. The order of the ideas presented in the argument section should follow the order presented in the thesis statement.

The contribution of the project may be included in the introduction in a number of other places, depending on whether the contribution is theoretical, empirical or both. If the contribution is in terms of the question posed, it may be included in the first section articulating the research question and/or puzzle. If it is in terms of the argument, it may be mentioned in this section of the introduction, and if it is in terms of the method employed or data used it may be discussed in the methodology section.

The methodology section ought to follow the argument section. In it, researchers should describe the methodology used to test their argument. They should also briefly mention the advantage of using this method to answer this question, and if appropriate, how this method is an advantage over existing methods used in the literature. In the final section of the introduction, researchers should present the results of their findings and the implications of these results for the broader literature in which the research question is embedded.

Some researchers include at the end of the introduction a roadmap describing the order and objective of the remaining sections of the paper. In an article-length research paper, this is unnecessary since the organization of the paper should follow the order of the paragraphs in the introduction. In a book-length project, a roadmap can be very helpful, however, since many people only read book-length projects for the parts of the project that are most relevant to their research interests. A roadmap of this kind allows readers to more easily identify the areas of interest to them.

Box 21.4   The Straphangers' Rule

All written research should pass the 'Straphangers' Rule'. The Straphangers' Rule is the ability of a person, while standing on a train holding a strap or poll with their one hand and your research in the other, to understand everything you have written despite the distractions of public transportation – loud music seeping out of headphones, panhandlers, buskers, performers, and so forth. To determine whether your writing meets the Straphanger's Rule, read it very quickly or in a distracted manner, as someone else might. If need be, turn on the radio or television to create a distraction and see if you are able to comprehend your own writing despite these distractions.

Puzzle Definition

Depending on the research question, it may be appropriate to include a section that substantiates the issues around which the research question is posed, defines any terminology related to it, and provides other necessary background information. Information that is not directly relevant to the research question should not be included in this section. A section of this kind is very helpful if the research puzzle is not well known or challenged.

In a study, for example, examining the consequences of Dalits leaving the Hindu faith to escape the Indian caste system, it would likely be helpful to have a section describing the caste system in India, how Dalits are restricted by it, and the frequency with which Dalits have converted from Hinduism to other religions. While many people are familiar with the caste system, the conversion of Dalits is much less well known. However, information about the development of Hinduism in the Vedic period would not be useful to include in this study because it is not directly relevant to understanding the consequences of the conversion process.

A puzzle definition section would be much less useful in a project offering a new explanation for a well-established puzzle, such as the democratic peace theory. Hundreds of articles and books, if not more, have already established that democracies do not tend to go to war with each other. It also would not be helpful if the goal of a research project is to explain why a certain phenomenon has not happened, like why North and South Korea have not unified, or why the Vatican is not a member of the World Trade Organization. It does not require very much to establish the absence of a phenomenon, as it does the presence of one.

Literature Review

The purpose, content, and structure of the literature review are discussed at length in Chapter 4.

Argument

An effective way in which to organize the argument section is to repeat the thesis statement used in the introduction at the outset of the section, and to structure the remainder of the section around each component of the argument in the order that it was introduced in the thesis statement. Each paragraph should contain a single idea although each component may require more than one paragraph.

Box 21.5   Making Your Voice Heard

Social scientific research is written from the point of view of the researcher. Therefore, always use the first-person singular in any write up of your research to refer to yourself, or the first-person plural when referring to you and your co-author, as in 'I argue' or 'we argue.' Only use 'we' when there are multiple authors. Never use 'we' to refer to the author and the reader.

Below is the thesis statement taken from the aforementioned paper on the diffusion of democracy protests.

> Democracy protests are not likely to diffuse across countries because the motivation for and the outcome of democracy protests results primarily from domestic processes that are either unaffected or undermined by the occurrence of democracy protests in other countries.

This thesis statement is comprised of three separate claims. The first contends that the motivation for democracy protests results primarily from domestic processes. The second contends that the outcome of democracy protests in countries results primarily from domestic processes, while the third asserts that both these things are either unaffected or undermined by the occurrence of democracy protests in other countries. The latter claim may even be divided into two separate claims – one about how protests do not cause protests in neighboring countries and one about how they can even reduce the likelihood of protests in other countries. The argument section should be structured around establishing each of these claims in the order presented in the thesis statement.

Box 21.6   Keep Your Thoughts to Yourself

Do not make the structure of your writing apparent with language explaining what you are doing, why you are doing it, and when you are going to do it. Examples of this kind are:

- 'As for the contribution this article makes to the academic literature ...'
- 'Now that I have established this point, I will move on to explain ...'
- 'A counterargument to my argument is ...'

This writing style is not only unsophisticated, but also verbose. If your writing is clear, a reader will know what you are doing without your having to announce it. In other words, your writing should have good bones but the reader does not have to see them.

In order to build a compelling argument, researchers may illustrate their claims using real-world examples, data, quotes, and so forth. This information can help to clarify points and make abstract ideas more concrete. This information is not a test of the researcher's arguments since the researcher has obviously cherry-picked this information to support his or her arguments. Researchers may also develop their arguments with reference to the work of others to demonstrate how the assumptions or logical consequences of certain aspects of their arguments are supported by existing research.

To build a strong argument, it is also important for researchers to anticipate and respond to potential counterarguments. Counterarguments are arguments that challenge either elements of an argument or the entire argument. Not every potential counterargument is worth considering, however. Researchers should only consider those that are likely to be raised by others and/or are reasonable and sound.

Addressing a counterargument does not necessarily mean dismissing it. Some counterarguments may present a compelling case against your argument. In this case, you ought to honestly recognize the counterargument as a distinct possibility. In some cases, it may be possible to test the validity of this counterargument in your analysis, but in other cases, it might not. Every research project has its limitations and it is important to recognize them, rather than sweep them under the rug. The goal of academic research is to find the answer to a question, not to defend a position by all means possible.

Box 21.7   Staying on Track

A major challenge for many writers is staying on track. It can be very difficult for researchers to cut material that they have spent a lot of time researching even if it does not fit, and disrupts the flow of the presentation. Save this material in a separate file, or as hidden comments in a typesetting program, such as Latex. After completing a full draft, sift through this material to determine if there is any material that you would like to re-integrate back into the paper. Chances are a lot of this material you will ultimately come to accept as extraneous.

Methodology

In the methodology section, it is important to explain why the methodology chosen is appropriate for the research question posed and the limitations, if any, it poses for the analysis. In this section, the reasoning behind the case selection may also be explained, as well as the advantages and disadvantages it presents for the research. Finally, in this section, it is important to discuss how the methodology used in this study differs from, and offers an advantage over, methodologies used to address the same research question in the existing literature. Depending on the method used, it may not be necessary to elaborate in great detail about how the specific procedures or estimation techniques of the method work. This may be addressed in the analysis section.

Analysis

The contents of the analysis section will differ significantly depending on the research methodology used. If the analysis is a qualitative single case study, the analysis section may present a narrative of events that is drawn from participant observation and interviews. If, in contrast, the analysis consists of an observational study or an experiment, this section may include an explanation of the measures and data used in the study as well as a description of the results of the statistical analysis. Usually, the measures and data are presented in a separate section prior to the results.

Researchers should discuss the empirical evidence used in the analysis at a level of detail sufficient for other researchers to replicate the findings unless confidentiality issues prohibit it. In presenting the evidence, it is generally very helpful to include visual elements to illustrate a study's key findings, such as figures, charts, photos, maps, tables, and so forth. These figures should stand alone – that is, a person should be able to understand the illustrations without further explanation provided in the text.

In many fields, including political science and economics, the analysis section contains a discussion of the significance of the results for the original research question posed – that is, whether the results confirm or disconfirm the original theory, and if they do not confirm the original theory, why this might be the case. In these fields, researchers also often address potential alternative explanations to their findings in this section.

In other fields, such as psychology, information about the importance of the results is included in a separate discussion section. In these fields, the discussion section may also identify new questions that are raised as a result of the analysis, as well as any potential extensions to the findings. In the absence of a discussion section, these issues are typically raised in the conclusion.

Box 21.8   Take a Note

Footnotes or endnotes should be used for detailed information that only a subset of readers would be interested in, and for information that would disrupt the flow of the writing. There are no hard and fast rules regarding the type of information that may be included in footnotes or endnotes. They may include direct quotes to support a statement, information to clarify, justify, or refine a point made in a sentence, or non-essential statistical tests used by the researcher.

Conclusion

At the outset, the conclusion should summarize briefly the results of the study and the significance of these results for the research question posed. However, the conclusion should go beyond a mere summary of the findings. In the conclusion, the researcher may discuss implications of the study's findings for other research or for public policy, and may suggest further avenues of research. These may include suggestions for different methodological approaches, data, cases, and so forth.

Box 21.9   Soliciting Feedback

Once researchers have written up their study results, it is essential that they solicit feedback from others on the presentation of their research. Other people can offer very helpful advice in this regard because they not only have different knowledge and experiences than the researchers, but they also have less familiarity and interest in a subject and are less vested in the outcome of the results.

Back Matter

The back matter of a research article typically includes the bibliography, which was discussed in Chapter 4, and an appendix. In a book-length project, the back matter also includes an index. An index is an alphabetized list of terms used in the text and the pages where the terms appear in the text. Although every research project, whether it is an article-length paper or a book-length project, contains a bibliography, not every research project contains an appendix. The appendix generally includes supplementary materials related to the empirical analysis. The materials will differ depending on the methodology used. It may include a list of names of persons interviewed, supplementary statistical models, mathematical proofs, survey questions, and so forth.

Often, with printing costs at a premium, researchers lack the space in journals and books to provide all the information about their research that they want even with the use of an appendix. For this reason, researchers generally make available the information that they cannot include in their publications online through journal websites, academic social media tools, and their own personal websites. Usually, this information is provided alongside the replication materials if the research involves a statistical analysis.

Key Points

- Social scientific writing is generally formal, objective, and analytic since the purpose of it is to inform, not to persuade.
- The key to good social science writing is rewriting.
- In order to improve the quality and presentation of your research, it is essential to expose it to others with different backgrounds and experiences.

Further Reading

The first and third books are general handbooks on the writing process and the second book provides advice to graduate students on how to revise their dissertations for publication as books.

Booth, Wayne C., Gregory G. Colomb, Joseph M. Williams, Joseph Bizup, and William T. Fitzgerald. 2016. *The Craft of Research*. Chicago: The University of Chicago Press.
Germano, William. 2013. *From Dissertation to Book*. Chicago: University of Chicago Press.
Rodenwasser, David and Jill Stephen. 2008. *Writing Analytically with Readings*. Boston: Thomson Wadsworth.

EXERCISE 21.1

To ensure that your paper passes the 'Straphangers' Rule', highlight the thesis sentence and the first sentence of every paragraph in your own research. Exchange your paper with another person and ask them to read only the highlighted parts, to summarize your argument based on these highlighted parts, and to mark the parts that they did not use to summarize your argument. Then ask yourself the following questions:

- Does my colleague's summary of my argument include every point that I wanted to make?
- Is the material that my colleague did not use to summarize my argument extraneous, or does it contain information that I should have included in my argument but did not?

If your colleague's summary does not include every point you made in your argument, review your writing to figure out why. Did you make the point further down in the paragraph? If so, rewrite the paragraph to include your point in the topic sentence. Also, review the information that your colleague did not use in his or her summary of your research, and decide whether the information is extraneous and should be deleted, or whether it should be re-written to make the point more apparent.

Glossary

Accuracy (data): the correctness of the values in a dataset.

Alternative explanation: an argument that claims that a given outcome was produced by a factor other than the one theorized.

Anchoring vignettes: a tool researchers use to standardize survey responses within and across countries through short stories known as vignettes.

Attrition bias: the bias that results when participants drop out of longitudinal surveys in a way that systematically differs from those that remain in them.

Case: an instance of a class of events (e.g., wars, protests, elections, and economic crises).

Close-ended questions: questions that have defined response categories.

Clustered sampling: random sampling method in which simple random samples are selected from subgroups of the total population. But, unlike stratified sampling, samples are only taken from certain subgroups of the total population, which are generally determined through simple random sampling.

Comparative case method: an umbrella term that refers to a set of qualitative research techniques used for both theory building and theory testing involving comparisons between and among classes of events, otherwise known as cases.

Completeness (data): the values representing the whole universe of cases.

Completion rate: the percentage of people who completed the survey, calculated as number of respondents who completed the survey/number of persons contacted, multiplied by 100.

Concatenation (mixed methods): the use of qualitative and quantitative research to analyze different components of a single phenomenon in a mixed methods research design.

Concept: an abstract idea or object.

Concept stretching: the distortion of a concept through its application to another case(s).

Confirmation bias: the tendency to search for or interpret information in a way that confirms one's pre-existing beliefs or expectations.

Consistency (data): the uniformity of the data across observations.

Construct validity: a term referring to the degree to which inferences from an experiment are relevant to the theory.

Content analysis: a research method used to construct quantitative data from written, spoken, and visual materials.

Continuous measures: measures that can take on any value or any value within a range.

Convenience sampling: a non-random sampling method in which respondents are selected based on the ease of their accessibility.

Counterfactuals: conditional statements about the past in which an event is supposed to have occurred when it did not (or vice versa), and about what would have occurred in the past as a result.

Crucial (or critical) case: a rare case, which arguably does not exist, that no other theory can explain.

Deductive reasoning: a top-down approach to reasoning in which researchers derive specific testable hypotheses to explain human behavior from theoretical axioms.

Design (mixed method): the use of either qualitative or quantitative research to inform the design of an analysis using the opposing method.

Design weights: a sample weight used in surveys to compensate for over- or under-sampling of specific observations or for disproportionate stratification. They are calculated for each case as 1/(sampling fraction). The sampling fraction is the ratio of the sample size to population size.

Deviant case: a case that does not conform to expectations.

Discrete measures: measures in which the data can only take on particular values and for which there are clear boundaries among those values.

Discriminatory power: a term that refers to the extent to which a measure is able to distinguish between two concepts. It is also used in the discussion of process tracing to indicate the degree to which a hypothesis distinguishes among competing explanations for a phenomenon.

Endogeneity: a problem that arises when an explanatory variable is correlated with the error term. It can occur as a result of simultaneous bias, omitted variable bias, or measurement error.

Epistemology: the study of the nature, scope, and production of human knowledge.

Equifinality: a term that refers to the possibility of there being multiple paths or combinations of different variables that produce the same outcome.

Experiments: a type of quantitative research method in which researchers randomly assign individuals to experimental conditions (i.e., a treatment condition where the explanatory factor is present and a control condition where it is not) in order to test the effect of an explanatory factor on a given outcome.

Expert surveys: surveys of individuals that have specialized knowledge on a particular subject.

External validity: a term that refers to the extent to which the inferences from an experiment are generalizable.

Falsifiable: capable of being proven false.

Field experiments: experiments in which researchers do not have control over the environment in which the experiment is conducted beyond the experimental manipulation.

Focus group: a semi-structured group interview designed to solicit information, perceptions, opinions, beliefs, and attitudes from participants of the group on a defined topic of interest.

Fundamental problem of causal inference: an axiom stating that for any given subject, it is impossible to observe an outcome under both the treatment and control conditions at a particular point in time.

Gap-filling (mixed methods): the use of qualitative and quantitative research to analyze different aspects of a single issue related to a given phenomenon in a mixed methods research design.

Generalizability: a term referring to the extent to which the research findings apply to or are representative of other cases.

Guinea pig effect: the idea that people behave differently knowing that they are participants in a research study than they would behave otherwise.

Hypotheses: propositions that are advanced to explain a given phenomenon.

Hypotheticals: statements about present conditions that do not exist and conjectures about the consequences that would occur from them in the future if they did.

Inductive reasoning: a bottom-up approach to reasoning in which researchers construct generalized theories from first observing patterns in human behavior and then developing hypotheses to explain these patterns.

Intercoder reliability statistic: a statistic that indicates the degree to which different individuals assign the same values to observations based on the same information.

Internal validity: a term that refers to the degree to which the relationship between the explanatory variable and outcome variable is causal.

Interpretation: the process by which the conclusions, significance, and implications of a study are understood.

Interpretation (mixed methods): the use of either quantitative or qualitative methods to explain the findings of research using the other method.

Interval-level measures: continuous measures in which the distance between units is known and equal.

Intervening variable: an explanatory variable that alters the effect of another explanatory variable on the outcome variable.

Interviews: a method for collecting qualitative information from individuals through a series of questions posed to individuals either face-to-face, by phone, or through another medium.

Lab-in-the-field experiments (LITFE): laboratory experiments that are conducted on theoretically relevant populations.

Laboratory experiments: experiments conducted in a common location in which the researcher has full control over the environment in which the experiment is conducted.

Least-likely case: a case that is unlikely to fit a theory but does.

List experiment: a method for eliciting honest responses to sensitive questions. In a list experiment, the survey sample is split into two groups. Both groups are asked to identify the number of statements (not which ones) in a list that are true for them. All but one of these statements is the same across the two groups. The one that is different is the sensitive issue.

Literature review: a synthesis of the existing academic and non-academic literature on a particular subject that characterizes the strengths and weaknesses of the existing literature in order to demonstrate the theoretical and empirical contribution of certain research to the existing literature or to identify important areas of future research.

Manipulation check: a test included in the experiment, generally in the form of a question, to determine if the participants received the treatment.

Margin of sampling error: indicates how much the results of a survey question may differ due to chance compared to what would have been found if the entire population was surveyed.

Mean (arithmetic): the average of a set of numbers.

Measures: quantitative representations of concepts used as a basis or standard of comparison.

Measurement error: the difference between the true value and the observed value.

Median (arithmetic): the middle value of an odd number of numbers listed in numeric order or the average of the two middle values of an even number of numbers listed in numeric order.

Method: the specific process used to collect and analyze information.

Method of agreement: a qualitative research method based on case comparisons in which the outcome is the same in the cases compared while the values of the explanatory variables are different, except for the factor believed to cause the outcome.

Method of difference: a qualitative research method based on case comparisons in which the outcome is different in the cases compared while the values of the explanatory variables are the same, except for the variable believed to cause the outcome.

Mixed methods research: the collection, analysis and interpretation of quantitative and qualitative data in a single study or in a series of studies examining the same phenomenon.

Mode (arithmetic) mode: the value that appears most often in a set of numbers.

Most-likely case: a case that should fit an existing theory but does not.

Natural experiments: observational studies in which the assignment to treatment and control groups is random or 'as if' random.

Necessary and sufficient condition: an explanatory factor that is required for an outcome to be produced and alone is enough to produce the outcome.

Necessary condition: an explanatory factor that must be present for an outcome to be produced.

Neither necessary nor sufficient condition: an explanatory factor that is not required for an outcome to be produced and alone is not enough to produce the outcome.

Nested case design: a qualitative research approach in which the cases analyzed are categories of another case.

Nominal measures: discrete measures in which there is no order or hierarchy among categories. The categories are also mutually exclusive (i.e., no observation may belong to more than one category) and exhaustive (i.e., all observations must belong to one of the categories).

Non-expert surveys: surveys of individuals that do not have specialized knowledge on a particular subject.

Non-observational data: data collected through researchers interacting with their subjects or intervening in their subjects' environments.

Non-positivism: a philosophical theory that posits that an objective reality does not exist independent of human perception and that a researcher is incapable of studying a phenomenon without influencing it or being influenced by it.

Observational data: data collected without researchers interacting with their subjects or intervening in their subjects' environments.

Observational study: a quantitative research method for testing arguments in which researchers do not randomly assign subjects to treatment and control conditions.

Observer bias: the bias that results when the researcher unintentionally affects the outcome of their study through their presence.

Omitted variable bias: the bias that results when a factor that is correlated with the outcome variable and one or more explanatory variables is not included in a statistical analysis.

On-the-regression-line case: a case that is consistent with theoretical expectations because the explanatory factor hypothesized to cause a given outcome is present and the outcome has resulted.

Ontology: the study of the nature of being or existence.

Open-ended questions: questions that do not have defined response categories.

Operationalization: a term that refers to the transformation of concepts into measures.

Ordinal measures: discrete measures in which there is, as the name suggests, an order among the categories, but in which the distance between categories is not necessarily equal. As in the case of nominal measures, these categories are mutually exclusive and exhaustive.

Outliers: an observation that is very different from the other observations.

Over/undersampling: random sampling method in which the selection of more or fewer individuals from a sub-population of the data known to participate in surveys at a low or higher rate in order to ensure that the sample includes a representative sample of this population.

Participant observation: a form of data collection that involves the immersion of the researcher for an extended period of time in the environment of the group that the researcher is studying.

Peer review: the process by which research is evaluated by experts in a given field in order to assess the quality of the research. Peer review may be double-blind, where neither the reviewer nor the author are known to each other, or single-blind, where the reviewer knows who the researcher is, but the researcher does not know who the reviewer is.

Positivism: a philosophical theory that maintains that an objective reality or truth exists in the world independent of the observer, and that it can be understood using the scientific method.

Post-stratification weights: sample weights used in surveys to compensate for the fact that persons with certain characteristics are not as likely to respond to the survey.

Power analysis: a calculation to determine the sample size required to detect an effect of a given size with a given degree of confidence.

Precision: a term that refers to the specificity of the data.

Process tracing: a qualitative research method used to evaluate causal process within cases, which involves the articulation of hypotheses regarding phenomena likely to be observable if the relationship between two factors is causal, and the marshaling of evidence, largely historical in nature, to evaluate the validity of these hypotheses. It also entails the evaluation of alternative explanations for this relationship through the same process.

Purposive sampling: a non-random sampling method in which respondents are selected based on characteristics of a population and the objective of the study.

Qualitative comparative analysis (QCA): a computer-assisted qualitative research method for analyzing the relationship between predictors and outcome variables for small- to medium-size datasets where statistical analysis is not possible.

Quantitative data: any data that is numeric in form.

Quota sampling: non-random sampling method in which respondents in the sample are in the same proportion as the entire population with respect to known characteristics, traits, and so forth.

Random measurement error: measurement error that is unrelated to the real value being measured.

Randomized response technique: a method for eliciting honest responses to sensitive questions. In it, the respondent is asked to toss a coin when the back of the person conducting the survey is turned, so that s/he does not know if the coin landed on heads or tails. The interviewer then tells the respondent not to tell him/her how the coin lands, and that if the coin lands heads to respond 'yes' to the question, and if the coins lands tails, to tell the truth.

Ratio-level measures: continuous measures in which the distance between units is known and equal. However, unlike with interval-level measures, with ratio-level measures, there is an absolute zero value that is meaningful.

Reliability: a term that refers to the extent to which a measure produces consistent and dependable results.

Replicability: a term that refers to the ability of another researcher using the same procedures under the same circumstances to research the same question and obtain comparable results.

Research ethics: the norms, standards, and legal rules regarding appropriate behavior in the conduct of academic research.

Research fraud: research misconduct involving the intentional falsification or fabrication of research or the reporting of misleading results.

Response rate: the percentage of people who responded to a survey, calculated as the number of respondents/number of persons contacted, multiplied by 100.

Reverse causation: refers to the situation where the explanatory variable does not cause the outcome variable, but the outcome variable causes the explanatory variable.

Sample weights: a numerical value that adjusts the weight of an observation in a survey in order to create a sample that is more representative of the given population.

Scientific method: a set of procedures used to test hypotheses about phenomena based on the collection and analysis of data either through observation, interaction, or experimentation. The scientific method involves six distinct steps in the following order: the identification of the problem, question, or puzzle; the formulation of hypotheses to explain the problem, question or puzzle; the development of measures to test the hypotheses; the collection of data representing these measures; the analysis of the data; and the confirmation or disconfirmation of the hypotheses based on the analysis.

Semi-structured interviews: a type of interview in which the same questions are not necessarily asked of all subjects using the same wording or order. The greater flexibility of this type of interview enhances the efficiency of the interview process, and potentially the quality of the information collected because it allows the researcher to tailor his or her questions to a particular interviewee.

Simple random sampling: random sampling method in which every member of the population has a known, equal, non-zero chance of being selected.

Simultaneity bias: a form of bias that arises when the explanatory variable and outcome variable are jointly determined. In other words, when the explanatory variable influences the outcome variable and the outcome variable influences the explanatory variable.

Simultaneous causation: a causal relationship in which the explanatory variable influences the outcome variable and the outcome variable influences the explanatory variable. It is also known as two-way or reciprocal causation.

Snowball sampling: a non-random sampling method in which respondents are chosen based on the recommendations of prior respondents.

Social desirability bias: the tendency of individuals to answer questions or behave in ways that they think are likely to be viewed favorably by others.

Spurious: a term that refers to a situation in which the hypothesized relationship between the explanatory variable and the outcome variable is false because of the presence of another latent (or confounding) factor that causes both the explanatory variable and the outcome variable.

Stable Unit Treatment Value Assumption (SUTVA): an assumption in experimental research that maintains that the treatment is the same across subjects and there is no cross-contamination between the treatment and control groups.

Stratified random sampling: random sampling method in which simple random samples are taken, in proportion to the population, from subgroups of the total population (e.g., regions, genders, and religions).

Structured interviews: a type of interview in which the same questions are asked of all interviewees without altering either the wording of the questions or the order in which the questions are asked.

Sufficient condition: an explanatory factor that alone is enough to produce a given outcome.

Survey: a research method for collecting information from a sample of individuals in order to construct quantitative descriptors of attributes of the larger population from which this sample is drawn.

Survey experiment: a type of field experiment in which the experiment is conducted via a survey.

Survey mode: the means by which the survey is administered (i.e., in-person, paper, telephone, or online).

Systematic measurement error: measurement error that results from problems in the test setup.

Systematic random sampling: random sampling method in which every k^{th} element of the population is sampled. The kth element is the ratio of the size of the sample to the population. Once k has been determined, the index of a starting element is selected within the first k elements by random selection. The indices for subsequent elements are formed by adding multiples of k to this starting index.

Tautology: a statement that is true by definition.

Triangulation: the use of different data, approaches or methods to validate and/or corroborate other data, approaches or methods.

Triangulation (mixed methods): the use of quantitative or qualitative research to corroborate the results of the other method.

Typical case: a case thought to be similar to other cases on certain dimensions and informative about these other cases for this reason.

Unstructured interviews: a very flexible type of interview in which the researcher improvises the questions based on the subject and the context in which the subjects are interviewed.

Validity: a term that refers to the extent to which a measure captures the concept it is intended to represent. It is also used in the discussion of data as a measure of the extent to which data represents the measures, and in process tracing to refer to the extent to which a hypothesis is a good test of the relationship between the explanatory and outcome variables.

Volunteer sampling: a non-random sampling method in which respondents self-select into the survey.

Notes

CHAPTER 1

1 United Nations Food and Agricultural Organization of the United Nations. www.fao.org/fao-stat/en/#home. Accessed 14 November 2017.
2 National Oceanic and Atmospheric Administration. National Centers for Environmental Information. www.ncei.noaa.gov. Accessed 1 February 2016; UN Data. http://data.un.org/Explorer.aspx?d=CLINO. Accessed 14 November 2017.
3 The Polity Project. www.systemic peace.org/polityproject.html. Accessed 17 July 2017.
4 Polyarchy Dataset. www.prio.org/Data/Governance/Vanhanens-index-of-democracy/. Accessed 14 November 2017.
5 UCDP/PRIO Armed Conflict Dataset. www.prio.org/Data/Armed-Conflict/UCDP-PRIO/. Accessed 14 November 2017.

CHAPTER 2

1 During the Second World War, the Nazis conducted a series of experiments, which came to be known as the Nuremburg experiments, on concentration camp prisoners to investigate the effects of dangerous conditions on the human body and treatments for these conditions. Many prisoners died or suffered grievous harm in the course of these experiments. A number of scientists who conducted the experiments were tried and convicted by Allied military tribunals after the end of the war, which led to the development of the Nuremberg Code, a set of research ethics principles regarding the use of human subjects in experiments.
2 David Chasan, 'Row Over "Torture" on French TV,' *BBC News*, 18 March 2010.
3 The BBC Prison Study. www.bbcprisonstudy.org. Accessed 15 November 2017.
4 An interesting exception is surrealist painter Salvador Dalí, who often signed his paintings with his name and the name of his muse and wife, Gala. See: Gala Dalí, *Biography.com*. www.biography.com. Accessed 15 November 2017.
5 John Kifner, 'Scholar Sets Off Gastronomic False Alarm,' *The New York Times*, 8 September 2001.

CHAPTER 3

1 'Alfred Nobel Quotes', 31 December 2015. www.alfrednobel.org/alfred-nobel-quotes/. Accessed 26 December 2017.
2 Appleton would not consent to an interview by *Time* magazine when asked but did agree to interview himself instead. One of the questions he asked himself was the secret of his success. 'What's the Secret of Successful Leadership and Living? Why it's Enthusiasm,' *The Rotarian*, February 1953, 8–9.

3   Ed Pilkington, 'How to Save the World,' *The Guardian*, 4 April 2008.

4   David J. Craig, 'Grave Decisions,' *Columbia Magazine*, Winter: 2010/11, 21–25.

5   Hilary Lamb, 'Saul Perlmutter: "Scientific Discoveries Aren't Made to Order",' *Times Higher Education*, 12 January 2017.

6   The Polity Project. www.systemicpeace.org/polityproject.html. Accessed 16 November 2017.

CHAPTER 4

1   A literature review, referred to in some fields as a narrative review, differs significantly from a systematic review, which is more common in the natural sciences. A systematic review provides a judgment as to the quality of evidence regarding a clinical question and restricts the literature reviewed to only high quality research meeting certain pre-specified eligibility criteria. A systematic review may include a meta-analysis. A meta-analysis is a statistical technique that combines the results from multiple studies in order to draw a conclusion regarding the validity of a hypothesis.

CHAPTER 5

1   Emily Swanson, 'Poll: Few Identify as Feminists, But Most Believe in Equality of Sexes,' *Huntington Post*, 16 April 2013; 'Only 7 per cent of Britons Consider Themselves Feminists,' *The Telegraph*, 15 January 2016.

2   'Can Men Be Feminists Too? Half (48%) of Men in 15 Country Survey Seem to Think So.' www.ipsos.com/sites/default/files/news_and_polls/2014-05/6511.pdf. Accessed 25 September 2017.

3   Asian Barometer. Fourth Wave. www.asianbarometer.org/. Accessed 9 September 2017.

4   'The Real Story of "Fake News".' www.merriam-webster.com/words-at-play/the-real-story-of-fake-news. Accessed 25 September 2017.

5   Certain components of the Polity IV index, a popular measure of democracy, include a factional category, where political competition is 'intense, hostile, and frequently violent,' whereby extreme factionalism can be manifested in civil war. See Vreeland (2008).

6   United States Department of State, *Patterns of Global Terrorism 2003*, April 2004, xii. www.state.gov/documents/organization/31912.pdf.

7   Terrorism Act. www.legislation.gov.uk/ukpga/2000/11/section/1.

8   Jordan Fabian, 'Spicer: Trump executive order "not a travel ban",' *The Hill*, 31 January 2017.

9   www.nobelpeaceprize.org/History/Alfred-Nobel-s-will.

10 The full statements of the prize announcements are available at: www.nobelprize.org/nobel_prizes/peace/laureates.

CHAPTER 6

1   National Archives of Australia. www.naa.gov.au/collection/explore/cabinet/by-year/1974-events-issues.aspx. Accessed 15 June 2017.

2   Splayd Eating Utensils 2016, Museum of Applied Arts and Sciences. https://ma.as/111703. Accessed 20 November 2017.

3   Ken Stern, 'Why the Rich Don't Give to Charity.' *The Atlantic*, April 2013; 'Why are the Poor More Generous than the Wealthy?' *Civil Society Voices*, 12 June 2013.

CHAPTER 8

1 A number of typologies have been developed to categorize the different ways in which qualitative and quantitative methods are combined in mixed methods research, but none is universally accepted as the best. The typologies are commonly based on the structure of the mixed methods design as opposed to the goals sought by them.
2 The International Property Rights Index. https://internationalpropertyrightsindex.org. Accessed 23 November 2017.

CHAPTER 9

1 The Panel Study of Income Dynamics. https://psidonline.isr.umich.edu.
2 The European Union Statistics on Income and Living Conditions (EU-SILC). http://ec.europa.eu/eurostat/web/microdata/european-union-statistics-on-income-and-living-conditions.

CHAPTER 10

1 Benedict Carey, 'Leading Psychiatrist Apologizes for Study Supporting Gay "Cure",' *The New York Times*, 18 May 2012.
2 Antonio Spadaro, S.J., 'A Big Heart Open to God: An interview with Pope Francis,' *America: The Jesuit Review*, 30 September 2013.
3 Evelyn Amony. 2015. *I Am Evelyn Amony: Reclaiming My Life from the Lord's Resistance Army.* Madison: University of Wisconsin Press.

CHAPTER 12

1 Ethnography is not in and of itself a method. Ethnography is the systematic description and analysis of a culture or society. It involves multiple methods of which participant observation is the primary one. Other methods used in ethnographic research include interviews, focus groups, and so forth.
2 Harper Lee. 1960/2006. *To Kill a Mockingbird*, reprint. New York: Harper Perennial Modern Classics, 33.
3 Graeme Wood, 'Anthropology Inc.,' *The Atlantic*, March 2013.

CHAPTER 13

1 The terms validity and discriminatory power are similar to those of certainty and uniqueness developed by Steven van Evera (1997, 31–32). The latter terms are not used here (although they are common in the process tracing literature) in order to draw parallels to the quantitative literature, and because the typology derived from Van Evera's terminology (e.g. straw-in-the-wind tests; hoops tests; smoking gun tests; and doubly-decisive tests) suggests that hypotheses either meet criteria or not, while the issue is more a matter of degrees.

CHAPTER 14

1 Stephanie Kirchgaessner and Lorenzo Tondo, 'Why has Italy been Spared Mass Terror Attacks in Recent Years?' *The Guardian*, 23 June 2017.
2 'South Korea's Protest Culture Gets Results, but its Roots are Nothing to Envy,' *Quartz*, 13 March 2017.
3 Statistics Korea. www.kostat.go.kr/eng/. Accessed 1 August 2017.
4 Eurostat. ec.europa.eu/Eurostat. Accessed 1 August 2017.
5 Gallup, Inc. www.gallup.com/home.aspx. Accessed 1 August 2017.
6 Corruption Perceptions Index. www.transparency.org/research/cpi/overview. Accessed 1 August 2017.
7 World Development Indicators. https://data.worldbank.org. Accessed 5 November 2017; 'Russia Masks Unemployment with Soviet-era Tactics,' *The Telegraph*, 18 August 2015.
8 'Questions and answers on Romania's anticorruption implosion,' *Clean Romania*, 6 February 2017. Accessed 5 November 2017. www.romaniacurata.ro; Anti-corruption Foundation. https://fbk.info. Accessed 5 November 2017.

CHAPTER 15

1 Presidential Inaugural Address to the General Meeting of the British Association, Edinburgh (2 Aug 1871). In *Report of the Forty-First Meeting of the British Association for the Advancement of Science* (1872), xci.
2 See: The Polity Project. www.systemic peace.org/polityproject.html. Accessed 17 July 2017; Freedom in the World. https://freedomhouse.org/. Accessed 21 December 2017; Correlates of War Militarized Interstate Disputes. www.correlatesofwar.org. Accessed 21 December 2017; World Justice Project Rule of Law Index. https://worldjusticeproject.org. Accessed 21 December 2017; Cingranelli-Richards (CIRI) Human Rights Project. www.humanrightsdata.com/. Accessed 21 December 2017; Liesbet Hooghe, Gary Marks, Arjan H. Schakel, Sandra Chapman Osterkatz, Sara Niedzwiecki, and Sarah Shair-Rosenfield. 2016. *Measuring Regional Authority: A Postfunctionalist Theory of Governance*, Volume I. Oxford: Oxford University Press.
3 World Health Organization. 2000. *The World Health Report 2000 – Health Systems: Improving Performance*. Geneva: Switzerland.
4 Justin McCurry, 'Did North Korea Photoshop its Hovercraft?' *The Guardian*, 27 March 2013.
5 Gallup World Polls. www.gallup.com/home.aspx. Accessed 1 August 2017.
6 Rachael Morarjee, 'China's Economic Statistics Aren't Fake Enough,' *Reuters*, 20 January 2017.

CHAPTER 16

1 This phrase has been attributed to mathematician W. Edwards Deming, but this attribution cannot be confirmed. The Deming Institute has no written or audio report of Edwards Deming making this statement. Email 2 January 2017.
2 Goldie Blumenstyk, 'Blowing Off Class? We Know,' *The New York Times*, 2 December 2014.
3 Jessica Benko, 'The Radical Humanness of Norway's Halden Prison,' *The New York Times*, 26 March 2015.
4 Organisation for Economic Co-operation and Development (OECD). www.oecd.org/dac/stats/officialdevelopmentassistancedefinitionandcoverage.htm. Accesse 26November 2017.

5   GDELT Project. www.gdeltproject.org/.
6   'China Underreporting Coal Consumption by up to 17%, Data Suggests,' *The Guardian*, 4 November 2015.
7   David Wertime, 'Meet the Chinese Trolls Pumping Out 488 Million Fake Social Media Posts,' *Foreign Policy*, 19 May 2016.

CHAPTER 17

1   William Bruce Cameron. 1963. *Informal Sociology: A Casual Introduction to Sociological Thinking*, 13. New York: Random House.
2   Andrew Piper and Richard Jean So, 'Women Write About Family, Men Write About War,' *New Republic*, 8 April 2016.
3   Chloe Farand, 'French Social Media Awash with Fake News Stories from Sources "Exposed to Russian Influence" Ahead of Presidential Election,' *The Independent*, 22 April 2017; Bob Dreyfuss, 'Russian Trolling of US Social Media May Have Been Much Greater Than We Thought,' *The Nation*, 23 October 2017.
4   'Google Settles Defamation Case from Morgan Stanley Banker Falsely Hounded as a Murderer and Money Launderer,' *Reuters*, 25 November 2004.
5   Christopher Heine, 'Mountain Dew Pulls "Arguably Most Racist Commercial in History",' *Adweek,* 1 May 2013.
6   Comparative Manifestos Project. https://manifesto-project.wzb.eu. Accessed 21 December 2017.

CHAPTER 18

1   TRIP Snap Polls of IR Scholars. https://trip.wm.edu/home/. Accessed 19 October 2017.
2   Academic Reputations Survey. http://ips.clarivate.com//m/pdfs/GIPP_AcamRep_report.pdf. Accessed 19 October 2017.
3   Electoral Integrity Project. www.electoralintegrityproject.com. Accessed 19 October 2017.
4   Asian Barometer. Fourth Wave. www.asianbarometer.org/. Accessed 9 September 2017.
5   Middle East Values Study. https://mevs.org. Accessed 19 October 2017.
6   A researcher may exploit another randomization device, such as a phone number or birthday, if a coin is not available or feasible.

CHAPTER 20

1   Trading Economics. https://tradingeconomics.com. Accessed 13 October 2017.
2   Global Retail Theft Barometer. www.globalretailtheftbarometer.com/. Accessed 13 October 2017.
3   Simultaneity bias, which occurs when the explanatory variable and outcome variable are jointly determined, is one form of endogeneity. In common usage, people often refer to an argument in which the explanatory and outcome variables are jointly determined as endogenous. This is a correct use of the terminology. However, endogeneity encompasses more than just simultaneity bias. In statistics, endogeneity arises when an explanatory variable is correlated with the error term. This can occur not only as a result of simultaneity bias, but also as a result of omitted variables (as in the case of a latent or confounding variable) or measurement error.

CHAPTER 21

1   Richard Lea, 'Penguin Cookbook Calls for "Freshly Ground Black People",' *The Guardian*, 19 April 2010.
2   Daniel Victor, 'Lack of Oxford Comma Could Cost Maine Company Millions in Overtime Dispute,' *The New York Times*, 16 March 2017.

References

Al-Olayan, Fahad S. and Kiran Karande. 2000. 'A Content Analysis of Magazine Advertisements from the United States and the Arab World.' *Journal of Advertising* 29(3): 69–82.

Ali, Ayaan Hirsi. 2007. *Infidel*. New York: Atria Books.

Amato, Paul R. 2000. 'The Consequences of Divorce for Adults and Children.' *Journal of Marriage and Family* 62(4): 1269–1287.

Amato, Paul R. and Bryndl Hohmann-Marriott. 2007. 'A Comparison of High- and Low-Distress Marriages that End in Divorce.' *Journal of Marriage and Family* 69(3): 621–638.

Anderson, John C. and Larry F. Moore. 1978. 'The Motivation to Volunteer.' *Nonprofit and Voluntary Sector Quarterly* 7(3–4): 120–129.

Angrist, Joshua D. and Alan B. Krueger. 1991. 'Does Compulsory School Attendance Affect Schooling and Earnings?' *The Quarterly Journal of Economics* 10(4): 979–1014.

Ansolabehere, Stephen, James M. Snyder, Jr., and Charles Stewart, III. 2000. 'Old Voters, New Voters, and the Personal Vote: Using Redistricting to Measure the Incumbency Advantage.' *American Journal of Political Science* 44(1) 1: 17–34.

Ariely, Dan and Gregory S. Berns. 2010. Neuromarketing: The Hope and Hype of Neuroimaging in Business. *Neuroscience Nature Reviews Neuroscience* 11(4): 284–292.

Art, Robert J. and Louise Richardson, eds. 2007. *Democracy and Counterterrorism: Lessons from the Past*. Washington, DC: United States Institute of Peace.

Artz, Sibyelle and Diana Nicholson. 2010. 'Reducing Aggressive Behavior in Adolescent Girls by Attending to School Climate.' In *Fighting for Girls: Critical Perspectives on Gender and Violence*, edited by Meda Chesney-Lind and Nikki Jones, 149–174. Albany, NY: SUNY Press.

Asch, Solomon E. 1951. 'Effects of Group Pressure upon the Modification and Distortion of Judgment.' In *Groups, Leadership and Men: Research in Human Relations*, edited by Harold Guetzkow, 177–190. Pittsburgh: Carnegie Press.

Avis, Eric, Claudio Ferraz, Frederico Finan, and Carlos Varjão. 2017. 'Money and Politics: The Effects of Campaign Spending Limits on Political Competition and Incumbency Advantage.' *NBER* Working Paper No. 23508. Cambridge, MA: National Bureau of Economic Research.

Awan, Imran. 2017. 'Cyber-Extremism: Isis and the Power of Social Media.' *Social Science and Public Policy* 54: 138–149.

Ayoub, Phillip M. 2016. *When States Come Out: Europe's Sexual Minorities and the Politics of Visibility*. New York: Cambridge University Press.

Bagnall, John, David Bounie, Kim P. Huynh, Anneke Kosse, Tobias Schmidt, Scott Schuh, and Helmut Stix. 2014. 'Consumer Cash Usage: A Cross-Country Comparison with Payment Diary Survey Data.' *European Central Bank*, Working Paper Series No. 1685, June.

Bailey, Drew H. and J. Michael Bailey. 2013. 'Poor Instruments Lead to Poor Inferences: Comment on Roberts, Glymour, and Koenen.' *Archives of Sexual Behavior* 42(8): 1649–1652.

Baker, Christina N. 2005. 'Images of Women's Sexuality in Advertisements: A Content Analysis of Black- and White-Oriented Women's and Men's Magazines.' *Sex Roles* 52(1–2): 13–27.

Barreca, Alan, Olivier Deschenes, and Melanie Guldi. 2015. 'Maybe Next Month? Temperature Shocks, Climate Change, and Dynamic Adjustments in Birth Rates.' *NBER* Working Paper No. 21681. Cambridge: National Bureau of Economic Research.

Barro, Robert J. and Rachel M. McCleary. 2003. 'Religion and Economic Growth.' *NBER* Working Paper No. 9682. Cambridge: National Bureau of Economic Research.

Beissinger, Mark R. 2007. 'Structure and Example in Modular Political Phenomena: The Diffusion of Bulldozer/Rose/Orange/Tulip Revolutions.' *Perspectives on Politics* 5(2): 259–276.

Bellamy, Carol. 1996. *The State of the World's Children: Focus on Child Labor*. New York: Oxford University Press.

Ben-Artzi, Ruth. 2016. *Regional Development Banks in Comparison: Banking Strategies Versus Development Goals*. New York: Cambridge University Press.

Bennett, Craig M., Abigail A. Baird, Michael B. Miller, and George L. Wolford. 2009. 'Neural Correlates of Interspecies Perspective Taking in the Post-Mortem Atlantic Salmon: An Argument for Proper Multiple Comparisons Correction.' Paper prepared for the 15th Annual Meeting of the Organization for Human Brain Mapping. San Francisco, CA, 18–23 June.

Benoit, Kenneth and Michael Laver. 2007. 'Estimating Party Policy Positions: Comparing Expert Surveys and Hand-coded Content Analysis.' *Electoral Studies* 26(1): 90–107.

Berman, Sheri. 1997. 'Civil Society and the Collapse of the Weimar Republic.' *World Politics* 49(3): 401–429.

Bertrand, Marianne and Sendhil Mullainathan. 2003. 'Enjoying the Quiet Life? Corporate Governance and Managerial Preferences.' *Journal of Political Economy* 111(5): 1043–1075.

Bertrand, Marianne, Simeon Djankov, Rema Hanna, and Sendhil Mullainathan. 2007. 'Corruption in Driving Licensing Process in Delhi.' *Quarterly Journal of Economics*, 122(4): 1639–1676.

Bianchi, Milo, Paolo Buonanno, and Paolo Pinotti. 2012. 'Do Immigrants Cause Crime?' *Journal of the European Economic Association* 10(6): 1318–1347.

Bieri, Franziska. 2016. *From Blood Diamonds to the Kimberley Process: How NGOs Cleaned Up the Global Diamond Industry*. New York: Routledge.

Bishop, Jacob Lowell and Matthew A. Verleger. 2013. 'The Flipped Classroom: A Survey of the Research.' Paper presented at the 120th ASEE Annual Conference and Exposition, 23–26 June.

Blair, Graeme, Kosuke Imai and Yang-Yang Zhou. 2015, 'Design and Analysis of the Randomized Response Technique.' *Journal of the American Statistical Association* 110(511): 1304–1319.

Blanco, Carlos, Jon Grant, Nancy M. Petry, H. Blair Simpson, Analucia Alegria, Shang-Min Liu, and Deborah Hasin. 2008. 'Prevalence and Correlates of Shoplifting in the United States: Results from the National Epidemiologic Survey on Alcohol and Related Conditions (NESARC).' *The American Journal of Psychiatry* 165(7): 905–913.

Blattman, Christopher and Jeannie Annan. 2016. 'Can Employment Reduce Lawlessness and Rebellion? A Field Experiment with High-Risk Men in a Fragile State.' *American Political Science Review* 110(1): 1–17.

Blaydes, Lisa and Mark Andreas Kayser. 2011. 'Counting Calories: Democracy and Distribution in the Developing World.' *International Studies Quarterly* 55(4): 887–908.

Bloch, Alice. 1999. 'Carrying Out a Survey of Refugees: Some Methodological Considerations and Guidelines.' *Journal of Refugee Studies* 12(4): 367–383.

Bloom, Mia, Hicham Tiflati, and John Horgan. 2017. 'Navigating ISIS's Preferred Platform: Telegram.' *Terrorism and Political Violence* (July): 1–13.

Blumenstock, Joshua E. 2008. 'Size Matters: Word Count as a Measure of Quality on Wikipedia.' Proceeding of the 17th International Conference on World Wide Web 2008, 1095–1096.

Boomsma, Dorret, Andreas Busjahn, and Leena Peltonen. 2002. 'Classical Twin Studies and Beyond.' *Nature Reviews Genetics* 3(11): 872–882.

Bound, John, David A. Jaeger, and Regina M. Baker. 1995. 'Problems with Instrumental Variables Estimation when the Correlation between the Instruments and the Endogenous Explanatory Variable is Weak.' *Journal of the American Statistical Association* 90(430): 443–450.

Boyd, Christina L., Lee Epstein, and Andrew D. Martin. 2010. 'Untangling the Causal Effects of Sex on Judging.' *American Journal of Political Science*. 54: 389–411.

Brajuha, Mario and Lyle Hallowell. 1986. 'Legal Intrusion and the Politics of Fieldwork: The Impact of the Brajuha Case.' *Journal of Contemporary Ethnography 14*(4): 454–478.

Brams, Steven J. and Peter C. Fishburn. 2007. *Approval Voting*. New York: Springer.

Brancati, Dawn. 2006. 'Decentralization: Fueling the Fire or Dampening the Flames of Ethnic Conflict and Secessionism.' *International Organization 60*(3): 651–685.

Brancati, Dawn. 2007. 'Political Aftershocks: The Impact of Earthquakes on Intrastate Conflict.' *Journal of Conflict Resolution 51*(5): 715–743.

Brancati, Dawn. 2009. *Peace by Design: Managing Intrastate Conflict through Decentralization*. New York: Oxford University Press.

Brancati, Dawn. 2014a. 'The Determinants of US Public Opinion toward Democracy Promotion.' *Political Behavior 36*(4): 705–730.

Brancati, Dawn. 2014b. 'Building Confidence in Elections: The Case of Electoral Monitors in Kosova.' *Journal of Experimental Political Science 1*(1): 6–15.

Brancati, Dawn. 2016. *Democracy Protests: Origins, Features, and Significance*. New York: Cambridge University Press.

Brancati, Dawn. 2018. 'The Domestic Politics of International Prestige.' Unpublished manuscript.

Brancati, Dawn and Adrián Lucardi. forthcoming. 'Why Democracy Protests Do Not Diffuse.' Unpublished manuscript.

Braumoeller, Bear. 2015. 'Guarding Against False Positives in Qualitative Comparative Analysis.' *Political Analysis 23*(4): 471–487.

Brotsky, Sarah. R. and David Giles. 2007. 'Inside the "Pro-ana" Community: A Covert Online Participant Observation.' *Eating Disorders 15*(2): 93–109.

Bucerius, Sandra M. 2011. 'Immigrants and Crime.' In *The Oxford Handbook of Crime and Criminal Justice*, edited by Michael Tonry, 385–419. Oxford: Oxford University Press.

Bunce, Valerie J. and Sharon L. Wolchik. 2006. 'International Diffusion and Postcommunist Electoral Revolutions.' *Communist and Post-Communist Studies 39*(3): 283–304.

Burgess, Melinda C.R., Karen E. Dill, S. Paul Stermer, Steven R. Burgess, and Brian P. Brown. 2011. 'Playing with Prejudice: The Prevalence and Consequences of Racial Stereotypes in Video Games.' *Media Psychology 14*(3): 289–311.

Bush, Sarah Sunn and Lauren Prather. 2017. 'The Promise and Limits of Election Observers in Building Election Credibility.' *Journal of Politics 79*(3): 921–935.

Cederman, Lars-Erik, Kristian Skrede Gleditsch, and Halvard Buhaug. 2013. *Inequality, Grievances, and Civil War*. New York: Cambridge University Press.

Ceron, Andrea, Luigi Curini, and Stefano M. Iacus. 2015. 'Using Sentiment Analysis to Monitor Electoral Campaigns: Method Matters – Evidence from the United States and Italy.' *Social Science Computer Review 33*(1): 3–20.

Cheibub, José Antonio, Jennifer Gandhi, and James Raymond Vreeland. 2010. 'Democracy and Dictatorship Revisited.' *Public Choice 143*(1–2): 67–101.

Chew, Cynthia and Gunther Eysenbach. 2010. 'Pandemics in the Age of Twitter: Content Analysis of Tweets during the 2009 H1N1 Outbreak.' *PLoS One 5*(11): e14118.

Chou, Eileen Y. and J. Keith Murnighan. 2013. 'Life or Death Decisions: Framing the Call for Help.' *PLOS One 8*(3): e57351.

Christian, Mervyn, Octave Safari, Paul Ramazani, Gilbert Burnham, and Nancy Glass. 2011. 'Sexual and gender-based violence against men in the Democratic Republic of Congo: Effects on survivors, their families and the community. *Medicine, Conflict and Survival 27*(4): 227–246.

Clary, E. Gil, Mark Snyder, and Arthur A. Stukas. 1996. 'Volunteers' Motivations: Findings from a National Survey.' *Nonprofit and Voluntary Sector Quarterly 25*(4): 485–505.

Coffey, Daniel. 2005. 'Measuring Gubernatorial Ideology: A Content Analysis of State of the State Speeches.' *State Politics and Policy Quarterly* 5(1): 88–103.

Coffey, John and Cale Horne. 2011. 'Measuring Public Opinion under Political Repression.' *American Diplomacy*, April.

Collier, Paul and Anke Hoeffler. 2002. 'On the Incidence of Civil War in Africa.' *Journal of Conflict Resolution* 46(1): 13–28.

Cooley, Alexander and Jack L. Snyder, eds. 2015. *Ranking the World: Grading States as a Tool of Global Governance*. New York: Cambridge University Press.

Crenshaw, Martha. 1981. 'The Causes of Terrorism.' *Comparative Politics* 13(4): 379–99.

Denham, Bryan E. 2014. 'Intermedia Attribute Agenda Setting in *The New York Times*.' *Journalism and Mass Communication Quarterly* 91(1): 17–37.

DeWall, C. Nathan, Richard S. Pond, Jr., W. Keith Campbell, and Jean M. Twenge. 2011. 'Tuning in to Psychological Change: Linguistic Markers of Self-Focus, Loneliness, Anger, Anti-Social Behavior, and Misery Increase Over Time in Popular US Song Lyrics.' *Psychology of Aesthetics, Art, and Creativity* (5): 200–207.

Doyle, Michael W. 1986. 'Liberalism and World Politics.' *The American Political Science Review* 80(4): 1156–1157.

Doyle, Michael W. and Nicholas Sambanis. 2011. *Making War and Building Peace*. Princeton: Princeton University Press.

Downs, Anthony. 1957. *An Economic Theory of Democracy*. New York: Harper and Brothers.

Dunning, Thad. 2004. 'Conditioning the Effects of Aid: Cold War Politics, Donor Credibility, and Democracy in Africa.' *International Organization* 58(2): 409–423.

Dunning, Thad and Lauren Harrison. 2010. 'Cross-cutting Cleavages and Ethnic Voting: An Experimental Study of Cousinage in Mali.' *American Political Science Review* 104(4): 21–39.

Eckstein, Harry. 1975. Case Study and Theory in Political Science. In *Handbook of Political Science*, Vol. 7, edited by Fred I. Greenstein and Nelson W. Polsby, 79–137. Reading, MA: Addison-Wesley.

Edelman, Benjamin, Michael Luca, and Dan Svirsky. 2017. 'Racial Discrimination in the Sharing Economy: Evidence from a Field Experiment.' *American Economic Journal: Applied Economics* 9(2): 1–22.

Eklund, Anders, Thomas E. Nichols, and Hans Knutsson. 2016. 'Cluster Failure: Why fMRI Inferences for Spatial Extent Have Inflated False-Positive Rates.' *Proceedings of the National Academy of Sciences of the United States of America* 113(28): 7900–7905.

Elder, Randy W., Briana Lawrence, Aneeqah Ferguson, Timothy S. Naimi, Robert D. Brewer, Sajal K. Chattopadhyay, Traci L. Toomey, Jonathan E. Fielding, and The Task Force on Community Preventive Services. 2010. 'The Effectiveness of Tax Policy Interventions for Reducing Excessive Alcohol Consumption and Related Harms.' *American Journal of Preventive Medicine* 38(2): 217–229.

Eubank, William L. and Leonard Weinberg. 1994. 'Does Democracy Encourage Terrorism?' *Terrorism and Political Violence* 6(4): 417–443.

Evans, Lorraine and Kimberly Davies. 2000. 'No Sissy Boys Here: A Content Analysis of the Representation of Masculinity of Elementary School Reading Textbooks.' *Sex Roles* 42(3–4): 255–270.

Eynon, Rebecca, Jenny Fry, and Ralph Schroeder. 2008. 'The Ethics of Internet Research.' In *The SAGE Handbook of Online Research Methods*, edited by Grant Blank, M. Raymond Lee and Nigel Fielding, 58–78. London: SAGE Publications.

Fearon, James and David Laitin. 2003. 'Ethnic Insurgency and Civil War.' *American Political Science Review* 97(1): 75–90.

Featherstone, Liza. 2018. *Divining Desire: Focus Groups and the Culture of Consultation*. New York: OR Books.

Feinstein, Matthew, King Liu, Hongyan Ning, George Fitchett, and Donald M. Lloyd-Jones. 2012. 'Incident Obesity and Cardiovascular Risk Factors Between Young Adulthood and Middle Age by Religious Involvement: The Coronary Artery Risk Development in Young Adults (CARDIA) Study.' *Preventive Medicine* 54(2): 117–121.

Festinger, Leon and James M. Carlsmith. 1959. 'Cognitive Consequences of Forced Compliance.' *Journal of Abnormal Psychology* 58(2): 203–210.

Festinger, Leon, Henry Riecken, and Stanley Schachter. 1956. *When Prophecy Fails: A Social and Psychological Study of a Modern Group That Predicted the Destruction of the World*. New York: Harper-Torchbooks.

Filiz-Ozbay, Emel, Jonathan Guryan, Kyle Hyndman, Melissa Kearney, and Erkut Y. Ozbay. 2015. 'Do Lottery Payments Induce Savings Behavior? Evidence from the Lab.' *Journal of Public Economics* 126 (June): 1–24.

Fish, M. Steven. 2002. 'Islam and Authoritarianism.' *World Politics* 55(1): 4–37.

Fishkin, James S. 2011. *When the People Speak: Deliberative Democracy and Public Consultation*. New York: Oxford University Press.

Fortna, Virginia Page. 2004. 'Interstate Peacekeeping: Causal Mechanism and Empirical Effects.' *World Politics* 56(4): 481–519.

Funk, Carolyn L. 1996. 'The Impact of Scandal on Candidate Evaluations: An Experimental Test of the Role of Candidate Traits.' *Political Behavior* 18(1): 1–24.

Gambetta, Diego and Steffen Hertog. 2016. *Engineers of Jihad: The Curious Connection between Violent Extremism and Education*. Princeton: Princeton University Press.

Gamson, William. 1992. *Talking Politics*. New York: Cambridge University Press.

Geertz, Clifford. 1973. *Interpretation of Cultures*. New York: Basic Books.

Gerber, Alan S., Donald P. Green, and Christopher W. Larimer. 2008. 'Social Pressure and Voter Turnout: Evidence from a Large-scale Field Experiment.' *American Political Science Review* 102(1): 33–48.

Gilligan, Michael and John Stephen Stedman. 2003. 'Where Do the Peacekeepers Go?' *International Studies Review* 5(4): 37–54.

Giuliano, Elise. 2018. 'Who Supported Separatism in Donbas? Ethnicity and Popular Opinion at the Start of the Ukraine Crisis.' *Post-Soviet Affairs*. 2–3(1): 158–178.

Gneezy, Uri and John A. List. 2006. 'Putting Behavioral Economics to Work: Testing for Gift Exchange in Labor Markets Using Field Experiments.' *NBER* Working Paper No. 12063. Cambridge: National Bureau of Economic Research.

Goffman, Alice. 2014. *On the Run: Fugitive Life in an American City*. Chicago: The Chicago University Press.

Golder, Scott A. and Michael W. Macy. 2011. 'Diurnal and Seasonal Mood Vary with Work, Sleep, and Daylength Across Diverse Cultures.' *Science* 333(6051): 1878–1881.

Gómez, Francisco R., Scott W. Semenyna, Lucas Court, and Paul L. Vasey. 2017. 'Recalled Separation Anxiety in Childhood in Istmo Zapotec Men, Women, and *Muxes*.' *Archives of Sexual Behavior* 46(1): 109–117.

Gross, Neil and Solon Simmons, eds. 2014. *Professors and Their Politics*. Baltimore, MD: John Hopkins University Press.

Guéguen, Nicolas. 2013. 'Weather and Courtship Behavior: A Quasi-experiment with the Flirty Sunshine.' *Social Influence* 8(4): 312–319.

Hadna, Agus Heruanto, Dyah Kartika, and Kar-wai Tong. 2017. Evaluation of Poverty Alleviation Policy: Can Conditional Cash Transfers Improve the Academic Performance of Poor Students in Indonesia? *Cogent Social Sciences* 3(1): DOI: 1295548.

Hamilton, Richard F. 1982. *Who Voted for Hitler?* Princeton: Princeton University Press.

Heckman, James T. 1979. 'Sample Selection Bias as a Specification Error.' *Econometrica* 47(1): 153–161.

Hegre, Håvard, Tanja Ellingsen, Scott Gates, and Nils Petter Gleditsch. 2001. 'Toward a Democratic Civil Peace: Democracy, Political Change and Civil War, 1816–1992.' *American Political Science Review* 95(1): 33–48.

Herrera, Yoshiko M. 2004. *Imagined Communities: The Sources of Russian Regionalism.* New York: Cambridge University Press.

Hibbing, John R. and Elizabeth Theiss-Morse. 2002. *Stealth Democracy: Americans' Beliefs About How Government Should Work.* New York: Cambridge University Press.

Himelboim, Itai, Stephen McCreery, and Marc Smith. 2013. 'Birds of a Feather Tweet Together: Integrating Network and Content Analyses to Examine Cross-Ideology Exposure on Twitter.' *Journal of Computer-Mediated Communication* 18(2): 40–60.

Homan, Roger. 1978. 'Interpersonal Communication in Pentecostal Meetings.' *Sociological Review* XXVI(3): 499–518.

Hornikx, Jos and Berna Hendriks. 2015. 'Consumer Tweets about Brands: A Content Analysis of Sentiment Tweets about Goods and Services.' *Journal of Creative Communications* 10(2): 176–185.

Huber, John D. and Ronald Inglehart. 1995. 'Expert Interpretations of Party Space and Party Locations in 42 Societies,' *Party Politics* 1(1): 73–111.

Huber, John D. and Charles R. Shipan. 2002. *Deliberative Discretion? The Institutional Foundations of Bureaucratic Autonomy.* New York: Cambridge University Press.

Hug, Simon. 2013. 'Qualitative Comparative Analysis: How Inductive Use and Measurement Error Lead to Problematic Inference.' *Political Analysis* 21(2): 252–265.

Hull, Alastair M. 2002. 'Neuroimaging Findings in Post-traumatic Stress Disorder.' *The British Journal of Psychiatry* 181(2): 102–110.

Humphreys, Laud. 1970. *Tearoom Trade: Impersonal Sex in Public Places.* Chicago: Aldine Publishing Company.

Humphreys, Macartan and Jeremy M. Weinstein. 2008. 'Who Fights? The Determinants of Participation in Civil War,' *American Journal of Political Science* 52(2): 436–455.

Hyde, Susan D. 2007. 'The Observer Effect in International Politics: Evidence from a Natural Experiment.' *World Politics* 60(Summer): 37–63.

Ichino, Nahomi and Matthias Schündeln. 2012. 'Deterring or Displacing Electoral Irregularities? Spillover Effects of Observers in a Randomized Field Experiment in Ghana.' *Journal of Politics* 74(1): 292–307.

Imbens, Guido W., Donald B. Rubin, and Bruce I. Sacerdote. 2001. 'Estimating the Effect of Unearned Income on Labor Earnings, Savings, and Consumption: Evidence from a Survey.' *The American Economic Review* 91(4): 778–794.

Irwin, Douglas A. 2011. *Peddling Protectionism: Smoot-Hawley and the Great Depression.* Princeton: Princeton University Press.

Jensen, Michael J. and Nick Anstead. 2013. 'Psephological Investigations: Tweets, Votes, and Unknown Unknowns in the Republican Nomination Process.' *Policy & Internet* 5(2): 161–182.

Jensen, Nathan M. 2006. *Nation-States and the Multinational Corporation: A Political Economy of Foreign Direct Investment.* Princeton: Princeton University Press.

Kadam, Prashant and Supriya Bhalerao. 2010. 'Sample Size Calculation.' *International Journal of Ayurveda Research* 1(1): 55–57.

Kahn, Kim Fridkin and Patrick J. Kenney. 1999. 'Do Negative Campaigns Mobilize or Suppress Turnout? Clarifying the Relationship between Negativity and Participation.' *The American Political Science Review* 93(4): 877–889.

King, Gary, Christopher J.L. Murray, Joshua A. Salomon, and Ajay Tandon. 2004. 'Enhancing the Validity and Cross-cultural Comparability of Measurement in Survey Research.' *American Political Science Review* 98(1): 191–207.

King, Gary, Jennifer Pan, and Margaret E. Roberts. 2017. 'How the Chinese Government Fabricates Social Media Posts for Strategic Distraction, not Engaged Argument.' *American Political Science Review 111*(3): 484–501.

Kirby, Douglas. 2001. *Emerging Answers: Research Findings on Programs to Reduce Teen Pregnancy*. Washington, DC: National Campaign to Prevent Teen Pregnancy.

Köbach, Anke. 2016. 'Psychotherapeutic Intervention in the Demobilization Process: Addressing Combat-related Mental Injuries with Narrative Exposure in a First and Second Dissemination Stage.' *Clinical Psychology & Psychotherapy*, 16 December.

Krogslund, Chris, Donghyun Danny Choi, and Mathias Poertner. 2015. 'Fuzzy Sets on Shaky Ground: Parameter Sensitivity and Confirmation Bias in fsQCA.' *Political Analysis 23*(1): 21–41.

Krugman, Paul R. 1979. 'Increasing Returns, Monopolistic Competition, and International Trade.' *Journal of International Economics 9*(4): 469–479.

Kydd, Andrew H. 2003. Which Side Are You On? Bias, Credibility and Mediation. *American Journal of Political Science 47*(4): 597–611.

Kydd, Andrew H. and Barbara F. Walter. 2006. 'The Strategies of Terrorism.' *International Security 31*(1): 49–80.

Lamontagne, Yves, Richard Boyer, Celine Hetu, and Celine Lacerte-Lamontagne. 2000. 'Anxiety, Significant Losses, Depression, and Irrational Beliefs in First-Offence Shoplifters.' *Canadian Journal of Psychiatry 45*(February): 63–66.

Laver, Michael and John Garry. 2000. 'Estimating Policy Positions from Political Texts.' *American Journal of Political Science 44*(3): 619–634.

Laver, Michael and W. Ben Hunt. 1992. *Policy and Party Competition*. New York: Routledge.

Law, David S. and Mila Versteeg. 2012. 'The Declining Influence of the United States Constitution.' *New York University Law Review 87*(3): 762–858.

Leiken, Robert S. 2012. *Europe's Angry Muslim: The Revolt of the Second Generation*. New York: Oxford University Press.

Levitt, Steven D. 2016. 'Heads or Tails: The Impact of a Coin Toss on Major Life Decisions and Subsequent Happiness.' *NBER* Working Paper No. 22487. Cambridge, MA: National Bureau of Economic Research.

Li, Quan. 2005. 'Does Democracy Promote or Reduce Transnational Terrorist Incidents?' *Journal of Conflict Resolution 49*(2): 278–297.

Lijphart, Arend. 1996. 'The Puzzle of Indian Democracy: A Consociational Interpretation.' *The American Political Science Review 90*(2): 258–268.

Lipset, Seymour Martin. 1960. *Political Man: The Social Bases of Politics*. Garden City, NY: Doubleday.

Lofland, John and Robert A. LeJeune. 1960. 'Initial Interaction of Newcomers in Alcoholics Anonymous: A Field Experiment in Class Symbols and Socialization.' *Social Problems 8*: 102–111.

López, Andrea, Alissa Detz, Neda Ratanawongsa, and Urmimala Sarkar. 2012. 'What Patients Say About Their Doctors Online: A Qualitative Content Analysis.' *Journal of General Internal Medicine 32*(9): 1031–1043.

Lowry, William R. 2003. *Dam Politics: Restoring America's Rivers*. Washington, DC: Georgetown University Press.

Lujala, Päivi, Nils Petter Gleditsch, and Elisabeth Gilmore. 2005. 'A Diamond Curse? Civil War and a Lootable Resource.' *Journal of Conflict Resolution 49*(4): 538–562.

Lum, Cynthia, Leslie W. Kennedy, and Alison Sherley. 2006. 'Are Counter-Terrorism Strategies Effective? The Results of the Campbell Systematic Review on Counter-Terrorism Evaluation Research,' *Journal of Experimental Criminology 2*(4): 489–516.

MacCallum, Robert C., Michael W. Browne, and Hazuki M. Sugawara. 1996. 'Power Analysis and Determination of Sample Size for Covariance Structure Modeling.' *Psychological Methods* 1(2): 130–149.

Magaloni, Beatriz. 2006. *Voting for Autocracy: Hegemonic Party Survival and Its Demise in Mexico*. New York: Cambridge University Press.

Mahoney, James. 2010. 'After KKV: The New Methodology of Qualitative Research.' *World Politics* 62(1): 120–147.

Mampilly, Zachariah Cherian. 2011. *Rebel Rulers: Insurgent Governance and Civilian Life during War*. Ithaca: Cornell University Press.

Mansfield, Edward D. and Jack Snyder. 2007. *Electing to Fight: Why Emerging Democracies Go to War*. Cambridge: MIT Press.

Martin, Lisa L. 1992. *Coercive Cooperation: Explaining Multilateral Economic Sanctions*. Princeton, NJ: Princeton University Press.

Martins, Nicole, Dimitri C. Williams, Kristen Harrison, and Rabindra A. Ratan. 2009. 'A Content Analysis of Female Body Imagery in Video Games.' *Sex Roles* 61(11/12): 824–836.

Martins, Nicole, Dimitri C. Williams, Rabindra A. Ratan, and Kristen Harrison. 2011. 'Virtual Muscularity: A Content Analysis of Male Video Game Characters.' *Body Image* 8(1): 43–51.

McCleary, Rachel M. 2008. 'Religion and Economic Development.' *Policy Review* 148(April/May): 45–57.

Mead, Margaret. 1928. *Coming of Age in Samoa: A Psychological Study of Primitive Youth for Western Civilization*. New York: William Morrow and Company.

Meger, Sara. 2016. *Rape Loot Pillage: The Political Economy of Sexual Violence in Armed Conflict*. Oxford: Oxford University Press.

Mellander, Charlotta, José Lobo, Kevin Stolarick, and Zara Matheson. 2015. 'Night-Time Light Data: A Good Proxy Measure for Economic Activity?' *PLoS ONE* 10(10): 1–18.

Miguel, Edward. 2004. 'Tribe or Nation? Nation Building and Public Goods in Kenya versus Tanzania.' *World Politics* 56(April): 327–362.

Miguel, Edward, Shanker Satyanath, and Ernest Sergenti. 2004. 'Economic Shocks and Civil Conflict: An Instrumental Variables Approach.' *Journal of Political Economy* 112(4): 725–753.

Munday, Jennie. 2006. 'Identity in Focus: The Use of Focus Groups to Study the Construction of Collective Identity.' *Sociology* 40(1): 89–105.

Netjes, Catherine E. and Harmen A. Binnema. 2007. 'The Salience of the European Integration Issue: Three Data Sources Compared.' *Electoral Studies* 26(1): 39–49.

Neuman, Yair, Yohai Cohen, and Golan Shahar. 2015. 'A Novel Computer-assisted Personality Profiling Methodology: Illustrating Psychological Analysis via Former Egyptian President Morsi's Speech to the United Nations.' *American Intelligence Journal* 32(1): 136–145.

Newman, George E. and Daylian M. Cain. 2014. 'Tainted Altruism When Doing Some Good Is Evaluated as Worse Than Doing No Good at All.' *Psychological Science* 25(3): 648–655.

Nicholls, John G., Ruth A. Pearl, and Barbara G. Licht. 1982. 'Some Dangers of Using Personality Questionnaires to Study Personality.' *Psychological Bulletin* 92: 572–580.

Noussair, Charles N., Stefan T. Trautmann, and Gijs van de Kuilen. 2014. 'Higher Order Risk Attitudes, Demographics, and Financial Decisions.' *Review of Economic Studies* 81(1): 325–355.

Okonofua, Jason A. and Jennifer L. Eberhardt. 2015. 'Two Strikes: Race and the Disciplining of Young Students.' *Psychological Science* 26(5): 617–624.

Open Science Collaboration. 2015. 'Estimating the Reproducibility of Psychological Science.' *Science* 349 (6251): 4716.

Ostrom, Elinor. 1990. *Governing the Commons: The Evolution of Institutions for Collective Action*. New York: Cambridge University Press.

Ostrom, Elinor. 1998. 'Coping with Tragedies of the Commons.' Paper prepared for delivery at the 1998 Annual Meeting of the Association for Politics and the Life Sciences (APLS), Back Bay Hilton Hotel, Boston, MA, September 3–6.

Paluck, Elizabeth Levy and Donald P. Green. 2009. 'Deference, Dissent, and Dispute Resolution: A Field Experiment on a Mass Media Intervention in Rwanda.' *American Political Science Review* 103(4): 622–644.

Pape, Robert A. 2003. 'The Strategic Logic of Suicide Terrorism.' *The American Political Science Review* 97(3): 343–361.

Persson, Torsten and Guido Tabellini. 1994. 'Is Inequality Harmful for Growth?' *The American Economic Review* 84(3): 600–621.

Phipps, Ronald and Jamie Merisotis. 1999. *What's the Difference? A Review of Contemporary Research on the Effectiveness of Distance Learning in Higher Education.* Washington, DC: Institute for Higher Education Policy.

Piff, Paul K., Daniel M. Stancato, Stéphane Côté, Rodolfo Mendoza-Denton, and Dacher Keltner. 2012. 'Higher Social Class Predicts Increased Unethical Behavior.' *Proceedings of the National Academy of Sciences* 109(11): 4086–4091.

Plomin, Robert, Michael J. Owen, and Peter McGuffin. 1994. 'The Genetic Basis of Complex Human Behaviors.' *Science* 264(5166): 1733–1749.

Primack, Brian A., Madeline A. Dalton, Mary V. Carroll, Aaron A. Agarwal, and Michael J. Fine. 2008. 'Content Analysis of Tobacco, Alcohol, and Other Drugs in Popular Music.' *Archives of Pediatrics and Adolescent Medicine* 162(2): 169–175.

Putnam, Robert D. 2000. *Bowling Alone: The Collapse and Revival of American Community.* New York: Simon & Schuster.

Qu, Zhe, Han Zhang, and Haizheng Li. 2008. 'Determinants of Online Merchant Rating: Content Analysis of Consumer Comments about Yahoo Merchants.' *Decision Support Systems* 46(1): 440–449.

Ragin, Charles C. 1987. *The Comparative Method: Moving Beyond Qualitative and Quantitative Strategies.* Berkeley: University of California Press.

Ragin, Charles C. 2008. *Redesigning Social Inquiry: Fuzzy Sets and Beyond.* Chicago: University of Chicago Press.

Redding, Stephen J. and Daniel M. Sturm. 2008. 'The Costs of Remoteness: Evidence from German Division and Reunification.' *American Economic Review* 98(5): 1766–1797.

Reiss, Matthias and Matt Perry, eds. 2011. *Unemployment and Protest. New Perspectives on Two Centuries of Contention.* Oxford: Oxford University Press.

Riker, William H. and Peter C. Ordeshook. 1968. 'A Theory of the Calculus of Voting.' *The American Political Science Review* 62(1): 25–42.

Rind, Bruce. 2013. 'Homosexual Orientation – From Nature, Not Abuse: A Critique of Roberts, Glymour, and Koenen.' *Archives Sexual Behavior* 42(8): 1653–1664.

Roberts, Andrea L., M. Maria Glymour, and Karestan C. Koenen. 2013. 'Does Maltreatment in Childhood Affect Sexual Orientation in Adulthood?' *Archives of Sexual Behavior* 42(2): 161–171.

Rose-Ackerman, Susan and Bonnie J. Palifka. 2016. *Corruption and Government: Causes, Consequences, and Reform,* 2nd edn. New York: Cambridge University Press.

Rosenbaum, Paul R. and Donald B. Rubin. 1983. 'The Central Role of the Propensity Score in Observational Studies for Causal Effects.' *Biometrika* 70(1): 41–55.

Rosenhan, David. 1973. 'On Being Sane in Insane Places.' *Science* 179(4070): 250–258.

Ross, Michael. 2001. 'Does Oil Hinder Democracy?' *World Politics* 53(3): 325–361.

Rothwell, Erin. 2010. 'Analyzing Focus Group Data: Content and Interaction.' *Journal for Specialists in Pediatric Nursing* 15(2): 176–180.

Rousseau, David L., Christopher Gelpi, Dan Reiter, and Paul K. Huth. 1996. 'Assessing the Dyadic Nature of the Democratic Peace, 1918–1988.' *American Political Science Review* 90(3): 512–533.

Rubin, G. James, Chris R. Brewin, Neil Greenberg, John Simpson, and Simon Wessely. 2005. 'Psychological and Behavioral Reactions to the Bombings in London on 7 July 2005: Cross Sectional Survey of a Representative Sample of Londoners.' *BMJ 301*: 606–612.

Rudy, David R. 1986. *Becoming Alcoholic: Alcoholics Anonymous and the Reality of Alcoholism.* Carbondale and Edwardsville: Southern Illinois University Press.

Rudy, Rena M., Lucy Popova, and Daniel G. Linz. 2010. 'The Context of Current Content Analysis of Gender Roles: An Introduction to a Special Issue.' *Sex Roles* 62(11–12): 705–720.

Rudy, Rena M., Lucy Popova, and Daniel G. Linz. 2011. 'Contributions to the Content Analysis of Gender Roles: An Introduction to a Special Issue.' *Sex Roles* 64(3–4): 151–159.

Russett, Bruce. 1993. *Grasping the Democratic Peace: Principles for a Post–Cold War World.* Princeton, NJ: Princeton University Press.

Sanders, Alan R., Eden R. Martin, Gary W. Beecham, S. Guo, Khytam Dawood, Gerulf Rieger, Judith A. Badner, Elliot S. Gershon, Ritesha S. Krishnappa, Alana B. Kolundzija, Jubao Duan, Pablo V. Gejman, and J. Michael Bailey. 2015. 'Genome-wide Scan Demonstrates Significant Linkage for Male Sexual Orientation.' *Psychological Medicine* 45(7): 1379–1388.

Sandøy, Ingvild Fossgard, Mweetwa Mudenda, Joseph Zulu, Ecloss Munsaka, Astrid Blystad, Mpundu C. Makasa, Ottar Mæstad, Bertil Tungodden, Choolwe Jacobs, Linda Kampata, Knut Fylkesnes, Joar Svanemyr, Karen Marie Moland, Richard Banda, and Patrick Musonda. 2016. 'Effectiveness of a Girls' Empowerment Programme on Early Childbearing, Marriage and School Dropout among Adolescent Girls in Rural Zambia: Study Protocol for a Cluster Randomized Trial.' *Trials 17*: 588–603.

Savun, Burcu and Brian J. Phillips. 2009. 'Democracy, Foreign Policy, and Terrorism.' *Journal of Conflict Resolution* 53(6): 878–904.

Schwindt-Bayer, Leslie A. and Margit Tavits. 2016. *Clarity of Responsibility, Accountability, and Corruption.* New York: Cambridge University Press.

Segal, Nancy L. 2013. 'Fullerton Virtual Twin Study: An Update.' *Twin Research and Human Genetics* 16(1): 1832–4274.

Segal, Nancy L., Shirley A. McGuire, and Joanne Hoven Stohs. 2012. 'What Virtual Twins Reveal About General Intelligence and Other Behaviors.' *Personality and Individual Differences* 53(4): 405–410.

Sen, Amartya. 1999. *Democracy and Freedom.* New York: Anchor Books.

Sharf, Barbara F. 1997. 'Communicating Breast Cancer On-Line: Support and Empowerment on the Internet.' *Women and Health* 26(1): 65–84.

Siegler, Robert S., Sidney Strauss, and Iris Levin. 1981. 'Developmental Sequences Within and Between Concepts.' *Monographs of the Society for Research in Child Development* 46(2): 1–84.

Simpser, Alberto. 2013. *Why Governments and Parties Manipulate Elections: Theory, Practice, and Implications.* New York: Cambridge University Press.

Smithers, Janice A. 1977. 'Institutional Dimension of Senility.' *Urban Life* 6(3): 251–276.

Spitzer, Robert L. 2003. 'Can Some Gay Men and Lesbians Change Their Sexual Orientation? 200 Participants Reporting a Change from Homosexual to Heterosexual Orientation.' *Archives of Sexual Behavior* 32(5): 403–417.

Staiger, Douglas and James H. Stock. 1994. 'Instrumental Variables Regression with Weak Instruments.' *NBER* Working Paper No. 151. Cambridge, MA: The National Bureau of Economic Research.

Stevens, Daniel, Benjamin G. Bishin, and Robert R. Barr. 2006. 'Authoritarian Attitudes, Democracy, and Policy Preferences among Latin American Elites.' *American Journal of Political Science* 50(3): 606–620.

Stock, James H. and Francesco Trebbi. 2003. 'Who Invented IV Regression?' *Journal of Economic Perspectives 17*(3): 177–194.

Stock, James H. and Motohiro Yogo. 2002. 'Testing for Weak Instruments in Linear IV Regression.' *NBER* Working Paper No. 284. Cambridge, MA: The National Bureau of Economic Research.

Stokes, Susan C. 2001. *Mandates and Democracy: Neoliberalism by Surprise in Latin America.* New York: Cambridge University Press.

Sussman, Abigail B., Eesha Sharma, and Adam L. Alter. 2015. 'Framing Charitable Donations as Exceptional Expenses Increases Giving.' *Journal of Experimental Psychology: Applied 21*(2): 130–139.

Tellegen, Auke, David T. Lykken, Thomas J. Bouchard Jr., Kimberly J. Wilcox, Nancy. L. Segal, and Steven Rich. 1988. 'Personality Similarity in Twins Reared Apart and Together.' *Journal of Personality and Social Psychology 54*(6): 1031–1039.

Tessler, Mark, Amaney Jamal, and Michael Robbins. 2014. 'New Findings on Arabs and Democracy.' *Journal of Democracy 23*(4): 89–103.

Todorov, Alexander, Anesu N. Mandisodza, Amir Goren, and Crystal C. Hall. 2005. 'Inferences of Competence from Faces Predict Election Outcomes.' *Science 308*(5728): 1623–1626.

Tumasjan, Andranik, Timm O. Sprenger, Philipp G. Sandner, and Isabell M. Welpe. 2010. 'Predicting Elections with Twitter: What 140 Characters Reveal about Political Sentiment.' Proceedings of the Fourth International AAAI Conference on Weblogs and Social Media, 178–185.

Tversky, Amos and Daniel Kahneman. 1973. 'Availability: A Heuristic for Judging Frequency and Probability.' *Cognitive Psychology 5*(2): 207–232.

Tversky, Amos and Daniel Kahneman. 1981. 'The Framing of Decisions and the Psychology of Choice.' *Science 211*(4481): 453–458.

Unger, Lynette S. 1991. Altruism as a Motivation to Volunteer. *Journal of Economic Psychology 12*(1): 71–100.

van Evera, Steven. 1997. *Guide to Methods for Students of Political Science.* Ithaca: Cornell University Press.

Vreeland, James Raymond. 2008. 'The Effect of Political Regime on Civil War: Unpacking Anocracy.' *Journal of Conflict Resolution 52*(3): 401–425.

Wacquant, Loïc. 2002. 'The Curious Eclipse of Prison Ethnography in the Age of Mass Incarceration.' *Ethnography 3*(4): 371–397.

Walther, Joseph B. 2002. 'Research Ethics in Internet-enabled Research: Human Subjects Issues and Methodological Myopia.' *Ethnics and Information Technology 4*(3): 205–216.

Warren, Mark E. 2014. 'What Does Corruption Mean in a Democracy?' *American Journal of Political Science 48*(2): 328–343.

Weyland, Kurt. 2014. *Making Waves: Democratic Waves in Europe and Latin America since the Revolutions.* New York City: Cambridge University Press.

Wood, Elisabeth Jean. 2006. 'Variation in Sexual Violence During War.' *Politics and Society 34*(3): 307–342.

World Bank. 2016. *Evaluating Tanzania's Productive Social Safety Net: Targeting Performance, Beneficiary Profile, and other Baseline Findings.* Washington, DC: World Bank Group.

Yanagizawa-Drott, David. 2014. 'Propaganda and Conflict: Evidence from the Rwandan Genocide.' *The Quarterly Journal of Economics 129*(4): 1947–1994.

Yelowitz, Aaron and Matthew Wilson. 2015. 'Characteristics of Bitcoin Users: An Analysis of Google Search Data.' *Applied Economics Letters 22*(13): 1030–1036.

Index